PRAISE FOR

# CAMELOT'S END

"Jon Ward captures the sound and the fury of [the 1980 Democratic primary] struggle in...a fast-paced, even-handed look at Kennedy's doomed challenge to a doomed president."

—*Washington Post*

"A masterful account of an all but forgotten episode in modern American politics. An accomplished journalist, Ward brilliantly re-creates an era when, in the aftermath of Watergate and the country's defeat in Vietnam, American power and prestige were waning and the country's faith in its institutions was being sorely tested...a must-read for anybody interested in American politics."

—Michael Isikoff, #1 *New York Times* bestselling author of *Russian Roulette*

"Well written, well reported, and compelling, CAMELOT'S END paints a picture of two flawed and ambitious politicians and destiny's collision course for them. It's a sheer joy to read."

—Jake Tapper, CNN anchor and chief Washington correspondent

"A dynamic telling of the Kennedy-Carter slugfest that defined the Democratic Party for two generations."

—Amie Parnes, #1 *New York Times* bestselling co-author of *Shattered*

"Anyone who wants to understand how our presidential campaigns came to be the way they are needs to read this rollicking, surprising account of an election season whose twists and turns have never, until now, been fully understood by anyone other than the participants. And there's a reason most of them didn't want the rest of us to find out."

—Sasha Issenberg, bestselling author of *The Victory Lab*

"CAMELOT'S END moves through an important time of testing with power and pace. The profiles drawn are sharp and memorable. This passion for politics is woven into our history and skillfully retold here."

—Major Garrett, chief White House correspondent, CBS News

"Ward skillfully resurrects the poisonous 1980 conflict between Jimmy Carter and Ted Kennedy that sowed new divisions in the Democratic Party and left it in a political wilderness for the next twelve years."

—Curtis Wilkie, author of *The Fall of the House of Zeus*

"A fabulous work of history... In novelistic fashion and with a keen eye for detail, Jon Ward plumbs the human drama behind a fight that tore apart the Democratic Party—a high-stakes confrontation that reverberates to this day."

—Del Wilber, *New York Times* bestselling author of *A Good Month for Murder*

"The story of two political titans whose clash defined the modern Democratic Party, expertly told by one of the best political reporters around. Jon Ward brings his tragic heroes to life on every page... A fresh breeze of a book."

—Matt Bai, author of *All the Truth Is Out*

"Ward's vivid telling of what may be the last missing chapter in the saga of the Kennedy family is compellingly told... a first-rate work."

—Craig Shirley, *New York Times* bestselling author of *December 1941*

# Camelot's End

*The Democrats' Last Great Civil War*

## Jon Ward

TWELVE

*New York   Boston*

Twelve
Hachette Book Group
1290 Avenue of the Americas, New York, NY 10104
twelvebooks.com
twitter.com/twelvebooks

Originally published in hardcover and ebook by Twelve in January 2019.
First Trade Edition: January 2020

Twelve is an imprint of Grand Central Publishing. The Twelve name and logo are trademarks
of Hachette Book Group, Inc.

The publisher is not responsible for websites (or their content) that are not owned by the
publisher.

The Hachette Speakers Bureau provides a wide range of authors for speaking events. To find
out more, go to www.hachettespeakersbureau.com or call (866) 376-6591.

Library of Congress Cataloging-in-Publication Data
Names: Ward, Jon (Writer of politics) author.
Title: Camelot's end : Kennedy vs. Carter, and the fight that broke the
democratic party / Jon Ward.
Description: New York : Twelve, [2019] | Includes index.
Identifiers: LCCN 2018003976| ISBN 9781455591381 (hardcover) |
ISBN 9781549194771 (audio download) | ISBN 9781455591374 (ebook)
Subjects: LCSH: Presidents—United States—Election—1980. | Kennedy, Edward M.
(Edward Moore), 1932-2009. | Carter, Jimmy, 1924- | Political campaigns—United States—
History—20th century. | Primaries—United States—History—20th century. | Democratic
Party (U.S.)—History—20th century. | Presidential candidates—United States—Biography.
Classification: LCC E875 .W37 2019 | DDC 324.973/0904—dc23
LC record available at https://lccn.loc.gov/2018003976

ISBNs: 978-1-4555-9139-8 (trade pbk.), 978-1-4555- 9137-4 (ebook)

Printed in the United States of America

LSC-C

10 9 8 7 6 5 4 3 2 1

If I could I would write with love...

—*The End of the Affair*

*To Alison: Because of you I can write with love*
*And to Joanne F. Crichton, 1928–2017*

# Contents

History is made up of living men whose work
is handed over defenseless to our understanding and
appreciation upon their death. Precisely because of this,
they have a claim on our courtesy, a claim that their
own concerns should be heard and that they should not
be used simply as a means to our ends.

—*Karl Barth*

# INTRODUCTION

I entered Jimmy Carter's personal office on a chilly winter day two weeks after the new year in 2015. The thirty-ninth president of the United States stood looking out of a large window onto the bucolic grounds of the Carter Center in Atlanta. His office was dimly lit by cloud-muted sunlight. Carter turned as I walked in and greeted me politely. At age ninety, he was sharp as ever. He had just returned from a trip to New York to promote a decades-long effort to eradicate worm-borne disease in Africa. That morning, he told me, he had sent his editor a finished manuscript for his latest book, his thirty-first.

Carter sat during much of our conversation with his right foot up on the coffee table in front of him, his leg bent, one or both of his hands resting on his knee. His eyes were a piercing blue. He wore his watch with the display on the inside of his wrist. "I learned that in the Navy," he said, referring to his days at the Naval Academy and as a nuclear submarine officer. Submariners wouldn't want a reflection from the watch to give away the submarine's position to enemy ships.

I was there to talk to Carter about Ted Kennedy. The last of the Kennedy brothers—the only one not cut down by an assassin's bullet or killed in World War II—had run against Carter for the Democratic nomination in 1980, at the end of Carter's first term in office. It was one of only a handful of times in American history that an incumbent president running for reelection had been challenged from within his own party. And the fight between Carter

and Kennedy turned ugly. We talked about one of the most igno-
minious episodes, when Kennedy embarrassed Carter on the final
night of the Democratic convention at Madison Square Garden in
New York. "Kennedy was drinking that night. Everybody knew
it," Carter told me. "On the stage when we were looking for harmony, I reached out to shake his hand. He obviously deliberately
avoided my hand. He refused to shake hands with me."

That wasn't quite right. I reminded him, having traveled to
Vanderbilt University's video archives to watch the footage of that
night, that the two of them had in fact shaken hands, more than
a few times, in the span of a painfully awkward few minutes. The
problem was that Kennedy had refused to join Carter in a pose of
unity, hands clasped together and raised above their heads. But
Carter remembered the most important part. Kennedy had humiliated him in front of the entire country on live television.

That night showed how divided the Democrats were. The party
was shattering. Key members of the coalition that gave Democrats
political dominance from the New Deal onward for almost half a
century—southern whites, blue-collar laborers from midwestern
cities—were deserting them for the Republican Party. Carter had
held things together in 1976, because he was a southerner who
won large swaths of that region but also appealed to an increasingly liberal party activist base. But the 1980s would be the age
of Reagan, and the 1990s would bring in Republican control of
Congress after decades of Democratic supremacy.

Carter still blamed his loss to Reagan in 1980 in large part on
Kennedy's defiant challenge to his reelection bid. He regretted not
having done more to prevent it. "The first year I was in office,
[Kennedy] was my best supporter in the whole Congress," he said.
"And when I saw that that was changing, particularly late in '78, I
believe, I should have gone out of my way, I could have gone out of
my way to accommodate him." In particular, Carter wished he'd

granted Kennedy's request to appoint Archibald Cox—the former solicitor general fired by former president Nixon in a dramatic showdown over a subpoena of Nixon's Oval Office recordings—to the First Circuit Court of Appeals. "I think it meant a lot to him in retrospect," Carter said. "I didn't do it, and I think if I had appointed that judge, Kennedy probably wouldn't have run."

The former president was overestimating the impact that such a gesture would have had, and underestimating the degree to which his and Kennedy's passions—in addition to forces well beyond their control—had drawn them into conflict. He had relished the chance to take Kennedy on. He wanted to "whip his ass," as he said publicly at the time. Kennedy was his polar opposite: a man of great appetites who struggled to exercise personal discipline, born into privilege, power, and wealth. Carter, who by sheer self-discipline and determination willed himself from a childhood on a southwest Georgia farm to greatness, despised Kennedy for being born on third base. Carter had anticipated a showdown with Kennedy for years before Kennedy even knew who he was.

And Carter was no dummy. He knew that Kennedy's challenge was driven by forces beyond Teddy's control, by the ghosts of his demanding father and his martyred brothers.

"I really relished Kennedy's support," Carter told me. "But then he decided, I don't know why, I think he felt that he in a way deserved to be president, that I didn't. Maybe inspired by his own family members—you know, 'You need to carry on the Kennedy heritage.' And since Bobby and John had been assassinated, I could see how he would be looked on as heir apparent."

He paused, sighed, and said, "Anyway, he changed."

Two months after I interviewed Carter in Atlanta, I traveled to Boston to attend the opening ceremony of the Edward M.

Kennedy Institute. The center was the equivalent—in size, prestige, and sheer ambition—of a presidential library. Kennedy had passed away only five and a half years earlier. It had taken sixteen years after JFK's death before his library opened, due to cost overruns and site changes. Bobby Kennedy's children were angry that no such building existed in their father's memory. But Bobby did not have any advocates in his death like Teddy's widow, his second wife, Victoria Reggie Kennedy. Vicki, a Washington attorney and a deft political operator, had seen to it that the taxpayers pitched in $38 million to the $78 million project. She had also assumed impressive control over Kennedy's legacy. Kennedy's own sons told me they had to check with her before talking to me.

Under Vicki's hawk-eyed direction, the massive Kennedy Institute—which included a full-size replica of the U.S. Senate chamber to be used for mock sessions to educate students—aspired to honor Teddy with as much grandeur as former presidents. There is a replica of Teddy's Capitol Hill office, and a room devoted to looking back over his life and career. Vicki said that Teddy had once told her that everybody knew about the presidency and each president got a library, but that few people knew about the Senate, and this could change that.

The dedication ceremony took place on a freezing cold, gray March morning. The weather, and some very bad planning on the part of the organizers, squelched the celebratory mood. Most attendees thought the event would be held in a heated tent, and did not wear coats. But the tent walls were removed in some places and pulled back in others. Massive heaters blasted hot air that quickly dissipated. The temperature was in the low thirties and snow flurries came and went. People had to be in their chairs for ninety minutes before the event started, thanks to the security precautions needed for President Obama. Kennedy family members and other attendees hunched over in their seats, burrowed into whatever clothing they had, and prayed for the ceremony to be over.

Broadway star Brian Stokes Mitchell sang one of Teddy's favorites, "Oh, What a Beautiful Mornin'," from Rodgers and Hammerstein's *Oklahoma!* And then Teddy's older son, Teddy Jr., strode to the lectern to introduce Senator John McCain. He made a brief aside about his father. "I just want to say one thing. It's not true that my father really wanted to be president. Who he really wanted to be is Brian Stokes Mitchell," Teddy Jr. said, pointing to the ebullient singer, who was a friend of the family. It was the only mention from the stage the entire morning of the fact that his father had at one time been a candidate for the highest office in the land.

After the ceremony, I went into the institute and looked through a multimedia display that reviewed the highlights of Teddy's career. I scrolled through the slides that made up the "1977–1983" portion of his career—his fourth term as a senator. Slide one was titled "Peace for Northern Ireland, 1977." Slide two: "Airline and trucking deregulation, 1978." Slide three: "The Refugee Act of 1980." Slide four: "Fighting budget cutbacks, 1981." Slide five: "Extending the Voting Rights Act, 1982." Slide six: "Small Business Innovation Research Program, 1982."

The overview slide for that 1977–1983 period included the famous closing line of his speech at the 1980 Democratic convention, widely viewed as one of the great political speeches of the modern era and the finest of Kennedy's long career. "For all those whose cares have been our concern," Kennedy had said, "the work goes on, the cause endures, the hope still lives, and the dream shall never die." But there was no mention that these lines were uttered at the end of Teddy's presidential campaign in 1980. There was no mention, anywhere in the institute, that Edward M. Kennedy ever ran for president.

The Kennedys' lack of appetite for the story told in this book is somewhat understandable. They are a family that doesn't like to lose. This is a story where the last of the Kennedys lost, where Carter lost, at a time in our history when America seemed to just keep losing.

But it is not just a story about endings and defeats. The best stories often begin in dark moments. This is also the tale of a deeply formative period in the life of a man who later became one of the nation's greatest lawmakers. It's about a president whose defeat propelled him to spend almost four decades reducing poverty, war, and disease. And the events described here marked a breaking point for the Democratic Party that ultimately led it—after a long decade out of power—back to the White House in 1992.

I got the idea for this book early in 2013. President Obama had just been reelected. Republicans were in the wilderness, lost, witless, clueless, seemingly destined to eternal minority status. But as I circulated around the Democratic Party's annual winter meeting in Washington, D.C., I ran into a veteran Democrat who remembered a time in the party's history when Democrats were in despair.

Jeff Berman was an intense, white-bearded man with a meticulous knowledge of Democratic Party rules and a constant supply of stories. He had run Obama's delegate operation in 2008, and thanks in part to his efforts, Obama was able to outlast Hillary Clinton as that protracted battle dragged on. He introduced me to Elaine Kamarck, who worked in the Clinton White House on Al Gore's "reinventing government" initiative. Berman told me that he had first met Kamarck when she was working for Jimmy Carter.

Kamarck and Berman began to reminisce about Carter chasing a drunken Kennedy around the stage of the convention in Madison Square Garden, in prime time. Kamarck said she was near the stage that night and got a close-up look at Kennedy. "He was loaded," she said. (Kennedy adviser Bob Shrum was with Kennedy then and disputes this.)

Kennedy had been dead for four years, and his legacy was that of an elder statesman, a lion of the Senate. He was widely respected for his long career as a lawmaker. His last major political gesture had been to endorse Obama, a passing of the torch. The idea of a young Teddy liquored up and making a fool of Carter on prime-time television was quite different from the image being broadcast by the protectors of his legacy.

I sensed that there was a story worth telling in full that for a variety of reasons had been swept under the rug, or at least into a dark corner of the attic, for many years: the collision between these two powerful men and all they represented. "It was ideological, it was personal, and it was very long," Tom Donilon, a key Carter aide who went on to become Obama's national security adviser, told me.

The effects of this episode were enduring. In 2008, advisers to Hillary Clinton encouraged her not to carry her campaign to the convention. They reminded her that it took Democrats a decade to recover from 1980. That year "was searing for the party," said Harold M. Ickes, a powerful Clinton adviser who had been a young operative on Kennedy's campaign against Carter. "We haven't had a challenge to a sitting president since. And I think it's unlikely that we're going to have one for a long, long time, unless there's a real bozo in the office. It . . . continues to haunt the party."

And this story helps us understand two men who played a major role in American politics for roughly a half century, and who are both, in their own ways, misunderstood and underestimated. Carter is remembered for sweaters and hostages and weakness. But that's an unfair caricature. He was a highly complex individual: cunning, ambitious, and competitive to the point of being ruthless. His remarkable personal story is not well known. And for all his adventures in Mideast politics, Carter blazed a trail in his post-presidency that no one before him had ever conceived of, and has done work of incredible benefit to many in need.

"He's really been like a great Bordeaux wine," said Ben Barnes, a legendary figure in Texas politics who was close friends with Kennedy but also knew Carter before he even became a governor. "With age he has gotten more and more visionary and more and more determined to work to the last day of his life to correct some things that need to be corrected."

Kennedy's experience in 1980 was metamorphic. After his run for president, not only did he shed significant parts of a burden he'd carried his entire adult life, but he also became something new. The Democratic Party was split between liberal and conservative wings, and Kennedy chose to side with the liberals. But over time he became known for bipartisan achievement in the Senate. This was only possible after fellow senators were no longer suspicious that he might use their cooperation to help elect himself president. "The period of '78 to '82 is as fundamental to understanding Edward Kennedy as any period of this [sic] life," said pollster Peter Hart, who worked on Kennedy's campaign. "I think he emerged from it with a sense of authority and resolve about what his life was," said Bob Shrum, a longtime adviser and friend.

---

Right after I spoke with Berman and Kamarck, I ran into Democratic consultant Anita Dunn. I was surprised to find she'd worked for the Carter White House. She shuddered at the memory of the period. "I cannot remember a time when the mood of the country was that sour. Certainly nothing in the last thirty years has come near to that," she said. "There was a sense of America spiraling. Things had spiraled out of control."

The seventies were an "anguished" decade, as novelist Madeleine L'Engle put it. Historic levels of prosperity after World War II led to ease and individualism. Growing awareness of racial injustice and of government malfeasance abroad led to protest. The 1960s had been tumultuous. The 1970s were the hangover.

In 1972, journalist David Broder described a nation in turmoil: "What we have is a society in which discontent, disbelief, cynicism, and political inertia characterize the public mood; a country whose economy suffers from severe dislocations, whose currency is endangered, where unemployment and inflation coexist, where increasing numbers of people and even giant enterprises live on the public dole; a country whose two races continue to withdraw from each other in growing physical and social isolation; a country whose major public institutions command steadily less allegiance from its citizens."

As I finished this book, while covering the 2016 presidential election, the 1970s didn't feel as foreign as they had just a few years earlier. We didn't have to imagine what that kind of cultural darkness felt like. We were living our own version. The economy was growing, but barely. Prosperity was abundant with some, but was eluding many others, and the gap between them was growing more drastic. Suicide rates were on the rise and had been since the 2008 economic crisis that cut the stock market in half and wiped out many Americans economically. Domestic terrorist attacks and mass shootings became more frequent, introducing a new level of fear about the threat of random violence in everyday life. Police brutality caught on video sparked protests and more violence.

And in the midst of all this, a candidate for president emerged to capitalize on the fear that was running rampant. We had caught up to the darkness of the 1970s, and surpassed it.

There were eerie similarities between 1980 and 2016. Until 2016, the 1980 election had been the last time there was any meaningful political fight on the floor of a nominating convention. But the Republican Party's resistance to Trump—whose candidacy was unthinkable in 2015 and remained so to many even as the 2016 convention approached—produced a protest on the floor, led by a sitting U.S. senator, Mike Lee of Utah. Two nights after that, another senator, Ted Cruz of Texas, gave a prime-time speech to the convention hall urging Republicans to vote their conscience, a clear slap at Trump, and was booed off the stage.

Like the Carter campaign in 1980, the Trump campaign had to whip and organize its supporters in response to an uprising on the floor of the convention. And like Carter, Trump fought to keep convention delegates bound to state primary results, rather than letting them vote according to their preferences. I walked the floor of Quicken Loans Arena in Cleveland and watched top Republican National Committee and Trump campaign officials twist arms, threaten delegates, and huddle in back hallways. And I stood three feet from Senator Lee as he and others screamed their opposition to Trump's nomination. Whether Trump is the last gasp of the Reagan coalition, just as Carter marked the end of the FDR era for the Democratic Party, remains to be seen.

This is a story about what happened to the Democrats when the country's long string of successes, luck, and global dominance following World War II had run their course. Like the country, they were coming apart. So they reached back in their minds to the time before America had gone down the drain. The Kennedy name represented the good old days. It had been just over a decade since Bobby was shot and killed. And since he'd gone down, many Democrats had been wondering when the last remaining Kennedy might be ready for the White House. Teddy was an imperfect product, to be sure. But if you didn't look too closely, there was still enough resemblance to his brothers that perhaps he could make Democrats, and America, great again.

It was thus that the Democrats plunged into civil war.

# CHAPTER 1

⸺ ◦∞◦ ⸺

# Sailing Against the Wind

*November 22, 1978*

He was alone with his thoughts at the gravesite in Arlington National Cemetery of his older brother, who had been struck down this very day fifteen years earlier. On an overcast, drizzly morning, he stood on a hill overlooking the Potomac River into Washington, D.C. He had to turn his back on the city to look down at the Cape Cod granite stones surrounding the gray slate tablet and the eternal flame that marked John F. Kennedy's resting place. The capital city behind him represented the present and the future. On the ground before him was the past. It was a personal history that carried obligations, driving him forward into a future he was not always sure he wanted, but that he felt compelled to pursue.

"Ted Kennedy had inherited a legend along with his name and he was almost as much trapped by the legend as propelled by it," wrote the famous political journalist Teddy White. Edward M. Kennedy had power, fame, and money, and looked the part in his formfitting suit, big-knotted wide tie, and full head of wavy, flamboyant hair. Dark cuff links dotted his wrists. But his face was drawn in on itself. His mouth was closed and slack. His brow was furrowed, pushing down on his eyes, which were half shut and held dark shadows in their recesses. All the lines on his forty-six-year-old face—the dimples, the cheekbones—pointed dramatically toward the center of his anxiety and melancholy: his inaccessible, heavy-lidded eyes.

It wasn't just a moment to reflect on his slain brother. It was a trying time for everyone. Since JFK's death, "Americans had been abused by history," White wrote. Vietnam, race riots, Watergate, inflation, rising levels of crime and squalor in America's cities. JFK was the last president "who had given Americans a sense of control of their own destiny," and he had presided over the nation at a time when the economy was stable and "working people grew comfortable and the rich got richer."

After JFK's tragic death, Bobby Kennedy took up the torch. He fused the Kennedy glamour with the increasingly progressive spirit of the age. JFK had been conservative on economics and hawkish on foreign policy. When he ran in 1960, Lyndon Johnson had been the "New Deal candidate." But after JFK's death, Bobby grafted the JFK legend onto the antiwar, pro–civil rights passions sweeping through the left.

Then in 1968, Bobby was killed by a crazed Palestinian who shot him in the head. And suddenly Teddy was the last Kennedy left.

Months before his death, JFK had sat on the Truman Balcony with his little brother Teddy and told him that he might someday inhabit the White House as commander in chief. Now Teddy was the only living son of Joseph Patrick Kennedy Sr., and he was the same age that JFK had been in the year of his death, president of the United States for three years. Teddy had been a U.S. senator for sixteen years, but if he had any plans of following in his brother's footsteps, the clock was ticking. He stood silently, holding a rose.

≈≈≈≈≈

Two weeks later, Kennedy's plane touched down in Memphis on a Saturday. He stepped onto the tarmac and into frigid cold. The temperature would sink well below freezing that night. Democrats were gathered there in early December for an unusual midterm convention, of which there have been only three in the party's history, in 1974, 1978, and 1982. Democrats held the first one two years after George McGovern failed to stop Richard Nixon from winning a second term in 1972. The midterm convention was symbolic of a party that was trying desperately to avoid disintegration. The miserable weather in the River City matched the mood of the Democratic Party and the nation.

Nixon's two wins had set off alarms inside the Democratic Party. His reelection in 1972 had given Republicans four out of the past six presidential elections. The New Deal coalition created by President Roosevelt had helped Democrats dominate American politics for decades, but it was splintering. The South was turning against the Democrats, labor was weakening, and big-city political machines were losing power. Nixon's Watergate disgrace and resignation in 1974 opened the door for a comeback, and two years before their Memphis gathering, Democrats had managed to win back the White House, with a southerner to boot. Jimmy Carter's election gave Democrats hope that the South, their geographical anchor, could be kept in the fold.

Carter's humble folksiness, embodied by his decision to walk down Pennsylvania Avenue after his inauguration rather than stay inside the presidential limo, was welcomed by many Americans exhausted by cultural turmoil, racial tension, and a loss of trust in government. His deep Christian faith was especially attractive to Southern Baptists, evangelicals, and other Protestants. But like a hasty marriage, the relationship between Carter and the nation, much less the Democratic Party, was fragile. Carter was not from Washington, and once he got to the capital he made little effort to adopt it as his hometown. He was not handsomely arrogant. He did not impress the TV cameras. And perhaps most significant, he took the country and the Democrats in a more conservative direction, especially on fiscal issues.

Carter's first two years as president had been hobbled by his lack of familiarity with the ways of Washington, by controversy over the financial dealings of top aide Bert Lance, and by his ideological clashes with the left wing of the Democratic Party. Carter wanted to rein in spending, which offended many Democrats who believed cuts would hurt the poor and vulnerable. Kennedy, for his part, wanted a national health care system, but Carter had put that on the back burner. Carter had promised to prioritize the issue during the 1976 campaign, but rising inflation, unemployment, the Soviets, and the Mideast peace process abroad had kept him occupied.

Still, the midterm convention in Memphis was not expected to be controversial or confrontational. There was grumbling about Carter's budget, but not outright revolt. Kennedy's health care push was getting some attention, but was not a dominant story. Teddy was "eager to play a minimal role" at the convention, Adam Clymer reported in the *New York Times*.

Carter had spoken to the gathering the previous evening. He stayed the night and on Saturday morning attended two panel discussions, submitting himself to questions from angry activists. The Associated Press called it "an extraordinary gesture for an incumbent president."

Carter left Memphis around lunchtime Saturday and headed

back to Washington. On his way to the airport, his motorcade made an unannounced stop at the Lorraine Motel and the president laid a wreath at the door of Room 306, where Martin Luther King Jr. had been killed. King's widow, Coretta Scott King, stood by Carter's side as he said, in his stilted way, "Let the people of the world know that I value what Martin Luther King was and what his memory is." He was trying, without much success, to win over the party's activist wing.

Kennedy took the stage at the convention late in the afternoon on Saturday. He was not a featured speaker but simply part of a panel on health care that included two of Carter's top advisers on the issue: Stuart Eizenstat, a top domestic policy adviser, and Joseph Califano, secretary of health, education, and welfare. All the panelists sat at a long table on the stage, facing the audience. The audience was arranged by state, like a regular convention, but the room lacked the same grandeur.

The moderator of the panel was a young southern governor-elect, Bill Clinton of Arkansas. A normal afternoon panel would have been a sleepy affair, but here the room was packed to hear and see Kennedy. And as Califano spoke, representing Carter, Kennedy's presence loomed over him. Califano pledged that the Carter administration would ask Congress to act on health insurance, an acknowledgment that Kennedy's pressure was having an effect.

Health care had been Kennedy's signature issue for several years. In 1972 he published a book called *In Critical Condition: The Crisis in America's Health Care*. The roots of his interest reached back even further, to his family experiences as a child. "As a young boy I had witnessed Rosemary's struggles," Kennedy wrote elliptically in his 2009 memoir. Rosemary Kennedy was the eldest of Teddy's five sisters, and her story is one of the most horrific in the family lore. She struggled in school as a young girl, and had a below-average IQ. But after she began to behave erratically in her early twenties, her father—without consulting or even informing his wife—had doctors perform a prefrontal lobotomy on their daughter. The experimental procedure was a total failure. Rosemary's intelligence was reduced to that of a two-year-old, and the attractive, once-vivacious young woman remained mentally disabled until her death in 2005 at age eighty-six. Teddy was nine years old at the time of her lobotomy.

Kennedy also attributed his focus on health care to watching older brother John "endure his many ailments, diseases, and near-death experiences," to his family's "shock" over his father's loss of speech after his 1961 stroke, and to the death of John and Jackie's two-day-old son Patrick in August 1963, just a few months before JFK's assassination. A year later, Teddy himself was hospitalized for half a year with a broken back after a small plane taking him from Washington to Massachusetts crashed on its approach to the airport in Westfield, killing the pilot and one of Teddy's aides. It was his first personal experience with a serious medical issue, and during his recovery it spurred an awareness on the young senator's part about the cost of care.

But Teddy himself referred to all of this as a "prologue." His passion for health care was even more personal. A year after he released his book on health care, his twelve-year-old son Teddy Jr. was diagnosed with cancer in his leg, requiring amputation above the knee. After the diagnosis, Teddy did not immediately tell his son what would happen, instead taking him home for a few days prior to the operation. He described throwing a football with Teddy Jr. and "fighting not to be crushed by emotion, knowing that this was probably the last time that Teddy would be able to run on two legs." When he finally broke the news to his son that he would lose more than half his leg, the boy started to cry, and Teddy held him close. During chemotherapy treatment, Teddy said he "slept beside [Teddy Jr.] in his hospital room. I would hold his head against my chest when the nausea overcame him."

In the halls of Boston Children's Hospital during those days, Kennedy met other parents in his situation, "mostly working people: salesmen, secretaries, laborers, teachers, taxi drivers," and concluded that the costs of the American health care system were unfair. After his son recovered, he began directing his Senate health committee staff to focus on uninsured and underinsured Americans.

Five years later, in Memphis, Kennedy took the podium and revisited his personal voyage. "More than most Americans, I know what it means to have serious illness in the family. We were able to get the very best in terms of health care because we were able to afford it," he told the delegates. "It would have bankrupted any average family in this nation." He cast the issue in historical terms, calling national health insurance "the great unfinished business on the agenda of the Democratic Party.

"Our party gave Social Security to the nation in the 1930s. We gave Medicare to the nation in the 1960s. And we can bring national health insurance to the nation in the 1970s," he boomed. The speech is best remembered for the line, "Sometimes a party must sail against the wind," a clear rebuke to Carter's argument that the Democrats must adapt to changing economic circumstances and adjust their priorities. It was received as a not-so-subtle signal from Kennedy that Democrats should gird themselves for a Macbethian intraparty coup.

The speech also challenged Carter over the rising cost of goods and services, a problem that had been growing since Nixon took the nation off the gold standard in 1971. "The party that tore itself apart over Vietnam in the 1960s cannot afford to tear itself apart today over budget cuts in basic social programs...at the expense of the elderly, the poor, the black, the sick, the cities, and the unemployed."

Kennedy emphasized leadership, a theme he would return to again and again as his chief intangible criticism of Carter, and a word that would become the vehicle for all of the Democrats' stylistic, personality-driven, and class-driven resentments toward the president. "To achieve the reform we need, we must have genuine leadership by the Democratic Party," he said. Far from Teddy's playing a "minimal" role, it was clear that a full-on revolt against the party's own president was brewing. Kennedy worked himself into a lather, giving "a shouting, lectern-pounding speech." The crowd of twenty-five hundred responded with passion. Carter's trade representative, Robert Strauss, told a reporter that it was "the orneriest audience I've ever seen."

As he came to the close of his brief "remarks" on the panel, Kennedy's voice rose to a shout. "I want every delegate at this convention to understand," he said, "that as long as I am a vote, and as long as I have a voice in the United States Senate, it's going to be for that"—and here he pounded the lectern, emphasizing each syllable in three words—"Demo-cratic plat-form plank that provides decent quality health care, Nooorth and South, Eeeeast and West, for aaall Americans as a matter of right, not of privilege." The room erupted, and Kennedy strode back to his seat in the middle of the long white table, receiving eager handshakes from the other speakers.

A photo of Kennedy, his right arm raised, index finger pointed, and his mouth open mid-shout, landed on the front page of the *New York Times*. Afterward, Kennedy tried to avoid the topic of a run for president. "No, no, no," he said when asked. "I presume [Carter will] run, he'll win the nomination and I'll back him, but I'm going to speak out on these issues and he understands that."

But during the speech, Kennedy had teased the audience about a presidential run, with his trademark self-deprecating humor. "I am often invited to address Democratic conventions," he said in the opening moments of the speech, "but it's always the wrong year." He flashed a Kennedy smile, and the crowd broke up in laughter. Even more telling, he had hired Carl Wagner, a political operative, just days before the Memphis speech. Wagner had worked on George McGovern's 1972 campaign and had carefully studied the Carter campaign's mastery of the newly important caucus system in Iowa—his home state. Hamilton Jordan (pronounced *Jer-dun*), President Carter's top political adviser in the White House, watched Kennedy's speech from the back of the room in Memphis and stormed out at its conclusion. "The son of a bitch is going to run," he yelled at fellow Carter advisers Pat Caddell and Stu Eizenstat. Caddell was not convinced, but Jordan had been sure for some time that Kennedy was going to challenge Carter. "I am tired of telling you guys. It's over and we are going to get ready for it," Jordan vowed.

Three months later, the fifty-four-year-old president sat on the same Truman Balcony looking over the sloping hill that led down toward the Washington Monument. It was a chilly night on the first day of March 1979. Jimmy Carter grappled with his thoughts, with his doubts. He was worried that the peace talks between Israel and Egypt that he had presided over the previous fall were now about to fall apart. His presidency would go down as well. *What in the world are we going to do?* he wondered to himself, sitting in the darkness on the balcony.

It was a moment of uncharacteristic self-doubt and uncertainty for the former peanut farmer from Georgia. He was a man who almost always knew where he was going and what he wanted to do, and was absolutely confident he would accomplish his objective. But the first two years of his presidency had been troubled. He had focused on the peace process with myopic intensity, to the detriment of several other pressing issues in the nation. Now Israeli prime minister Menachem Begin had arrived in the United States that same day, and did not sound interested in finalizing the deal with Egyptian president Anwar Sadat.

In addition, inflation was ticking up. Gas prices were doing the same. So was unemployment. The nation was anxious about its place in the world. Carter's poll numbers had been bolstered by the Camp David agreement in September, but in December, as the rift between the Israelis and the Egyptians became more clear, his approval began to fall. He was now upside down in the polls, with just a 37 percent approval rating, down from 52 percent in November. His disapproval rating was at 46 percent.

The year had gotten off to a rotten start as well. In January, the shah of Iran had fled his country, chased out by Islamic radicals who two weeks later welcomed the Ayatollah Khomeini back to Iran from exile in France. So now Iran, which Carter had just over a year ago called "an oasis of stability" in the region, was controlled by religious extremists who held enormous power over global energy prices due to their nation's proximity to the Strait of Hormuz, through which about a fifth of the world's oil supply passed.

Strange things were happening in the United States as well. On January 29, Brenda Ann Spencer, a rail-thin red-haired sixteen-year-old with freckles, woke up at her father's house in San Diego. She picked up her father's rifle, went to the window of the house, and started firing live rounds at elementary school children across the street. Spencer wounded eight children and one police officer, and killed two adults: the principal and the custodian. During a nearly seven-hour siege at her house after the shooting, Spencer told a reporter over the phone, "I don't like Mondays. This livens up the day."

Carter was under strain, and it showed. "It is just disgusting," he had told the press two days before Begin's arrival, "almost to feel that we are that close and can't quite get [a deal]." The differences between the Israelis and Egyptians, he insisted, were "absolutely insignificant."

"The failure of the Camp David accords would be a costly

personal defeat at a time of doubt about [Carter's] leadership," the *New York Times* editorialized.

Carter had taken on plenty of water because of his efforts with American Jews, who thought he was a weak supporter of the Jewish state in Israel. Those concerns had grown since the Camp David agreement. As Begin arrived in Washington, Vice President Walter Mondale was in Los Angeles to speak at a $1,000-a-plate Democratic fund-raiser. He faced sharp questioning from leaders of the California Jewish community in meetings before the dinner. Other Jewish leaders organized a dinner to protest Carter the night before Mondale's arrival.

The problem for Carter was that it wasn't just Jewish leaders now publicly protesting his vice president's visit. A full-page newspaper ad appeared the day of Mondale's arrival, signed by a number of California political leaders, charging Carter with creating a "crisis of leadership." They called on Kennedy or "other gifted leaders" to challenge Carter in the 1980 campaign. The dinner protesting the president was attended by representatives from a wide range of interest and advocacy groups: leaders from the African American and Latino communities, women's groups, and farmers' protest groups.

The political furor over Mondale's appearance was so significant that the vice president did something he'd never done during his time in the office. He called a televised news conference with reporters to answer questions. There, he argued that Carter's political future was not doomed, hardly a compelling message. Mondale even had to answer questions about whether Carter intended to run for reelection. Polls showed Kennedy beating the incumbent by a two-to-one margin in a head-to-head matchup.

"It is not in the nature of the Democratic Party to make a Democratic president feel comfortable. They like you to feel lousy as much as possible so you'll work harder," Mondale said, referring to the criticism being leveled against Carter by many on the left. "But that does not mean the president is in trouble. I think the president is in good shape."

But Hamilton Jordan knew Carter was vulnerable. Kennedy, however, still wasn't entirely sure what he was going to do. Presidential campaigns did not have a history of lasting a year or more, as they have come to. So in the early spring of 1979, Kennedy, given historical precedent, had plenty of time to make up his mind. Teddy was consulting others and would ramp up those discussions in the coming months. But as was his habit, he was largely keeping his own counsel. "When Teddy wanted advice from somebody he really trusted, he found a quiet place, and locked the door, and talked to himself," said Burton Hersh, one of Kennedy's biographers.

It would be a historic and audacious thing to challenge a sitting president. Republican Ronald Reagan had done it just four years earlier, taking on President Gerald Ford. But Ford had never been popularly elected, so there was a rationale for someone to run against him. Carter's name had been on the ballot in 1976. He'd won the presidency himself. And before Reagan it had only happened a few times in American history.

But these two men had differences that at the bottom of it all were intensely personal. Their mutual dislike bordered on loathing. It was a rivalry between two highly ambitious men that had been building for nearly a decade. It would be hard to imagine two men more different from each other, shaped by more disparate and opposed backgrounds. They might as well have been raised on different planets.

# CHAPTER 2

❈❈❈

# Origins of Dirt and Riches

James Earl Carter Jr. came into a world dominated by white supremacy and racist ideology. Carter was born on October 1, 1924, in southwest Georgia. The Ku Klux Klan had just defeated an attempt to denounce them at the Democratic convention in New York a few months earlier, with the help of the overwhelmingly supportive Georgia delegation. Two weeks after Carter was born, Georgia governor Clifford Walker, a Democrat, admitted to reporters that he had addressed the KKK's annual convention in Kansas City the previous month.

The Klan was in its second iteration. It had first emerged in American life at the end of the Civil War, as a way for ex–Confederate soldiers to unofficially continue fighting the conflict, to keep white southerners in power. It lacked organization, however, and by the turn of the century it had crumbled. But then it had been reborn in 1915, this time largely in reaction to Catholic and Jewish immigrants taking jobs and acquiring influence in cities at a time of rapid urbanization and industrialization.

Atlanta was the epicenter of the Klan's revival. In August 1915, a thirty-one-year-old Jewish New Yorker who had moved to Atlanta, Leo Frank, was abducted from prison and lynched by a mob for the murder of a thirteen-year-old girl. On Thanksgiving Day that same year, a thirty-five-year-old itinerant preacher named William Joseph Simmons, inspired by the movie *The Birth of a Nation*, took a group of men with him to the top of Stone Mountain, where they put an American flag on an altar and burned a small cross. It began the Klan's adoption of the tactic.

This was the world that Carter was born into, his culture, his people. He was the first son of James Earl Carter, a World War I veteran and industrious farmer, and his wife, Lillian, a nurse. Carter would become known as the "man from Plains," but he actually grew up in a place called Archery, two and a half miles west of Plains. This was Carter's term for it: not a town or a village, but "a place." The town of Plains, 130 miles south of Atlanta, was founded in 1827 after the Creek Indians were pushed out, and in the 1880s was moved a mile south to be closer to a local railroad that helped transport cotton crops to market.

Carter grew up amid poverty and isolation. There was no running water in his home until he was nine years old, and so he and his family would relieve themselves either in one of the "slop jars" in each of the three bedrooms, or out back in the outdoor privy. "We wiped with old newspapers or pages torn from Sears, Roebuck catalogues," Carter would later write, in a perhaps characteristic moment of oversharing that is nonetheless illustrative. And that was a step up from other poor families, who "squatted behind bushes and wiped with corncobs or leaves." When his father bought a small windmill in 1935, it powered a toilet, a sink, and a rudimentary shower. The showerhead was a can with holes poked in it. Electricity would not arrive on most farms until President Roosevelt's Rural Electrification Administration, so artificial light came from kerosene lamps.

And the farming process in the Deep South until the 1940s was basically the same as during colonial times nearly two hundred years before. Tractors or other forms of mechanized power were rare, so plowing was done with mules, and harvesting was done by hand and depended on manual labor, usually from black tenant workers who lived in shacks on the farm property in exchange for a job, and who had little prospect of ever earning much money. The southern farm population actually grew from 1930 to 1935, as city workers lost jobs during the Great Depression and moved to places like Archery.

Carter's father, Earl, owned 350 acres. It was a good-sized farm, especially since many other family estates were still undergoing a multidecade process of being subdivided by descendants of plantation owners after the Civil War. And Earl made the most of it. He was smart, very thrifty, and a good businessman. "He developed the reputation of having everything he touched turned to gold," wrote Carter biographer Peter Bourne. Earl Carter increased his wealth modestly and cautiously, buying land with cash and selling the timber. He harvested cotton, but by the time Jimmy was born he was growing peanuts as well, after the 1915 boll weevil infestation had severely damaged that year's cotton harvest. He also ran a small store where he sold a number of items he made or produced himself: syrup from sugarcane grown on the farm, jars of honey, ketchup, jams and jellies from various fruits, milk and butter from their cows' milk. He grew potatoes, sweet potatoes, velvet beans, and corn. He raised pigs, which they slaughtered each year to make hams, pigs' feet, sausages, and Brunswick stew; cows; a bull; sheep; geese, whose feathers they plucked to make down pillows and comforters; chickens; and mules for plowing the fields.

Earl could be stoic and restrained, and sometimes severe. The family did not speak at the dinner table, although they were allowed to bring books to read while they ate. Carter strove to please his father and rarely felt that he succeeded. He would write a poem later in life, after his presidency, titled "I Wanted to Share My Father's World." Carter wrote of "those rare times when we did cross the bridge between us" and described them as "pure joy." His father was dead, and he was an adult, but Carter wrote: "Even now I feel inside, the hunger for his outstretched hand, a man's embrace to take me in, the need for just a word of praise." He concluded the poem by revealing that he didn't overcome his "resentments" until he sat with his father on Earl's deathbed. Some of Earl's austerity was due to the Depression, which hit when young Jimmy was five years old. And some of it was just his personality.

Carter lived an existence that would have been foreign to any member of the Kennedy clan. He spent his free time in the summer roaming through creeks and forests with friends, shirtless and shoeless. "I don't remember that my parents ever put any limits on my explorations around the farm, even including the more remote woods and swamps," Carter wrote. "I was completely free to roam throughout the 350 acres" as long as he did not neglect his chores and was on time for meals. He collected "little white round rocks" from the railroad bed and kept them in his pockets as ammunition for his slingshot.

He also engaged in demanding physical labor from a young age. He picked cotton in the fields alongside black field hands. He learned to plow the fields by guiding the mules, and engaged in many other forms of physical labor and farm work. Most of his playmates were black, the children of field hands. When his parents went on trips, he would sleep in a small one-bedroom shack with his father's chief farmhand, a black man named Jack Clark, who had a son Carter's age. Carter spent most of his childhood with two sisters, Gloria and Ruth. His only brother, Billy, was not born until he was twelve years old.

Carter learned to be industrious early on. He would pick peanuts from an acre given to him by his father, boil them at home, and then walk along the train tracks to Plains's small downtown, where he sold them in paper bags for a nickel each. At age nine, he had saved around $125, which he used to buy five bales of cotton. Thanks to the Great Depression, the price of cotton had fallen to 5 cents a pound. Carter stored the cotton in his father's warehouse for four years, and watched the price of cotton go up to 18 cents a pound. He sold the five bales for $450, and used the money to buy five small local shacks. For the next ten years, until he left Plains for college, Carter rented the shacks to poor black tenants for a combined $16.50 a month.

There were around thirty other families in Archery. Only one of those families was white. The rest were made up of black farmhands who worked on Earl's farm, earning subsistence wages. There were 260 farmhands at one point.

Earl Carter's politics were segregationist and white supremacist, as were most Georgians' at the time. But Carter's mother, Lillian, was a progressive on racial questions from a young age. Earl "was tolerant if not supportive of Lillian's views." Earl was "above all, a Talmadge man," meaning he was a devoted supporter of Eugene Talmadge, the arch-segregationist governor of Georgia in the 1930s and '40s.

Earl Carter would drive his one-ton truck to Talmadge rallies, the flatbed loaded down with friends and neighbors sitting on hay bales. These were social events, but only for men, and they would chant for Talmadge to take off his suit jacket and reveal the red suspenders underneath. "For some reason," Carter wrote years later, "this seemed to be the highlight of the entire event." Carter sounded like he was feigning surprise, to disguise his disgust for the simplicity of the masses. "Talmadge was a populist, I guess," he wrote. He didn't try to hide his disappointment in his father's choice of political hero.

---

In contrast to Carter, Edward M. Kennedy was born into great wealth. His father, in addition to being rich, was a potential presidential candidate. Teddy was born eight years after Carter, on February 22, 1932. He was the youngest of nine children. The family lived in a mansion in the New York suburbs fifteen miles north of Manhattan, and spent summers in Cape Cod. Teddy's childhood was filled to overflowing with experience and travel and luxury. But his father was absent for most of his early childhood.

Teddy entered a family that was already a swirling vortex of activity, in which he was often an afterthought. Unlike his brothers, he did not get a family name. Teddy was named after his father's closest business partner and best friend, Edward Moore, who had worked for his mother's father, former Boston mayor John "Honey Fitz" Fitzgerald. "There was an unvoiced suspicion around the household that he was one more than the family really needed," wrote Kennedy biographer Burton Hersh. When guests would spend the night, Teddy sometimes slept in a bathtub.

That was about the roughest it got in Teddy's early years, however. For the first six years of his life he lived in a three-story, twenty-room white house in Bronxville, New York, with a large colonnade out front and a red-tiled roof. The house had a garage with room for five cars, a billiards table in the basement, and an electric toy train set on the third floor that Teddy's older brothers, John and Bobby, jealously guarded. Teddy's mother, Rose, had a household staff of eight: four maids, a waitress, a cook, a nurse, and a governess. Teddy's siblings called him "fat stuff" and "biscuits and muffins."

Summers for young Teddy were spent at the family compound

in Hyannis Port, Massachusetts. Teddy's father, Joseph Patrick Kennedy Sr., had bought the house in 1928 after renting in the small Cape Cod village for two years. He expanded the house, which sat on two and a half seafront acres, to make it a fifteen-room, nine-bath home, with an outdoor tennis court and a small movie theater in the basement.

Joe Sr. had come up in the Boston banking scene and willed and wiled his way to fortune in the 1920s as a distributor of low-budget films. Despite the persistence of a myth that he made a fortune from bootlegging illegal liquor during Prohibition, David Nasaw wrote in his definitive biography, *The Patriarch,* that "not only is there no evidence of Kennedy's being a bootlegger... [but] it flies in the face of everything we know about him."

The year Teddy was born, Joe Sr. was named chairman of the Securities and Exchange Commission by the new president-elect, Franklin Delano Roosevelt. That job kept Joe Sr. in Washington. In 1938, President Roosevelt named Joe Sr. his ambassador to Great Britain. The Kennedy family arrived in London in March. At the age of six, young Teddy was living in an urban metropolis across the Atlantic. He cut the ribbon to reopen a renovated Royal Children's Zoo. He received his first communion from Pope Pius XII.

The Kennedys' lodgings in London were even grander than their home in the United States: six floors and thirty-six rooms just off Hyde Park, with an elevator and a full staff of personal valets and servants. The house had belonged to banking giant J. P. Morgan, who donated it to the American government. Teddy's bedroom on the third floor was "almost as big as a school room," with twin beds, a large fireplace, dressers, a chaise, and a small table with two chairs. His father had an American freezer shipped overseas because the freezers in Britain did not keep their ice cream cold enough for his liking.

Joe Sr. was Irish Catholic, which was an obstacle to him in business and social life in the United States and could have been an impediment in the United Kingdom. An American president had never sent anything but "Anglo-Scottish Protestants" to the Court of St. James's. Roosevelt had chosen Joe Sr. to represent him in Britain in part because he knew he would retain some independence instead of going native. He would "remain an American," as Senator James Byrnes, a South Carolina Democrat, wrote to Joe Sr. But the British press loved the ambassador's family, and fawned over his children.

For Teddy's older brothers and sisters, it was a glamorous time of balls and parties. For Teddy himself, he later wrote, it was a time of loneliness. He struggled to make friends, to understand cricket, and was whacked with a ruler on the palms of his hands anytime he misbehaved in school. The silver lining for Teddy was that his father, who had mostly been absent from his life to this point, was now with him and went out of his way to ease the discomfort of his youngest son. Joe Sr. attended Teddy's cricket games, took him along on his morning horseback rides through Hyde Park, and would often read to him before bed.

London was preparing for war. As Teddy and his older brother Bobby walked through the city streets on their way to and from school, they saw the sandbags piled around buildings as the prospect of bombing became more imminent, and at school they strapped on gas masks and filed with the other children into air raid shelters. Joe Sr.'s political fortunes were on the wane as the Nazi threat grew. Because he believed Hitler should be appeased rather than fought, he was an adamant opponent of FDR's sending weapons or military equipment to Britain, arguing that it would fall into German hands once Adolf Hitler's army overwhelmed the Royal Air Force and invaded Great Britain. "He believes that Germany and Russia will win the war and that the end of the world is just down the road," FDR told Harold L. Ickes, who served as his secretary of the interior for thirteen years and who warned Roosevelt that Joe Sr. was a dangerous rival for the presidency in 1940.

Great Britain declared war on Germany on September 3, 1939, and within two weeks, Joe Sr. began sending his large family home to the United States, on three separate ships in the event one of them was sunk. He was kept in place by FDR only because the president didn't want him to return home and endorse Wendell Willkie, the Republican candidate. "The ambassador was too rich, too outspoken, too charming, and too well connected to the national media to have as an enemy," Nasaw wrote. Joe stayed in London for the first six weeks of the Blitz, only because he didn't want the public to think he was running away from the bombs. Finally, at the end of October he returned to America. He gave a radio address endorsing FDR, a critical piece of support for the president in winning the Irish Catholic vote.

But after he told a reporter, "Democracy is finished in England. It may be here," any political future Joe Sr. might have had was badly damaged. It was a tough blow for a man who had had such high hopes that FDR might retire, opening the way for him to make a play for the presidency. He never served in public office after that.

For Teddy, the return home ushered in the start of the bleakest portion of his childhood. "These did not prove to be happy, joyous years," Teddy wrote in his memoirs. His mother wanted him to go to boarding school, but for some reason she sent him to the school Bobby was attending, Portsmouth Priory, in Rhode Island. The school only taught students beginning in the seventh grade, but the Benedictine monks who ran it agreed to let Rose send Teddy there anyway. And so he spent the spring of 1940, at age eight, going to math and Latin classes that were incomprehensible, and only barely grasped a few measures of French class. "It was a recipe for disaster. My time at Portsmouth Priory was not an education; it was a battle," Teddy said. "My classmates did not befriend me."

Teddy's only friend was his pet turtle. When the turtle died, Teddy buried it in the yard and cried himself to sleep. He woke to find the dead turtle back in his bed. The older boys in his dorm had dug it up, thrown it around the hall, and then put it under the poor kid's sheets while he slept. "I buried him again that morning," Teddy wrote in his autobiography.

Joe Sr. sold the house in Bronxville that same year, with the youngest kids all off at boarding schools or colleges. Rose, Teddy's mother, was often traveling during the year. They felt they no longer needed a home base. For Teddy, this meant that the rest of his childhood was, as he put it, a rather "nomadic" experience. "I was essentially without a central home," he wrote. The fall after Portsmouth Priory, he endured the worst experience of his school years, when he was moved to Riverdale Country School for Boys, in the Bronx. It was an elite educational institution, but Teddy's dorm master was "an abuser" who "specialized in terror and humiliation." Teddy did not name the man in his autobiography, referring to him only as "R." But he strongly implied that some boys were sexually abused, and that he escaped this fate only by hiding under his bunk. He described those nights as "terror-filled."

"I could not believe this was happening," he wrote. "I kept telling myself that this would pass. That I would get through this nightmare. That my brothers had survived boarding school and I would too. *It's going to be okay*, I told myself. I had to believe that."

Teddy was saved by his mother's desire to have him near her during the winter semester. She moved him and her youngest daughter, Jean, to a day school in Palm Beach while they lived with her. In the spring, Teddy developed whooping cough. The pertussis vaccine was not yet widely available and children often died from the sickness. He had pneumonia as well, and the cough "nearly killed" him. But after being released from the hospital, he went to Hyannis Port with his mother to recuperate. They walked on the beach together, and she read to him each evening, something she had been too tired to do with him when he was younger. "As sick as I was, those days were a tonic for me," Teddy wrote. "And they cemented a special bond between my mother and me that survived until her death at the age of 104."

Teddy also felt strong love and admiration for his father, who for all his faults was an affectionate and devoted parent. Joe Sr. wrote letters to each child throughout his life during his many travels. And Teddy remembered how he "always kissed us when we came home." He wrote, "Not many fathers kissed their children back then. And even as grown men, we kissed our father on the cheek when greeting him or saying goodbye. I continue that tradition with my sons."

The fall of 1941 brought what Rose would call "the first of the tragedies that were to befall us," when Rosemary disappeared from the Kennedy family after her lobotomy. She was rendered severely retarded by the procedure, unable to speak and completely dependent on others. Her parents moved her to a nursing home, and nine-year-old Teddy would not see her again until he was well into adulthood. Rose would not mention her in letters to the children for two decades. A month after the operation, the Japanese bombed Pearl Harbor, and the United States entered World War II.

Three years later, at the height of World War II, Teddy's oldest brother, Joseph Jr., volunteered for a mission to take out launch sites in Belgium for V-1 guided missiles, which had been introduced by the Germans in June 1944 as a new way to bombard London. Joe Jr.'s Navy PB4Y-1 Liberator bomber was stripped down and loaded with explosives. His assignment was to fly it close to the target and then abandon the aircraft by parachute, turning control of the aircraft over to two B-17s flying with him, who would guide the plane via radio control to the launch site. On August 12, as Joe Jr. attempted to carry out his mission, the explosives on board the plane detonated prematurely, killing him instantly. Back in Hyannis Port, Teddy and his siblings sobbed at hearing the news, until Jack—now the oldest boy—told Teddy and his friend Joey Gargan to come sailing with him because that's what Joe Jr. would have wanted them to do.

In high school, Teddy finally stayed in one place, attending Milton Academy south of Boston. From his constantly uprooted, uncertain childhood, he had learned how to make friends quickly and easily. But he also "tended to travel light emotionally," as his future college classmate Burton Hersh put it. Teddy claimed to have no anger at his parents for his childhood experience. And as he moved into early adolescence, he learned to play a new role in the family and with his parents as the Kennedys endured one tragedy after another.

But then in May 1948, Teddy's second oldest sister, Kathleen, died in a plane crash in France. She was twenty-eight years old and a widow at the time; her husband had been killed by a sniper in World War II less than a month after Joe Jr. died. When Kathleen, known as "Kick," died, Teddy was sixteen, ensconced at Milton Academy. "Even though it was spring, I remember that morning as exceptionally cold and dark," he wrote.

Kick's death devastated her parents. "The sudden death of young Joe and Kathleen, within a period of three years, has left a mark with me that I find very difficult to erase," Joe Sr. wrote to a friend. The tragedies to befall three of the Kennedys' four eldest children were, sadly, just a prelude to the family's suffering.

# CHAPTER 3

❧

# The Pull of Home and Politics

When Jimmy Carter left his hometown and headed to the U.S. Naval Academy in the summer of 1943, his father, Earl, went off with a buddy to get drunk. Despite all the stoicism that characterized Earl's relationship with his firstborn son, their bonds of love ran deep.

Carter, at the preposterous age of seven, had set a goal of going to the Academy but had failed to earn a sponsorship from his congressman after graduating from Plains High School. So he spent a year at Georgia Southwestern College in Americus, eleven miles east of Plains, and got his sponsorship at the end of that year, on the condition that he complete some prerequisite classes at Georgia Tech over the following year.

Carter was a bright and hardworking student, but his sponsorship wouldn't have happened without Earl's stature as a community leader. It was a role Earl had first embraced after the Rural Electrification Administration was created. Earl became a member of the rural electric cooperative in the region, and would attend national conventions and travel to Washington to urge lawmakers to continue funding the REA, which handed out low-interest loans to utilities in rural areas in order to hold down the cost of electricity.

And Carter's gifts were nourished and enhanced by the woman whom he credited with doing more to influence his intellect than anyone else, Julia Coleman. The daughter of a Baptist preacher, she never married, devoting her life to education. Coleman was blind in one eye and relied on others to read to her. Despite this, she was a highly educated, highly motivated learner and educator. "I don't think there is any way to explain my life or to explain Rosalynn's life, or to explain our advancement after school, without understanding the Plains High School and what it meant," Carter wrote, referring primarily to Coleman, according to biographer Peter Bourne.

Once he got to Annapolis, Carter was far from a standout or a leader. Confronted as a freshman plebe with hazing from upperclassmen, he "settled into a strategy of anonymity," wrote Bourne. "My main trouble was that I smiled too much," Carter later wrote. He was physically small, at five foot nine inches and weighing only around 120 pounds. He did well at cross-country, and was labeled "a loner" by one classmate, Dr. Francis Hertzog. "He did not make close intimate friendships," Hertzog said. "He didn't need other people's close bond of friendship to support his own ego and personality—he had a very strong character."

There were also early signs during his college years of a tendency to dramatically downplay his own disappointment and failure, which would hurt him politically in the future. A year after graduating from the Naval Academy, Carter applied for a Rhodes Scholarship, and the choice for the selectee from his home state came down to him and one other young man. Carter, who was already discouraged about the state of the Navy during the postwar era, badly wanted the scholarship, but did not get picked. His mother, Lillian, said the rejection was "devastating" and that Carter was depressed for weeks. Carter, however, would recall the incident as little more than a minor disappointment. "I didn't even feel bitter about it," he said. He noted that "as a matter of fact," the man who did get selected "had a nervous breakdown" not too long afterward.

A year before he graduated from the Academy, Carter and Rosalynn were married on July 7, 1946. Rosalynn had grown up in Plains, but was three years younger than Carter and they'd not known each other. When she became friends with Carter's sister Ruth, however, he met her during a trip home from the Academy in the summer of 1945. Carter had dated several other girls in Plains over the years, but on their first date, he kissed Rosalynn, something she had never allowed another boy to do on a first date. When Carter got home that night, he told his mother, "She's the one I'm going to marry."

Over the years, their marriage would become a rock, a tight bond between them, and an equal partnership. But in their early years as a couple, Rosalynn simply followed Carter from naval post to naval post after his graduation. Carter spent one year on the USS *Wyoming*, a beat-up old battleship in Norfolk, Virginia, and their first son, Jack, was born during this time, in the summer of 1947. After spending his second year on another ship based in Norfolk, the USS *Mississippi*, Carter rebounded from the Rhodes Scholarship rejection by applying for submarine service, a prestigious and sought-after post.

He got in, and in the summer of 1948 he and Rosalynn moved to New London, Connecticut, for six months of submarine officer training. His first tour on a sub, the USS *Pomfret*, took him to China early the next year, and it was on that voyage that Carter had his closest brush with death. Not long after departing Honolulu, the *Pomfret* ran into a massive storm in the Pacific. Carter, who was badly seasick, drew duty on the bridge at night when the vessel had to surface to recharge its batteries, and an enormous wave tore him from the handrail and swept him off the deck. He was separated from the ship and considered it a miracle that when the wave receded he landed on the *Pomfret* thirty feet away from where he had been standing before.

Just as at the Naval Academy, Carter was "not one of the guys" on the *Pomfret*, a shipmate said, despite the close quarters. While the others played poker at night, Carter could be found reading a book on sonar or some other aspect of submarining. "He was always apart...he never really got close to anybody," another sailor on the *Pomfret* recalled. But he was an outstanding officer, well suited for submarine life. He had masterful knowledge of the vessel but carried himself with an understated yet confident demeanor, and thrived under the kind of pressure and confined spaces that drove one of his shipmates insane. He learned a different kind of leadership style on a submarine than he might have on a surface vessel; life underwater in such cramped quarters required a collaborative style that was based as much on example as it was on command.

At the beginning of 1951, Carter moved his family back to New London, where he had been appointed a senior officer on a newly commissioned submarine, the *K-1*. In June, he was promoted to full lieutenant. He had a growing family now. Their second son, James Earl "Chip" Carter III, was born in early 1950, and their third son, Donnel Jeffrey, was born near the end of Carter's eighteen-month tour on the *K-1*, in August 1952. During his time on the *K-1*, he qualified to be a submarine commander. That was his future.

But the restless Carter always looked for new challenges. So he applied for a position in a newly created nuclear submarine officer school, and was accepted. The program was run by Captain Hyman Rickover, a brilliant but controversial figure in the Navy, who held himself in high regard as "not so much a manager but as a charismatic figure...surrounded by dedicated followers." He eschewed bureaucracy, cared only for results, was notoriously stingy with praise, and held his subordinates to extraordinarily high standards.

Carter would never forget his first interview with Rickover, in which the older man quizzed him repeatedly on various topics far beyond Navy life, such as classical music, literature, and current events. Rickover ended the interview by asking Carter about his time at the Naval Academy. "Did you always do your best?" he asked. Carter began to answer that he had, but then reconsidered. "No, sir. I didn't always do my best," he said. Rickover stared at him for several seconds, and then said only, "Why not?" He turned his chair away from Carter, who sat there stunned for several moments before leaving the room. Rickover deeply influenced Carter and his leadership style. "We feared and respected him and strove to please him," he wrote. "He scared me." Carter compared him to his own father, and would later title one of his books *Why Not the Best?*

But Carter was only in Rickover's program for a few months before news came from Plains that his father was sick. A few weeks after that, his mother, Lillian, called with the bad news: Earl, at age fifty-nine, had pancreatic cancer, and would not live long. Carter got off the phone, lay down on his bed, and cried. He returned home to visit, and sat with his father by his bedside, where he got to know Earl in a way he had not before. He heard from others of his father's compassion and generosity, and his quiet acts of charity that he never talked about. And he saw the way in which much of the town of Plains now depended on his father's farm. Earl's various parcels of land amounted to more than five thousand acres now, and through his seed and fertilizer business, he extended credit to many farmers in the area who could not pay up front. "It was almost like a medieval idea. . . . Without his father, those 1,500 people were not going to have any means to live," said Carter's friend Frank Andrews.

Earl died at 9:30 a.m. on July 22, 1953, with his wife and children around him. Not long afterward, Carter and his sister Ruth went around visiting with the tenants on his land to inform them one by one of the news. Ruth said these visits deepened Carter's conviction that his father had led a more consequential life than he had previously thought.

Carter returned to his naval post in Schenectady in the midst of a personal identity crisis. He was on a steady upward trajectory in the Navy. Rosalynn was busy with three young children, but very happy with their life. But Carter's mother, in particular, had made no bones about what she thought he should do. "He had to come back," she said. "Everything we had was on the line." And as Carter assessed his life in the Navy, he began to argue with himself that a return to his hometown could be a more enriching life, spiritually and relationally. He would be stepping into his father's shoes, picking up his mantle, carrying on his tradition and his name, upholding his honor. There was just one problem: Rosalynn was dead set against the idea. The thought of going back to their hometown scared and horrified her.

But Carter had made up his mind. The decision nearly severed his marriage. Rosalynn "almost quit me," he said. She wouldn't speak to him. But they were going back. It was a turning point in Carter's life. On October 9, 1953, at the age of twenty-nine, he was honorably discharged from the Navy and returned home to Georgia with his wife and three children.

———— ⊗ ————

A month before the Carters' tense car ride from New York to Georgia, Teddy Kennedy had been readmitted to Harvard University, after two years of exile. He was still paying the price for having been kicked out of the school in the spring of his freshman year for cheating on an exam. Teddy's rocky college career was an inauspicious entry into adulthood for the youngest of Joe Sr.'s nine kids. Teddy's father had always made clear to his children, and more specifically to his sons, that he expected high achievement from them. "We don't want any losers around here. In this family, we want winners," Joe Sr. often told them.

When Teddy was thirteen or fourteen years old, he said, his father sat him down and said, "You can have a serious life or a nonserious life, Teddy. I'll still love you whichever choice you make. But if you decide to have a nonserious life, I won't have much time for you. You make up your mind. There are too many children here who are doing things that are interesting for me to do much with you." And Teddy could see that his older brothers were well on their way. When he was expelled from Harvard, Jack had been in Congress for five years, and Bobby was a high-powered Senate committee staffer.

Teddy's father had made a great fortune in order to make his kids financially independent, and he told them he wanted them to go into public service. Joe Sr. tried to instill a sense of responsibility into his children, rather than pampering them at every turn. But his youngest son was having trouble growing up. After getting kicked out of Harvard, Teddy knew he needed to atone for his sins. He decided to enlist in the Army. He did basic training at Fort Dix, New Jersey, as one of the grunts, among other recruits from all walks of life.

Teddy intended to volunteer to go fight in the Korean War. Jack and Bobby said it was selfish and inconsiderate of their parents and talked him out of it. Teddy instead took an assignment in counterintelligence, but was transferred out after two months. He suspected he had been blacklisted by an ambitious prosecutor named Roy Cohn who viewed Bobby as a rival. (Ironically, Bobby and Cohn both ended up working for anticommunist senator Joe McCarthy. Cohn would go on to work for and advise

Donald Trump as his attorney for thirteen years in the seventies and eighties.)

Teddy landed in Camp Gordon, Georgia, to be trained as a military policeman, and then in June 1952 went to France to help guard the Supreme Allied Headquarters in the Paris suburbs. After this less than spectacular military career, Teddy—whose obligation of service had been shortened from four years to two years by his father's political influence—was discharged from the Army as a private.

Teddy finally graduated from Harvard in 1956. His main accomplishment was to letter in varsity football as a senior, playing defensive end and tight end. He then spent three years at the University of Virginia School of Law, where for a brief time he "stopped worrying about 'catching up' and savored the moment." He savored some a bit too much, apparently, for he was regularly ticketed by the local police for speeding and one time led cops on a high-speed chase at up to ninety miles per hour. And his own future beyond law school weighed on him more than he would acknowledge. He developed an ulcer during this period.

The same fall that Teddy entered UVA, Jack told his parents and siblings at Thanksgiving that he intended to run for president in 1960. Teddy wrote that "a charge of energy ran through our family" when they heard the news. "Getting Jack reelected to the Senate, and then helping him become president—this had become our mission," he said.

In the fall of 1957, Teddy, who was now twenty-five, met twenty-one-year-old Joan Bennett. Ted's sister Jean introduced her little brother to Joan after he gave a speech at Manhattanville College of the Sacred Heart, the women's college that his mother, sisters Eunice and Jean, and sister-in-law Ethel Kennedy all attended. Joan was a tall blonde who had done some modeling, and the daughter of an advertising executive, Harry Bennett, a Republican. Teddy's courtship with her moved quickly, and in a year, they were married.

There were plenty of warning signs leading up to the wedding that it might not be a good idea. Joan had grown up in a family where politics was rarely discussed; the political arena was foreign to her. Teddy, for his part, was something of an absentee suitor after proposing to Joan late in the summer of 1958. The pair saw each other just twice during their three-month engagement as Teddy traveled around Massachusetts campaigning for Jack's reelection to the Senate. He gave her a ring that his father had bought for him, having never even looked at it. And most tellingly, as the wedding approached, Joan and her parents decided they wanted to put the nuptials off for a year, but Joe Sr. would hear nothing of it, insisting that they go through with it.

On the day of the wedding, November 29, 1958, Jack was Teddy's best man. As the two stood at the altar waiting for Joan to walk down the aisle, the newly reelected senator told his younger brother that being married didn't mean he had to stop sleeping with other women. Jack had forgotten he was wearing a microphone, as was Ted, for a film being made of the wedding, and Joan heard the comment when she watched the video.

Teddy finished law school, and then in the summer of 1959 he and Joan took a delayed honeymoon. On his return, he jumped headfirst into Jack's presidential campaign. He was sent out west to wrangle up support in far-flung places like Arizona, Colorado, and even Alaska. At one stop in Madison, Wisconsin, a group of ski jumpers challenged him to give it a try. Not wanting to back down or make his brother look bad, he took them up on it. He somehow avoided serious injury or death, despite having never before attempted anything like it. In Miles City, Montana, he got on the back of a rodeo steed and, again, survived. In Arizona, he flew himself between small towns in a chartered single-engine prop plane; he'd earned his pilot's license while in law school.

Teddy's performance was mixed. JFK lost most of the Western

states. But Teddy helped wrangle delegates in a number of hard-to-reach places, and by his telling, he played a vital role in securing JFK's presidential nomination. It was Teddy's close relationships with the Wyoming delegation, he said, that helped put JFK over the top on the first ballot.

Teddy returned from the 1960 campaign with his mind set on the West. It's not entirely clear what he wanted to do with his life at this point, but he wanted to move himself, Joan, and young Kara Anne, born in February 1960, somewhere far away from his family. He and Joan had "seriously discussed living in California," he wrote in his memoir. Kennedy biographer Adam Clymer wrote that Joan preferred Arizona and wanted to get some distance from the Kennedys, and that Teddy himself had his eye on New Mexico, both of whose senators were growing old. As Joan put it at the time, "His main reason for wanting to move was a feeling that in a new state he would have to succeed or fail on his own."

What is less apparent is what Teddy wanted to do with his life. Politics was clearly on the table for him. But biographer Burton Hersh said he toyed with the idea of buying a small newspaper out west, or going into law. The widely repeated story is that Joe Sr. told Teddy he had to run for Jack's Senate seat: "I paid for it. It belongs in the family," the patriarch said. According to Joan Kennedy, he told her and Teddy, "It's your turn. Get your fat asses up to Boston." But Teddy denied this. He insisted years later to Hersh that he had gone into politics of his own accord. "Nobody forced me to run. I wanted to. It wasn't a situation of my father pressing me into the breach," he said. He also told Clymer that his father "never used the word 'ass' in his life."

In Teddy's telling, he informed his father of his desire to run but wasn't sure if Joe Sr. would even approve. But it was not far-fetched to believe that Joe Sr. had made the decision rather than Teddy. "Dad didn't think too much of the idea" of moving out west, Teddy wrote in his memoir. And so he yielded to his father's will that he stay in Massachusetts. As Joan put it, "Eventually, of course, we both decided that you can't run away from being the president's brother."

As with Carter, there were deep ties to family pulling Teddy toward a destiny he did not fully control.

By 1960, Carter had survived his first few years in Plains, overcoming an initial drought, and was beginning to think beyond the small town. He had solidified his standing in the community, but not without some major challenges, which came primarily from his more liberal views on race at a time of great upheaval over the matter.

Six months after he returned home, the Supreme Court had issued its ruling in *Brown v. Board of Education*, mandating that schools nationwide desegregate and integrate black and white students. The tectonic plates were shifting, and great forces had been set in motion. The South would fight the ruling, and desegregation policies in general, for decades longer.

Jimmy and Rosalynn, then, chose to walk something of a fine line. Their priority was building up their farm and warehouse business, and they took a political approach to it, attending many weddings and funerals in and around Plains, and assuming a place in the larger community as business and civic leaders. Yet when the local chapter of the White Citizens' Council tried to get Carter to join, he refused. When a member of the group produced a five-dollar bill and said he would pay Carter's entry fee, Jimmy lost his cool, telling them he'd rather flush the money down the toilet than join up with them. A boycott of the Carter business resulted. It didn't last, but the Carters were kicked out of the Americus Country Club.

Still, Carter continued to flourish financially. "We wanted to have a successful business and be rich one day," he said. And by

1961, he was on his way. He had built up the farming operation, as well as a warehouse that provided peanut seed and many other supplies to local farmers. He had been elected chairman of the Sumter County school board, was a member of the regional hospital authority, and held a leadership position in the Lions Club. He paid off a modest ranch-style home in Plains in three years.

Carter encountered the volatile politics of the South when he tried to consolidate county schools. Many southerners saw the consolidation plan as the first step in eventual desegregation. Carter believed that if he simply presented people with the simple facts of what consolidation meant, he could win them over. The vote was close, but did not carry, and was defeated overwhelmingly in Plains. Carter's own cousin, Hugh, organized the opposition.

Some in Plains believed Carter ran for the state senate because he wanted to get away from the bitter fight over desegregation in Sumter County. To have spoken out in favor of integrating the schools in the years leading up to that "would have been unthinkable and pointless," wrote Bourne. The idea was regarded by many whites with the same horror as child molestation, according to Warren Fortson, a local attorney and friend of Carter's. Carter had not been a public advocate for it up until that point, even if he privately might have favored it.

Carter himself described his integration efforts as "relatively unobtrusive." He did things like organize a biracial steering committee to help plan an evangelism effort around a Billy Graham crusade. But he had seen during the consolidation fight the venom that would be unleashed at anyone on the school board who presided over any measures of integration. Someone had put a sign on the Carter warehouse that read COONS AND CARTERS GO TOGETHER. The local service station refused to fuel up Carter's truck, so he went and installed his own underground fuel tank and pumping station on his farm.

Carter considered leaving Plains and going to work for a ship-building company that desired his expertise on nuclear-powered vessels and his top-secret clearance. But in the end, he decided to stay and to run for the state senate in 1962, with the goal of improving the state's education system at the forefront of his mind. A state senate seat had just become a much more valuable asset, during a time of immense political upheaval in Georgia. Federal court rulings had done away with the county unit system, which gave white rural voters outsize influence, and the state legislature had drawn new districts and changed senate seats from temporary positions that rotated between counties to permanent offices. The new Fourteenth District included Sumter County and six other smaller counties, and Carter thought he could win it.

Carter declared his candidacy in a notice he placed in the Americus newspaper only fifteen days before the primary election. Rosalynn and other family members made phone calls from the family warehouse. But on election day, Carter was stymied by a corrupt local official in the smallest county in his district, Quitman County. A man named Joe Hurst ran the small town of Georgetown, about fifty-five miles west of Plains and right on the state line with Alabama. Hurst used his political influence to bring roads and bridges and other state-funded projects to the county, and his wife, Mary, was the local welfare director. More than half of the county's population was on welfare, and the Hursts arranged for the checks to be sent to them, so that they could personally hand them out to recipients.

On election day, the overweight Hurst, wearing an open-necked white shirt and a gray fedora, smoking a cigar, greeted voters as they entered the Georgetown courthouse and escorted them inside. Instead of a voting booth where citizens could vote in private, he had them do so on a counter in front of his lackey, a county functionary named "Doc" Hammond. Hammond would instruct the voters how to vote, telling them to scratch out Carter's name because Hurst wanted Homer Moore, Carter's opponent, to win. One woman came in and announced that she would be voting for Carter. Hammond harangued her until she submitted to voting for Moore. Another elderly couple tried to hide their ballots in the cardboard ballot box by mixing them in. Hurst reached in, pulled them out, and when he saw that they were for Carter, tore them up. He filled out six ballots instead for Moore, put them in the ballot box, and threatened the couple that he would burn their house down if they crossed him again.

Perhaps most amazingly, a known friend and supporter of Carter's named John Pope sat watching all of this, and it was no restraint on Hurst at all. Pope tried to intervene once and was cursed out by Hammond. When he confronted Hurst, the man waved his cigar in Pope's face and told him, "I have been running my county my way for twenty years and no one from Sumter County, or any other county, is going to come in here and tell me how to run my county." He then added an ominous and wholly believable physical threat. "Mr. Pope, I want you to know that I have put three men in that river out back for doing less than you are doing here today." Carter himself showed up and confronted Hurst, who casually deflected all his questions. Carter couldn't even get a local newspaper reporter to write about what Hurst was doing. The reporter's response summed up the attitude in the South to much that was culturally wrong: "Everybody knows it's not right, but this is the way they always run elections over here," the reporter said. And later that night, when the results came in, the fraudulent returns in Quitman County put Moore narrowly over the top against Carter.

Many would have grudgingly accepted defeat, believing nothing could be done to change the result. But Carter was incensed. He did not like losing, but he would not tolerate being swindled. It deeply violated his strong sense of right and wrong. His request for a recount likely would have been a lost cause if not for the advice of his cousin Hugh, the same cousin who had opposed him on consolidation, who connected Carter with an investigative reporter in Atlanta, John Pennington. Pennington's exhaustive reporting into Joe Hurst's election-day antics ran on the front page of the *Atlanta Journal* on October 22, two weeks before the general election. A few days later, Pennington published another deeply reported piece on Quitman County's historical pattern of election abuses. It brought the story to the public's attention around the state and in the capital city, and led to Carter's meeting with a high-powered Atlanta attorney, Charles Kirbo. Kirbo took their case a little reluctantly, but would likely never have done so without Pennington's initial article.

The weeks between the primary and the general election on November 6 were a mad dash of depositions, legal filings, and court hearings, but with the help of Pennington and Kirbo, Carter succeeded in getting the Quitman County ballots thrown out. He won by a count of 3,013 votes to 2,182, and faced no Republican opponent in the general election. After the election, a man came by the Carter warehouse and made a veiled threat about burning down the building. When Carter was away at the General Assembly, Rosalynn made her sons stay with her at the warehouse after school, and at night would leave the lights on in her house and barricade the doors with chairs.

But for all that, Carter had prevailed.

That very same fall, up the East Coast, Teddy was chasing a slightly bigger quarry—a seat in the U.S. Senate. In Boston, Joe Kennedy Sr. was asked by a reporter what challenges his youngest son might face in his own first campaign for elected office. The patriarch paused for effect and then said succinctly: "None."

Through the compressing lens of time, that might seem accurate. Teddy had at his disposal his father's vast fortune and the most highly efficient and effective political operation in the nation, which had just gotten his brother elected president. But in actuality, Teddy's candidacy was regarded as a joke and an insult. He did not turn thirty, the minimum age required to serve in the Senate, until February 1962. And more important, he had no résumé to offer the state of Massachusetts. He had yet to do anything with his life.

"His academic career is mediocre. His professional career is virtually non-existent. His candidacy is both preposterous and insulting," wrote leading Harvard law professor Mark A. De Wolfe Howe, an occasional adviser to JFK, in a publicly distributed letter. James Reston of the *New York Times* wrote that Teddy's candidacy was "widely regarded here [in Washington] as an affront and a presumption." The editorial page of the *Times* called Teddy's choice to run "demeaning to the dignity of the Senate and the democratic process."

Teddy's only work experience had been in a low-level spot in the Boston district attorney's office, procured for him through political connections. Teddy worked hard and did respectably, but "hardly made a ripple." In the evenings, he would hit the rubber chicken circuit, speaking at whatever local community or political meeting his family's fixers could find for him.

The Kennedy White House did not want him to run. JFK's close adviser Kenny O'Donnell was dead set against it. Bobby, too, reportedly was not in favor of the run. Even JFK himself had reservations. Teddy's opponent in the Democratic primary was the thirty-eight-year-old attorney general in Massachusetts, Edward McCormack, who was nephew to the brand-new Speaker of the House, John McCormack. JFK needed the Speaker's help in shepherding his agenda through Congress. Teddy himself understood the sentiments against his candidacy. "If I'd been somebody else I'm not at all sure I would have supported the idea," he told Hersh.

He knew he didn't have much of a leg to stand on when it came to matching experience and accomplishments against McCormack, or anyone, really. But he knew the opportunity was there, and as his father was fond of saying, "If there's a piece of cake on the table, you eat it."

And despite his youth and inexperience, Teddy had plenty of self-confidence. He understood the way that fame and television and sex appeal could sway voters. "If they've seen you on TV, they can't think anything bad about you," he said of female voters. He "understood his own appeal with the calmness of a natural matinee idol," Hersh wrote. In one meeting with Betty Taymor, the influential Boston activist, organizer, and politician, she asked him when his thirtieth birthday was. "The same day as Washington's birthday, only two hundred years later," Teddy replied brashly. *My God*, Taymor thought. *You're already running for president!*

At the end of 1960 he took a trip to Africa, and then in the summer of 1961 another trip to Latin America. These were intended to give him something to talk about back home and to bolster his credentials as a serious politician. But then a week before Christmas in 1961, Joe Sr. had a serious stroke while playing golf in Florida. He survived it, but barely, and lost the ability to speak. For Teddy, it was a heavy blow. His father had treated him as a peer for the first time in his life and they were enjoying a growing closeness. The loss "was almost more than I could bear," he wrote. "Some people around me thought my political plans would end with dad's illness." But brother-in-law Steve Smith, who had run JFK's presidential campaign, stepped in to run Teddy's, and the ship sailed on. Teddy announced his candidacy on March 14, 1962.

There was a big iceberg in the way, however: Teddy's cheating scandal and expulsion from Harvard. President Kennedy himself intervened, meeting three different times with hotshot *Boston Globe* reporter Bob Healy. The president wanted Healy to bury the details of Teddy's cheating incident in a longer profile on him. "We're having more fucking trouble with this than we did with the Bay of Pigs," the president said at one point. National Security Adviser McGeorge Bundy responded, "Yes, and with just about the same results."

On March 30, the *Globe* ran a front-page story on the matter, but softened its language dramatically. "Ted Kennedy Tells About Harvard Examination Incident," ran the headline. Teddy's expulsion from Harvard was described in the first paragraph as a "withdrawal." Not until the fifth paragraph was it disclosed that Teddy had, in his own words, "arranged for a fellow freshman to take the examination for me." In his own press release that went out at the same time, Teddy said he had been "asked to withdraw." Healy admitted he had gone easy on Teddy because others inside the *Globe*, particularly the paper's publisher, Davis Taylor, "believed in not hurting the presidency."

In the fall, Teddy's biggest test was his first debate with McCormack. McCormack's advisers wanted their candidate to attack Teddy and bait him into losing his temper. Teddy's advisers wanted to get McCormack to go too far in his attacks on their candidate, and said they had agreed to holding it in South Boston, McCormack's home turf, so he might be encouraged by a supportive crowd to burst any restraints and in the process come across as "too hot" to the television audience.

McCormack did indeed savage Teddy, again and again. And the effect on the first-time candidate—who had been instructed not to respond in kind—was devastating. Teddy physically shook as McCormack ripped into him. "I ask my opponent: What are your qualifications? You graduated from law school three years ago. You never worked for a living. You have never run or held an elective office," McCormack said, pointing accusingly at Teddy. "I say that we do not vote on influence or favoritism or connections. We vote for people who will serve. . . . We need a senator with experience, not arrogance . . . and the office of United States senator should be merited and not inherited." The crowd roared its approval at McCormack's broadsides.

McCormack closed with a final insult. "If his name was Edward Moore, with his qualifications, with your qualifications, Teddy, if it was Edward Moore, your candidacy would be a joke," he said, turning to look at Kennedy. "But nobody's laughing because his name is not Edward Moore. It's Edward Moore Kennedy, and I say it makes no difference what your name is, in a democracy you stand on your own two feet."

Teddy's voice shook throughout the debate, and as it ended he wobbled off the stage. He and Joan drove home thinking his candidacy might be over. But by the next day, initial polling conducted by the campaign suggested McCormack had come across on television as a bully. Teddy crushed him in the primary election, 559,303 votes to 257,403.

Teddy did not need much help from the president in his general election matchup with George Lodge. Lodge was the son of former senator Henry Cabot Lodge, the man whom JFK had defeated in 1954 to win his Senate seat for the first time. Teddy won with 54 percent of the vote.

In the end, Teddy had defeated McCormack because his campaign was vastly superior in its funding, its organization, and its execution, all advantages of his family. But the young man did perform the one task he was capable of. He may have been a clumsy candidate who barely knew what he was talking about half the time, but he plunged each day into the campaign and shook as many hands as he could. It wouldn't have been enough on his own, but without it, he might not have prevailed.

"That was the question: was there anybody there?" Steve Smith said. "Turned out there was."

# CHAPTER 4

—&#8250;&#8226;&#8226;&#8226;&#8249;—

# A Sense of the Void

Outside the U.S. Capitol on November 22, 1963, there was occasional drizzle, but the temperature was climbing from an early morning low in the high forties to almost seventy degrees by midafternoon. Inside the Capitol, the Senate was debating whether to expand federal aid to local libraries at 1:30 p.m. when Lee Harvey Oswald fired the shots in Dallas that killed the president. For eleven minutes, the lawmakers on the Senate floor continued their low-key speechmaking, unaware that the world had changed. In the chair at the head of the chamber, presiding over the Senate, was thirty-one-year-old freshman senator Edward M. Kennedy. He was signing letters, paying little attention to the remarks from the floor. He was going to hold a party that night to celebrate his and Joan's fifth wedding anniversary.

At 1:41 p.m., Teddy looked up from his desk, hearing a shout from the lobby just off the floor. It was a female staffer, an aide to Oregon senator Wayne Morse, who was monitoring the Associated Press teletype machine for her boss. Hearing the staffer's shout, a Senate press gallery aide named Richard Riedel walked over to the machine and read the following:

*…AP Photographer James W. Altgens said he saw blood on the President's head. Altgens said he heard two shots but thought someone was shooting fireworks…*

Riedel rushed into the chamber. It was the first time he had ever walked onto the Senate floor in roughly fifty years as an aide. He frantically told a few senators that the president had been shot. Teddy's attention was roused, but he did not yet know the news Riedel bore. As Riedel made his way toward the rostrum where Teddy sat, his face wore a "strange expression."

"The most horrible thing has happened! It's terrible, terrible!" Riedel said.

"What is it?" Teddy said, his pen still in his hand.

"Your brother," Riedel said. "Your brother the president. He's been shot!"

Teddy stared at Riedel for a moment. "How do you know?" he said in disbelief.

"It's on the ticker. Just came in on the ticker," Riedel replied.

Teddy gathered his papers and rushed from the chamber, overwhelmed by shock. He could barely hear the growing tumult around him as he exited into the lobby, as reporters and aides crowded to see the news clattering across the wire.

"The world lurched apart from me. I felt unmoored," Teddy wrote. Bobby asked him to call their mother and sisters. So Teddy called his parents in Hyannis Port. His mother answered. She knew. She said she was worried about Teddy's father, who lay in bed unable to speak from his stroke two years earlier, still ignorant of what had happened. Teddy was rushed to Andrews Air Force Base by helicopter, and then up to Cape Cod on a military aircraft.

Teddy waited until the next morning to tell his father. To keep him from watching any TV broadcasts, Teddy yanked the wires

out of the set near his father's bed. When he finally told the patriarch the next morning, with Eunice beside him, Joe Kennedy Sr.
broke down and wept, as did his son and daughter sitting with him.

About twelve hundred miles to the south, Jimmy Carter was in his
warehouse when he heard the news of President Kennedy's death.

Carter, a thirty-nine-year-old successful farmer and newly
elected state senator, walked out the back door of the warehouse
to be alone, and wept. He had not cried over the death of anyone
since his father had passed away a decade before, he told me. But
he felt an affinity for President Kennedy. His mother had been a
fervent supporter in 1960, and he too had voted for JFK. In his
younger days, he even bore a resemblance to JFK, which was noted
by those around him who became his political supporters.

Being a cautious progressive on the race issue, Carter had reason to mourn the way that the South would respond to Kennedy's
death. Schoolchildren in Plains, Carter's hometown, celebrated
the president's assassination, resentful of Kennedy's decision to get
involved in the civil rights fight. Carter's son Chip was in his high
school class when a teacher announced the news of JFK's death and
said, "That's good!" The students applauded. Chip, who had been
a volunteer for Kennedy in the 1960 campaign, was so angered by
this that he reportedly picked up his school desk and threw it at
the teacher, earning a three-day suspension.

Racial tensions were exploding in Carter's rural southwest corner of Georgia at this time. White and black student organizers
had arrived in Americus in 1963, leading to an escalation of protests by the activists and local blacks. They were met with beatings
by police and mobs. After one demonstration, police sent twenty
young black girls between the ages of nine and thirteen to prison
in nearby Leesburg, where they were kept in a single cell with no

beds for an entire month. The situation in Americus was so bad in the summer of 1963 that it drew national attention. Carter, however, kept his head down. Whatever he said privately on the matter, he did not speak out publicly or get involved. The focus of his efforts in his district was on economic development.

Carter was firmly on the side of integration, but did not endorse it publicly, and he also did not demonize those who were against it. He worried about the political consequences of speaking out publicly. But racial issues became unavoidable for Carter. His church, First Baptist Church in Plains, voted in the summer of 1964 to bar blacks from services. Carter stood and spoke against the resolution. Many in the congregation did not vote out of fear, but of those who did, only Carter's family and a nearly-deaf farmer who may not have comprehended the issue opposed the proposal. It passed, 54 to 6. When almost two thousand local signatories demanded that Sumter County attorney Warren Fortson be fired for his efforts to create a biracial committee to resolve tensions in Americus, Carter spoke there publicly as well in Fortson's defense. "There was a testing time that came," Fortson said. "And when it did he stood up."

Carter's burgeoning political ideology was driven more by personal experience than anything else. He identified with the rural poor and, having worked hard to earn financial self-sufficiency, resented those who were born into wealth (like Kennedy). He was fiscally conservative, a lesson learned from his father and during the Depression. But he was also a populist, opposed to favors for big special interests, whose ambitions often ran counter to those of individual farmers.

After an easy reelection in 1964, he began eyeing a run for Congress in 1966. His younger brother, Billy, was back in Plains and able to run the family business, and the idea of moving to Washington was an appealing one for him and Rosalynn, who still yearned to escape small-town life. For both of them, the racial tensions they'd been living through in Georgia were unpleasant.

Unlike during his first run for office in 1962, Carter had a campaign plan mapped out well in advance of his run for Congress. But then suddenly the congressman Carter was trying to unseat, Republican Howard "Bo" Calloway, decided to run for governor, after former governor Ernest Vandiver dropped out due to health concerns. It appeared that Carter had a clear path to winning the congressional race. It would be a remarkable ascent, from unknown farmer and school board chairman four years earlier to U.S. congressman. Carter, however, made a decision that in the short term would come to look like a miscalculation. The Democratic Party was fearful that Calloway would become the first Republican to win the governorship since 1868. Carter tried to help find moderate Democratic candidates, but, finding none, decided to run himself.

Carter's youthfulness and personal charisma evoked comparisons to the recently departed President Kennedy. "Many think [Carter] resembles the late President," the *Atlanta Constitution* wrote. Most of his appeal to his supporters was biographical. His campaign material was "entirely devoid of any discussion of issues," according to Bourne, who called the devotion to Carter from his most fervent supporters "almost cult-like." Carter had this effect because he was personable and warm in one-on-one interactions, highly intelligent, and he emphasized his personal faith and integrity. "The bottom line for Jimmy Carter was a conviction that if people knew him they would vote for him." To younger and more progressive-minded Georgians, he represented a break with the past that many felt embarrassed by, a leader who could help move the state into the future.

Carter made outreach to black voters a key part of his long-shot candidacy, and he tried personally to reach as many voters of all types as he could. He set a methodical plan to shake hands with what he estimated were 250,000 people for a primary in which almost 800,000 people voted. But he still came in third, behind fifty-nine-year-old former governor Ellis Arnall and fifty-one-year-old Atlanta restaurant owner Lester Maddox, who had become a racist folk hero in 1964 for standing in the entrance of his Pickrick Restaurant with an axe handle when black activists tried to enter. Carter got 21 percent of the vote to Arnall's 29 percent and Maddox's 23 percent.

The Atlanta press, having expected little from Carter, was impressed. "A new Democratic star is born," the *Constitution* wrote. The campaign of 1966 did end up connecting Carter with advisers Hamilton Jordan and Gerald Rafshoon, who would remain with him for the rest of his political career. But Carter, who had naively expected he could win, was devastated, and wept in a hallway away from supporters.

Carter left his election-night rally without thanking his supporters. He had passed up an easy election to Congress. He had spent most of his savings, and then taken out a loan that was still unpaid after the election and was the responsibility of four close friends. And Maddox had won the runoff with Arnall and then defeated Calloway in the general, giving Georgia an avowed racist as its governor. Carter wrote a thank-you note to John Girardeau, an Emory University student who had served as his driver during the campaign, saying he hoped he could repay him for all his hard work "whether I ever amount to much or not."

Carter turned his attention quickly to running for governor again in 1970. But he did not believe he had much of a chance. It was more that he needed something to do. He was forty-two years old, and he was questioning his purpose in life. "I had very little genuine interest in other people and I was quite disconsolate and dissatisfied with myself," he told Bourne in an interview a decade later.

A conversation, a book, and a trip changed his life. Six weeks after his loss, Carter's youngest sister, Ruth Carter Stapleton, visited with him. He saw in her an inner peace that he felt he lacked, and asked her, "What is it that you have that I haven't got?" Ruth told Carter that through her struggles she had reached a point of "total commitment" to Jesus Christ. "I belong to Jesus, everything I am," she said. Carter replied, "Ruth, that's what I want." He began reading the Bible more closely and questioning how his faith applied to modern life and to politics.

He already thought of politics as a quasi-pastoral calling. But he questioned the inherently self-promotional nature of politics and sought to understand how he could advance the ideals of his faith through elected office without violating the separation of church and state, in which he believed. He was deeply influenced during this time by the writings of Christian socialist Reinhold Niebuhr.

Carter called a collection of Niebuhr's essays his "political Bible." Niebuhr articulated a form of political realism captured succinctly in his quote that "man is the kind of lion who both kills the lamb and dreams of when the lion and the lamb shall lie down together." Niebuhr helped Carter reconcile his exacting approach toward religion and ethics with the messy realities of life and politics at a time when he was seeking to sharpen his own sense of purpose.

At the end of May 1968, two months after the assassination of Martin Luther King Jr., Carter traveled with three other men from his church to Lock Haven, Pennsylvania, a coal-mining town in the center of the state, to help start a new church there. They walked door-to-door for ten days and told residents about a new Southern Baptist congregation in the town. At each home Carter or his counterpart, Milo Pennington, would talk about their personal faith in Jesus Christ and invite anyone interested to nightly services that they organized at the local YMCA.

Carter later described his time in Lock Haven as "a miracle." It was, he said, "where I first experienced in a personal and intense way the presence of the Holy Spirit in my life." He said his time "witnessing" in Pennsylvania gave him the "genuine interest in other people" that he felt a lack of after his 1966 loss. He would go on another trip in the fall to the Kennedys' home state, evangelizing Spanish-speaking immigrants in Springfield, Massachusetts.

If this process clarified Carter's vision, it also imbued him with a sense of higher calling that would at times border on the messianic. And the Niebuhrian lens through which he came to view politics, combined with his belief in divine calling, created a man whose toothy grin masked a determined and competitive politician. Already confident in his own logical approach to problems, Carter became more comfortable with a realpolitik approach to problem-solving if he thought it was the righteous thing to do. "Increasingly, he conceptualized politics as a vehicle for advancing God's kingdom on earth by alleviating human suffering and despair on a scale that infinitely magnified what one individual could do alone," Bourne wrote. "His absolute determination to win became less a troubling matter of egotistical ambition and more a prerequisite for fulfilling the commitment he had made to carry out God's work."

And if a few lambs got killed along the way to accomplishing his goal, well, that was the cost of justice in a fallen world.

———— ◆◆◆ ————

The 1960s had begun hopefully for the country, with the election of JFK as president. And for the Kennedy family, things had progressed apace as well, with Teddy scraping his way into the Senate.

But JFK's death set in motion a chain of events that would turn the decade into a nightmare for the Kennedy family, and in many ways for the nation itself.

Only seven months after the nightmare in Dallas, Teddy himself nearly died. It was June 10, 1964, and after the Senate voted to move President Lyndon Johnson's civil rights legislation past a filibuster (it passed nine days later), Teddy hopped on a small two-engine plane to western Massachusetts, where the state Democratic Party was waiting to nominate him for reelection to his first full term as a senator. There were four other passengers: fellow senator Birch Bayh; Bayh's wife, Marvella; an aide named Ed Moss; and pilot Edwin Zimny.

A few miles from the convention that night, a dairy farmer's teenage daughter, Joanne Bashista, was watching television inside her father's home in West Springfield. Outside, there was thick fog. Just before 11 p.m., Bashista heard a noise outside that sounded like a sputtering motorboat engine, then a collision of some sort, and a tearing noise. She and her father, Walter, rushed out into their apple orchard and found the Aero Commander in pieces. Zimny had brought the plane in too low on its approach and had collided with a number of trees.

Zimny was dead. Moss, Teddy's aide, who had been up front next to Zimny, was badly hurt. Birch and Marvella Bayh were staggering from the wreckage, having suffered only minor injuries. And Teddy, who had been sitting behind the pilot facing the tail of the plane, where the Bayhs had also been sitting, lay inside the plane still, with two cracked ribs, one vertebra crushed and two others badly broken, a punctured left lung that was partially collapsed, and massive internal hemorrhaging.

Joan rushed to the hospital, as did Bobby. Still reeling from Jack's death the previous fall, Bobby told reporters, "I guess the only reason we've survived is that there are more of us than there is trouble." Teddy survived, but narrowly. Doctors would discover that every one of his upper twenty-four vertebrae were cracked. He would be in the hospital for six months, as part of an arduous recovery. Most of his time in the hospital was spent in a special Stryker bed that immobilized most of his body with a frame and straps and could be flipped to allow him to rest on his stomach and then back again.

This recovery period, however, held some blessings in disguise. Teddy decided to make the most of it by reading a lot, holding seminar sessions with policy experts, and reflecting. It was "perhaps the only time in his adult life he was utterly by himself," wrote Hersh. A family friend noted as well that Teddy "never really had any time alone before to really think." It's not known how much of this time he spent introspectively. His focus appears to have been on preparing himself to return to the Senate with not only a deeper knowledge of the issues, but also a more robust sense of his priorities. But there was undoubtedly some personal reflection as well. "I had a lot of time to think about what was important and what was not and about what I wanted to do with my life," Teddy told *Good Housekeeping* after his release from the hospital ten days before Christmas.

Teddy had already been a cautious, deferential senator before the one-two punch of JFK's murder and his own brush with death knocked him down. When he returned to the Senate in January 1965, he had more reason to be so: Bobby had been elected to the Senate from New York, and the older brother's presence now loomed large in the chamber, and over his younger brother. Yet Teddy also had grounds to be more quietly confident than he had been just two years prior. He had now been reelected to the Senate to serve out a full term: his own term, not his brother's. And he was gaining a sense of direction and expertise in the areas he wanted to focus on: the nation's health care system, unfair tax laws, voting rights, and inequities in the military draft.

From 1965 to 1968, Teddy did yeoman's work on an immigration bill, on the 1965 follow-up to the Voting Rights Act, and on a redistricting bill in 1967. In the 1965 Voting Rights debate, Teddy led an insurgency against the Dixiecrats to outlaw poll taxes, which were used to block African Americans and the poor from voting. The measure was narrowly defeated, but in the following year Teddy was vindicated when the Supreme Court struck down poll taxes in the few states that still used them.

Key to Teddy's success was his tortoise-like approach, which grew out of his sense of inferiority from his early days as an interloper in the Senate. "He avoided reporters. He knew he needed time badly," Hersh wrote. "At a loss by his own admission for the wit of John and most of the bite of Robert, Edward presented himself to himself as ruminative. While Ted Kennedy was in no way a 'quick study,' as he put it himself, he was determined to put in the hours, months, years required to be a surpassingly thorough study. If piercing, erratic little Robert tended to personalize… Ted Kennedy went about things by working through expanses of detail until he felt ready to propose a legislative remedy." Members of both parties were already, by Teddy's third and fourth years in the Senate, expecting him to be more prepared on the issues he championed or attacked than anyone else.

Teddy also did not personalize politics. He in fact went out of his way to befriend even the most racist members of the Senate, like Senate Judiciary Committee chairman James Eastland, the Mississippi Democrat who held enormous power. His ability to get along with the segregationists inside his own party and with Republicans paid dividends.

As his Senate career slowly built steam, Teddy's personal life was showing more strain. He worked long hours and was home infrequently, even though Joan gave birth to their third child, Patrick, in July 1967. Teddy's extramarital affairs became more matter-of-fact. He and Joan had separate bedrooms in the new home they built for themselves in McLean, Virginia. As Joan's alcoholism began to show itself, Teddy himself combined his overwork with overdrinking. Partly this was his response to his own inability to fully process his feelings about Jack's death.

Bobby had always been more intensely emotional and introspective than Teddy. His grief in response to JFK's death had "veered close to being a tragedy within a tragedy," Teddy wrote in his autobiography. Those around Bobby had feared for his "psychic survival." Teddy claimed that he ignored his own feelings as a result. "I was so worried about Bobby that I tried to suppress my own grief," he wrote. "I was afraid to allow grief to swallow me up. So I just pushed it down further and further inside."

But when Bobby leaned toward a run for president in 1968, Teddy grumbled that "Bobby's therapy is going to cost the family eight million dollars." Yet he lent his full support to the effort when Bobby jumped in against his advice. He told his older brother he should wait until 1972, after President Lyndon Baines Johnson had served out his second term. And he also feared Bobby might meet the same fate as Jack. But Bobby ran anyway, and Teddy became an integral part of his campaign and a trusted adviser. The relationship between the two brothers became more equal than at any previous point in their lives.

It was a chaotic year. American opinion was swinging decisively against the Vietnam War, sparked by the Tet offensive (Teddy had been behind the war in 1965 but had turned deeply pessimistic by 1968). College campuses were the site of increasingly militant actions by student protesters, who staged sit-ins and took over administration buildings at Howard and Columbia. Martin Luther King Jr. was shot and killed in Memphis on April 4, sparking major riots in cities around the country.

During the same week that Carter was in Pennsylvania on his missionary trip to save souls, Teddy traveled to San Francisco to campaign for Bobby's presidential campaign in the California primary, which took place on June 4. He was in the northern part of the state to make sure voters turned out there. His days in California that week were spent at campaign events and rallies, while nights found him at dinners and parties with his main extramarital flame at the time, Austrian-born Scientologist Helga Wagner. Joan was in Paris.

On the night of the primary, Teddy rallied campaign workers at a raucous late-night party in the city. The returns were coming in and Bobby was going to win. Before Bobby spoke from Los Angeles, Teddy addressed the supporters in San Francisco. "California is coming through for us!" he said. Moments later, he watched on TV as Bobby delivered a rousing victory speech at the Ambassador Hotel in Los Angeles.

As Teddy headed for his San Francisco hotel, Bobby was making his way out of the Ambassador ballroom, through the crush of the crowd and into a back hallway on his way to a car. In the hotel kitchen, a crazed Palestinian Christian named Sirhan Sirhan stepped forward and fired a .22 caliber revolver three times into Bobby Kennedy's head and back.

Surgeons operated to remove bullet fragments from Bobby's brain, and the father of nine children clung to life for twenty-four hours before doctors allowed him to expire at 1:44 a.m. on June 6.

<hr />

Teddy was now the only Kennedy boy left. He disappeared for a week the day after the funeral in New York and the burial at Arlington National Cemetery. He retreated to the sea and spent most of the rest of the summer on a sailboat. Sometimes Joan and the children came along. Other times it was just Kennedy and a buddy like Joe Gargan or Bill vanden Heuvel or Dun Gifford. And sometimes he sailed alone. He grew a beard.

Politics, however, could not be kept at bay forever. The Democratic Party was being torn apart by antiwar sentiment that would soon be on full display for the nation to see in the violent protests on the streets of Chicago during the Democratic convention. Democratic front-runner Hubert Humphrey did not match up well against Republican nominee Richard Nixon. The nation wanted law and order and calm, and Nixon promised that.

Some thought Kennedy should join Humphrey on the ticket or even run himself for the nomination. Chicago mayor Richard J. Daley, who controlled the Illinois delegation, pushed Kennedy the most aggressively. Kennedy didn't want to do it, but he toyed with the idea nonetheless, sending Steve Smith to Chicago days before the convention. Smith and others ran a whip operation and told Kennedy they had the votes to get him the nomination. But Kennedy, still only thirty-six years old, walked away from it. "I am not yet qualified to be President of the United States," he said.

Those words would prove more prophetic than anyone could have predicted. For a time, however, it looked like Kennedy was perfectly positioned to run against Nixon in 1972. He took over the number two leadership post inside the Senate the following year, unceremoniously defeating Russell Long of Louisiana. He would use that post, he told fellow senators, to confront and challenge the Nixon administration and fight for Democratic priorities and programs in a manner the more genteel majority leader, Mike Mansfield, would not. Kennedy would be the leader of the Democratic Party against the new Republican president. When he unseated Long from the majority whip post, the *New York Times* wrote that it was "a stepping stone to the Presidency."

Richard Nixon certainly saw Kennedy as his most likely rival in 1972. When Kennedy in the spring of 1969 opposed the White

House plan for an antiballistic missile system to protect U.S. cities against the possibility of a Chinese attack, H. R. Haldeman, Nixon's White House chief of staff, wrote in his diary that it was "the first battle of '72, vs Kennedy, and we *must* win."

But then came a night that would haunt Kennedy for the rest of his life. Thirteen months after Bobby's death, on Friday, July 18, 1969, Teddy attended a small party on Chappaquiddick Island, which sits just off the southeast corner of Martha's Vineyard. He was one of several men there, most of whom were in their late thirties or older and married. There was a group of single women at the party as well, all of them in their twenties, who had worked on Bobby's campaign and were known as the "Boiler Room Girls."

The next morning, one of the women—twenty-eight-year-old Mary Jo Kopechne of Wilkes-Barre, Pennsylvania—was dead. Her body lay trapped in the backseat of a black four-door Oldsmobile Delmont 88, underwater in a channel not far from the party. The car was registered in Kennedy's name.

Kennedy did not go to the police until 10 a.m. that morning, as Kopechne's body was being pulled from the water by police. He dictated a statement saying he had been driving the car a little before midnight, intending to take Kopechne to the Edgartown ferry and back to the main island, when he got confused, took a wrong turn, and ended up driving off the small Dike Bridge. He claimed he had been able to escape the car, but could not rescue Kopechne. He gave a wild account of asking friends to help with no success, trying to swim back to the island, and going to sleep in his motel room, hoping it had all been a dream. The diver who retrieved Kopechne's body would later say she had survived for some time in an air bubble in the backseat, and could have been rescued if he had been called soon after the accident.

It appeared that at the very least, Kennedy had let a young woman die while he tried to figure out how to find a way out of this pickle. The Kennedy political operation went into high gear, spiriting the party attendees off the island before reporters could find them, and forming a hedge around Kennedy himself. He secluded himself at the family compound in Hyannis Port while an army of advisers and lawyers spent days plotting how to respond.

Incredibly, Neil Armstrong and Buzz Aldrin were about to become the first human beings to set foot on the moon—fulfilling a goal set out by President John F. Kennedy—on Sunday evening, just as the news of Kennedy's accident and Kopechne's death was reverberating around the country. President Nixon, waiting to speak live on national television about the moon landing, remarked to his chief of staff, Haldeman, "It marks the end of Teddy."

Authorities never performed an autopsy on Kopechne's body. A week after the accident, Kennedy was let off with a small wrist slap, pleading guilty to leaving the scene of an accident after causing an injury, and receiving a two-month prison sentence that the judge suspended. That evening, he made a highly rehearsed speech on national television from the library of his parents' Hyannis Port home. He claimed he could not have commented previously because of the police investigation, and denied he was drunk that night or that Kopechne had engaged in "immoral conduct."

Kennedy claimed he had "made immediate and repeated efforts to save Mary Jo by diving into the strong and murky current." He did not have a good answer for why he had waited ten hours to tell police what had happened. "My conduct and conversation during the next several hours, to the extent that I can remember them, make no sense to me at all," he said.

"All kinds of scrambled thoughts—all of them confused, some of them irrational, many of them which I cannot recall, and some of which I would not have seriously entertained under normal circumstances—went through my mind during this period. They were reflected in the various inexplicable, inconsistent, and inconclusive things I said and did, including such questions as whether the girl might still be alive somewhere out of that immediate area, whether some awful curse did actually hang over all the Kennedys, whether there was some justifiable reason for me to doubt what had happened and to delay my report, whether somehow the awful weight of this incredible incident might in some way pass from my shoulders," Kennedy said. "I was overcome, I'm frank to say, by a jumble of emotions: grief, fear, doubt, exhaustion, panic, confusion, and shock."

The scandal could easily have resulted in prison time, and probably should have. Kopechne's death should have cost Kennedy his Senate seat, but it did not. It did have other consequences, however. Joan suffered her third miscarriage soon after, and blamed it on the stress and strain of dealing with Chappaquiddick. And there was another outcome. The presidency was out of the question in 1972. Kennedy's father died a few months after the incident, in November, going to his grave with his son's disgrace fresh in his memory.

Chappaquiddick moved Kennedy's name off Richard Nixon's "enemies list." But Ted would never be at rest until he ran for president. His dead father and his martyred brothers would hover over him until he fulfilled his destiny. He had wanted to pledge, in his televised speech apologizing for Chappaquiddick, that he would never run for president. His older sister Eunice, her political antennae still intact despite the shock of the episode, had the promise taken out.

But even if Kennedy was no longer a threat to Nixon, there was another man eyeing the presidency in 1976, a largely unknown governor from Georgia. And to Jimmy Carter, Ted Kennedy loomed large.

# CHAPTER 5

—◆◆◆—

# A Rivalry Begins

The yelling of an agitated man disturbed the morning quiet outside the governor's mansion in Atlanta on the morning of May 4, 1974.

At the front gate, a Georgia state trooper slammed his hand down on the hood of a taxicab that had pulled up and shouted at the driver to shut off his engine. A passenger climbed out of the backseat. Despite the early hour, the grungy-looking man held a beer can in his hand. This further raised the ire of the trooper, who berated him loudly. To his surprise, however, the passenger swore he had arrived to have breakfast with Governor Jimmy Carter and with his overnight guest, Senator Edward M. Kennedy.

The trooper asked the sweaty, manic-looking man with the beer for his name. It was Hunter S. Thompson, the celebrated godfather of gonzo journalism who two years earlier had published *Fear and Loathing in Las Vegas*. That meant little to the officer, who held Thompson at bay.

After finally being let in the back door, an agitated Thompson was greeted by Carter himself, wearing blue jeans. Carter ushered him into the mansion as the journalist raved and ranted about the trooper to anyone who would listen. When Thompson calmed enough to take stock of his surroundings, he saw Carter and

Kennedy sitting a few feet from each other in the dining room, surrounded by more than a dozen aides and hangers-on. The mood was tense.

Both men were scheduled to speak at a luncheon that day at the University of Georgia, seventy miles away in Athens, and Kennedy had planned on hitching a ride with Carter on the governor's plane. But Kennedy told Thompson that Carter had informed him at rather the last minute that he and his entourage could no longer be accommodated on the plane. Kennedy aides scurried to locate their Secret Service detail so they could drive to Athens.

Kennedy was less than pleased. He had just returned from a weeklong trip to the Soviet Union, where he'd discussed nuclear arms control with Soviet leader Leonid Brezhnev. Kennedy was treated as a potential president-in-waiting, since President Nixon was engulfed in the Watergate scandal. And now here Kennedy was being yanked around by some no-name backwoods peanut farmer who was limited by the Georgia constitution to one term and would be back in overalls in less than a year. Kennedy's aides treated Carter "politely but with mild disdain."

In contrast to Kennedy's agitation, Carter was calm and confident in this, the first meeting between the two men. Unlike Kennedy, who had probably never given one moment's thought to Carter before this weekend, Carter had been thinking about Kennedy constantly for the previous two years. Carter had decided almost two years earlier to run for president. He saw two men in the way of his goal: Alabama governor George Wallace, and Kennedy.

———✦———

After his gubernatorial loss and his spiritual rebirth, Carter had been more motivated than ever to ascend to the governor's mansion in 1970. But he faced a complicated electoral environment.

The race issue remained definitive in 1970 in the Deep South. Many Georgians thought changes brought on by the civil rights movement and by the federal government's desegregation efforts were moving too fast. Many others were just plain opposed.

Hamilton Jordan tried to persuade Carter to run for a lower office, either lieutenant governor or agricultural commissioner. He did not think Carter could beat the popular former governor Carl Sanders. But Carter was determined to win the prize that had eluded him in 1966, and saw vulnerability in Sanders's moderation on the race issue. He believed he could win over the state's rural areas with a populist message that tapped into the energy in the state among white voters who felt besieged by the civil rights movement.

Carter made some overtures to black voters. He campaigned with Reverend Andrew Young, one of Martin Luther King's top lieutenants, who was attempting to become the first black U.S. congressman from the South since Reconstruction (Young lost in 1970 but went on to win a seat in Congress two years later). Carter was the first white politician running for statewide election in Georgia to visit MLK's Ebenezer Baptist Church, where MLK Sr. remained the pastor. "Daddy King" gave Carter his endorsement. A successful businessman, David Rabhan, introduced Carter to black preachers around the state, and Carter visited many of their churches over the course of two years.

Carter portrayed himself as a workingman, a man of the people. "Can you imagine any of the other candidates for governor working in the hot August sun?" one TV ad said, showing Carter working on his farm. "Isn't it time someone spoke up for you?"

Carter paired his positive biographical message with brutal and relentless attacks on Sanders as an out-of-touch fat cat. His ads called Sanders "Cufflinks Carl." One ad zoomed in on the well-manicured hand of a man writing a check inside a country club private room. The narrator said, "People like us aren't invited. We're too busy working for a living."

Carter himself displayed the street-fighter political instincts hiding behind his toothy grin, the ruthlessness and "functional meanness" that would a few years later so awe Hunter S. Thompson. Carter's own wife, Rosalynn, once said that her husband "appears kind of meek or something. People always underestimate him."

Carter attacked Sanders for using his first term as governor to enrich himself after he left office, through the granting of TV licenses, through retainers paid to him by large businesses, and by purchasing property that he knew would increase in value once the state moved forward on highway projects. Carter launched such fusillades at Sanders nearly every day, making the issue of Sanders's integrity a central part of the campaign. But when Carter finally provided the "proof" of his allegations, late in the summer, the press deemed it laughable.

More disturbing were the appeals to voters who had supported Wallace when he ran for president as a third-party candidate in 1968. Wallace had won five southern states and ten million votes. One out of every five Americans who voted in that election had cast a ballot for him. The "Cufflinks Carl" ad, which ran in early June, closed with an exhortation to vote for Carter, "our kind of man, our kind of governor." The "our kind of man" line was an overt reference to Wallace, who used the same phrase.

Wallace's 1969 campaign for governor had been openly racist. The Wallace campaign had distributed leaflets with a photo of a young white girl seated on the ground and surrounded by seven young black boys, with a caption that screamed in large letters, "WAKE UP, ALABAMA!" "Is this the IMAGE you want?" the flyer said. "Blacks vow to take over Alabama."

Carter's aides distributed racist flyers too, though they were milder. Ham Jordan and press secretary Bill Pope were responsible, according to Bourne, for flyers that showed a newspaper photo of Sanders—who was part owner of the Atlanta Hawks—standing next to an African American player for the Hawks named Lou Hudson who was pouring champagne over Sanders's head after a big win. Carter denied any knowledge of the leaflets, and no evidence ever surfaced to suggest that he was aware of them. But Pope would tell the *Washington Post* years later that he had run a "nigger campaign" for Carter.

The message of the flyer, Sanders said a year before his death in 2014, was, "Here's Carl Sanders making love with the blacks." Carter, he said, "hoodwinked enough people" into thinking he would work to undermine segregation if elected. At the same time, the Carter campaign was also distributing flyers that criticized Sanders for negligence as governor in the case of a black inmate who died in a Putnam County prison in 1966.

Carter also regularly criticized Sanders for the time as governor that he blocked Wallace from speaking on state property, and told audiences that if he was elected he would invite Wallace to Georgia to address the state legislators. He also criticized Sanders for supporting Hubert Humphrey and the national Democratic ticket in the 1968 presidential election, despite having voted for Humphrey himself. The criticism was seen as a subtle signal to voters that Sanders should have supported Wallace for president.

A week before the primary, Carter visited an all-white school in Swainsboro, Georgia, that had been created by whites to take their children out of integrated schools, and he promised to do "everything" he could for private schools.

When I asked Carter in early 2015 about the 1970 campaign, he blamed the *Atlanta Constitution* and its political reporter Bill Shipp. "The *Atlanta Constitution* did everything they could to defeat me," he told me. He then mentioned offhandedly that Shipp had "just died last year." And he said that Shipp "constantly claimed that I was taking a racist attitude to get support. But I would say my involvement with the black community far exceeded what Sanders or anyone else had done before or since then. I was a constant presence in the black churches...I knew every black pastor in Atlanta.

"I never made a racist statement," Carter added, "but I did get the more conservative country votes there in Georgia because I never did anything to alienate them."

Indeed, when the votes were counted on primary day, September 9, 1970, Carter won a large majority of the state's white vote, while only receiving about 5 percent of the black vote. He beat Sanders 48.6 percent to 37.7 percent, but the primary nomination fight went to a runoff nonetheless because Carter had not passed the 50 percent threshold. Civil rights pioneer C. B. King, a courageous and brilliant black attorney, won almost 9 percent of the vote, and a Ku Klux Klan leader got 2 percent.

During the primary runoff, Carter sought and received support from the state's best-known white racist leaders. One of these was Roy Harris, the former president of the state chapter of the White Citizens' Council, the very group Carter had refused to join more than a decade prior when he'd first come back to Plains. Others followed Harris's lead: Marvin Griffin, the former governor who had briefly been George Wallace's running mate in 1964, and Ernest Vandiver, another arch-segregationist from the 1950s. Lester Maddox, the sitting governor best known for standing in the doorway of his restaurant with an axe handle to keep blacks out, did not endorse any candidate but did refute Sanders's claim that he was backing the former governor against Carter. Maddox would, after the primary was over, praise Carter for "running a Maddox-type campaign."

Black leaders in Georgia like Julian Bond, Andrew Young, Vernon Jordan, and others were horrified. Sanders denounced Carter as a "smiling hypocrite" and an "unprincipled grinning chameleon." But it was to no effect. Carter trounced Sanders in the runoff, winning with 60 percent of the vote. He again, however, won only 7 percent of the black vote. It was a startling reversal from four years earlier when he had eagerly sought and received the votes of black Georgians.

On election night after the results were in, Hamilton Jordan sensed that Carter lacked enthusiasm about his win. "I said, 'Well, Jimmy, I guess it's about time to start calling you governor,' and he just shrugged and said, 'Well, whatever you want.' He didn't seem the least bit excited about it." In his Carter biography, titled *Redeemer*, progressive evangelical Randall Balmer speculates that Carter was upset about the campaign he had to run in order to win. *New York Times* White House correspondent James Wooten quoted "close friends" of Carter's as saying the governor-elect told them the same thing. "Carter's only prospect for redemption," Balmer wrote, "lay in his conduct as governor."

When he had easily dispatched the Republican nominee in November and mounted the stage on inauguration day in January, Carter admitted as much. "I realize that the test of a man is not how well he campaigned, but how effectively he meets the challenges and responsibilities of the office," he said in his inaugural speech. And he recast himself once again as a racial progressive.

"I say to you quite frankly that the time for racial discrimination is over," he said. There was some applause from the audience, but also plenty of groans. To those who had voted for Carter hoping he would uphold white supremacy, this "did not sound like the man for whom they had voted."

---

As Carter ascended, by morally dubious methods, to a prominent political perch, Kennedy at times contemplated leaving politics altogether because of his own compromised standing. Chappa-quiddick loomed over him in 1970 as he ran for reelection to the Senate. An inquest was held in January 1970. The grand jury showed interest in pursuing the case, but the district attorney decided to drop it anyway. Mary Jo Kopechne's parents spent time with Kennedy alone in New York not long after that. Kennedy family friend Dun Gifford told Adam Clymer in 1996 that after that conversation with Kennedy early in 1970, the Kopechnes were "satisfied."

Kennedy was unsure if he had a future in politics. "The voters need reassurance," he told the *New York Times*'s Johnny Apple. "You can't counter the Chappaquiddick thing directly. The answer has to be implicit in what you are, what you stand for and how they see you."

To help blunt the damage from Chappaquiddick, Kennedy's campaign paraded Joan around the state at numerous events. She would say years later that she felt "used" during this campaign, and that this experience turned her into a full-blown alcoholic. Her travails may not have been necessary. Kennedy was not seriously threatened in his reelection. He won easily over businessman Josiah Spaulding, 62 percent to 37 percent.

Nonetheless, Chappaquiddick had changed everything. Once seen as the national leader of the Democrats, Kennedy now couldn't even influence the process inside the Senate. Aides advised him to walk around the Senate floor and have conversations with other senators during votes so reporters watching from the gallery would think he was helping round up votes. And in January 1971, Kennedy was ignominiously dumped from the leadership post in the Senate he had won just two years earlier. Fellow Senate Democrats elected Robert Byrd, the West Virginia Democrat, in his place. It was a total humiliation for Kennedy.

Kennedy did begin to work on national health insurance more seriously than before during this period, an issue that would come to define his Senate career. And he was involved behind the scenes in other matters, such as changing the voting age to eighteen from twenty-one, efforts to increase cancer research, government-funded meals for elderly poor, and money to improve the lives of Native Americans. He also began to speak out more forcefully about the situation in Northern Ireland, which would become another life-long passion. But when he did so, he was mocked by British news-papers, which pointed immediately to Chappaquiddick.

Kennedy's private life—specifically his constant extramarital affairs—was also now fair game for the press, post-Chappaquiddick. *Newsweek* and *Time*, the dominant national newsmagazines of the time, wrote about Kennedy's "ever-ready eye for a pretty face" and the "countless rumors" about his extramarital affairs. Report-ers asked Kennedy and Joan in public why they were not more affectionate with each other. President Nixon, who still feared a challenge from Kennedy in the 1972 presidential election, loved to hear stories of Kennedy's lechery. Henry Kissinger, who was national security adviser to Nixon in 1971, told the president that Kennedy was "a total animal."

But in spite of Teddy's troubled personal life, the Kennedy name still caused the hearts of many Democrats to skip a beat. "The Kennedys," wrote Jules Witcover at the time, "had become a kind of royal family in exile, awaiting in their Washington and Cape Cod homes an eventual return to the political summit from which they had been so brutally banished on the tragic day in Dal-las. They wanted the promise of John and Robert Kennedy to be realized and fulfilled in Edward Kennedy."

By the time 1972 rolled around, there were polls that indicated he could win the Democratic presidential nomination if he ran. Chicago mayor Richard Daley again made noises about draft-ing Kennedy once Senator George McGovern, the South Dakota Democrat, looked ready to win the nomination. And McGovern himself pleaded with Kennedy to be his running mate, arguing that such a run could help him move past Chappaquiddick. But Kennedy ultimately said no to it all.

But after Nixon destroyed McGovern in the election, winning forty-nine out of fifty states, Kennedy began talking to confidants about running in 1976. He knew that any Democrat would have to win back southern Democrats who had deserted McGovern for Nixon, who had played to racism and white fear just as Carter had in the 1970 gubernatorial election.

With that in mind, Kennedy made a pilgrimage to pay tribute to George Wallace in 1973. He attended a July 4 ceremony in Decatur, Alabama, where Wallace was awarded the Audie Murphy Patriotism Award. Kennedy posed for photos onstage in a dark suit next to Wallace as the segregationist, seated in a wheelchair and wearing an all-white suit, held a plaque given to him.

When Kennedy rose to speak, he praised Wallace and attacked the Nixon White House, which was under the full withering heat of the Senate Select Committee on the Watergate scandal. In fact, it had been discovered by the committee that both Kennedy and Wallace were on Nixon's enemies list. That created a thin pretext for Kennedy to claim some form of solidarity with Wallace.

"All of you know Governor Wallace and I have different opinions on some important issues," Kennedy said as the audience applauded, "and there are many in the Democratic Party and across this country who disagree with both of us. But we have one thing in common: We don't corrupt, we don't malign, we don't abuse the trust which the people have given us.

"We don't compile lists of enemies whose careers and lives are to be shattered because of their disagreement. We don't use the tactics of a criminal or the power of the law to silence those whose ideas or politics are different than our own," Kennedy continued, blasting Nixon. He added a line of commendation for Wallace that must have struck many as horrifying: "For if there is one thing that George Wallace stands for, it is the right of every American to speak his mind and be heard, fearlessly and in any part of this country."

He also softened a critique of the region's legacy of racism and slavery by noting that bigotry existed in the Northeast as well. "Let no one think I come to lecture you on racial injustice, which has proven to be as deeply embedded and resistant in the cities of the North as in the counties of the South," he said. "We are no more entitled to oppress a man for his color than to shoot a man for his beliefs."

Kennedy was excoriated by liberals and African American leaders. The Southern Christian Leadership Conference, founded by Martin Luther King Jr., passed a resolution declaring Kennedy's visit to Alabama and his speech honoring Wallace as "the height of political opportunism." "The crisis in our nation demands electoral leadership uncompromising with racism, police statism and mob rule," the resolution said.

The trip was seen by some as a clever political move. But it also made clear to Kennedy that Chappaquiddick remained a problem for him. Like the British newspapers' response to his comments on Northern Ireland, his discourse on race drew a rebuke from Republican senator Barry Goldwater of Arizona. "Until all the facts involving the Chappaquiddick tragedy are made known, the American people can do without moralizing from the Massachusetts Democrat," Goldwater said. Letters flooded into his Senate office in Washington in the wake of that trip; they were overwhelmingly focused on Chappaquiddick in a negative way. "People had not forgotten, and the slightest stirring that suggested a Kennedy presidential candidacy," as the trip to visit Wallace had, "flushed out their animosity," Jules Witcover wrote. "The issue remained, submerged but potent."

And then, a few months after the trip to Alabama, Kennedy noticed a nasty red lump on his twelve-year-old son Teddy Jr.'s knee. It was cancer. After a few days of tests, doctors told him that Teddy Jr. would need to have his leg amputated above the knee, but that they were hopeful they could remove all the cancer. Joan was traveling in Europe and was summoned home immediately.

Kennedy did not tell Teddy Jr. that he would lose his leg until the day before the surgery. "I'd heard and delivered more than my share of bad news in my life, but this was the worst of the worst," he wrote in his autobiography. As the boy absorbed the shock and dissolved into tears, his father held him in his arms.

The surgery was successful, and Teddy Jr. began his recovery and rehabilitation quickly. But not long afterward, doctors studying tests of the tumor they had removed found bone cancer cells. Kennedy, determined to fight back against the disease, called around the country to different physicians and found doctors at Boston Children's Hospital who could treat the disease with an early form of chemotherapy.

For the next two years, every three weeks Kennedy would take Teddy Jr. from Washington to Boston for three days of treatment. And so when he arrived in Atlanta in the spring of 1974 to spend the night as Governor Carter's guest, he was still getting used to this new reality. Kennedy was conflicted about running for the White House in 1976. He still wanted to be president, but Chappaquiddick still lurked ominously in the background and Teddy Jr. needed him. He was leaning toward no this time around.

———— ∞∞∞ ————

Carter didn't know that. Like most people, he assumed Kennedy would be the front-runner for the nomination. By the time Kennedy spent the night at the governor's mansion in Georgia in May 1974, Carter had been plotting a presidential run for almost two years. Hamilton Jordan, Jody Powell, Jerry Rafshoon, Charles Kirbo, Peter Bourne, and others were all in on it.

The topic had first come up in the summer of 1971, when Bourne was with Carter in Washington and asked him if he'd ever thought about running for president. Carter said he hadn't, but then immediately switched gears and started talking about how he'd do it. Bourne soon afterward wrote a ten-page strategy memo for Carter. The most liberal among Carter's advisers, he tried to nudge him to take strong left-leaning stands on issues. Carter ignored that part, but clearly relished the larger idea of running.

Those closest to Carter, however, were far more skeptical. When he first told his mother, Lillian, that he might run for president, she responded, "President of what?" And even Carter's closest advisers could hardly believe what they were doing when they held their first meeting with him in late September 1972. "We all knew it looked kind of preposterous," Jordan said years later about their first meeting. "It was hard to really talk about. It was almost embarrassing."

Carter was not as overwhelmed at the idea. "It was obvious he was two or three steps ahead of us," Jordan said. "It was not an idea we had to force upon him."

Carter and his advisers discussed the need for "moral leadership" in the country in the wake of the Vietnam War's divisive effect. A national leader was needed, they thought, who would be more transparent and open and say things that might be unpopular.

After a six-hour conversation, Carter did not explicitly give his advisers the green light, but they saw he wanted to go for it. For the next month, the twenty-seven-year-old Jordan worked on a fifty-eight-page memo that laid out a detailed plan of attack for what he described as Carter's "national effort." It was dated November 4, 1972, three days before the presidential election in which Nixon pasted McGovern. In the section outlining the political challenges in Carter's way, the first heading was "George Wallace." The second was "Senator Edward Kennedy."

Jordan argued that a Carter candidacy for president should "encompass and expand on the Wallace constituency and 'populist' philosophy by being a better qualified and more responsible alternative." Jordan said he hoped that Wallace would not run himself. "A <u>serious</u> national effort" by Wallace, Jordan wrote, "would preempt your candidacy." He later scratched out "would" and wrote in "could." If Wallace did not run, Jordan recommended that Carter could hope to win the support of the segregationist governor "if he saw in your candidacy an extension and continuation of his earlier efforts."

As for Kennedy, Jordan wrote that many in the Democratic Party, desperate to regain the White House after Nixon's two terms, "are ready to give Senator Kennedy the nomination today." Jordan acknowledged that Kennedy was "the only visible candidate at present" who could unite the party's establishment wing and its liberal McGovernite wing. But, he said, Kennedy's ability to win a general election was in serious question because of his integrity problems related to Chappaquiddick. He attached a July 1972 article from *Harper's Magazine* that included a survey of voters in Illinois, at the time a leading swing state, which found that the stigma of Chappaquiddick "not only persists; it may be getting worse." Kennedy did well among young voters, liberals, and blue-collar workers, but high numbers of college-educated and higher-income voters retained "grave doubts" about his actions in the summer of 1969.

Kennedy's lack of trustworthiness and integrity, Jordan wrote, were major problems at that particular national moment. "Perhaps the strongest feeling in this country today is the general distrust and disallusionment [*sic*] of government and politicians at all levels. The desire and thirst for strong moral leadership in this nation was not satisfied with the election of Richard Nixon." In the scope of history, Jordan's comment that the desire for moral leadership would "grow in four more years of the Nixon administration" looks like staggering understatement. But he couldn't have known at the time how Watergate would play out.

"The unanswered questions of Chappaquiddick," Jordan concluded, "runs [*sic*] contrary to this national desire for trust and morality in government." He also discussed the possibility that Kennedy might not run for president in 1976, noting that his marriage was troubled and adding, "There are many (myself included) who believe he will be shot if he runs for the presidency." But the memo assumed Kennedy would run, and theorized that he might actually welcome a Carter candidacy, seeing it as a vehicle to collect support from southerners who otherwise would have supported Wallace. A Carter candidacy might be much more easily subsumed into a Kennedy candidacy than would a Wallace one, the memo calculated Kennedy might think.

"I would place a high priority on an early meeting with Kennedy and a discussion on the future of the party and your intention to play an active role in the 1976 elections," Jordan wrote.

And so by the fall of 1972, Kennedy was in Carter's sights. "Carter had a thing about Kennedy all along, [and] it began when we first started making plans for Carter to run for president," Bourne told me.

Kennedy arrived late to the University of Georgia that day in May 1974, but still in plenty of time to give his speech, which went generally unremarked upon.

As the Law Day luncheon progressed, Hunter S. Thompson busied himself with multiple trips to the trunk of one of the Secret Service cars that had carried Kennedy and his entourage to Athens, for refills of Wild Turkey bourbon. The first sign that something was off in the room came a few minutes after Carter started speaking. Thompson said he noticed a "general uneasiness in the atmosphere of the room, and nobody was laughing anymore."

Carter, now in his last year as a governor, had decided that Kennedy's speech was too similar to what he planned to say. He scrapped his prepared remarks and decided to give Georgia's political and legal elites a piece of his mind. With at times barely disguised anger in his voice, he laid bare what he thought of the state's justice system. He said he was "deeply concerned about the inadequacies of a system of which it's obvious that you are so patently proud."

The state's judges were unaccountable, Carter said, and he had helped establish a commission to change that by hearing complaints. He said he had instituted a judicial review process after reading "an analysis of some of the sentences given to people by the Superior Court judges of this state" that had "grieved me deeply and shocked me as a layman." He castigated a criminal code that penalized alcoholics rather than helping them seek treatment, and called for a prison system that aimed to rehabilitate prisoners and to treat them with compassion and humanity.

But Carter's greater concern was that after he left office, the state would become complacent or would go backward in the effort to serve its underprivileged, its poor, and its black populations. The speech was in essence an attempt to shame the audience into continued action. "We still have a long way to go," he said.

Repeatedly, Carter prefaced his most biting critiques with clever diminutions of his own stature or qualifications to make such judgments. "As a farmer, I'm not qualified to assess the characteristics of the ninety-one hundred inmates in the Georgia prisons, 50 percent of whom ought not to be there. They ought to be on probation or under some other supervision and assess what the results of previous court rulings might bring to bear on their lives," he said.

"I don't know, it may be that poor people are the only ones who commit crimes. I don't think so. But they're the only ones that serve prison sentences," he said, lamenting that at one prison, an investigator had discovered "people that had been in solitary confinement for ten years."

Carter assailed the way in which "the powerful and the influential" fear and resist change because they "have carved out for themselves or have inherited a privileged position in society of wealth or social prominence or higher education or opportunity for the future." He placed himself on the side of the poor, reminding the audience that he had grown up without electricity or running water. And he blasted the South's legacy of racism and discrimination against blacks as an "embarrassment."

And then he went for the jugular, stating that Martin Luther King Jr. had been "perhaps despised by many in this room because he shook up our social structure that benefited us, and demanded simply that black citizens be treated the same as white citizens." King "wasn't greeted with approbation and accolades by the Georgia Bar Association or the Alabama Bar Association. He was greeted with horror."

Rhetorically, the speech was a "king hell bastard of a speech," Thompson would later write. "I have never heard a sustained piece of political oratory that impressed me any more," he said.

The response in the room was palpably hostile. "The tension in the room kept increasing.... The audience muttered uneasily and raised their eyebrows at each other," Thompson wrote. "They had not come there to hear lawyers denounced as running dogs of the status quo."

But here was Carter, the man who had won the governorship by appealing to racist sentiment, brutally castigating those sentiments

near the end of his term. He closed with a plea, calling on the audience to "eliminate many of the inequities that I've just described."

"I've done all I can in the governor's office," he said.

After the speech, Thompson told Carter he wanted to get a
copy of his prepared remarks. Carter responded that there wasn't
one. He had sat down in a side room after hearing Kennedy speak
and had written down a page and a half of scrawled notes. He'd
then stood up and let loose. It was "the voice of an angry agrarian
populist," Thompson wrote. Bourne told me decades later that
Carter was more "strident" than normal because "he was angry he
had been relegated. He thought he would have a bigger role. He
thought he had been upstaged by Kennedy."

Perhaps it was a road test of a message that Carter intended to
take to the national stage as a way to co-opt the Wallace constituency in the South, as Jordan had recommended in his memo two
years earlier. It was not the message that Carter ultimately went
with, in large part because Watergate so completely reshaped the
political landscape and created a desire among the nation's voters
to be, as Thompson described it, "cleansed, reassured and revital-
ized." But it was more than enough evidence that Carter possessed
a unique set of political skills, and the guts to utilize them.

And there was an element of primal political will as well,
Thompson thought. He'd later say that he had seen Carter "push
Kennedy around" during that trip. "I had never seen Kennedy
pushed around anywhere, in any room, and I was stunned," he said
on a talk show in 1977. "He just beat the hell out of them. . . . The
whole establishment had been against him and he just stomped on
them in public. I had never seen a politician do that before. And he
just pushed Kennedy aside: 'Get out of my way. I got work to do.
Move aside.' And Kennedy was stunned. I was stunned."

Kennedy had been "impressed" by the speech, Clymer later wrote,
though Thompson noted at the time—with all the observational

skill he could muster in his chemically altered state—that Kennedy appeared to be "uncomfortable and preoccupied."

For Carter, it had been a big moment. "It was a little bit like prizefighters at the weigh-in where they try to psych themselves up in terms of hostility toward their opponent," Bourne told me. "He was psyching himself up to run against Kennedy.... That was the beginning of the real serious dislike and hostility toward Kennedy."

The speech would turn Thompson into something of an evangelist for Carter. He took the tape of the speech he had made and began sharing it with journalists and political operatives. "I probably would have chuckled along with the others if Carter had said something about running for president at the *beginning* of his 'remarks' that day," Thompson wrote. "But I would not have chuckled if he'd said it at the end."

# CHAPTER 6

————◇◇◇————

# The Outsider

One year after the Law Day speech, Jimmy Carter still wasn't being taken seriously. As the 1976 presidential race took shape, he remained an afterthought. At best, he was seen as a pawn in a scheme to rid the Democratic Party of George Wallace once and for all.

In the summer of 1975, two Democratic activists from Florida flew from Miami to Washington, D.C., to pay a visit to Mo Udall, a congressman from Arizona. Udall, a six-foot-five Mormon who had played a year of pro basketball, and who possessed a mirthful sense of humor, was the early favorite of the liberal wing of the party.

Udall took the meeting with the two political operatives from Florida because Mike Abrams and Sergio Bendixen—both of them in their late twenties—were highly influential in the Sunshine State. They had cut their teeth on the McGovern campaign in 1972, and were drawn to Udall's liberal policies. They had shown him around the state earlier in the year and introduced him to people who might help his campaign.

But Abrams and Bendixen came to Udall's congressional office on Capitol Hill with an unusual request. They asked him not to campaign in Florida's 1976 presidential primary. The request was extraordinarily audacious. It was not out of the ordinary for candidates to skip states. Carter, in fact, was an anomaly in that he was campaigning and competing in virtually every primary state. But for two state-based twenty-somethings to be so bold with a presidential candidate twice their age was unheard of. Thirty years later both Abrams and Bendixen shook their heads in disbelief when recalling their impudence.

The Floridians' goal was a one-on-one showdown in Florida between Wallace and Carter, who had announced his candidacy less than a month after Udall's, in December 1974. Carter was the only other southern candidate in the race, and the Floridian youngsters believed that if their state could get a clear choice between the brazenly racist Wallace and the "New South" Carter, voters would go with the future. But they needed to keep the primary to a two-man race. In 1972, Wallace had won Florida, but with only 41 percent of the vote. Six other candidates had split the rest of the vote.

Abrams and Bendixen had made similar asks of the other moderate to liberal Democrats in the race at that point: Sargent Shriver, the vice-presidential nominee from 1972, former senator Fred R. Harris of Oklahoma, Senator Birch Bayh of Indiana, and Senator Henry M. "Scoop" Jackson of Washington. Their argument to each was two-pronged. First, Wallace had to be stopped for the sake of the Democratic Party's future, they said. Wallace was a poison and could not represent their party to such a large swath of the country.

And second, Carter was harmless. He had no shot at the presidency, so it was a low-stakes gamble to let him win Florida. "We just saw him as some obscure governor from an obscure state, not to be taken very seriously," said Udall aide Iris Jacobson Burnett.

Udall, like all the others except for Jackson, went along with the plan. "I didn't think that the party was really going to nominate Jimmy Carter," Udall told Jules Witcover. "If Carter could be used as an engine to destroy Wallace, well, then, fine." Jackson was the only candidate to tell Abrams and Bendixen to get lost.

But by the time the spring of 1976 rolled around, Carter had come out of nowhere to win the Iowa caucuses and the New Hampshire primary, emerging from a huge field of roughly a dozen candidates. By this time, Udall was not in a good position to change his mind about Florida if he wanted to. It is a massive state that requires a lot of money and organization to travel and to advertise on TV, and Udall was beset by chaos inside a fractured campaign staff.

But just one week before the Florida primary, Carter stumbled badly in Massachusetts on March 2, coming in fourth behind Jackson, Udall, and Wallace. The Massachusetts loss presented the Carter campaign with "the crisis of our lives," said Carter pollster Pat Caddell. Carter was still viewed with deep skepticism by political elites, and a Florida loss could knock him out of the race.

Udall's absence in Florida likely made the difference. Carter defeated Wallace by just a few points, 34 percent to 30 percent, with Jackson getting 24 percent. Udall took 2 percent despite assiduously staying true to his promise not to campaign there. Wallace had been "suddenly transformed from a powerful vote-getter into a sad has-been." A week later Carter trounced Wallace in Illinois, and the Alabama governor's spell had been broken.

The Democrats had finally defanged Wallace, but in the process had made Carter a front-runner who—despite massive vulnerabilities—now had staying power. Carter still had to overcome a series of challenges from Udall and other candidates in a prolonged primary, but he ultimately won the nomination with a helping hand from Chicago mayor Richard J. Daley at just the right moment.

"He's got courage. I admire a man who's got courage," Daley said of Carter just before the last three primary states held their elections. "The man talks about true values. Why shouldn't we be sold on him? All of us recognize the violent and filthy movies and the newspapers with all the mistresses on the first page stripped down to the waist. What are the kids going to do in the society that see that all around?" the mayor said.

Carter had courted Daley for years with visits and calls. But Daley, one of the last dominant machine politicians, knew that Democrats had to nominate someone who could win southern voters to have any chance of winning back the White House. He threw his delegates to Carter, as did Wallace, and the two of them helped Carter avoid a contested convention.

How had he done it? Strategically, Carter's decision to enter every primary and caucus, and to win the early states, was unprecedented and transformative. It was the beginning of the modern primary system, in which it is now the norm for every candidate to contest every state. Carter's cover-the-map playbook ensured that he built an early delegate lead that he kept adding to in every state, which was just enough to repel the late charge by California governor Jerry Brown, who closed strong with wins over Carter in Maryland, Rhode Island, Nevada, New Jersey, and his home state of California. Carter also had won far more contests than any other candidate, and was "the nearest thing the Democrats have to a demonstrated popular choice."

Ham Jordan was largely responsible for this strategic choice. It was Jordan who had written the series of memos from 1972 to 1974 plotting out how to win the race, even creating an intricate point system that weighed the value of every delegate available and allowed the campaign to marshal its resources as efficiently as possible in pursuit of each. The run-everywhere approach also matched Carter's temperament. Carter hated to lose anything, and approached any undertaking with total commitment. After he had lost the 1966 governor's race in Georgia, Jordan had tried to persuade him that Carl Sanders couldn't be beaten and that he should run for another office. Carter replied, "If I don't get but two votes, mine and yours, I'm going to run for governor."

The Carter campaign also saw opportunities in the crowded field that the other campaigns did not. Jody Powell focused their media outreach efforts on local newspapers and TV stations, knowing that especially in the early going of the race no one candidate would dominate coverage and so the best way to stand out would be to gain maximum exposure for Carter's campaign trips in the local media markets. And Jordan was savvy enough to get inside the heads of other campaigns, anticipating they would build their efforts around an expectation that the nomination would be decided at the convention, because of the large field and the rules changes. Jordan chose to go after wins early in the process to build name recognition for Carter. They could amass a delegate lead and cement a position in the public consciousness as the front-runner, which would be hard for the party to undo. It was a way to make an end run around the convention and the party insiders.

And the campaign also saw that Iowa was a good match for Carter, at a time when the New Hampshire primary was still considered by the political press to be the first real contest. Carter's advisers wanted to jump out ahead of the rest of the field before New Hampshire. And in fact, five states held caucuses before New Hampshire's primary: Iowa, then Mississippi, Oklahoma, Alaska, and Maine. Carter could have chosen to focus on any of those states, and it would have changed the arc of American political history. But Iowa's agricultural and religious culture fit him best, and he visited it seven times in 1975. He was guided to key parts of the state by operative Tim Kraft's diligent organizing.

The press, in addition, was primed to award Iowa more significance than it had in the past. The media had overlooked George McGovern's candidacy in 1972 until he started winning primaries, and they were determined not to miss any early signs of momentum in 1976. The rules reforms of 1972 had opened up the process and would favor a populist, which Carter aimed to be. The campaign finance changes following Watergate had muted the advantage of a well-financed candidate or a party insider favorite, and leveled the playing field. That also advantaged an outsider like Carter.

None of this would have worked, however, if Carter had not won Iowa, and if he was not an effective and eager campaigner. He is remembered as an inept communicator, but in person, he converted followers with the success—and the methods—of a traveling preacher. "A strange calm came over the audience as he talked of America's basic goodness," Jules Witcover observed early in the campaign. Wrote Charles Mohr in the *Times*, "His speeches are mostly received with a strange quietness."

Carter said the nation's decency had been only "temporarily obscured by the debasings perpetuated by Nixon." He repeated, over and over, "I want a government that is as good, and honest, and decent, and truthful, and fair, and competent, and idealistic, and compassionate, and as filled with love as are the American people." Witcover, who compared Carter to Christian evangelist Billy Graham, called this phrase Carter's "personal rosary" and noted that "in crowd after crowd, it worked."

The country was not only disillusioned by Nixon and Watergate. Americans were disquieted and anxious by the rise of inflation in the early 1970s, by the energy crisis of 1973 that created lines of cars at gas stations, and by a slowing economy. Wages were flatlining, jobs were disappearing, and the cost of living was going up. People may have wanted someone to redeem the country, but they also wanted someone who could restore their confidence and ease their economic pain.

Carter paired his pastoral and personal approach with an indomitable, relentless work ethic. He would talk to anyone, go anywhere, and take as long as necessary to win someone over or to answer questions from a small-town newspaper or radio station. He "would listen long" and "with a vengeance," Witcover wrote. That description, of such an aggressive, almost martial way of conducting what is usually a more passive activity, got to the core of what made Carter unique. As *Washington Post* columnist Sally Quinn put it, in a rather backhanded compliment, "The conventional image of a sexy man is one who is hard on the outside and soft on the inside. Carter is just the opposite."

Those who knew Carter from the statehouse in Georgia would not have been surprised. "Don't pay any attention to that smile. That don't mean a thing," said Ben Fortson, the long-serving Georgia secretary of state. "That man is made of steel, determination and stubbornness."

This interplay between Carter's soft, approachable exterior and the unsmiling, ferocious core within him drove to the heart of the man's duality. There were essentially two Jimmy Carters, and he struggled to balance and reconcile the two. He was a man who had grown up in rural poverty, but who had traveled abroad and domestically and had lived much of his adult life among elites. On the one hand, he was "a simple, straightforward common man of common tastes and virtues who had come out of the peanut fields of south Georgia to lead a nation back to its basic strength and goodness," Witcover wrote. But on the other hand, he was "a well-traveled and well-read man, urbane in many ways for all his folksy style and manner of speaking...a man with homespun charity and love in his heart, yes; but also a tough, competitive, cold-eyed political professional with a steely determination to reach his lofty objective."

Carter played up his rural persona to voters as he campaigned for president, but the press wanted policy detail, and either looked down on the simplicity he projected or suspected it was a fraud. For supporters, critics, and observers alike, "it was difficult to grasp that one man could be so simple and straightforward and so complex and conniving at the same time," Witcover wrote. Carter himself was highly aware of how he projected himself. He once tossed a *Time* photographer out of a meeting after spokesman Jody Powell had allowed the journalist in. "I don't want a picture in *Time* that shows my senior staff and has only one black and one woman, and her my wife," Carter told Powell after the photographer left.

Nonetheless, Carter's willingness to spend time talking in depth with real-life voters was a startling contrast to the antiseptic, sealed-off styles of both Richard Nixon and Lyndon Johnson. He would engage in conversation with a man or woman he met at an event, and end by asking, "Have I answered your question?" This was a curious contrast with the way he had interacted with the Georgia legislature during his time as governor, when his closest adviser, Ham Jordan, had remarked that Carter had curiosity "about process, not people" and that he "doesn't understand the personal element in politics."

Rosalynn Carter was also a huge asset. She campaigned in forty-two states, just as tenaciously as her husband. The formerly quiet, shy woman had become a full partner of her husband's, and was his closest confidante. She and a friend spent two weeks driving through Florida in April 1975, with very few meetings or events planned. She would arrive in a small town and head for the courthouse, which she said "tend[s] to be the center of political activity and gossip," or she would look for the TV and radio antennas to guide her to the local station, and then ask to be interviewed. She even wrote down a list of questions for the disc jockeys to ask her. She stayed in people's homes and barged into all-male rotary meetings. Each new person she met, she wrote down their name and contact information on a three-by-five index card. All told, Rosalynn spent seventy-five days in Florida and visited 105 communities in Iowa, with many trips to several other states. "She wants to be first lady as bad as he wants to be president," Ham Jordan once said of her.

There were no themes to Carter's candidacy except "faith in Jimmy Carter and the sense of hope he sought to inspire in the American people," wrote Bourne. Witcover picked up on this as well. "He asked of voters the same 'leap of faith' that is at the core of religious belief," he wrote.

The electorate was ripe for this approach, as Carter pollster Pat Caddell had discovered. Voters wanted "nonideological change and the restoration of values." George Reedy, the former spokesman for Lyndon Johnson, said that "the real issues in the campaign are spiritual. . . . The average American today is lost. He doesn't know what to believe, where to go, what to do."

There was an element of sheer demagoguery to Carter's approach. Unlike a populist who stirs people's passions, Carter simply stroked voters' egos by telling them how virtuous they were. "I want a government always to tell the truth. What we need is for our government to be as good as our people," he told a room of elementary school children in New Hampshire days before the primary there. He smiled widely. "Wouldn't that be a great thing?" Witcover observed that when Carter spoke to adults this way, he was essentially treating them as gullible children.

"He has tenaciously stuck to a 'basic speech' that, more than anything else, flatters the voters," Mohr wrote. Journalists covering Carter rolled their eyes at much of his rhetoric.

Carter's soft-spoken, mild-mannered delivery overshadowed

some of the positions he did take that would have seemed radical coming out of the mouth of a more strident speaker. Carter voiced support for abolishing preferential tax treatment for capital gains, and for big tax increases on higher incomes. But Mohr said conservative audiences seemed not to notice these comments, though they would applaud when Carter asserted that there were more than a million people on the welfare rolls who should not be.

But Carter was able to be all things to most people. "He was a conservative to the conservatives, he was a moderate to the moderates and he was a liberal to the liberals," his presidential aide Bert Lance said. "He covered the whole spectrum of political philosophy and feeling and emotion. And he covered it very well, because he fragmented himself. Fiscally he was conservative. On people issues he was liberal. He was liberal in terms of the needs of the needy who are dependent on the government. On social issues, the broad spectrum, he was probably moderate."

Carter was viewed suspiciously by Jewish groups, but otherwise was popular with blue-collar whites as well as minorities. He was capable of impressive rhetorical achievement, and in fact, two days after the last primaries, he gave one of the best speeches of his career. He traveled to Los Angeles and dedicated a new psychiatric wing of the Martin Luther King, Jr. General Hospital in the predominantly black Watts neighborhood, which had been burned out in the riots after King's assassination eight years earlier. In his speech, Carter positioned himself as the rightful heir to both MLK and Bobby Kennedy, because he was a bridge between the Deep South and the rest of the country, who could bring his own region into the future and unite the nation. His remarks were populist in flavor, a continuation of his Law Day speech.

He brought Robert Kennedy into his remarks, quoting Kennedy's speech in Indianapolis on the night MLK was killed. "We lost Martin Luther King. We lost Robert Kennedy," Carter said.

"We lost the election that year to men who governed without love or laughter, to men who promised law and order and gave us crime and oppression.

"But the dream lived on," he continued, bringing the point home, and in essence stealing the very thunder that Teddy Kennedy saw as his own. "It could be slowed, but never stopped." After Carter finished, a moderator read a telegram from the Reverend Martin Luther King Sr. "I have a dream too," King Sr. had written, "that a Southerner, Jimmy Carter, is going to be President of the United States.... I love you and ask all Americans to love you."

The audience's reaction was captured by Mohr, who was covering the event for the *Times*. "An almost physical wave of love seemed to pass from the black listeners to Mr. Carter," he wrote.

Teddy Kennedy watched all this—this interloper taking his part and reading his lines—from the sidelines. He was seen by many as the most prominent potential stop-Carter figure, but after Daley's intervention on Carter's behalf, Kennedy saw the writing on the wall. "I expect the nominee will be Mr. Carter," he said, without much enthusiasm.

In late September 1974, Kennedy had announced he would not run for president in 1976. The announcement came four months after his trip to Georgia and his first meeting with Carter. It was also soon after the ghost of Mary Jo Kopechne had once again been resurrected. On July 14, 1974, the *New York Times Magazine* published an eight-page piece revisiting the Chappaquiddick incident. The piece, written by liberal journalist Robert Sherrill, mentioned early on that Kennedy's "reputation as a ladies' man" had provoked widespread talk that "Kopechne was pregnant and that her death was no accident."

Sherrill resurrected all the unanswered questions and contra-
dictions in the evidence from that night, including Kennedy's own
statements. "The questions are endless, and most of them seem not
at all to have stirred the curiosity of officialdom, which from the
very beginning was much more interested in protecting Senator
Kennedy," he wrote.

It was a shot across Kennedy's bow that if he ran for president,
he could expect far more scrutiny of the incident than he'd under-
gone so far. "The piece attracted great attention," Kennedy would
remember decades later in his autobiography. He wrote that the
Sherrill piece "was not a determinant" in his decision not to run
for president. But, he added, "I also knew that it did not help my
presidential prospects."

Jimmy Carter had actually relished the prospect of taking on
Kennedy, and when that opportunity vanished, his path to the
nomination became more complicated. Beating Wallace in the
South and Kennedy elsewhere had been a tall task, but easy to
understand. Once Kennedy was out, however, every Democrat
with presidential ambitions was thinking about putting his or her
hat in the ring. That made things far more unpredictable.

And tension between Carter and Kennedy continued throughout the primary. There was talk of drafting Hubert Humphrey to
run, and Kennedy was mentioned frequently as a potential running
mate. News reports in late May said that Kennedy might run himself. Kennedy denied it, but he also criticized Carter's vagueness on
policy matters. Carter had "made his position on some issues indef-
inite and imprecise," Kennedy said. He was particularly concerned
about Carter's lack of commitment to national health insurance.

Carter lashed out publicly and privately. In a prepared speech
in Cincinnati on May 27, he said that those trying to stop his
nomination opposed his dream of "a better America" and were

obsessed with keeping "at all costs their own entrenched, unresponsive, bankrupt, irresponsible political power.

"We have seen this campaign come full circle from 'Jimmy Who?' sixteen months ago to 'Stop Carter.' The people who ignored me then are opposing me now," he said.

An even more provocative comment Carter made in private was reported in the *Atlanta Journal* by David Nordan, who had been granted behind-the-scenes access to Carter. Nordan brought up Kennedy's criticism of Carter's lack of policy detail, and Carter lashed out. "I'm glad I don't have to depend on Kennedy or Humphrey or people like that to put me in office," he said. "I don't have to kiss his ass."

After Carter wrapped up the nomination, Kennedy offered to enter Carter's name into nomination at the convention, a symbolically important gesture. The Carter campaign rejected him, and Kennedy promptly left the convention. It was the first time in twenty years that a Kennedy had not played a prominent role at a Democratic convention.

Carter's remark that he didn't have to "kiss [Kennedy's] ass" exposed more than just a dislike for Kennedy. It revealed his independent approach to the presidential campaign in general. And in fact, he was able to win the nomination without much help from anyone outside his small, insular group of Georgians. "To those who for years had controlled the party and the convention mechanism, he was an unknown quantity, an outsider, a loner who had triumphed without them."

But because of reforms to the primary system after 1968, outsiders like Carter were able to defy the party establishment and mount successful campaigns. Big-city bosses no longer controlled as many delegates. Carter's independence was a double-edged sword, however. His estrangement from the political establishment, from the grass roots of the Democratic Party, and from the political press left him isolated and politically weakened.

The liberal wing of the party did not trust Carter, because he was a southerner, and because he had been vague on the issues important to them. This pushed him to choose as his running mate a Minnesotan, Senator Walter Mondale, to pacify the left. That calmed liberals for a moment, but their suspicions remained, and would fester.

Relations with the press were mixed, but the seeds of much bigger problems had already been planted there as well. It started with Carter, who held much of the media in contempt for seeking to nail him down on answers to complicated questions that he thought he should have time to sort through. He called many of the pack's questions "frivolous."

The journalists covering Carter saw him as vague and evasive, and especially hated the way he cloaked his lack of specifics— or even his flip-flopping answers on abortion during the Iowa primary—in self-righteousness. "It would be a very serious viola-tion of my word of honor if I pretended to know those answers," Carter told Witcover early in the primary. Witcover wrote of this comment, "Carter had a distinct way of converting his every act, even a refusal to give a plain answer to a plain question, into an act of political morality."

The more obvious reason for Carter's vagueness was that he was a master at assembling a diverse coalition of supporters by avoiding offending each of them. Speechwriter Bob Shrum, who quit the Carter campaign in April after working for him for only nine days, said in a letter to Carter that his strategy was "designed to conceal your true convictions, whatever they may be." Shrum's bitter con-clusion: "I am not sure what you believe in, other than yourself."

The press also suspected Carter was a fraud. His preference for running on his own character and persona, and his aversion to getting into the details of policy and issues, led him to attack his rivals for the same. He tended toward "impugning their motives and accusing them of being subservient to this or that powerful interest group." Reporters like Witcover viewed Carter's talk of love and unity as hypocritical. Witcover referred to Carter's attacks on opponents as him "sticking his love-coated needle into a foe."

And Carter's vow never to tell a lie or even to mislead voters was like throwing chum in the water, especially right after the Watergate scandal, when the entire press corps felt both burned by Nixon's misdeeds and lies and empowered by the *Washington Post*'s uncovering of it all. Speechwriter Patrick Anderson described an average day with the traveling press corps as a "moveable madhouse." He wrote, "After every stop, the reporters played their tapes over and over, furiously seeking some inconsistency. Carter could have delivered the Sermon on the Mount and no one would have cared unless it contradicted what he'd said the day before."

Relations with the press and with the Democratic establishment were not helped by the fact that Carter's campaign team was a highly insular bunch, suspicious of those who were not from Georgia. Shrum's betrayal only increased the campaign's mistrust of outsiders, and further consolidated power in the people closest to Carter, namely Jordan and Powell. These two, for all their talents, still personified what Bourne described as "the dark side of the South, a regional inferiority complex reflected as resentment and paranoia."

The suspicion that Carter was a hypocrite also was given oxygen by the conduct of Jordan and others in the Carter high command. "Our candidate may have been a saint, but he surrounded himself with sinners," wrote Anderson, who replaced Shrum as Carter's main speechwriter near the end of the primary season, after writing a positive profile of the candidate for the *New York Times Magazine* in 1975.

Jordan, who was married and would divorce his wife, Nancy, in 1978, made racist jokes about blacks voting for Carter because they thought he had a warehouse of watermelons in Plains, and openly caroused with much younger staffers and volunteers. He boasted of it. Carter's advisers were described as being as "hard-drinking, fornicating, pot-smoking, free-thinking a group as has been seen in higher politics."

As Kraft said, others in the campaign followed Jordan's example, according to Bourne, whose perch inside the campaign gave him a front-row seat to what he described as "a deeply embedded southern attitude" of chauvinism that "pervaded the campaign." Carter advisers or supporters such as Barbara Blum and Connie Plunkett were "demeaned and regularly excluded from meetings." Taken altogether, along with a "disdain for the intellectual," the campaign set a tone that cut against what Jimmy and Rosalynn stood for, and undermined their credibility with the press, which then influenced the way they were covered.

To top it all off, Carter's fervency of faith was regarded as foreign and strange by many in the press, and that impression was only heightened by his infamous interview with a freelance journalist for publication in *Playboy* magazine. Over five hours of questions and answers during the course of a few visits with the writer, Robert Scheer, Carter—at least in Scheer's telling—enjoyed engaging on topics that were "a bit more challenging and philosophical than the routine inquiries about political tactics." Many of Scheer's questions touched on the matter of how Carter's faith would influence his decisions if he were elected president, including his private and religious views on sexuality.

When they discussed his views on homosexuality, Carter said the issue "always makes me nervous.... It's political, it's moral, and it's strange territory for me." He said he couldn't "change the teachings of Christ" on the matter, which convinced him that to commit adultery as a heterosexual or to engage in homosexuality were both sins, but that as a private citizen his faith told him to worry about his own shortcomings more than those of others, and as a government official, he would not focus on such personal matters. In Georgia, he said, "I didn't run around breaking down people's doors to see if they were fornicating."

At the end of the last interview, Scheer asked Carter if he thought he'd "reassured" people who might be "uneasy" about his religiosity. Carter launched into a long answer about the importance of humility, and of not looking down on others. And he punctuated his point with an example of his own weakness. "I try not to commit a deliberate sin. I recognize that I'm going to do it anyhow, because I'm human and I'm tempted. And Christ set some almost impossible standards for us. Christ said, 'I tell you that anyone who looks on a woman with lust has in his heart already committed adultery.' I've looked on a lot of women with lust. I've committed adultery in my heart many times. This is something that God recognizes I will do—and I have done it— and God forgives me for it." He added, "Christ says don't consider yourself better than someone else because one guy screws a whole bunch of women while the other guy is loyal to his wife. The guy who's loyal to his wife ought not to be condescending or proud because of the relative degree of sinfulness."

Religious conservatives were offended by his use of the word "screw" and by the fact that he'd been interviewed by *Playboy* in the first place. For many others, the comments about lust in his heart—in Jordan's words—"increased the weirdo factor." Within a week, Carter's 10-point lead in his campaign's internal polls evaporated, and pollster Pat Caddell reported that he was now narrowly trailing incumbent president Gerald Ford.

Nevertheless, for the moment the times were still in Carter's favor, despite his missteps. But as he went along in the general election against Ford, a Republican, Carter realized that Ford was seeking to avoid open confrontation with him by holding most of his events at the White House or in other official settings that emphasized his standing as the commander in chief. This frustrated Carter to no end. He complained that while Ford often had to face the press only once a day and at that could stroll into the Rose Garden, make a statement, and walk away, "I make a hundred different statements a day."

Carter's frustration boiled over into personal attacks on Ford that made him look petty and mean-spirited, hurting his reputation as a uniter and a healer. He directly associated Ford with Nixon: "The spirit of this country has been damaged by Richard Nixon and Gerald Ford. We don't like their betrayal of what our country is, and we don't like their vision of what this country ought to be." He said Ford was "even worse" than Nixon on economics. And he accused the president of "callous indifference" to the poor who had been hurt by inflation and unemployment. Having led Ford by around 15 points at the start of the fall after Labor Day, he saw his lead slipping away.

But Ford contributed some significant missteps of his own, which arrested his momentum. In the end, Carter narrowly defeated him in the popular vote, 40.8 million votes to 39.1 million, and in the Electoral College, 297 to 240. It was the smallest margin of victory in electoral votes for a president since 1916. And Carter won four fewer states than did Ford. In addition, the negative tone of the campaign had taken a toll. The presidential election saw the lowest voter turnout in twenty-eight years, at only 54 percent.

Carter entered Washington as an outsider, and the presidency without much of a mandate. His speechwriter, Anderson, pointed to the *Playboy* interview as the pivotal moment in the campaign. Anderson called it "the turning point of [Carter's] political career because of the way it altered Carter's trajectory as he entered the White House.

"It destroyed his lead, soured his press relations, threw him on the defensive and his campaign into chaos, and probably cost him the big electoral victory he had expected. Moreover, Carter's remarks first raised the possibility to millions of voters that he might be a bit too different, too strange."

Teddy White wrote that Carter "arrived in Washington having won both his nomination and his election on personality alone, without an organized party behind him."

# CHAPTER 7

# Lanced

The one thing about Jimmy Carter I think that will ultimately be said about him in a proper sense of study of his presidency, he never made a popular decision.

—*Bert Lance*

Despite the brevity of Jimmy Carter's inaugural address, the fifty-two-year-old new president mentioned the phrase "new spirit" five times. Carter said his inauguration was the mark of "a new beginning, a new dedication within our government, and a new spirit among us all."

The former submarine commander, peanut farmer, state legislator, and southern governor was not triumphalist in his rhetoric. He told the nation that without their support and participation, he would fail. To the American people, he promised "to stay close to you, to be worthy of you, and to exemplify what you are."

"A president may sense and proclaim that new spirit, but only a people can provide it," he said. "Let us create together a new national spirit of unity and trust. Your strength can compensate for my weakness, and your wisdom can help to minimize my mistakes."

To the extent that there was substance or policy in his address,

Carter emphasized defending human rights abroad as a core part of American foreign policy, and standing up for the poor, weak, and vulnerable at home. The change to foreign policy "would become the most widely acknowledged and enduring legacy of the Carter presidency," according to Peter Bourne, a longtime adviser to Carter. For decades, the U.S. government's organizing principle abroad had been anticommunism, and any foreign government that joined it in this cause received friendship, regardless of how it treated its own people.

Carter broke with precedent and walked the parade route from the Capitol to the White House. Every president since has to some degree copied his man-of-the-people routine. He reviewed the parade for almost two hours, toured the residence, held a few meetings in the Oval Office, and then had dinner with Rosalynn, his nine-year-old daughter, Amy, his three sons and their wives, and his mother, Lillian.

Carter's honeymoon period as president was pleasant. He immediately commenced a flurry of activity. He reached out to the Soviet Union with a new arms reduction plan, and to the Israelis and Palestinians about a peace deal. He proposed an economic stimulus package and a plan to reorganize the executive branch. At home, inflation was down to 6 percent after having reached 12 percent three years earlier. Unemployment was still high, though, around 8 percent. Republicans, having expected Carter to be a typically high-spending Democrat, were pleased with his fiscal restraint. Two months into his presidency, his approval rating was 75 percent.

"In his first two months as President, Jimmy Carter has achieved a triumph of communications in the arena of public opinion," the *Washington Post*'s David Broder wrote. "He has transformed himself from the very shaky winner of a campaign into a very popular President whose mastery of the mass media has given him real leverage with which to govern."

His first trip abroad to a meeting of foreign leaders—the Group of Seven summit in London in early May—won him the admiration of other leaders for his knowledge of the subject matter and his personal warmth.

Carter was obsessed with showing that if he could save money in the executive branch, the rest of the government could too by being more efficient. "Even our great nation has its recognized limits. . . . We cannot afford to do everything," he'd said in the inaugural. He instituted a 10 percent pay cut for executive branch staff (but not for himself) and cut the number of White House staff by a third. He even briefly had the National Park Service turn off the lights illuminating the Washington Monument and the Jefferson Memorial at night, until aides convinced him it was a terrible idea. And he instructed the Secret Service to take him the seventy-five miles from an Air Force base in Georgia to his hometown of Plains by car rather than helicopter, during his first trip back to the Peach State in the second week of February.

That plan was foiled, however. "I discovered that because of the tremendous amount of effort that has to go into traffic control for intersections, it's much less expensive to go by helicopter, which we will do in the future," Carter wrote in his journal. Even his plan to reduce White House staff met resistance immediately from inside his own family. First Lady Rosalynn Carter did not want to see her staff cut from twenty-three to twenty, and prevailed. "I think we took those cuts somewhere else for the sake of peace and harmony in the first family," said White House budget chief Bert Lance.

But finances and energy were on Carter's mind. One of his most ambitious proposals was the creation of a new Department of Energy, and to address the nation's dependence on imports of foreign oil. Carter came before Congress in late April to pitch his energy plan, aimed at moving utilities from natural gas and oil to coal plants, at getting American auto manufacturers to produce more fuel-efficient cars, and at encouraging Americans to better insulate their homes. After the speech, the *New York Times*'s James Reston summed up the conventional wisdom of the moment about the nation's still new president. "He still baffles the capital," Reston wrote, noting that in the weeks leading up to the energy plan's unveiling, Carter had proposed and then backed off $50 tax rebates and the cancellation of various local water projects he had deemed wasteful. "He talks like a populist but acts like a conservative."

Carter failed to build a strong working relationship with Congress. In these early days, however, he still had a new car smell, and while he was frittering away any favor he might have had inside Washington's establishment, Americans were willing to give him a chance. "It is with Carter a sense that there is something very good at the bottom of the barrel, a purpose in his human rights arguments, in his insistence on cutting down strategic arms and pork-barrel projects, and facing up to the energy problem," Reston wrote on April 24. "He doesn't have a sense of humor, but he clearly has a sense of history. . . . Nobody quite knows where he is going, but it is clear after the last couple of weeks that he is leading the parade."

Anthony Lewis noted in mid-August that America in the latter half of the 1970s was "in an essentially conservative period, continuing the swing to the right noted at the end of the turbulent 1960's." He continued, "The country is hardly eager for social experiment. There is a backlash against sexual permissiveness. Further steps to help blacks and other minorities are difficult. Economic fears have aroused protectionist feelings and resistance to environmental safeguards. One of Jimmy Carter's principal functions in history may be to keep the reaction from going too far."

But there were signs early on of Carter's myopic, obsessive managerial style that would cause him trouble later on. It emerged in July that the president would sometimes scrutinize the list of government officials scheduled to accompany him on a foreign trip and scratch out names of those he did not think needed to come. And any staff who wanted to use the tennis court on the White House grounds had to receive permission from the president himself. "He has his eye on anything that moves," said an aide.

As the summer of 1977 wound down, there were more serious warning signs. The House had passed most of Carter's energy plan, but polling showed declining public support for the legislation. Carter and his administration were pushing the Senate to ratify the treaty they had negotiated with Panama over transfer of the canal, but Senate Majority Leader Robert Byrd was in no rush. And the president's relations with the Jewish community were declining.

—————— ∞ ——————

And then, during Carter's first summer as president, the Bert Lance affair happened.

Thomas Bertram Lance, a small-town banker from northern Georgia, had met Carter in 1966 during his first run for governor. He was seven years younger than Carter, but over time the two developed a relationship that was honest, leavened with humor, and largely coequal. Carter chose Lance to run the Transportation Department in Georgia, and then asked him to run for governor in 1974 to prevent former governor Lester Maddox from retaking the governorship and undoing his many reforms. Lance lost, but Maddox did too, to George Busbee.

When Carter won the presidency two years later, he brought Lance to Washington as his budget chief. The two men scheduled a weekly tennis game. "I had a different relationship with him where I could try to knock his eyes out with a tennis ball and he knew full well that's what I was going to do," Lance said.

"I was the only person in Washington who had a peer relationship with the President other than Rosalynn," Lance remembered years later. "Hamilton [Jordan], Jody [Powell], Stu [Eizenstat], Jack [Watson]—all were staff people, and there was no social relationship or personal relationship. [Charles] Kirbo has that relationship with him. I had it with him, and there probably wasn't anybody else in Washington that ever developed it.

"Kirbo was not there," Lance added. "He didn't have any idea."

Lance was also an extremely gregarious, extroverted personality who provided badly needed relational tissue between the Carter White House and the cabinet secretaries, as well as with the Congress. Lance had played a similar role in Georgia when Carter had shown little interest in schmoozing with members of the legislature in order to get his agenda passed into law.

Lance had paid special attention in Georgia to backbench members of the legislature. "They all have a vote and they all have egos and they all want to be stroked and made to feel that they're something special. If you don't do that, then you lose a relationship with them that can help," he said. He felt later that Carter had overestimated his ability to steamroll Congress the way he had the Georgia legislature.

"He did involve himself and he had called the leadership of the House and the Senate down to his office and he talked to them and he'd tell them what he stood for and he'd go through all that process," Lance said. "But he was stern and he was determined and with the same way that he said to the Congress, 'If you don't do what I ask you to do I'm going to go over your heads and go to the American people.'"

Carter's executive approach to dealing with legislatures had much to do with his own self-confidence. But it was also a function of his loner tendencies. "He had very few personal relationships in my opinion," Lance said. "I like people. I like to be around them. I try to be cordial to them. Not that he doesn't, but he'd just rather be by himself."

E. Stanly Godbold noted in his biography of Carter that during his time as governor, "Apart from Rosalynn, he saw as few people as possible.... Usually he ate lunch alone in his office, ordering the food from the cafeteria.... In the afternoons he studied serious academic books about politics and society." Carter may have been in politics, Teddy White wrote, but he "simply did not like politicians.... He wasn't offering friendship."

Carter's approach to working with the Georgia legislature had been like that of a "South Georgia turtle," said friend Warren Fortson. "He doesn't go around a log. He just sticks his head in the middle and pushes and pushes until the log gives way." Carter was willing to sling dirt during a campaign, but in governing, he did not like to sully himself. Rather than trade favors and cajole legislators into supporting his reorganization plan as governor, he hosted meeting after meeting with lawmakers, activists, and interest groups, trying to rationally persuade them of his plan. If that did not work, he sought "primarily to shame legislators into supporting it," said Peter Bourne. As a result, Carter was "more of an outsider when he left the governor's office than when he came in," said Lance.

After Carter became president, this blind spot persisted. He could not or would not understand that sending a congressman a set of presidential cuff links or taking them on Air Force One during a trip to their state was worth far more than rational argument about why they should support Carter's energy plan or some other part of his agenda.

Lance was ambitious and had designs on becoming treasury secretary or Federal Reserve chairman. But in mid-July, the press picked up on a letter that Carter had sent to the Senate Committee on Governmental Affairs asking them to let Lance off the hook from a promise he'd made during confirmation hearings earlier in the year when he had pledged to sell 190,000 shares of National Bank of Georgia stock—then valued at $15 a share—by the end of the year, to avoid a conflict of interest with his ability to influence national economic policy. But the stock had fallen in value to $9.50 a share, and Lance was now set to take a massive loss.

Lance was also deeply in debt, having taken out loans to buy the stock in the first place, and the media raised questions about the impact of his indebtedness on his policymaking decisions. The stories dragged on for a month, and the Carter administration complained about an unfair feeding frenzy, especially after Congress left town in the first week of August and the press looked around for fresh stories. But Carter was in a difficult position. "The hands of the Carter entourage are tied," wrote Hedrick Smith in the *Times*. "In post-Watergate Washington, the President cannot afford the risk of appearing to allow any cover-up to take place, especially because of the image of purity that he has sought to have his top Administration appointees project."

By mid-August, the problem appeared contained. But the press would not let go of the story, and Lance's sloppy banking practices—including a pattern of massive overdrafts by him and his family—gave them plenty of material. For another month, into mid-September, the saga dragged on, with pressure mounting day after day for Lance to resign or be fired. After some resistance from his wife, LaBelle, he resigned his budget director job on September 21.

A somber, bitter Carter told the press that he believed Lance had "exonerated himself completely" of any wrongdoing. The obvious implication was that the press wanted their pound of flesh from Carter and wouldn't let up on Lance until he gave in. Carter later called it "probably one of the worst days I've ever spent."

"Lance's departure was a profoundly significant turning point in Carter's presidency," Bourne wrote. The episode greatly damaged Carter's moral authority. The two months of daily stories poisoned an already contentious relationship with the press. And the impact on public perceptions of the new president was extremely negative. Carter's approval rating dropped from 66 percent to 54 percent in about a month. All of this emboldened Congress to resist him. Carter was further weakened when he backed off an appointment of Ted Sorensen to run the CIA, and reversed some of his cuts to local water projects after he faced a furious reaction from members of Congress who were affected.

Carter could have had a productive relationship with Congress, where Democrats held an overwhelming majority in the House and Senate when he arrived. He was an outsider, and so were many new members of Congress: 118 of the 289 Democrats in the House had been elected in either 1974 or 1976. And the new members of Congress had run for public office during a time of intense anti-Washington sentiment stirred up by the Nixon presidency. "These people didn't come up through state legislatures, they never ran for city council or county office; they ran against the system," House Speaker Tip O'Neill of Massachusetts told Teddy White. "The same emotions rebelling against the 'imperial presidency' and the 'insiders' of Washington had brought both [Carter] and the new Congress to power at the same time," White wrote.

But neither Carter nor Congress were naturally predisposed to view each other favorably. Carter lumped in the new members of Congress with the old Washington establishment. And Nixon's abuses had been the culmination of the expansion of presidential power by a string of chief executives. This created in Congress a strong push to be more adversarial toward the president, regardless of his party. The executive branch had usurped power that was rightly the legislative's, many felt, and balance needed to be restored. Carter was not helped by a team of advisers who, with the exception of Lance, by and large did little to show respect for and win over congressional leadership. Hamilton Jordan wouldn't return O'Neill's calls, and the Speaker began referring to the president's top adviser as "Hamilton Jerkin."

The Lance affair, by destroying whatever goodwill remained in Congress toward Carter, also stopped the momentum of his domestic agenda, and brought almost everything—all the balls in the air—crashing down. "We simply had more issues of a policy nature than we could deal with," Lance said later. "We were dealing with so many different things that we were terribly frightened by our inability to focus in on certain basic issues that needed to be dealt with.... [Carter] just had the supreme confidence, which I guess from your viewpoint would be viewed as overconfidence, that he could deal with that many issues. Human rights this week, the B-1 decision the next week, the tax things the next week, the Panama Canal this week. There's so many things going on that it got to be too much." The Department of Energy was created by Congress on August 4, but other than that, the White House agenda ground to a halt.

Losing Lance also deprived Carter of a key adviser who would tell him when he was wrong, and left him exposed to an organization without an effective structure. It was a crucial weakness as he entered a new environment where he needed to overcome his loss of strength with organizational and strategic efficiency. Instead, he was beset by the unique and unorthodox organizational structure he had created in the White House.

Carter had insisted when he came into the presidency that a chief of staff was not necessary. It was a reflection of his own desire for control, and it was aided and abetted by Hamilton Jordan's thirst for power and aversion to responsibility. Carter fought off attempts by those around him to create a chief of staff. Jack Watson, a Harvard-trained attorney who was a mentee of Kirbo's, created a transition plan but ultimately went along with Carter's wish for a "spokes of the wheel" management structure around Carter, rather than having one central organizer and manager under the president, even though "everybody I had ever talked to said, 'It won't work.'"

A wider range of people coming to Carter made him more powerful and those around him less so, Peter Bourne wrote, giving Carter "maximum control while deliberately leaving people in ignorance of exactly where they stood in the overall scheme." The arrangement was also a reflection of Carter's micromanaging instincts. "He made everything come through him," said Griffin Bell, attorney general under Carter.

Jordan was happy to go along with this structure, because it allowed him to retain the control and influence he had on Carter without having to deal with the management and organizational tasks that confront a traditional chief of staff. He wanted to continue "writing thoughtful memos and developing narrow political strategy" without "having to assume any managerial responsibility," wrote Bourne. And Jordan knew that while it was hard to win an argument with Carter, it was possible to influence him through writing. "Whatever Hamilton pretty well laid out in memo form, he showed respect for and generally went along with," said Lance.

Jordan was a phenom who at age twenty-six had helped Carter get elected as governor of Georgia. He had been with the president almost since the beginning of his political career. The two had met when Jordan volunteered for Carter's first campaign for governor, which Carter lost. He went on to become a trusted aide, and a decade later, when Carter became president, Jordan was the top political adviser in the White House at age thirty-two.

Jordan was a fast-talking, quick-thinking Georgia native whose easygoing demeanor masked an intensely competitive core. He had a thick head of fine dark brown hair, combed to the side, and deep-set eyes that accurately suggested a quick wit. He attracted attention with his casual dress code in the White House. Jordan would often wear a blazer and jeans to work. He thought of himself as a rebel, as did most of Carter's aides—outsiders in Washington's political culture.

Carter had infinite confidence in his own ability to handle the job of president without a chief of staff. But his staff lacked "a cohesive plan" day in and week out, because everything ran through the president and there were no regular staff meetings to plan strategy. Carter would instead meet with individual aides or advisers. And now, with the news media and Congress turning on him, and his agenda stalled, Carter's presidency began to totter. This was when his own party began to desert him.

On the very day that Bert Lance resigned, Ted Kennedy visited the White House to have lunch with the president. The two men ate on the patio outside the Oval Office for about forty-five minutes. When they returned to the Oval Office, Bert and LaBelle Lance were waiting to speak with Carter, and for three minutes Kennedy remained in the room with Carter and the Lances.

Kennedy was pushing Carter to take action on a national health care program, but was becoming increasingly suspicious that Carter's campaign promises were not going to amount to much. In May, Kennedy had publicly called Carter out. "It is time," he said, for the president to move forward on a national health insurance bill. Carter had stalled for time, saying he'd get going on the issue in 1978.

Kennedy had floated rumors late in the spring of the 1976 campaign that he might run, in an attempt to push Carter to the left on health care. And in the one campaign rally that Kennedy spoke at for Carter in the fall of that year, he'd made sure to emphasize Carter's promise during a speech in April to push for a health care plan.

During Carter's first year in office, however, Kennedy was an ally. He supported the president's plan for a tax rebate until the administration scrapped it, and he backed his energy plan. Kennedy was also thrilled with Carter's statement of support for a political settlement in Northern Ireland that would end the British occupation there. Carter took his position against the vehement opposition of the British government, issuing his statement at the end of August, in the midst of the Lance affair. Kennedy sent him a handwritten note that said, "No other president in history has done as well by Ireland."

After the Lance affair, Kennedy continued to work with Carter's White House. He consulted with Zbigniew Brzezinski, Carter's national security adviser, ahead of taking a trip to China over the Christmas and New Year holiday at the end of 1977. But Kennedy and Carter were headed for an inevitable clash, because of their different priorities. Carter was most concerned with keeping inflation in check, while Kennedy's top priority was health care.

Carter was prescient in his economic outlook. He was trying to lead "a party whose coalition was forged during depression and sustained by decades of economic growth," and that was now grappling with "the threat posed by slower growth and rising inflation." Dick Moe, the chief of staff to Carter's own vice president, Walter Mondale—who was far more liberal on spending than Carter—acknowledged two decades later in hindsight that "the world had changed" and that "Carter, more than any other Democrat, acknowledged the fiscal realities, and congressional Democrats, Mondale included, did not."

But Carter was rapidly losing altitude. By February 1978, his approval rating had dropped to 47 percent. By April, he was down to 40 percent. His public approval rating would rise above 50 percent only twice for brief periods during the rest of his presidency.

It was during this time that speculation began that Kennedy

would challenge Carter in 1980. A Gallup poll showed Democrats preferred Kennedy to Carter, 53 percent to 40 percent. For the time being, Kennedy downplayed any such talk. "Give President Carter a chance," he told the U.S. Conference of Mayors in June 1978.

Kennedy had other things on his mind in the fall of 1977 and spring of 1978 as well. His daughter, Kara, was in high school and was running away from home sporadically. And Joan moved out of the family's home in the fall and took up residence in Boston, where she could attend Alcoholics Anonymous meetings without attracting attention. Chappaquiddick continued to lurk in the background. Even in China, Kennedy couldn't escape the horrible incident. When he visited a prison, he asked a prisoner why he had been jailed. The prisoner, obviously prepped by government officials, responded, "I am in for negligent homicide. The bus I was driving went over a cliff and killed nine people."

But the idea of challenging Carter was impossible to ignore. He had been asked in 1974 whether, "deep down," he still wanted to be president. Kennedy couldn't lie. "Yes," he said. And as the Carter presidency entered a tailspin at its halfway mark, the door appeared to be opening for Kennedy to walk through and claim the mantle of his party's leadership.

# CHAPTER 8

—⁂—

# Malaise

The people out there are getting frantic, they know the
great American ride is ending.
—*John Updike*, Rabbit Is Rich

After the Memphis convention and Kennedy's fiery speech, the
Carter reelection campaign began preparing for a primary challenge from Kennedy. But Carter's clinching of the Egyptian-Israeli
peace agreement in the spring of 1979, and his successful normal-
ization of relations with China—concluding a process begun by
Nixon—once again showed the nation that he possessed unusual
abilities.

"Suddenly, they're not laughing at Jimmy Carter anymore,"
wrote Martin Tolchin in the *New York Times Magazine* at the end
of 1978. The Camp David agreement had "laid to rest the competency issue" and "made [Carter] a man to be reckoned with at home
and abroad."

That was a premature conclusion. Carter's charisma and grit
may have paid off in his pursuit of a Middle East peace agreement, but he wasn't having much success on issues that more
directly impacted the average American. Inflation was up again to

11 percent in May 1979, up from 6.8 percent at the beginning of 1978. By the end of 1979 it would be at 13 percent. The purchasing power of the middle class had been under strain for years, and now it was being obliterated. Buying a home or a car was increasingly out of reach for many Americans.

The economy was stuck in neutral, with the industrial sector in full collapse, roiling the middle portion of the country where jobs and pensions had been easy to come by for years. The Soviet Union was building up its military. And there was great concern about the rise of Japan as an emerging economic superpower. Violent crime had been rising in the nation for over a decade, with murders doubling since 1966 to the highest point in American history. There were 21,460 murders in 1979. By comparison, in 2010 the U.S. population had grown by almost 100 million people yet homicides were down to just over 14,000, though that number rose to 15,696 in 2015.

The nation needed strong leadership, but Carter struggled to provide it. "For the part of his job that involves leadership, Carter's style of thought cripples him," former Carter speechwriter James Fallows wrote in an *Atlantic* magazine article published in the spring of 1979. "He thinks he 'leads' by choosing the correct policy; but he fails to project a vision larger than the problem he is tackling at the moment." Fallows felt that Carter's weakness was that he approached problems as "technical, not historical" and that he had a "lack of curiosity about how the story turned out before. He wanted to analyze the 'correct' answer, not to understand the intangible irrational forces that had skewed all previous answers." Teddy White would write a few years later that Carter "seemed to believe that if he could grasp all the facts and figures of a problem, he would understand its dynamics."

Fallows also charged that Carter was actually "bored and

impatient" with the domestic challenges facing everyday Americans, like inflation. He accused the president of becoming distracted and entangled by the "allurements of foreign affairs: the trips on fabulous Air Force One, the flourishes, twenty-one-gun salutes, and cheering multitudes along the motorcade routes. More important," Fallows wrote, "was the freedom to negotiate with foreign leaders without constant interference or nit-picking from congressmen and senators, the heady dips into worldly secrets in rooms lined with lead to protect against eavesdroppers—all the excitement and trappings that go with dealing in momentous global matters that can mean life or death for all mankind."

The heightened anxiety of the time—from gas lines, to rising costs for basic goods, to unemployment—was reflected in the public's desire for a stronger form of leadership in the White House. More than half of the country—55 percent—still thought Carter was honest in a June CBS News/*New York Times* poll, despite the Lance affair. But 66 percent said they wanted someone "who would step on some toes and bend some rules to get things done." Democrats in the poll overwhelmingly said they wanted Kennedy to be their nominee in 1980, with 52 percent for Kennedy to 23 percent for Carter, and 8 percent for Jerry Brown.

The *Times*'s Tom Wicker noted that many of those polled about Kennedy supported him despite holding less liberal views on health care and government spending. "He is a glamorous figure with a great name," Wicker wrote. "Those who are trying to draft him are looking for a winner."

Carter remained publicly defiant about his political future, despite his tanking popularity. One day after the June numbers appeared, he hosted several dozen congressmen at the White House for a briefing on the Panama Canal treaty, which was struggling to gain support. The House members were seated at round tables, in groups of ten or so. Carter went from table to table. While he spoke to one group, he was asked by Representative Toby Moffett of Connecticut how he felt about the 1980 election. Carter claims that Moffett asked him if he was even going to run for reelection, "which was kind of an insult to an incumbent president."

"Of course I am," Carter told Moffett.

Moffett persisted. "What about Ted Kennedy?" he asked.

"I'm going to whip his ass," Carter said.

Representative William Brodhead, a Michigan Democrat, was taken aback. "Excuse me, what did you say?" he said.

Moffett cut him off. "I don't think the president wants to repeat what he said," he told Brodhead.

Carter corrected him. "Yes I do," he said. "I'm going to whip his ass."

Carter claimed years later that he "didn't intend" for the remark "to be publicized all over the world." But there were multiple reports that week that White House staff encouraged congressmen like Brodhead to talk publicly about the comment by making it clear they wouldn't be upset if he did.

Kennedy sniped back: "I'm sure the president must have been misquoted. I think what he meant to say was that he was going to whip inflation." Kennedy was "amused" by Carter's comment, reported Mondale aide Dick Moe, relating a conversation with a person "very close to Kennedy." But Kennedy was "upset at the glee and eagerness with which the White House pumped it up with the press," Moe related.

But Carter pollster Pat Caddell said the poll numbers were cause for great alarm, noting that in addition to a cratering job approval rating, the public's personal approval of Carter had plummeted to 33 percent from 54 percent earlier in the year. "The significance of this result cannot be over-emphasized," Caddell wrote in a June 11 memo. "This result tends to suggest that frustration with the

President is moving toward personal hostility as opposed to indifference or disappointment." Carter's failure to slow inflation was hurting him the most with voters, Caddell reported.

But Caddell saw a bigger problem in the nation. He had labeled it "a psychological crisis of the first order" in a break-the-glass memo on April 23 to try to rouse Carter and alert him that his reelection prospects were in grave danger because of strains on the nation's psyche that had been decades in the making. Beyond economics, Americans were worried that their country was "in deep and serious trouble" because of "moral threats which cut right through the social fabric," according to one survey by Democratic pollster Peter Hart in Wisconsin. Hart's results showed widespread concern over "a lack of morality and religion and the breakdown of the family structure." People said they were "afraid that people have become too selfish and greedy, that the people are apathetic and just don't care."

Hart's survey in Wisconsin showed a desire for "a reemergence of the more traditional approach to life and a turning away from the more publicized free-wheeling attitudes of the 1960's and 70's." This should have given the Carter White House some reassurance that Kennedy, whose life bore all the hallmarks of excess and privilege, might not be as formidable a foe as the polls showed. But when things are going badly and you're getting blamed, it's hard to think clearly, and the Carter White House was spooked.

Days after the Fallows article came out, Senator Daniel Patrick Moynihan said that the move among Democrats away from Carter and toward Kennedy "seems like destiny to me." The very next day, five liberal Democratic congressmen, including Representative John Conyers of Michigan, announced they were starting an effort to "dump Carter" and "make it irresistible" for Kennedy to run for president. A write-in effort on Kennedy's behalf was already under way in New Hampshire.

"It seems hardly debatable that the dump Carter/draft Kennedy activity is sapping Mr. Carter's thin reserve of political authority," Tom Wicker wrote in the *Times*.

Events in Iran pushed a nation already on edge into full-blown crisis. The U.S.-backed shah of Iran had fled the country in January and been replaced by Islamic fundamentalists deeply hostile to the West, led by Ayatollah Ruhollah Khomeini. The instability drove up the price of oil. And the Three Mile Island accident in Pennsylvania, in late March, further increased Americans' anxiety about the reliability of their energy supply.

Remembering the gas lines that had formed a few years earlier in 1973, when the Arab states of OPEC cut the supply of oil and raised prices in response to U.S. aid to Israel during the Yom Kippur War, American motorists began to show panicky behavior at the pump. They started filling up their cars even when their tanks were half or three-quarters full. In the spring, gas lines appeared in California. On the first weekend of May in Los Angeles, some motorists had to wait three hours in line, and tempers flared. Police arrested a twenty-six-year-old man for assaulting a pregnant woman he said had cut in front of him in line.

On May 15, Carter gave an "I told you so" speech to business leaders at the White House. He reminded his audience that more than two years earlier he had told the nation they faced a looming energy crisis and asked them to face it as "the moral equivalent of war." The response from the American people, from business, and from Congress had been one of "frivolity," the president lectured. Now, Carter added, "the American people refuse to face the inevitable prospect of fuel shortages" and were looking for "scapegoats" by blaming the government, the oil companies, and OPEC. A day later, he tried to do damage control, assuring the nation that shortages would ease by June.

Privately, Carter was angry. "This country is going to hell. This government has fucked up from end to end," he told his inner circle, according to Teddy White's account of a May 20 meeting on the Truman Balcony.

A group of public intellectuals who met with Carter to discuss the nation's malaise left the White House confounded by the president's lack of clarity about how to lead the country. Carter's rivals in the Democratic Party could sense an opening in his weakness. Jerry Brown visited Carter at the White House and then told reporters outside he was thinking of running for president. "The seeds of division are sprouting," he said.

And the gas crisis got worse. At the end of May, most gas stations in and around New York City shut down the day after Memorial Day weekend, having run out of gas. And then later that week, on the last day of May, twenty-one-year-old Andrew Medosa, a coffee sampler, pulled into a line at a gas station in Brooklyn with his pregnant young wife, Jean, in the passenger seat. Medosa tried to move his 1971 Buick into a shorter line just as twenty-three-year-old Dennis Rosales, an unemployed former U.S. Marine in bartending school, swerved his brand-new tricked-out 1979 Pontiac TransAm into the same spot. The two cars briefly touched, the two men got into an argument, and Rosales shot and killed Medosa in front of his wife.

Just over a week later, twenty-nine-year-old Fritz Boutain was stabbed to death by a fifty-year-old man named Charles Butler in another gas line dispute in Brooklyn. A day later, a gas station attendant was arrested for pointing his gun at an irate customer.

On June 24, the *Times* carried a front-page story that reported motorists waiting in line for as long as five hours to get gas the day before, and that 90 percent of the gas stations in the New York area had not even opened the previous day. Some people parked their cars in line at closed stations, intending to come back a day or two later whenever the station opened up. That same day in Dallas, a man was shot in the head during a fight in a gas line. By the end of June, much of the nation was dealing with gas lines.

Adding to the chaos, independent truckers went on strike to protest the rising price of diesel and began blocking highways and gas stations with their rigs. The protests started out west and spread across the country quickly during the month of June. A meeting with Carter adviser Stuart Eizenstat on June 18 failed to produce any agreement, and the strike went national. At its height, the strike cut off 40 percent of the major carriers' hauling capacity, squeezing the nation's distribution system.

There were violent attacks on truck drivers who sought to break ranks with the strikers. One was shot and wounded by a sniper in Tennessee. On June 20, a trucker trying to drive his rig was shot and killed in Alabama, and two others were wounded by gunfire.

The frustration over the gas lines and the trucker protests came to a boiling point at the end of June in a place called Levittown, Pennsylvania. A planned community just north of Philadelphia that in many ways symbolized the rise and fall of postwar America, Levittown was the brainchild of William J. Levitt, the father of the American suburb. His company, Levitt and Sons, built 17,311 nearly identical houses in six variations over the course of six years, starting in 1952. The homes were bought by blue-collar workers at a nearby U.S. Steel mill, and also by white-collar commuters who worked downtown. The residents of Levittown were so dependent on automobiles that they had more than a hundred gas stations in their community in the early 1970s, with nine on a single block.

On June 23, a Saturday, a group of truckers decided to stage a protest against the gas prices. They drove their rigs to a central intersection in Levittown called Five Points, where there were four gas stations, some of which were closed or about to close because of dwindling fuel supplies. The town's residents cheered them on, but in the evening the largely festive atmosphere turned dark when police arrested a trucker who refused to move his rig out of the center of the intersection. The rough police treatment of the trucker prompted a backlash from the crowd, which began to throw projectiles at the officers. Police made arrests and dispersed the gathering, but the protests continued the next day and turned even more violent. Protesters dragged a sofa and a mattress into the intersection and lit it on fire. Then a tow truck pulled a junked 1974 Ford Torino and a van from a nearby gas station into the intersection, and those too were torched.

The increasingly out-of-control crowd—which often broke into chants of "More gas! More gas!"—added tires and motor oil from the gas stations to the blaze, creating a massive bonfire with huge clouds of smoke billowing over the formerly idyllic community. They rampaged through local businesses, smashed the windows of gas stations and the carts of a farmers' market, and pelted law enforcement with firecrackers, bottles, rocks, and vegetables. The police reacted with fury, arresting nearly two hundred people over two nights and smashing the windows of passing motorists without discretion. The *New York Times* reported that two hundred protesters and forty-four officers were injured. None of the injuries were serious, but about forty or fifty individuals required treatment at local hospitals.

While all this was happening, Carter was abroad on a weeklong trip to Japan. He had departed the country for Tokyo the same day that the Levittown riots had kicked off, arriving in Japan on Sunday ahead of a global economic summit that did not start until Thursday. He was in Tokyo all week, which set off alarm bells at the White House.

"There are two questions that will obviously be on everyone's mind during these meetings," wrote Rudd Poats, a member of the National Security Council, in a memo to Vice President Mondale.

"With gasoline lines, shootings on the highways and the crisis we have at home, what is the President doing in Tokyo? [And] with OPEC devasting [sic] us on prices, what will the summit do to help?"

"I do not need to detail for you the political damage we are suffering from all of this," Carter adviser Stuart Eizenstat wrote to the president. He lamented that "nothing which has occurred in the Administration to date—not the Soviet agreement on the Middle East, not the Lance matter, not the Panama Canal treaties, not the defeat of several major domestic legislative proposals, not the sparring with Kennedy, and not even double-digit inflation—have added so much water to our ship."

The president and Rosalynn had planned to spend four days in Honolulu on their return from Japan to recuperate from the grueling travel of the previous few weeks, which had included a quick trip to Vienna and then the Asia jaunt. "Almost no one's body can take such a jolting of the circadian rhythm in so short a time; jet lag addles the senses, the perception, the mind," noted Teddy White. The Carters had skipped a customary overnight in Hawaii on the way over to Japan, looking ahead to relaxing there on the return leg. The talks in Tokyo were contentious and unpleasant, and Carter was running ragged. He arrived in Korea on June 29 to see that he was scheduled to run with the 122nd Signal Battalion soldiers at 5:15 the next morning. "I didn't see how I could possibly survive," he wrote in his diary. Nevertheless, he boasted to himself in his entry next day of leaving the young soldiers gasping for breath after a one-and-a-half-mile run that he described as "very easy for me."

The president needed to rest. But America was melting down, and Carter's advisers in Washington told him to get back as soon as possible. The Carters' four days of rest were whittled down to less than two hours. They landed in Honolulu, spent fifteen minutes at a reception in their honor on the grounds of Hickam Air Force Base, and waited for Air Force One to finish refueling.

Carter flew back to D.C. and promised to address the nation-wide energy crisis. The White House reserved time on national television for July 5. Carter went to Camp David on July 3 to prepare. But then, one day before the speech, he abruptly canceled it. He had given so many speeches on the energy issue that he felt the country was no longer listening to him. But the impression of panic that he gave off upset even those who were supportive, such as Senator Abraham Ribicoff. "Why ... the man doesn't deserve to be president," Ribicoff exclaimed when told of Carter's decision to cancel his speech.

---

And then Carter disappeared from public view. It emerged that he was staying at Camp David with no explanation of when he would return. The nation was stunned. The commander in chief had fled to his mountain hideout with no word as to what he was up to. Even after Carter had been at Camp David for a day and a night, White House staff largely had no idea what was going on. "Most White House officials remained in the dark as to who particularly was in on the discussions, how long they would go on and when the President would return," the *Times* reported on July 7.

The mystery surrounding Carter's unplanned, abrupt decision to disappear from public sight was so thick that when a group of eight governors—all of them supportive of Carter—were summoned at a day's notice to visit with the president, they were asked questions by the press about whether Carter was seriously ill. It was left to the governors to reassure a flustered public about the well-being of their commander in chief. "My observation, as a physician, is he looked very well and healthy," said Indiana governor Otis R. Bowen, a Republican. "I know for a fact that he ran a couple of miles this morning."

Brock Adams, Carter's secretary of transportation, called Bert

Lance and asked him to intervene with Carter. "Brock said, 'Bert, I think you ought to talk to the president. I'm concerned about the situation. I've lost accessibility to him, I think other people have and I'm just concerned about where we're going.' And nobody had ever said that to me before," Lance said. "So I called the president early the next morning and it must have been four-thirty or five o'clock because I never had lost any sleep over my own circumstances but I was losing sleep over what I thought was happening to him and happening to the country as a result.

"He just obviously was not in control," Lance said. He told Carter "things were crumbling not only here but around the world and he ought to start making some move to restore his position as being the leader of our country."

Carter, according to Lance's account, admitted to his friend that he had returned from Japan and essentially panicked. "When I came back from Tokyo and I saw what was taking place I felt like the walls of the White House were crumbling in around me," Carter said. Lance bucked him up with a pep talk, telling him he was listening too much to other people.

"There are some things that you can see that he did extremely well as long as he was what he was, and that's a tough-minded individualistic leader who knows his own mind, knows what he wants to do," Lance said. "He was getting to the point where he was not in control. Other folks were trying to remake him and remold him and you don't remake him and you don't remold him."

To the degree that Carter was overwhelmed, his confusion was not helped by the fact that his inner circle of advisers had split into two warring factions over how he should respond to the multiple crises engulfing the nation in the summer of 1979.

Pat Caddell, Carter's pollster, had been the loudest voice urging the president to postpone his July 5 address and to instead give a speech that addressed the nation's psychological and spiritual crisis. Caddell had enlisted the First Lady and Jody Powell in support of his idea. But Vice President Mondale and domestic adviser Stuart Eizenstat were completely opposed to Caddell's advice. And Hamilton Jordan pretended to be ambivalent while privately working to undermine Caddell's approach.

Much of Caddell's thesis was that the American people had stopped listening to Carter—who had given several speeches on energy already—and he needed to do something dramatic to recapture their ear. "Pat continues to argue that we need first to make our 'America is going to hell speech' to grab the attention of the American people and then to focus their attention on the energy problems," Jordan wrote in a memo to the president.

Jordan utterly rejected Caddell's theory. Because of the gas lines and trucker strikes and Levittown riots, "people are finally focused on the problem." But Carter's long trips away from the United States had angered the nation and they needed to hear from their president soon, he wrote. "I feel strongly that a long delay in addressing the American people will only contribute to the physchological [*sic*] panic in the country and further damage us poltically [*sic*]."

Jordan wrote in conclusion, "The speech is badly needed." But Carter disregarded his advice. And so on Thursday, July 5— one day after Carter had canceled his speech and fled to Camp David—Caddell handed out a memo to Carter's inner circle ahead of their first meeting. "The theme was the same" as Caddell's April 23 memo, wrote Teddy White. "America was afflicted by self-doubt, its people no longer had the old patriotic spirit, they were too self-centered."

Carter thought Caddell's memo was "brilliant" and endorsed his line of thinking "100 percent," as did Rosalynn and Powell. But Mondale called the Caddell memo "crazy." He would days later implore the president in a memo not to speak to the nation as if he were Puritan minister Jonathan Edwards, talking about a topic akin to "Sinners in the Hands of an Angry God." The Mondale group wanted Carter to give a straightforward speech on energy, not play armchair psychiatrist and pastor in chief.

Instead, Carter spent ten days at Camp David doing exactly what Jordan had advised against, which was to "hype up" the situation. White reported that this was intentional on the part of the Carter administration, calling it "a ten-day production."

A parade of public figures and ordinary citizens came through Camp David over those ten days. Among those summoned to the Maryland retreat was Clark Clifford, the ultimate Washington insider, who had been a key adviser to Presidents Truman and Kennedy, and defense secretary under President Johnson. Clifford told reporters that Carter was "steeping himself... in the basic fundamental problems of the country and attitudes of people—the cynicism, loss of respect for institutions." Carter looked back over the previous two decades and saw a marked decline in national morale, starting with JFK's assassination in 1963, then carrying on through the Vietnam War and the Watergate scandal, up to the present moment and the nation's energy and economic crises.

The *Post*'s David Broder astutely pointed out that Carter himself had contributed to this public mistrust of government institutions by positioning himself in his 1976 campaign as an outsider running against "a political and economic elite who have shaped decisions and never had to account for mistakes nor to suffer from injustice."

In his deliberations at Camp David, Carter was beginning to see the energy crisis as an opportunity "to revive ourselves as a nation, make ourselves proud of our country again," one U.S. senator told the *Times* anonymously. He hoped to help the American people think of the energy crisis in the same way they had approached the space race with the Soviets, the same way JFK had inspired the country by setting a goal in 1961 of getting a man on the moon before the end of the decade.

Carter spoke with members of Congress, cabinet secretaries, energy experts, economists, religious and civil rights leaders, labor leaders, mayors, state legislators, and a few members of the press. He made two brief excursions to meet with citizens in Carnegie, Pennsylvania, and Martinsburg, West Virginia. Arkansas governor Bill Clinton told him to relax in his speeches and to not "worry so much about the teleprompter." And Vernon Jordan, head of the National Urban League, told the president, "Somebody needs to pray the right prayer, sing the right hymn, preach the right sermon, and that gets to leadership.... Only you can do that, and you need to do it when you come off this mountain."

After all this, expectations for Carter's new speech were high. But when Carter descended from Catoctin Mountain and returned to Washington, he did actually have something substantive to say. At 10 p.m. on July 15, 1979, he sat behind his desk in the Oval Office as a lone TV camera in front of him blinked red, the signal that he was now appearing live in the living rooms, bars, hospital waiting areas, and airports of millions of Americans.

He started awkwardly. "Good evening, this is a special night for me," he said. Looking sharp and freshly scrubbed in a blue suit with a blue-and-gray-striped tie, Carter explained that it was the third anniversary of his nomination for president by the Democrats. It was an introduction that came across as lacking in self-awareness, since the topic was of such gravity.

But Carter used the reference point to talk about how he had promised the nation back when he first ran for president that he would be a leader "who feels your pain and who shares your dreams and who draws his strength and his wisdom from you."

He said he'd fallen short in this regard and had let Washington's perspective dominate his field of view. He explained that he had spent ten days at Camp David to "listen to the voices of America."

The question he was asking himself, he said, was a simple one: "Why have we not been able to get together as a nation to resolve our serious energy problem?" He clenched his fist just for a moment when passing over the word "nation." He chopped at the air throughout the opening minutes with his hands as he spoke, with gentle, precise hand gestures. His body language was decisive and forceful, if a bit stiff and rehearsed.

He continued, "The true problems of our nation are much deeper—deeper than gasoline lines or energy shortages, deeper even than inflation or recession." Here he began to channel some of the southern preachers he must have seen growing up in Georgia. As he repeated the word "deeper," he emphasized it, raising his voice and pointing down at his desk. Then he read nineteen one-liners from various conversations he'd had with people at Camp David, and then summed up his findings. The problem, he explained, was a "fundamental threat to American democracy . . . a crisis of confidence."

"All the legislation in the world can't fix what's wrong with America," he said. Gropingly, he tried to put his finger on a sense of existential disorientation. Few politicians have ever ventured to raise such deep philosophical questions in the modern era.

Carter's tone bordered on that of a lecture. "In a nation that was proud of hard work, strong families, close-knit communities, and our faith in God, too many of us now tend to worship self-indulgence and consumption," he said reproachfully. There was no mistaking his disdain when he said, "Two-thirds of our people do not even vote."

But he diagnosed a real trend in American life: a sense of cynicism and despair, a loss of faith in institutions that in the past had held people together. He ticked off the tragedies, crises, and scandals that had done so much to undermine trust in society: the murders of JFK and MLK, the Vietnam War, Watergate, inflation, the energy crisis. "This is not a message of happiness or reassurance, but it is the truth and it is a warning," he said. "The people are looking for honest answers, not easy answers.... We must face the truth, and then we can change our course."

These were some of the most authentic, self-deprecating, and honest words any president had spoken in public since the advent of television, when image and style trumped substance. No one could accuse Carter of sugarcoating things. He was perhaps not the best messenger to give it: a dour, uncompromising man who lacked a sense of humor. But he did call the country to action. "We know the strength of America. We are strong. We can regain our unity. We can regain our confidence," he said.

Carter promised government action, laying out a number of things he would do, and that he wanted Congress to do, to increase America's energy independence. But his request to the nation itself lacked specificity, beyond a plea that citizens "take no unnecessary trips," carpool or use public transportation whenever possible, "obey the speed limit," and "set your thermostats to save fuel."

The speech's greatest weakness was that it attempted to do too much, to connect "a theme that is primarily moral and cultural to a 'cause' or 'crusade' that is so complex as energy," said Daniel Bell, a Harvard sociologist whom Carter had consulted months earlier.

Carter never uttered the word "malaise." That was a term that the political press began to use in the days before the speech. It came from Clark Clifford, who was part of a group that met with Carter on his second day at Camp David, Saturday, July 7. "He said he had a lot of time to think during his recent travels, and he had the feeling that the country was in a mood of widespread national malaise," Clifford said. The *Post* quoted a second anonymous person using the word. Caddell had also used the word in his April 23 memo. The *Post* put the word "malaise" on its front-page headline, in quotation marks: "Camp David Talks Cover Wide Range: Carter Wants to Improve His Leadership, Counter 'Malaise.'" From then on the word began to be used in newsprint without quotation marks, but attributed to the president or his thinking.

The speech at first was extremely well received. Roger Mudd of CBS News came on the air moments afterward to anchor the network's analysis of the address, describing it as "really an extraordinary speech, a very strong one, very upbeat." The American public loved Carter's speech. The White House switchboard was flooded with enthusiastic, encouraging phone calls. Letters of support poured in. White House press secretary Jody Powell told reporters on Air Force One, as Carter flew to Kansas City the morning after, that 84 percent of the calls and telegrams to the White House were favorable. Carter's approval rating jumped 11 points in a few days. "We've taken down the for-sale sign!" John White, chairman of the Democratic National Committee, exclaimed.

Some noticed an attempt by Carter to recapture the status of a Washington outsider taking on the establishment, a theme that had helped him win the presidency in 1976. He referred to D.C. as an "island" cut off from the concerns of everyday Americans. But, Steven Roberts wrote in the *Times*, Carter had "become an islander himself."

Nonetheless, Mondale said, "There was a feeling we'd done it, for a few days. I think the press felt something was happening. The people did, I know that based on my travels. There was a sense of almost joy in the country...joy, expectation, we're on our way again."

But the president halted his own momentum. Two days after the speech, Carter, seeking to project strength and boldness, asked for the resignations of the head of every single one of his major cabinet departments: Treasury, Health, Education and Welfare, Transportation, Energy, and his attorney general, Griffin Bell.

After spurning Jordan's advice about the speech, Carter was now following the counsel of his top adviser. The day after the "malaise" speech, Jordan wrote Carter another long memo about how the president should transition from "manager of the government to the leader of the people." Jordan identified five different "negative perceptions" about Carter, and created a chart explaining how he should try to reverse each of them.

"Carter is not tough" was one negative perception. Under "Actions Required to Change Perceptions," Jordan typed: "Cabinet firings." In the next column, labeled "Desired Perception," Jordan entered: "Carter is getting tough and is getting a grip on his government."

"Six weeks from now, the skeptics in the media and the political community of this country will measure the degree of change and 'toughness' by your actions against the Cabinet," Jordan wrote in his memo. "The Cabinet changes are the 'litmus test' for most of the persons who will be interpreting your actions to the American people."

In Jordan's defense, he had originally conceived of much of this plan before Carter's big speech, while the president was in Japan and Korea, and at a time when Jordan was advising Carter to give a more straightforward energy speech and then to consolidate power in the White House. Jordan had not wanted to link the firings to Carter's response to the energy crisis. "A White House shakeup should not be seen as the response of the Administration to our energy problems," he had written in his July 3 memo. "We don't need to hype any of these things up—the American people need to see action and change, not rhetoric."

Nevertheless, Jordan did still advise the president to fire his cabinet officers the day after the speech, knowing full well the political environment that Carter had created. Perhaps his instincts for the dangers of such a move were dulled by the initial positive reaction to the speech.

After the firings were announced, Carter went to the White House press room to brief the press on the changes. "Every single change has been a positive change," he said. "There is no doubt in my mind that I and my administration will now be able to better serve this country."

But the press and the nation didn't interpret it that way. The changes backfired horribly, and came off as chaotic and weak. "The firings were meant to be part of the new picture, but were actually an opportunity seized upon by his aides to get him to do what they had long urged him to do.... The manner in which they were executed ... gave off that he had capitulated to his own aides—young men without much national stature—made him appear to many people not strong but weak," Elizabeth Drew wrote in the *New Yorker* a month later.

Rather quickly, the goodwill Carter had created with his dynamic and risky speech came crashing down. "Suddenly, bang, we were right back down in the ditch again," Mondale said. Wrote Drew, "There was a strong feeling on Capitol Hill in July that the Carter Administration had collapsed."

Kennedy had watched the speech carefully. He would years later say that Carter had failed to lead and sound a tone of optimism. "It was in the aftershocks of this speech that I began thinking seriously about running for the presidency in 1980," he wrote in his memoir.

But he'd already been deliberating before the speech. Kennedy had held two big meetings with close advisers and family members to debate whether to run against Carter in February and again in May.

Carter's resurgent poll numbers at the end of 1978 had given Kennedy pause. It was a perilous, divisive thing to challenge a sitting president who remained popular with more than half the country, even if it was barely half. Democratic Party insiders might have wanted to dump Carter, but that wasn't enough. The country had to agree.

Circumstances intervened on Kennedy's behalf, and by the summer of 1979 that hurdle was gone. And according to Kennedy, Carter's "malaise" speech was the final straw. Still, Kennedy remained "torn" over the prospect of dividing the party, Mondale aide Richard Moe told the vice president, in a memo prepping him for lunch with Carter on August 1. "I think we are unnecessarily contentious with him, and appear outwardly to be uptight, petty and sometimes paranoid about him," Moe advised Mondale.

Moe argued that Kennedy "doesn't want to run but feels the White House is sniping at him and thinks, why go through four more years of this?" He advised Mondale to tell Carter to invite Kennedy to lunch or dinner before he left for Cape Cod to "try to bury the hatchet" and to "try to work something out" regarding the nomination of Archibald Cox for a federal judgeship. "Too often we let our emotions govern our reason when it comes to Kennedy," Moe wrote. "It's in our own political interest to be friendly to him and keep him out of [the] race."

Kennedy was also upset with Carter's neglect of the health care issue. Kennedy still thought a national health care system should be a top priority, but Carter had already resolved not to pursue it, deciding that the $60 billion price tag was too steep at a time when the government needed to cut spending, not increase it. "We were losing what I thought was the most powerful and important issue and opportunity of our time. I was convinced that under different leadership we would be able to get this passed," Kennedy said.

During August, Kennedy talked it over with his wife and

children. Close friends, family, and advisers had been meeting since February to discuss whether he should run. By Labor Day, he had decided. He told trusted aide Paul Kirk at a Labor Day barbecue, in words that revealed all the forces at work inside him, "If the thing doesn't work out, I think I'll just be able to live with myself better for having taken up the cause that's drifting away."

Kennedy may have been thinking about the possibility of a loss, but he was in the distinct minority on that count.

# CHAPTER 9

—⊗⊗⊗—

# The Inevitable Return of Camelot

On a sunny afternoon in late September, *Newsweek*'s Eleanor Clift accompanied Kennedy in a convertible from his home in McLean, Virginia, to his Senate office in Washington. "Heir to all the magic of the family name and ahead of Carter 2 to 1 in the polls, Kennedy could reduce the President to a lame duck by spring," Clift gushed in her column.

Jimmy Carter was helpless to lead America out of its malaise. As a result, his prospects for future employment looked increasingly dim in the fall of 1979. As Kennedy neared the launch of his campaign, he debated how best to contrast himself with Carter. There were issues to talk about, such as health care, but more than anything, he simply thought Carter was a terrible leader who had squandered his opportunity to be president. Kennedy "loved government, its mechanics and practices, and thought he knew how to make government work for the people," Teddy White wrote. And as he watched Carter stumble again and again, he concluded—like Fallows had—that the president was not up to the job. Kennedy held for Carter "the contempt of a master machinist for a plumber's helper."

"We wanted the same things," Kennedy told White, acknowledging that in fact there weren't that many differences between them on policy. "But this outsider can't solve our problems. Even on issues we agree on, he doesn't know how to do it."

White put things in historical perspective. "This was remarkable enough—never before had a sitting President, an elected President, with command of both houses of Congress and the party machinery, been so challenged by his own people. What was even more remarkable was the nature of the challenge—a charge of incompetence," he wrote.

Things were so bad that in mid-August Carter felt the need to tell Kennedy that he had no intention of backing off a run for reelection, like LBJ had in 1968. An Associated Press/NBC News poll in September showed Carter's approval rating at a stunning 19 percent.

And so the Democratic nomination for president looked to be Ted Kennedy's for the taking. "It's amazing," Hamilton Jordan thought to himself on November 6, 1979. "A sitting President is the long shot in the fight for the nomination of his own party."

Republicans took great pleasure in Carter's woes. "The question Carter must ask himself is this: Other than satisfying his own ego and ambition, and saving himself from personal humiliation, to what end this struggle for renomination and reelection?" wrote Patrick Buchanan, a Republican operative who had worked in the Nixon White House. Buchanan cited a poll showing Kennedy ahead of Carter in New Hampshire 59 percent to 19 percent. He said Carter faced "the near certainty" of losing the Iowa caucuses and the New Hampshire primary, and then a series of northeastern primaries, before he could hope for a win in Florida.

Inside the Carter White House, Pat Caddell's memo to the president on November 6 sent a tremor through Carter's advisers. Caddell put his finger on the same theme of leadership that

Kennedy planned to hit. "We are not simply the victim of 'not getting our story out,'" he wrote. "We are hostage to real events and to the appearance of how we respond to those events.

"I fear that we may slaughter Kennedy on character and yet given the inability to visibly lead by signal, to dominate the debate over real events, lose because enough people will gamble to try the signal of leadership despite apprehensions over character," Caddell warned.

But the Carter forces did have one thing going for them: They had been preparing to take on Kennedy since the beginning of the year, and they had the vast resources of the federal government at their disposal with which to reward friends and punish enemies. Their ability to govern might have been in question, but this was still the same group of folks who had outwitted and outworked the field of 1976 to win the White House. They knew how to run political campaigns.

Before Kennedy formally launched his candidacy, a few episodes would test his organizing capability and the support for him among party activists. The first of these was in Florida, in a straw poll at county caucuses in October. Democratic activists in Florida had been building a draft-Kennedy organization since June, and allies had begun to quietly funnel money to them.

Sergio Bendixen and Mike Abrams had worked for Carter in 1976. In fact, they were the very Democrats who had cleared the way for him to win Florida that year. At the time, Bendixen and Abrams hadn't been in love with Carter, but they had wanted to repudiate George Wallace in the South and prove that not every southerner was a racist. During the course of Carter's campaign, however, the pair came to fully support the Georgian candidate. And early in his presidency, they were with him.

"We had evolved from people who just wanted to beat Wallace to people who were true Carter believers," Abrams said. "The day

Jimmy Carter got nominated, I was on the floor wearing jeans and they invited me to sit in his family box. That's how close I was."

The move by Abrams and Bendixen from Carter to Kennedy resulted from the insularity and pettiness of Carter's aides. The Floridians were at odds with Ham Jordan, who was not much older than them. They disagreed over which Florida Democrats should be named delegates to the 1976 convention, and Abrams went behind Jordan's back to get Carter to intervene.

"Hamilton Jordan killed me with a thousand pinpricks ever after that," Abrams said. Jordan isolated and humiliated the Floridians. Abrams complained at one point directly to Rosalynn Carter when she visited the state, and was invited to eat dinner at the White House with the president and spend the night there. But over time, Abrams and Bendixen drifted away from Carter and grew tired of Jordan's games. Ultimately, the two men started the draft-Kennedy group.

"In my mind, I was always a Kennedy-phile. That was the reason I got into politics. So when people in Washington started whispering to me that we could be the catalyst in Florida—just like we were the catalyst to defeat Wallace, we could be the ones to knock off the president and elect a Kennedy—at the age of thirty-one, thirty-two, that was heady stuff," Abrams said. "All of a sudden we were having fund-raisers on Park Avenue with people we had never met."

In September, Bendixen received a mysterious phone call. "I represent the Kennedy family," the anonymous voice on the other end of the line said. "Steve Smith wants to meet with you, but nobody can find out about it."

Bendixen was summoned to hop on a plane to New York for a meeting with Stephen E. Smith, who had been one of John F. Kennedy's closest advisers and was married to Jean, the youngest Kennedy girl. Smith had managed Bobby's presidential campaign in 1968 and was now in the same role for Teddy. He also managed much of the Kennedy family's financial fortune.

Bendixen traveled to New York, but Smith refused to see him in his office, insisting they meet in the parking lot outside. "He kept looking over his shoulder. He wanted to make sure that nobody saw us," Bendixen said. Kennedy had not declared his candidacy yet, so there could be no trace of official Kennedy involvement.

Smith inquired into the state of their operation, and let him know that the draft effort had Kennedy's support. Soon after, some money, funneled from Kennedy backers, began to show up, followed by the arrival of a few operatives. And so it was decided, at the highest levels: This was where the Kennedy wave would begin its surge.

The Florida straw poll began to take on monumental significance, as the political world's appetite for a Kennedy candidacy reached the level of bloodlust. Media from around the planet descended on the Sunshine State. The Florida result, though technically meaningless, would be seen as an indicator of Kennedy's political strength. Pressure from the Kennedys on the activists in Florida was increasing. Paul Corbin, an infamous Kennedy fixer, made frequent calls to Bendixen and Abrams. "You better win if you know what's good for you," Corbin would tell them menacingly. Bendixen, who had been an unknown just weeks before, was interviewed by the two most prominent reporting teams of the day—Bob Novak and Rowland Evans, and Jack Germond and Jules Witcover—and by the editorial board of *Time* magazine.

"I was a twenty-five-year-old nobody and here were all these people coming to see me wanting to know how we were going to defeat the president," Bendixen said. "It was just a lot of attention, too much attention. It kept us from concentrating when it was very much an organizational battle that required a tremendous amount of careful planning."

There were fifty thousand or so delegates to the county caucuses, where the straw polls would be held. The epicenter of press
attention was Miami, a natural location for members of the media
to base themselves. And as it turned out, it was Miami that decided
the straw poll result.

Miami became a perfect storm that demonstrated the powerful
forces that came together to thwart the Kennedy operation's coup
attempt. The press attention overwhelmed the operation. And Bendixen said the Carter forces directed federal money to a key local
organizing group—the James E. Scott Community Association—
that he believed made the difference in putting the incumbent
over the top and securing a win in the statewide contest.

"To be perfectly honest, they made a— Let me be kind: They
made a deal with a group called JESCA, where they funded their
effort to get people out to vote in a major way, and they brought
hundreds of people that were involved with that community to
vote, and they swamped the caucus," Bendixen said. "They didn't
win by that much, but they brought enough people from that
operation."

Carter's operation was helped by a Kennedy campaign error.
Bendixen and his fellow activists controlled much of the state
party, and because of that they wielded significant influence over
where caucuses would be held. But they had placed the Miami
caucus site in the heavily African American Liberty City area,
which would turn out to be a mistake. This allowed JESCA to
easily move people to the caucus site.

Miami's caucus was decided by a few hundred votes, which
turned the statewide result in Carter's favor. Despite all that, the
result was seen as a close call for Carter. The *Washington Post*'s
David Broder wrote in his nationally syndicated column that the
win was a "hollow victory" for Carter, "a claimed 'win' that really

dramatized the vulnerability of his southern political base to a challenge from [Kennedy]." The straw poll "certainly did nothing to discourage a Kennedy candidacy," Broder wrote. However, he also noted that Florida had exposed Kennedy's organizational weaknesses and had "left no doubt that Sen. Kennedy's personal reputation—meaning Chappaquiddick, among other things—remains a major barrier to his reaching the White House."

Chappaquiddick was damaging to Kennedy beyond the awful facts of what had happened. It played up the caricature of him as an out-of-touch, elitist northeastern patrician who didn't have to play by the same rules as normal people. Anita Dunn was at the time a young aide in the Carter White House. She remembers being at her grandmother's house in Waynesboro, Mississippi, in 1969 when the story hit the news.

"My grandparents didn't have a lot of use for the Kennedy family, as many southerners did not," Dunn said. After Chappaquiddick, "my grandparents, like many others in the country, made some fundamental decisions about Ted Kennedy. When he ran for the presidency eleven years later, they had not forgotten those things," she said. "There was a sense . . . that he needed to be honestly confronted. . . . They felt that he had never answered those questions, and that a family that is wealthy can get away with a lot that others can't."

A poll conducted by four Florida papers had shown Kennedy and Carter tied among Democrats in the state, but had also shown that Kennedy's character was a concern for many. Chappaquiddick had been "a lively topic" on talk radio in the weeks leading up to the straw poll, Broder wrote. That issue was about to become an even more prominent problem for Kennedy, on the national level. The Kennedy campaign-in-waiting, however, was not alert to this. They were still in the process of hiring Peter Hart and Morris Dees to do polling for them, and so they had no detailed data on voter attitudes about Kennedy.

A few days later, one U.S. senator spoke more circumspectly to Elizabeth Drew about Kennedy's chances. "People here still think he'll be the nominee, but not as easily as before," he said. Momentum continued slowly to shift. In mid-October, Illinois congressman Dan Rostenkowski said that "the realization that they're not going to roll Jimmy Carter over is making some people sit back."

Former secretary of state Henry Kissinger was skeptical even then of Kennedy's chances. During a private breakfast with Chile's foreign minister, Hernán Cubillos, in October, Kissinger dismissed Kennedy as more flash than substance, labeling him little more than a "movie star." When the campaign got tough, Kissinger predicted to Cubillos, Kennedy would be "torn apart by Carter."

One week after the Florida straw poll, Kennedy and Carter came face-to-face in a remarkable coincidence of history. On Saturday, October 20, 1979, they shared the same stage at the dedication of the John F. Kennedy Presidential Library in Boston. When the president arrived in his motorcade, Teddy was standing on the sidewalk, waiting to greet him and Rosalynn. They shook hands and then took a tour of the library.

When they emerged onstage for the ceremony, Carter greeted JFK's widow, Jacqueline Kennedy Onassis, with a kiss on the cheek. Some said they saw her wince. Carter himself remembered it years later more dramatically. "I started to kiss her on the cheek and she flinched away ostentatiously," he told me. He added that he'd greeted her with a kiss "just as a matter of courtesy." Carter shook hands with Teddy again. Then he and Rosalynn took their seats on the stage beside Teddy and Joan. The Carters were surrounded by Boston Brahmins. They were outnumbered and out of place. But they were used to that.

When he stood to speak, Carter smiled and paid tribute to JFK and to the Kennedy family. It was a warm fall day and a soft breeze blew his thin wisps of hair straight back, creating a disheveled look. An orchestra sat perched behind him with their violins and cellos ready, wearing tuxedos, as if the president had wandered into Connie Corleone's wedding celebration. And in a way, he had. Teddy Kennedy often referred to his family as "the Family." Some of the orchestra members behind the president had to twist around in their seats to watch him as he spoke, as if his comments were an interruption.

Carter wore a friendly grin. But that masked a hostility to Kennedy's coming challenge, which both men knew by that time was imminent. Teddy had informed Carter all the way back on September 7 of his intention to run. Three days after that, Carter aide Landon Butler wrote a memo to Ham Jordan titled "Response to Kennedy." Butler was looking ahead to this day. "The President's speech at the Kennedy Library could well be a pivotal point," he wrote. "We must make plans, now, to insure that this speech is among the best the President has ever given."

As he stepped to the lectern, Carter got the obvious fact of his outsider status out of the way up front. "I never met him," he stated declaratively, raising his voice a level. "But I know that John Kennedy loved politics. He loved laughter, and when the two came together, he loved that best of all." It was a setup for a story that he would use to bash Teddy's teeth in. Carter told a story of JFK speaking with the press. The press, he said, had asked JFK a question: "Mr. President, your brother Ted said recently on television that after seeing the cares of office on you, he wasn't sure he would ever be interested in being president."

The audience at the library dedication laughed in knowing appreciation of the reference toward Kennedy's expected announcement. Carter glanced back over his right shoulder at Teddy, grinning widely, chuckled and looked down, and then looked over again at him for a few seconds, still smiling, as some in the audience began to applaud.

"And the questioner continued," Carter said, " 'I wonder if you could tell us whether, first, if you had it to do over again, you would work for the presidency and, second, whether you can recommend this job to others?' The president replied, 'Well, the answer to the first question is yes, and the second is no. I do not recommend it to others—at least for a while.' "

Carter looked over again at Kennedy. Then he drove the point home. "As you can well see, President Kennedy's wit—and also his wisdom—is certainly as relevant today as it was then." There could be no mistaking the sting of Carter's remarks. There it was again, the bulldog behind the big smile. The Kennedy forces had to recognize that Carter's speech was "one of the best speeches of his career," wrote Adam Clymer.

After Carter finished speaking, a White House advance man dashed to the podium and removed the presidential seal. There would be no pictures of Teddy speaking from a lectern with the commander in chief's seal on the front.

When it was Kennedy's turn to speak, he treated Carter's broadside with the indifference of an adult brushing aside the chatter of a young child. He wore spectacles and looked down at the notes in his hands, which he held tightly to protect them from the wind. And he talked about his own close link to JFK, in direct contrast to Carter's more removed remembrance of the political legend.

Teddy described the bond between himself and the brother fourteen years his senior. "He was the best man at my wedding. He taught me to ride a bicycle, to throw a forward pass, to sail against the wind," Kennedy said.

There it was again, that phrase: *sail against the wind*. It was a reprise of his speech in Memphis a year earlier, a return shot across the bow of the president. Only this time, there was a jaunty confidence to the way Kennedy employed it. It was as if he were saying to Carter, *You may have played the part of national leader for the past three years—and not very well—but I am here now, and I am of a bloodline which you know not of, and I am destined to replace you.*

❈

Two weeks later in Washington, D.C., around 10 p.m., political fortunes were turned upside down. While Washington was winding down, the sun was coming up in Tehran. And there, 6,320 miles away, radical Iranian student leaders were gathering inside the Amirkabir University of Technology. They spread out crude sketches of the U.S. embassy, preparing an assault.

It would be the second time the American embassy in Tehran would come under attack and the walls would be breached. Earlier in the year, on February 11, the non-Islamist government had collapsed, and a new regime under the control of the fundamentalist Shia cleric Ayatollah Ruhollah Khomeini had taken over. Three days later, on February 14, the embassy had been overrun by anti-U.S. demonstrators, who took hostages from among the embassy personnel. The new government intervened and ordered the hostages released hours later, and the embassy had been returned to U.S. control. This second time, order would not be so easily restored.

Around 4:30 a.m. on the East Coast, on Sunday, November 4, Hamilton Jordan was woken by a phone call to the vacation home of a Maryland businessman on the Eastern Shore. Jordan was spending the weekend away from D.C. in hopes of getting some planning and strategy work done for the upcoming reelection campaign. The call came from the duty officer in the White House Situation Room.

"We wanted to advise you," the duty officer told Jordan, "that the American embassy in Tehran has been overrun by demonstrators and the American personnel are believed to be held in captivity." The nation woke up soon after to the news that its embassy in Iran had been seized by Islamic radicals, and that sixty-six people had been taken hostage.

The roots of this incident traced back years, of course, to American meddling in Iranian affairs. In 1953 the CIA had organized a coup to reinstall Mohammad Reza Pahlavi as shah, or monarch, of Iran. Pahlavi and his father, Reza Shah, had both long been opposed by large segments of fundamentalist Muslim clergy in Iran. Pahlavi had continued his father's policy of modernization and secularization, increasing women's rights and banning the hijab in public. So by the time that Carter, on New Year's Eve 1977, had called Iran an "island of stability" in the region, the shah's hold on power was slipping. Only one year later the shah left Iran and went into a roving exile in several different countries, and Khomeini returned from his own exile in Paris to take control of the government.

The shah wanted to come to the United States, but Carter resisted. He knew it would destroy any chance of establishing any kind of relationship with the new government in Iran. But powerful figures in the U.S. foreign policy establishment—Henry Kissinger foremost among them—argued forcefully that the United States could not turn its back on a leader who had been a loyal ally. Carter's national security adviser, Zbigniew Brzezinski, lobbied the president in meetings to allow the shah in.

By the fall of 1979, the shah was saying he needed medical treatment for cancer, which put new pressure on Carter. He continued to resist, however. Ham Jordan was now arguing in White House meetings that they should let the shah come to the United States.

"Mr. President, if the shah dies in Mexico, can you imagine the field day Kissinger will have with that? He'll say that first you caused the shah's downfall and now you've killed him."

Carter glared at Jordan and spat out, "To hell with Henry Kissinger. I am president of this country!"

But Secretary of State Cyrus Vance, who had opposed letting the shah come, had relented because of his medical condition. And by the end of that October 19 meeting—the day before the JFK Library event—Carter was close to yielding, but was not happy about it. "What are you guys going to advise me to do if they overrun our embassy and take our people hostage?" Carter said.

Three days later Carter gave the green light, and the shah arrived for a two-month stay before moving on to Panama and finally to Egypt. The hostage crisis erupted two weeks later.

Jordan assumed that the hostage episode would end like the incident in February had. "It'll be over in a few hours," he told a fellow White House official during the first twenty-four hours after the hostages were taken.

Many Americans felt the same way. Around eighty million of them tuned their television sets to ABC on Sunday evening for the *Sunday Night Movie Special*, the television premiere of *Jaws*. "The most exciting movie ever made comes to television," Ernie Anderson intoned in the ABC promo. "Get ready for *Jaws*."

And so because of *Jaws*, most Americans missed a bloodbath of a different kind, which was airing on CBS.

# CHAPTER 10

———— ❧ ————

# Mudd

"Why do you want to be president?"

That's the question everyone remembers from Roger Mudd's infamous interview with Kennedy that aired days before Kennedy announced his candidacy. Kennedy's bumbling answer is mentioned as a major gaffe that hurt him badly. But the truth is that Mudd's in-depth interviews were harmful to Kennedy for many other reasons.

What has gone unremembered is that by the time Kennedy fumbled Mudd's most famous question, the damage had already been done.

The introduction to the special made it clear that this would be no wet kiss to Camelot, but in fact a look beyond the myth and the image to the more troublesome elements of Teddy's biography. "His coming candidacy seems almost seductive: the Irish charm and self-deprecating humor, the painful evocation of Jack and Bobby, the powerful pull of nostalgia," Mudd narrated. "But there is more to Edward Kennedy than those familiar images, and for the next hour, we will report on the quality of character, his performance as a senator, and his conduct at Chappaquiddick." And then in came soaring cinematic music, similar to the kind of soundtrack one would hear on an epic western like *Gunsmoke* or an iconic film like *Gone with the Wind*, as a single word appeared on the screen in enormous golden letters, all uppercase: TEDDY.

After the intro and a commercial break, the Mudd special resumed with an opening shot of Teddy walking down a gravel driveway in Hyannis Port with his mother, Rose, the famous and beloved matriarch of the Kennedy clan. Teddy wore a tight-fitting red short-sleeved collared shirt and white pants. He was taking a rollicking crew of Kennedy youngsters on their annual camping trip, but he looked like he was dressed for a night at the disco. "We've got a good trip for them. They've got their sleeping bags. They've got their mosquito repellent," Teddy said, prompting a laugh from Rose.

Teddy continued to brief his mother on the banal details of what her grandchildren and their friends had packed for the trip, in an attempt to make sound for the TV cameras. "They've got their flashlights," he said.

"Their wha?" she said.

"Their flashlights," Teddy repeated. "Their sandwiches."

"This is probably the way a mother whose son is running for the presidency would like a documentary about him to begin," Mudd broke in with narration over the footage. "A nice walking shot of the two of them, as he sets off with her grandchildren on a summer camping trip." Perhaps it was a gentle warning to the aging grandmother of twenty-seven grandchildren. Mudd gave Kennedy credit for the importance of his family, calling it the "driving force" in his life. "In recent years he has become its male head," Mudd proclaimed.

But the CBS reporter quickly changed gears, insinuating that the camping trip was more of a press junket intended to create pro-Kennedy propaganda images for his presidential campaign. "No Kennedy camping trip can ever be just a family camping trip, not with a driver and an advance man," Mudd said as the pictures showed the clan rolling away in a large mobile home trailer. "Not when the route and the stops are made public. Not when the senator and the children are on almost constant display." There was footage of Kennedy and the children coming out of the camper amid a swarm of TV cameras, and Kennedy answering questions about his presidential aspirations.

"This is the raw material for magazine cover stories," Mudd continued. "Less than an hour in an amusement park near Springfield gives the press plenty of time to watch and compare notes." A few journalists were shown standing by as Teddy and the rest of his young entourage rode a roller coaster.

Mudd then switched, somewhat abruptly, to footage of an annual Kennedy family tennis tournament fund-raiser and a discussion of Teddy's marriage. Joan was shown sitting next to Teddy as they were surrounded by a phalanx of photographers at the tournament. She looked nervous and uncertain, bright-eyed but unsettled and off-balance. Ted sat next to her, sweaty, red-faced after a match, sprawling in his seat, wearing a look of amusement.

Mudd lowered the boom, noting over the footage that Joan's "appearances with her husband are now so rare that the marriage seems only to exist on select occasions." He did not mention that Joan had been living in Boston for some time, separated from Teddy and receiving treatment for alcoholism. Mudd's narration noted the plainclothes security around Teddy that day at the tennis tournament, and he moved on quickly to the shadow over the Kennedy family after the assassinations of his two brothers.

After a little over five minutes of introduction, Mudd's first interview with Kennedy—he conducted two for the special—became the focus.

Mudd interviewed Kennedy at his seaside house at Squaw

Island, a half mile from the family compound. Kennedy called his place "the cottage." The two men sat on the back patio, which was made of large stone tiles, next to a lawn, in white metal outdoor chairs with removable cushions. Mudd, who was fifty-one years old at the time—four years Kennedy's senior—sat with his back facing the house. He wore a gray tweed jacket over a light blue open-collared shirt, blue jeans, and black loafers. Visible behind him was a swimming pool and two outdoor pool lounge chairs. A large notepad lay on his lap. He had spent months preparing for this interview.

Kennedy sat with his back to the sea. He wore a black polo shirt under a dark peacoat. He also wore jeans, which were a little wider around the ankle than Mudd's, and dark shoes. His hair was long and looked grayer than normal. The weather was overcast. The whole thing had a dreary feel, amplified by the fact that Kennedy appeared to have just woken from a nap. He looked haggard and, as he answered Mudd's questions, confused.

If Kennedy was expecting light, breezy talk about the meaning of the ocean to him and his family, as he later claimed, that might have explained the perplexed expression he wore during the interview. Mudd bore into him with a calm, steady, unrelenting focus on questions about matters of the most personal nature: the state of his marriage to Joan, his fitness to run for the presidency, and an extensive look at his conduct that night in 1969 on Chappaquiddick Island.

Even on the question of a Kennedy curse, Mudd had a provocative way of posing his questions, hoping to pry loose some new response, some measure of self-disclosure or self-reflection from the senator.

"Someone said that when you, Senator Kennedy, talk about performing a great public service—and this is not a Republican talking—but they say that the greatest public service you could perform would be not to run, so that you would save the country this trauma again," Mudd said, looking intently at Kennedy.

Teddy grunted as Mudd finished his question, and then diplomatically batted it back, ignoring the bait that his interlocutor had put out for him to take. "Well, I appreciate the concerns of people for my safety," he said, with a hint of sarcasm. "I don't think that there's probably any group or any people that have more of an interest in that than the members of my family, clearly."

And then the stumbling, halting diction emerged, a problem that would mark Kennedy's answers throughout both interviews with Mudd: "And, uh, the, uh, but, uh, I think, uh, uh, one does what one feels that, uh, one, one must do, and out of the basis of, of, uh, deep views and, uh, deep concerns."

Mudd asked about whether Teddy thought the press had been fair to him and his family, and then closed in on his prey. "What kind of separatism should the press maintain between your public life and your private life, or any public official?" he asked.

Teddy responded in a tone of voice he might have used to remark to a friend about the weather, starting off on a sunny, bright note. "I think there's a natural inquisitiveness of people about all aspects of people's lives. I sort of understand that," he said.

Kennedy had opened a door. Mudd strode through it. "What's the present state of your marriage, Senator?" he asked.

Teddy's tone was not as sunny this time. "I think that, uh, it's, it's a, uh, uh, uh, you've had, um, uhh, some, uh, difficult, uh, uh, times, but I think we've, uh, have, uh, uhh, we've, I think been able to make some very good progress, and, uh, uh, it's, uh, uh, I would say that it's, uh, uh, it's, it's, uh—delighted that we're able to, uh, to share the time and the relationship that we, uh, that we do share."

The *Washington Post* editorial board would, months later, refer to this interview as "uh-strewn."

It had already become the type of interview that, years later in the Internet age, politicians and their press aides would cut short. But this was a time when the TV networks and a few big newspapers had the run of American politics. Roger Mudd was the leading candidate to replace Walter Cronkite as the next anchor of *CBS Evening News*, which at the time had a nightly audience of about sixteen million people. Mudd held the cards, and he continued to push Kennedy about his personal life.

"Are you separated, or are you—just—what, how do you describe the situation?" Mudd asked.

Kennedy cut in, showing obvious irritation. He would later write in his memoir, "My discomfort and unhappiness with the line of questioning was more than apparent on my face and in my halting answers." He also said that his then twelve-year-old son Patrick was "struggling" to get a twenty-five-foot sailboat to the dock so the two of them could go sailing. Kennedy's face wore a look of growing consternation.

"I don't know whether there's a single word that should, uh, have for a description of it. Uh, um, Joan's involved in a continuing program to deal with, um, the problems of uh, of, uh, alcoholism and she's doing magnificently well. I'm immensely proud of the fact that she's faced up to it, made the progress that she's, uh, made," Kennedy said.

"Um, I'm, uh, that, that, uh, process continues and it's, uh, the type of disease that one has to continue to work on, and she continues to work on it. The program that's been devised is, uh, is, uh, in Boston," he said.

"Is there a prospect that she will, uh, soon resume her life with you in Washington?" Mudd asked. Kennedy responded that they were "taking it day by day, or week by week."

It was nearing the end of the first quarter-hour segment. The first portion had been highly uncomfortable and unflattering. But that was just a foretaste. The last question of the first segment included the word that Kennedy knew would be raised at some point, the word that raised ghosts from his past and demons that he had hoped would no longer haunt him if he ran for president.

"Senator, uh, when you gave, uh, your television, televised speech after Chappaquiddick"—there it was, that word—"you mentioned, uh, thinking that there was some awful curse that was hanging over the Kennedy family. Do you still think about that?"

"Well, uh," Kennedy said, exhaling. He sounded exhausted by the question, by the prospect of having to think about what to say in response. "I don't, uh, I don't think so, uhh, anymore. I mean, the set of circumstances which happened in fairly, uh, rapid sequence, uh, at that time, which I think, uh, probably, uh, helped me to reach that, uh, that observation—in the period of the last, uh, ten years I think life has been, uh, been, uh, much more, uh, probably, uh, normal by general, uh, standards and, uh, it's been, uh, been able to, uhh, reach a sense of, of, uh, of, uh, perspective of life, uh, on it, which, uh, uh, I, I wouldn't say that that, uh, viewpoint is mine any, any longer."

The video stopped, with Teddy's face frozen in mid-frown. Mudd and the editing team at CBS held it there for a few seconds as Teddy's name in those big gold letters came on the screen again, and the network went to a commercial break.

After the ads, Mudd dove right back into Kennedy's darkest chapter. "The mystery of what happened at Chappaquiddick ten years ago still hangs over Martha's Vineyard like a summer ground fog, and still is impenetrable," Mudd began, talking over pictures of the Cape in summer.

He launched into a disquisition of the known facts about what happened the evening of July 18, 1969. He started with the precise details of the route that Teddy had driven to get to the bridge where his car went off the road and into the water. Mudd pointed out that Kennedy had been over the route he was driving before, but in a car driven by a chauffeur.

This was possibly the most damning minute of the entire hour-long special. Mudd had his producers affix TV cameras to his car as he drove the route that Kennedy had taken in his 1967 Oldsmobile Delmont 88 when he and Kopechne left the party around 11:15 p.m. a decade before. Kennedy's story was that he was taking Kopechne to the ferry back to Edgartown, but got lost and disoriented and found himself on the wrong road, which led to a narrow bridge, which he then drove off. Mudd retraced the route, at the same time at night that Kennedy had driven it, with the TV camera attached to the side of the car's left front fender. The footage, and Mudd's narration, made clear that if Kennedy truly were headed for the ferry, it was hard to believe he would have gone as far as he did on the wrong road.

"After a minute or two of driving, the reflector sign, the yellow line, and the hard surface of the road all indicated that the main street to the ferry bore sharply to the left. But Kennedy turned sharply to the right...onto an unpaved, bumpy road, leading to the Dike Bridge," Mudd said. And here the footage showed a dirt road riven with potholes and deep ruts. The camera bounced up and down. "Kennedy later testified that he became generally aware that the road was unpaved, but he kept going, at about twenty miles per hour, he estimated. He kept going for approximately half a mile, until he hit the Dike Bridge. Only then, he said, did he realize he had taken the wrong road, and it was too late."

Mudd then noted that Kennedy had not reported the accident for ten hours afterward, and quoted Kennedy as saying that his behavior had been "irrational, inexcusable, inexplicable, and indefensible." He noted that the judge who presided at the inquest "thought

Kennedy was not telling the truth." Dukes County District Court judge James Boyle said in his report that "Kennedy was driving the car so negligently that there was probable cause to believe him guilty of criminal conduct." Mudd did not mention that a sheriff's deputy had, more than an hour after Kennedy left the party, seen a car resembling Kennedy's parked on a private side road in that area, which had sped off toward the Dike Bridge when he approached it.

"We are left with two questions ten years later," Mudd concluded. "Is Kennedy's account truthful? And why did the Martha's Vineyard authorities fail to prosecute their famous senator for anything more than leaving the scene of an accident?"

And so, after covering all that ground in just over three minutes, the second fifteen-minute segment of the Kennedy special really dug in. Mudd noted by way of introduction that Kennedy "still does not seem at ease" talking about Chappaquiddick, and did so "in a rather bloodless, third-person way." Kennedy described his actions that night, Mudd said, as "the conduct."

The interview footage opened with Kennedy talking, saying, "Well, I expect I'll be asked about the incident during the course of the campaign, and I'd be prepared to respond to any of the questions, as I have been in the period of the time that I've been in public life."

And then he issued the first of several direct challenges to Mudd. "I mean I'd respond to any particular questions that you'd have," he said, emphasizing the word "you'd."

"But you don't think, because of your rapidly changing position as a national leader rather than as a senator from Massachusetts, that you on your own ought to say something more to illuminate in people's minds what indeed went on that night, other than saying it's all in the record?" Mudd asked.

Mudd would argue later that he was not trying to get into a back-and-forth with Kennedy over the details of that night, and instead wanted Kennedy to address it as "a political question." In other words, how should voters who were considering him for the first time as a possible president think about what happened? But Mudd's questions were also inextricably linked to a sense of doubt about the veracity of Kennedy's account, making it hard for Kennedy to avoid the conclusion that Mudd wanted to litigate facts and details.

Kennedy looked like a cornered animal, and became aggressive toward Mudd. "Well, um, I'll answer any question that you have, or that you have right now," he said. "I'll answer any question that you want to ask me. I'll answer any question that is asked me during the course of a campaign."

Mudd tried to put the question more clearly in a political context, asking Kennedy what he would say if a "heckler stood up at a rally" and yelled, "Kennedy, you know, you were drinking, you lied, and you covered up."

"What are you going to tell him in a situation like that?" Mudd asked. "Because that's the way those questions would come at you, I would think."

"Sure," Kennedy said, trying to counter Mudd's own clever positioning of the question by remaining as calm as he could. "As I say, I'll, uh, answer any of the, any of the questions that, uh, that do, uh, come up, during the course of a campaign, whether they, uh, if it's, if it's a particular heckler on X, Y, or Z issue."

But then, suddenly, Kennedy switched back to what Mudd later called a "defiant" dare to plunge into the gory details of the case. "But I will answer the questions," he said, raising his voice. "If you have questions right now, you ask them to me, because I'll answer them. I've answered them in the past. I've answered them completely, honestly, and to the best of my ability. And I'm glad to answer any question that you have right now, on any of the aspects of it."

Mudd later called this "a very sweaty moment." He said, "I think he was trying to make me back down. I was a guest in his home. When you sit and interview him, he's an imposing person physically. . . . I had a choice. I could back down and destroy myself professionally, and not be true to my calling, or I could just go on through the wall."

Mudd plunged ahead, noting that after looking at the inquest record, the maps, the timeline, and everything else, "the toughest question for me, and for a lot of people, is how was it that you took that right-hand turn, when all signs led you to the left, the surface of the road led you to the left? How was it you could possibly have turned right?"

A sneer appeared on Kennedy's lips. "First of all, it isn't as described, as all the signs, uh, led to the, uh, uh, different way," he replied. "I was on my way back to what I thought would be the ferry, and back to the, uh, back to Edgartown, and the, uh, difference between paved and unpaved for anyone that lives in, on Cape Cod or, or visits the island, uh, the roads are indistinguishable in, in, in most parts of the islands and in many of the areas, still the areas of Cape Cod."

Mudd shot back, "But that unpaved road is like a washboard, Senator."

"Oh, there, uh, if you've traveled in the, um, either on Cape Cod or in the islands of Martha's Vineyard or Nantucket, you go from paved to unpaved, really without interruption," Kennedy returned.

"You were not aware—you did not figure that the main road—"

"No, that day was the first day that I had been on, on that island in terms of, I'd been on the beach part of the island over various sailing races. But that was the first day that I'd been on the, on the, uh, island itself."

"But you'd been across that road twice that day to swim, had you not?"

"I'd been driven at that particular time. I was not driving during those particular occurrences. And maybe I should have recognized the difference of it. Probably I should have. But I didn't."

"And you continued to believe, even though that road is rough and unpaved, you continued to believe until you saw the bridge, that you were indeed on your way to the ferry?"

"Exactly," Kennedy said, with some exasperation. There was a pause as he fumbled for words. "Exactly right."

"When you came back to the cottage," Mudd pressed, "after your car had left the bridge, and you got Mr. Markham and Mr. Gargan to go with you, you noticed the time was approximately 12:20, 12:15, because of the clock in the Valiant in which you were riding. It later turned out there was no clock in the Valiant. How do you explain that?"

"Well, it later turned out that, uh, one of them, Mr. Markham, had a watch on. Whether it was I made that determination from what I thought was a clock in the car or looking at his wrist, I was very conscious of time at that moment, because I knew time was ticking by. I knew that every moment that passed was, uh, the greatest sense of danger, even though, you know, I sensed internally that, uh, it'd be difficult to expect that you'd have a sense of rescue. But I knew that moments were important. And, uh, whether it was from a watch that was on Mr. Markham, or whether it was from a clock which I thought did exist in the car, I couldn't, uh, I couldn't tell. I mean, clearly there wasn't a clock in the car, there wasn't a clock in the car."

"Yeah, yeah," Mudd said quietly. "You think, Senator, that anybody will really fully believe your explanation of the Chappaquiddick—"

Kennedy cut in again. "Well there's, the problem is, is from that night, uh, I found the, the, the conduct and behavior almost, sort of beyond belief myself. I mean, that's why it's been, uh—but I think that that's, that's the way it was. That happens to be the way it was. Now, I find it, as I've stated, I found that the conduct that, in, in, that evening, and in, in, the, uh, as a result of the impact of the accident, and the sense of loss and the sense of hope, and the sense of tragedy, and the whole set of circumstances, that, uh, the, uh, the behavior inexplicable. So I found that those, those, uh, those types of questions as they apply to that—questions of my own soul as well. But that happens to be the way it was."

Amazingly, there was still more. Mudd asked Kennedy how a citizen could be assured that he would not again "act, as you said, irresponsibly or inexplicably, when your own career came in conflict with the public's right to know."

Here Kennedy's language reached perhaps the apex of clinical detachment and antiseptic dissembling. "Well, uh, I didn't make that, uh, distinction. I was asked a series of, of questions where others drew that conclusion. But, uh, but I have pointed out is that the, uh, circumstances of that, uh, particular evening did involve, uh, physical trauma, did involve an accident, did involve, uh, enormous, uh, uh, sense of, of, of loss, in terms of the, uh, the life of an individual, uh, and did involve, uh, the, uh, uh"—and here a plane flew overhead, forcing Kennedy to speak over the noise of its engine—"what I have recognized, uh, basically, as, um, uh, irresponsible behavior in not reporting the accident earlier. Now I think that that is, uh, uh—I have served in the United States Senate for a position of seventeen years. I've taken the positions. I've spoken on issues. I've spoken on questions. And there have been other factors which have impacted my life. And, uh, people will have to make that judgment."

Mudd pressed Kennedy after that on why he needed a whole crew of advisers and attorneys with him when he made a televised statement about the incident a week after it took place, on the evening of the day when he pleaded guilty to the minor charge of leaving the scene of an accident and received a suspended jail sentence of two months. "What were all those advisers doing at your home here if your motive was just to lay out the truth?" Mudd asked.

"Well, the accident report, no but the accident report was a very, just a, uh, factual document, uh, on the accident itself. And because of the enormous interest in the whole set of, uh, circumstances, it was, uh, felt it necessary to give a more elaborate explanation of the circumstances that surrounded that, uh, you know that occasion. And I felt that my first responsibility had been to the court, prior to the time of reporting to the people of Massachusetts."

"But still," Mudd continued, "if all that was needed to explain to the people of Massachusetts what had happened, uh, and to present them with the political realities of what had happened, why couldn't you have done that yourself? Why did you need all those people to—"

"Well the question wasn't just sort of the factual circumstances, like a traffic, uh, uh, accident. You go through a square and you hit a particular fender. There were obviously kind of circumstances to describe what the nature of that particular gathering had been, what the background had been of the people that were involved, and what happened that evening. There was a more fuller elaboration and explanation of the circumstance that evening."

Mercifully for Kennedy, the segment was drawing to an end. Mudd asked him how Chappaquiddick had changed him. "Well it, uh, I suppose in the sense of, uh," and here Kennedy paused for several seconds. "Um, I've been impacted by a number of, of tragedies in my life: the loss of life of people who were members of my family. Those were circumstances in which I really didn't have control. I could feel a sense of regret and a sense of sadness and a sense of loss. But this was a circumstance in which I did have a responsibility. And that, in that sense it was quite different from other life's experience. And so, uh, I'm a very different person than prior to that tragedy. The way that, uh, I'm a different person I think is probably reflected in perhaps the way others see myself. I know from just my own interviews or inner attitudes or view about, sort of, life and people, and, uh, and, uh, faith in God. I'm a different person. And I know that."

Finally, Kennedy was done talking about it. It had been an excruciating fifteen minutes or so, most of it filled with him talking about the most embarrassing, most shameful episode of his entire life, on the eve of his declaring his candidacy for the presidency of the United States.

<hr />

Mudd had known going into the interview that there was a potential for Kennedy to come off badly if he had to give coherent answers to tough questions. "He had never sat down for a serious interview," Mudd wrote in his memoir. Most Americans, he wrote, knew Kennedy "mostly from clips on the nightly news" or from his appearances on the Sunday talk shows, "when the issues were what he wanted to discuss." The candidate who appeared onscreen was nothing at all like the image many held in their minds of Teddy Kennedy.

The second interview, filmed in Kennedy's Washington Senate office two weeks after the first, took up the second half hour of the special. Kennedy sat stiffly in an armchair facing Mudd, wearing a blue suit and striped tie. His hair was combed about as neatly as possible for his lengthy coif.

Despite the presence of minders on Kennedy's staff in the room, Mudd began by launching back into more questions about Chappaquiddick, according to his account of it later. That again went nowhere, and the footage of that exchange did not get aired. Somewhat flummoxed, he said, Mudd asked Kennedy a basic question: Why did he want to be president? There was a long pause...one Mississippi, two Mississippi, three Mississippi...

"Well, I'm, um," Kennedy began...four Mississippi, five Mississippi... "Were I to make the announcement—" And he launched into a rambling 336-word answer with a look of consternation on his face that he later said was aggravation at being asked, in early October, about a decision he would not announce for more than a month. However, most viewers watching a month later, days before his announcement, took the expression as one of confusion. The conclusion by many was that Kennedy did not have any animating ideas or philosophy, and was running for president based solely on pure ambition, or, possibly worse, that he was ambivalent about it.

"Oh my God," Mudd thought. "He doesn't know. He doesn't know why he's running."

Mudd said later, "It was like, 'I want to be president because the sea is so deep and the sky is so blue.'" Kennedy outlined how the country was headed in the wrong direction, but said not one word about his own desire and ability to lead it. He didn't even make a general reference to the need for stronger leadership, which later on did become a theme. How he was so badly unprepared for such a simple question was a mystery. For much of the rest of the second interview, Kennedy wore a distant, almost vacant look, and continued to speak haltingly and with frequent pauses and switches of direction.

The Mudd special was "not the way you'd like to launch the campaign," Patrick Luccy, one of Kennedy's campaign advisers, said, in a vast understatement. Steve Smith tried to kill the special by lying to Mudd about when Kennedy would announce his candidacy. If the program did not air before the announcement, federal law would require the network to give Carter and any other candidate an equal amount of airtime. But Mudd fought for his program, and CBS rearranged its November 4 schedule so that it could air the entire special that night, three days ahead of Kennedy's announcement.

The only problem for Mudd, and for Carter backers who wanted the country to see this inferior version of Kennedy, was that the network premiere of *Jaws* was what most Americans watched that night. Ham Jordan was immensely frustrated. "Everybody's going to be watching mechanical sharks eating swimmers instead of Roger Mudd eating Ted Kennedy alive," he thought to himself. "I wanted everyone to see what I saw: the Kennedy legend reduced to a bumbling, inarticulate man." In addition, newspaper and TV coverage in the following days was dominated by the capture of the U.S. embassy in Tehran. The next morning's newspapers carried front-page stories about the hostages, and that would be the dominant story on TV all week and for weeks to come.

Nonetheless, the impact was huge among the political class: the press, activists around the country, donors, lawmakers, and operatives. Political columnists in the important newspapers had been given advance copies of the interview and had written critical columns for Monday's papers. It was a disaster for Kennedy. It was not so much that it knocked him out or disqualified him as much as it destroyed an image of him as the imperial candidate coming to sweep Carter and Reagan out of his way in an unstoppable show of brilliance and eloquence.

"It gave everybody pause," said Harold Ickes, a Kennedy adviser. "Everybody knew that Mudd was very favorable towards Teddy and he couldn't answer?"

Anita Dunn, a junior aide to Carter adviser Jerry Rafshoon at the time, said the Mudd interview "was such a shock to the political class who had assumed that [Kennedy] was going to be a great candidate. The mythology around the brothers had grown."

Senator Robert Dole, a Kansas Republican who was running in the Republican presidential primary, captured the moment well. He noted that "seventy-five percent of the country watched *Jaws*, twenty-five percent watched Roger Mudd, and half of them couldn't tell the difference."

The back story of how the special came to be was filled with intrigue. Kennedy had agreed over the summer to sit down for a pair of interviews with Mudd for an hour-long special focused on his life and political career. The interviews had been filmed on September 29 in Cape Cod and on October 12 in Washington, D.C., and then they were edited into the special.

Neither interview had gone well at the time they were conducted. Kennedy had been entirely unprepared for the first one, in Hyannis Port. He was alone with Mudd and his crew, without a single staff member there to ward off unwelcome questions. He was blindsided by the continuing relevance of Chappaquiddick. During his meetings in the winter and late spring of 1979 to talk about whether to run against Carter, there had been little discussion of the matter. Kennedy, said Paul Kirk, "felt anything he had to say about it had been said, and there wasn't anything he could do to redress or correct or alter the situation."

The matter of how Kennedy had possibly ended up in this situation would later take on the intensity of a federal investigation, with both Mudd and Kennedy airing details of their respective versions of the story, predictably diverging in significant ways. Mudd was friendly with the Kennedy family. He had comforted Bobby Kennedy's wife, Ethel, moments after Bobby was shot a decade earlier. So it's possible that Kennedy expected the interviews, and the documentary, to be friendly. "I'm sure he knew better," Mudd wrote in his 2008 memoir. "Given what Richard Nixon had put the country through, we agreed that character, truthfulness, steadiness, and strength would be critical in the 1980 presidential campaign."

Kennedy had been badly wounded, in the view of political elites, by the Mudd interview. The hostage crisis in Iran rallied regular Americans to the president's side. It would also dominate the news for weeks. In one day, then, a series of events put him quite suddenly on the defensive and out of sight at the same time.

Kennedy sought to put the Mudd debacle behind him three days later, on November 7, when he announced his candidacy. He chose to make the announcement in Boston, unlike his brothers, who had made their presidential bids official from the Senate Caucus Room in the Capitol, in Washington. It would have been natural for Teddy, a senator for seventeen years by this point, to do the same. But that would have been too similar for a younger brother who was insecure about his ability to forge his own path. So instead Kennedy held the event at historic Faneuil Hall.

He stood on a stage that Wednesday morning that was empty except for Joan and their three children seated in chairs behind him against the wall, under a giant painting of the founders signing the Declaration of Independence. Joan's platinum blonde hair stood out against the mahogany paneling and somber art. Kennedy's remarks began in a droll manner, as he recited his personal and family connections to Boston. He sounded defensive, explaining why he chose to announce there rather than in the tradition of his brothers. And when he began to talk about why he was running, for a moment it appeared he had little more to say than he had offered up to Roger Mudd.

"As a senator, I've taken positions on thousands of issues. I gladly offer that record as witness to my qualifications for higher office," he said.

Then he got in his first shot at Carter, telling his listeners that his career in the Senate had taught him how "good intentions can be translated to achievement.... I have learned to deal with the continental diversity of interests that my colleagues have been elected to represent," he said. There was a pitch to elect a president who could cultivate and work with Congress, as Carter had so badly failed to do.

"Only the president can provide the sense of direction needed by the nation," Kennedy said, picking up steam. "For many months, we have been sinking into crisis, yet we hear no clear summons from the center of power. Aims are not set. The means of realizing them are neglected. Conflicts in directions confuse our purpose. Government falters. Fear spreads that our leaders have resigned themselves to retreat. This country is not prepared to sound retreat. It is ready to advance. It is willing to make a stand. And so am I."

The crowd applauded for the first time, and Kennedy nodded to them, in his way. Then, as he told them he was formally announcing his candidacy, he said he was "compelled by events and by my commitment to public life." That word, "compelled," spoke volumes about the degree to which Teddy's choice was driven by forces larger than himself.

# CHAPTER 11

# Upended

*The Iranian revolution is the Pearl Harbor of our day....*
*Unlike the thunderbolt of Pearl Harbor, it grinds its effect*
*upon the West slowly.*
—*Charles Malik, a former ambassador to*
*Washington from Lebanon*

Circumstances were pushing against Kennedy now. In one momentous day, the Mudd interview had put him on the defensive and the hostages had pushed him out of sight. Americans now wanted to rally around their president.

The day after the Mudd interview aired, Kennedy was scheduled to have lunch with the *New Yorker*'s Elizabeth Drew. "He seems tired," she wrote of their time together. She noted that "much is being made" of the Mudd interview.

In the weeks leading up to the Iowa caucuses, the daily news cycle came to be dominated by developments in Iran and Afghanistan. Carter cleverly fused his own political fortunes with the nation's standing in the world. He argued that a win in Iowa would send a clear message to the world that the United States was united behind its leader. One month after Kennedy jumped into the race, Carter led him 48 percent to 40 percent in one national poll. Carter's approval rating since the hostages had been seized—two days before Kennedy announced—had doubled in only a month, from 30 percent to 61 percent.

The race had been flipped upside down. "One day it's sunny and people are pissed at Carter and they want a real liberal, and the next it's raining and people are going, 'Why are you against the president?'" said Joe Trippi, whose career as a Democratic operative was launched while working for the Kennedy campaign.

Suddenly, the Kennedy strategy, crafted for a different universe, was badly flawed. The Kennedy campaign had believed for some time that they were on a wide avenue leading to an easy victory. "The Carter campaign will be like the French army in World War II, an obstacle but not a deterrent," boasted Kennedy's delegate counter Rick Stearns, in an odd comparison of the Kennedy campaign to the Third Reich. Kennedy's high command, at the direction of Carl Wagner, had banked everything on beating Carter in the first contest, the Iowa caucuses. "The whole idea was to replay what happened to LBJ in New Hampshire in '68: Deal the president such a crippling blow early that he was forced to drop out," Trippi said. "The only strategy was to win in Iowa."

This was despite the fact that the second and third states in the process, Maine and New Hampshire, were more natural fits for Kennedy. Iowa was also where Carter had built a massive, sophisticated political operation four years earlier, propelling him to the nomination.

And as Kennedy plunged into the business of wooing Iowa voters, it became clear rather quickly that he was a rusty campaigner. Giving speeches in the Senate was one thing. This was another. The press scrutinized every slip of the tongue or verbal stumble, and that became the storyline. At one stop, Kennedy referred to "fam farmilies." Then he said it again at a second stop the same day. Another time, he lost himself in his words: "Roll up your sleeves and your mother and your fathers," he said.

The press pounced on these gaffes. In response, Kennedy began to read his speeches, further sapping him of energy and vitality. Probably the only way he could gain back the momentum that was slipping away was to reignite his ability to inspire. And he was unable to summon it.

Then, on December 2, Kennedy dared to say what he really thought about the shah. After a long day of campaigning and fund-raising in California, Kennedy spoke to San Francisco TV reporter Rollin Post. Post asked Kennedy whether the shah, who had arrived in America in late October, should be allowed to stay. Kennedy blasted the former ruler, telling Post that the shah had presided over "one of the most violent regimes in the history of mankind—in the form of terrorism and the basic and fundamental violations of human rights, in the most cruel circumstances, to his own people." Kennedy added that the shah had stolen "umpteen billions of dollars from his country." Why let him in to the country, Kennedy said, "and at the same time say to Hispanics who are here legally that they have to wait nine years to bring their wife and children to this country?"

Kennedy advisers gave different accounts of this episode. Bob Shrum would later write that Kennedy's comments were spontaneous. It was late, Kennedy was tired, and on West Coast time to boot. He was sick of giving the same old boosterist line about how "we're all united as Americans," and he was frustrated by the way the campaign was going. "Carter's approval rating had risen in one month from 32 percent to 61 percent—not on the basis of something he'd accomplished, but because of a crisis he'd inadvertently provoked by admitting the Shah into the country for medical treatment," Shrum wrote in his memoir. But at the time, Kennedy's press secretary Tom Southwick said the comments "had been thought out carefully." Kennedy was desperate to get into the news, which was being dominated by coverage of the hostage crisis, and so he decided to go after the shah.

The blowback to his comments was "a phenomenon," Drew wrote. The editorial boards of the *Times*, the *Washington Post*, the *Los Angeles Times*, the *Atlanta Constitution*, and the *Baltimore Sun* all criticized him. John B. Connally, the Republican presidential candidate and former Texas governor who was riding in the same car as JFK the day that he was shot and killed in Dallas, said Kennedy's comments would bolster Ayatollah Khomeini's standing. "The president is entitled to all the support any of us can give him," Connally said. A Carter White House adviser told the *Times* that if the Iranian radicals holding the U.S. hostages thought their efforts were supported by any group of Americans, "they'll hold onto the hostages that much longer." George H. W. Bush, the former CIA director also now running for president as a Republican, said Kennedy's comment "might endanger the lives of the hostages." The incident raised "serious questions about [Kennedy's] judgment of foreign policy," Bush said.

"The roof caved in," said Shrum.

The next morning, in Reno, Kennedy had to clarify that he supported Carter's efforts to free the hostages. But he doubled down on his criticism of the shah. "We all support our country's efforts to end the crisis in Iran. But [that] . . . does not and cannot mean that this nation must condone the Shah and the record of his regime," he said, describing the monarch's reign as a "repressive dictatorship."

Adam Clymer called this episode "the single most damaging event in the campaign" in the weeks leading up to the Iowa caucuses. "Sloppily done, it invited doubts about his judgment when tired and pressed," Clymer wrote. "Even worse than the visible damage was the lasting case of shell shock inside the campaign, leaving it afraid to take any risk." That would keep them from pressing the attack against Carter until it was too late.

Kennedy was also uncomfortable, even miserable at times, campaigning in the Iowa cold, meeting people who often viewed him with suspicion because of their regional and cultural differences. Teddy's mix of celebrity and infamy added to the stiffness and awkwardness of his interactions. Dressed in a tweed overcoat, his long hair slicked back, looking like a cross between a Boston businessman and a movie star, he trudged through snow to tour farms, trailed by Joan and his two oldest children, Kara, nineteen, and Teddy Jr., eighteen. He would ask farmers about the price of hogs, of feed, and of farming combines. But his heart wasn't in it, Drew thought as she observed him, and it showed.

"How do you like Knoxville?" one woman asked him in a small town forty miles southeast of Des Moines, as he stepped into her drugstore, out of the two-degree cold.

"Nice, nice," Kennedy answered her with a smile. "Nice and cool."

*Boston Globe* columnist Ellen Goodman also followed Kennedy around Iowa and noticed the same thing Drew had. "His voice is strained, his timing is off, his eyes are glazed and his energy is drained by bad news or bad back or bad timing or bad karma," Goodman wrote. "One sentence keeps recurring in my brain: The guy doesn't want it. It's written in his body language. It's in his eyes, his speech patterns, his erratic behavior. It's even in the calm, almost depressed affect. The man doesn't really want to be in Iowa, Maine, New Hampshire. He doesn't want to be asked again about Chappaquiddick, about his sex life, about the shah."

Goodman put her finger right on the pulse of Kennedy's zombification. "I see a man running for President dutifully, fatalistically, unhappily. I see a complicated man with a lot to win by losing. Privacy, peace, family, personal freedom," she wrote. "If Ted runs and loses, he exorcises the past. He's done it, he's run for President and doesn't have to do it again. If he runs and loses, he exorcises the fear. He has survived. He is, in a very real sense, a free man."

To make things worse, Iowa was a bad fit for Kennedy. It wasn't just superficial differences that were keeping Iowans on guard around him. Teddy's character—Chappaquiddick, his personal life, his marriage—was playing a major role in the minds of the midwestern, socially conservative farming-state voters. "They don't trust his judgment," one Kennedy adviser told Drew. "Everybody underestimated it."

Joan's presence, which was intended to tamp down concerns and reassure voters, seemed to do the opposite. She rarely spoke, and when she did, she gave off the appearance of a "fragile and vulnerable woman...treated as if she were a frail creature."

Burton Hersh, a Kennedy friend from his Harvard days, would write years later that Joan's appearances on the campaign trail, when she appeared by herself, did more harm than good. In her first speech of the campaign, written with the help of historian Doris Kearns Goodwin, after the Iowa caucuses, she spoke openly about her separation from Teddy but cast it as part of her "journey back to health," which was necessary to "regain my strength to be the mother and woman I wanted to be." She talked of regaining self-confidence while studying music education.

And she said her absence from the family's home in Virginia had allowed Teddy to grow closer to their son Patrick, who was twelve at the time. "Perhaps the best result of my absence has been how close my husband Ted has grown to Patrick; in these months he has often been both mom and dad to Patrick," she said. "Why should men be denied that central human experience of being a parent?" But Joan added that if Ted were to win, she would of course rejoin the family and live with her husband at the White House, and advance the cause of women's rights.

Columnist Mary McGrory called Joan's campaign appearances "unnerving." "Some people who did not like her husband liked him less after hearing about her troubles," McGrory wrote.

Kennedy suffered another blow when his "womanizing" was written about by the *Washington Monthly*'s Suzannah Lessard, in a cover story for the magazine's December issue. "Within the world of politics and journalism, Kennedy's womanizing is widely known," Lessard wrote. She described "a pattern" of "a series of short involvements" with women that suggested to her "a kind of narcissistic intemperance."

She went on, "How strange it is that despite all that has been written about this man, and despite all of his exposure to the public eye, he is still so unclear to so many of us. Could that be because he actually is a rather unclear, unformed person? This is the aspect of the philandering that concerns me the most—the immaturity of it."

Lessard concluded that "we have kept alive the possibility that the great aborted promise of John and Robert Kennedy will some day be realized fully. It is as though, despite all our scrutiny of Edward Kennedy on one level, on another we've averted our eyes, saving our hope, putting off the moment of judgment, saying to ourselves: when he runs for president, then we'll see, then we'll take a really close look. Well, now he is actually running for president....As the abstract haze of hope begins to thin in the atmosphere of a concrete candidacy, we find ourselves squinting at the particular human being inside that haze. Who is he?"

Carter didn't shy away from drawing attention to the character issue either. "I don't think there's any way you can separate the responsibility of being a husband or a father or a basic human being from that of being a good president," he said in a TV ad. "What I do in the White House is to maintain a good family life, which I consider crucial to being a good president."

Carter supporters in Iowa didn't bother with a veneer of subtlety. "Ted Kennedy leads a cheater's life—cheats on his wife, cheats in college," John Pope, one of Carter's closest friends, told voters.

Chappaquiddick was the dark cloud that lingered in many voters' minds. Just over half of all Iowans told the *Des Moines Register* in December that they did not believe Kennedy's tale of what had happened, and one third said the accident "revealed basic problems in Edward Kennedy's character which still will affect his performance as a public official." Only one third of Iowa voters disagreed with that statement, and the rest said they weren't sure.

Kennedy's message was also predicated on circumstances that had changed dramatically over the course of just a few months. Rather than going after Carter directly, Kennedy felt constrained by the national mood to subdue his attacks on the president and to talk about inflation and energy instead. These were the pressing issues of the day, to be sure, but Kennedy was not as passionate about them or as knowledgeable as he was on health care. And the reason he was running against Carter in the first place was because he thought Carter had shown a failure of leadership. It had been a good strategy until the hostages turned the president's leadership into a sacred cow.

Kennedy's advisers had also wanted him to downplay his more liberal positions—national health care, higher taxes, wage and price controls—thinking their real challenge would be winning the general election and not the primary. "Our mistake was thinking we were at 65 percent, so why would we take tough positions?" said Bob Shrum. It took too long to recalibrate this approach.

So Kennedy the passionate liberal was replaced by an uncertain, fumbling northeasterner who talked in Iowa of controlling inflation, projecting greater American strength abroad, and even balancing the federal budget, but without any detail. "He seemed to have lost the voice he had found at Memphis," Clymer wrote in his biography of Kennedy. Wrote Hersh, "When he censored him-self his delivery got so stilted audiences clawed toward the exits."

Perhaps most consequentially, Teddy walked the snow-covered fields of Iowa stalked by the shadows of his older brothers. "Virtually each day Kennedy was faced with what was probably the most painful criticism of all: that he was not as good as his brothers," Drew wrote. "All his life, it seemed, he had been measured against them, and now, in the largest and most visible test, he was held to be falling short."

Even so, Carter's pollster Pat Caddell walked into the Oval Office in December with some sobering polling results. He had done a ninety-minute focus group with Iowa voters that showed Carter ahead three-to-one over Kennedy at the beginning of the session. But after asking the voters to imagine Kennedy as president, the group shifted to favoring Teddy. "You won't believe this," Caddell said. Carter looked at the results, listened to Caddell's summary, and gave him simple instructions. "I want these burned," he said. Only Caddell, Ham Jordan, Jody Powell, and Jerry Rafshoon even knew about the survey. Caddell left the room and took the study results to his office, where he put them in a safe and locked them up.

---

On Christmas Day, events in the Middle East once again intruded into the presidential contest. The Soviet Union began an invasion of Afghanistan that unfolded over the next several days. Carter denounced the move. At the same time, he decided to withdraw from an upcoming debate in Iowa with Kennedy and California governor Jerry Brown scheduled for January 7, ahead of the Janu-ary 21 caucuses. Carter put most of his emphasis on the ongoing hostage situation in Iran.

The caucuses would now "revert to a battle of organizations," the *Times*'s Adam Clymer wrote. "Mr. Kennedy's appears stron-gest, Mr. Carter's strong, and Mr. Brown's weak." Even after

Carter's incredible Iowa showing in 1976, his organizational abilities continued to be underestimated.

Kennedy was restrained in his criticism of Carter's withdrawal from the debate, but Paul Tully, Kennedy's Iowa director, said that "there's no question in our minds that this is calculated politics." Back in Washington, Kennedy's press secretary, Tom Southwick, soft-pedaled Tully's attack, saying the operative was "not speaking for the Senator, but we're not going to tell him not to say things." Kennedy's carefulness not to criticize Carter too harshly illustrated the new environment, which had put Kennedy off-balance.

And Kennedy remained restrained into January at the very moment he needed to ignite some kind of spark. Even as he campaigned down the home stretch toward the January 21 caucuses in Iowa, on a six-day trip back and forth across the state, he held himself back from attacking Carter too directly, from speaking too extemporaneously, and from coming across as too "hot" for TV or for the conservative Iowa voters. And this was despite the fact that his own internal polls in December had showed him getting beaten almost three-to-one among likely caucusgoers.

Drew, along with Kennedy for the entire trip, noticed that he was talking "slowly, in a sort of singsong." It was the type of elocution one uses when one has been told over and over to talk differently than one is used to. Drew wrote that Kennedy was "being advised not to try to stir the excitement that he in his own way can...being programmed and reprogrammed....He seems battened down and unnatural."

Kennedy expressed occasional displeasure with the strategy— "Geez, when can we go out there and have some fun?" he asked aides at one point—but for the most part stuck to the plan. He tried to overcome Carter's years of organizing and visits to the state by shaking hands with every single person after his multiple meetings and speeches a day. A Secret Service agent would often hold a chair behind him to support his aching back, a result of that plane crash sixteen years earlier.

But Carter's advantage in Iowa was beyond formidable. He had virtually lived in the state for a year ahead of the 1976 caucuses, he had come back often as president, and he had invited Iowans to the White House as well over the previous few years. During the fall of 1979, Jimmy and Rosalynn would spend good chunks of their weekends making as many as sixty calls each to important activists and supporters in Iowa and other early primary or caucus states. They knew who these people were. And even though the president himself wasn't campaigning, he had Rosalynn, his sister Ruth Carter Stapleton, Joan Mondale, and many other surrogates in Iowa advocating for him.

Carter implemented a "Rose Garden strategy" against Kennedy, just as Ford had done to Carter in 1976. "We're being smothered," said Paul Tully. He noted with admiration and resentment that the Carter White House was "very astute at having the president seem above the political fray back in Washington, but meanwhile they're flooding the state with his relatives, cabinet people, and his own phone calls, all of them milking patriotism."

Agriculture Secretary Bob Bergland, for example, toured Iowa talking to farmers about the need to support the embargo on grain shipments to the Soviet Union imposed by Carter on January 4, even though it would cost them 10 to 15 percent of their annual income. "We are being tested, you and I, by the Russians as never before," Bergland said. "The Russians are a rough-and-tumble bunch and they'll skin you alive if you let them."

The Soviet invasion of Afghanistan and the hostage crisis had taken attention away from the inflation problem, and Carter's representatives were even asking these Iowa farmers to sacrifice more to stop the communist nation from taking over a country in the desert. The White House told reporters that the Iowa caucuses would be a referendum, watched around the world and by the Soviets, to see if the American people would stand behind their president's action.

The Carter campaign ran an ad in the closing days before the caucuses that showed Carter sitting in front of a map with the red-colored Soviet Union on it and saying, "On Monday night, Iowa will send a clear signal to the rest of the world. Do we or do we not support the president?"

Nonetheless, Carter and his advisers were concerned about the political cost in Iowa of the grain embargo. Mondale was "strongly opposed" to it before Carter announced it, but when Kennedy criticized the embargo, Mondale lashed out at him and questioned his love of country. Support for the embargo was "the patriotic route to take," Mondale said. Kennedy responded, "I don't think I or the members of my family need a lecture from Mr. Mondale or anyone else about patriotism."

Kennedy did have many members of his own clan racing through the state to drum up support. But he had difficulty prying farmers away from Carter over the grain embargo. Those who moved away from Carter seemed to be landing in the uncommitted lane rather than firmly with Kennedy. Patriotism and concerns about Kennedy's character were working in tandem against him. Even his own family's appearances undercut his cause at times. "Here we are in the middle of a cornfield with some farmers we're trying to impress and this Kennedy relative comes in wearing purple boots, like she was just out of Studio 54," one Kennedy campaign volunteer in Iowa told the *Boston Globe*'s David Nyhan. "How do you think that goes over with a bunch of guys in denim and muddy shoes?"

A week before the caucuses, the *Des Moines Register* released its final poll. The *Register*'s poll was and remains the gold standard in Iowa. The newspaper's survey in December had shown the race to be a dead heat. This one showed Carter leading Kennedy 57 percent to 27 percent.

Once again Elizabeth Drew had a scheduled interview with Kennedy just as he was dealing with the aftershocks of bad news. She rode with him that afternoon during an hour-long drive from the Quad Cities area in southeastern Iowa up the Mississippi River along the state's border with Illinois to the town of Clinton. It was his third event of the day, after a morning event in Council Bluffs on the other side of the state, and a plane ride to Iowa City. He had two more events after this as well. It would be a late night.

As he talked to Drew in the car during the afternoon drive to Clinton, Kennedy smoked a cigar and was reflective. Drew asked him if he'd imagined he'd be trailing Carter by such a large margin. "I didn't expect so, no," Kennedy said. He looked off into the distance and didn't say anything for a moment. "I never assumed gaining the nomination or winning the election would be easy. I never assumed that," he said. He sounded defensive. But then he chuckled. "And I don't assume it now."

He admitted that he had not been prepared for the challenge of running for president when he announced. The switch from being a legislator to a presidential candidate was "like getting your equipment one day and playing in the Super Bowl the second day."

There was undoubtedly some truth to that analogy, but it wasn't as if Kennedy had no idea of what was to come, given his firsthand experience in both of his brothers' presidential campaigns. And if he'd failed to take steps to be more prepared than he was, that was his own fault, and that of his campaign.

It was break-the-glass time for Kennedy. He didn't show signs of panic, however. In fact, he became a more effective candidate in those days after the *Register* poll was released, according to Drew's firsthand account. He was looser, more himself, more energetic, and began connecting with audiences more. At his very next stop after the Drew interview, he rallied about a thousand people and praised the local high school basketball team, stretching words out with his northeastern drawl. "I bet you didn't know that we knewwwww about the St. Mary's team back in the United States Senate. But you'd be amaaaazed at what you learn when you run for president," he bellowed.

Later that night, at his 11 p.m. rally in Davenport with three hundred caucus organizers, he mentioned Carter by name for maybe the first time all week, a sign that the gloves were coming off, finally, after he had held back from hitting the president all these weeks. "I refuse to accept the comments and the statements of Mr. Carter when he talks about 'malaise,'" Kennedy said, overlooking the fact that Carter never actually used that term. "I say no malaise. No malaise!" He began voicing a more muscular, effective message in his stump speech.

But the shadow of the *Register*'s poll numbers hung over him. At each stop, and even when he returned to Dulles Airport in northern Virginia at 2 a.m. on Sunday morning and was greeted by a hundred or so campaign workers, Kennedy couldn't help but mention the survey, if only to say that "we'll show them what a real Iowa poll is."

Kennedy began lowering expectations, telling the press that Carter had to win 50 percent in Iowa for it to be a victory. And he continued to tear into the president more aggressively as the caucuses loomed ever closer. His campaign broadcast into Iowa homes a fifteen-minute speech by the senator in which he blasted Carter's foreign policy as being "out of control." The nation, he said, was "adrift, buffeted by events, tossed like a cork on uncertain and stormy seas. America's prestige is at its lowest point since we became a world power." Almost as if he were reading off of Pat Caddell's memo to President Carter from the previous summer, he said, "Constantly, we seem to be reacting to events that take us by surprise."

But the same day that Kennedy was beamed into Iowa homes,

one week before the caucuses, Chappaquiddick surfaced again, with a vengeance. *Reader's Digest* published an in-depth investigative article by John Barron that claimed Kennedy's account of his swim across Edgartown harbor was false. One day later, the *Washington Star*—where Barron had previously worked—published a similar article.

The *Reader's Digest* article claimed that based on an "elaborate scientific study," they had concluded Kennedy was driving at thirty-four miles per hour when his car went off the Dike Bridge, not the twenty miles per hour he claimed. And they argued that the current in the water would have been far weaker than Kennedy claimed. If that were true, it would undermine Kennedy's claim that he was traumatized by his swim and forgot to tell anyone that Mary Jo Kopechne was still in the water.

The *Digest* story forced Steve Smith to go to the remarkable length of holding a press conference in which an MIT ocean engineer and two admiralty lawyers from Boston offered evidence in support of Kennedy's account.

The next day, January 15, Kennedy was scheduled to accept the endorsement of the United Auto Workers in Washington, a big win for him. But that was overshadowed by the *Star*'s report, which reached the same conclusion as *Reader's Digest*: that the tide had not been all that strong and was not pulling Kennedy out to sea. Kennedy this time was forced to call a press conference to respond. He called the *Star* story "dead wrong, irresponsible, shoddy and incomplete." But he knew, as he said, that the reports made his path to the nomination "more complicated and difficult."

The issue only became more of a focus, though. And so Joan herself had to weigh in, during a dramatic news conference in Sioux City, Iowa, on January 18, just three days before the caucuses. Teddy took questions from reporters in a plane hangar, and the first was not for him, but for Joan. Do you believe him? That was essentially the question. Nervously, Joan—with daughter Kara watching—stepped up to the microphone and vouched for her husband.

"I believe my husband's story," Joan said, as Teddy stood watching, twisting a pen in his hand. Joan charged that the articles were politically timed. "I happen to believe that these stories are coming out now because of this crucial time," she said. "It's just too bad."

Joan had said the year before that she wanted Teddy to run. She didn't want to be blamed for his not running. "She didn't want the monkey on her back," a Kennedy friend told Jack Germond and Jules Witcover. She might have been reconsidering that opinion by this time.

Chappaquiddick would continue to be an issue in the press. The *New York Post* published an article the day of the caucuses in which they interviewed four Martha's Vineyard residents who said they'd seen Kennedy on Chappaquiddick Island multiple times before the 1969 accident, contradicting his assertion that he had never been there before then.

Despite all this, on the eve of the caucuses, Adam Clymer wrote in the *New York Times* that it was "clear" that Kennedy aides believed their man had "a chance to finish first." The Kennedy campaign was sitting on 30,000 "hard ID's." In other words, they knew they had 30,000 Iowans going to caucuses for them. And just four years earlier, only 38,000 people in total had taken part in the Democratic caucuses. The *Washington Post* would, the day after the caucuses, call the Kennedy turnout operation "one of the most impressive ever seen in the state."

"The polls weren't looking good, but what mattered in Iowa was intensity and who actually showed up at a caucus," Bob Shrum said, summing up Carl Wagner's presentation to Kennedy's top brain trust the day before the caucuses.

Kennedy spent caucus night at his home in northern Virginia, just outside Washington, where he watched results come in. Carter was at the White House after giving an evening speech to the National Association of Religious Broadcasters.

Kennedy was obliterated in the January 21 Iowa caucuses, 59 percent to 31 percent. Turnout had far exceeded anyone's expectations. Most observers had expected it to surge to 50,000 or 60,000, out of Iowa's 550,000 registered Democrats. In 1976, 38,000 people had attended a Democratic caucus. But in 1980 that number nearly tripled, as 100,000 Democrats caucused.

The increase came in part because in 1980, for the first time, the caucuses were a national event. The national press had overlooked them in 1976, but had greatly increased their coverage four years later. That raised voter awareness of the caucuses.

The Kennedy forces were not prepared for the massive increase in caucusgoers. The Carter team had outworked and out-organized them. Carter's team had expected to get 60,000 votes, said Bill Romjue, who ran the state for the president, and that's what they got. "I could not believe it," Kennedy wrote in his memoir.

"You still have me," Eunice Kennedy Shriver, Kennedy's older sister, told him after the loss. Kennedy replied bluntly, "I'd rather have Iowa."

The Republican caucuses also yielded a shocker. George H. W. Bush defeated Ronald Reagan by five points, resetting the GOP primary. Reagan had been expected to win, and his loss in Iowa meant that the New Hampshire primary became a must-win for him.

Kennedy's two-to-one pummeling at the hands of Carter was a stunning turnaround from just a few months earlier. For a decade he had waited for the right moment to reactivate the Kennedy legacy. Three months earlier, the nomination, and the presidency, had been his for the taking. He had been lured into a presidential run by an inviting set of circumstances, only to see the landscape shift dramatically. Now, after just one defeat, he was out of money and the path to victory looked narrow. His candidacy was on life support.

# CHAPTER 12

---

# "I Didn't Ask for a Challenger"

Late on the night that Teddy Kennedy lost the Iowa caucuses, he found himself crammed into a tiny bathroom in an old Cadillac showroom on 22nd Street NW, now his campaign headquarters in Washington, D.C., with two other men. It was closing in on 11 p.m. and the last of Joe Kennedy's sons was staring the first concession speech of his life in the face.

"What wonderful words do we have?" Kennedy asked speechwriter Bob Shrum and Carey Parker, a longtime adviser.

Shrum had already helped draft a speech conceding the race. Kennedy had instructed him to do so the day before the caucuses. "This baby's going down," he told Shrum then, holding his hand out like a plane falling from the sky.

But when Kennedy emerged after his loss to greet a roomful of a few hundred supporters, he was defiant. "Wellll," he drawled with a wry smile, "we could have done a little better in Iowa." But while he congratulated Carter on his win, he noted that the president needed 1,634 delegates to clinch the nomination, and he himself needed only a few more than that. "We need 1,657, and we're going to get it," Kennedy vowed. It was on to Maine and

New Hampshire, though those contests were not to be held until February 10 and February 26, respectively.

"Here and there, a few politicians think that Mr. Kennedy's campaign cannot recover," Hedrick Smith wrote in the *Times* two days after the caucuses. "But the prevailing view is that his national constituency is loyal and large enough to carry and finance him for a time to come, but that he must win convincingly in New England."

Yet Kennedy had not done much preparation for a campaign in Maine or New Hampshire, having put all his best people in Iowa. "The whole idea was to kill Carter [in Iowa]," Joe Trippi said. Kennedy's all-out focus on Iowa had led to a myopic allocation of resources. "People who should have been running states were running counties in Iowa," Trippi said.

They called themselves "the Cornstalkers." John Sasso was running Iowa for Kennedy. Two years later he would head up Michael Dukakis's gubernatorial campaign in Massachusetts, and then the governor's presidential campaign in 1988. Paul Tully, Mike Ford, Steve Murphy, Jack Corrigan, and Trippi were all running separate counties in Iowa. They would all go on to either manage presidential campaigns in the future or play prominent senior roles in them.

But there was virtually no personnel in the states that would vote after Iowa. Kennedy campaign offices in Maine, New Hampshire, and elsewhere were populated by cronies and friends and friends of friends. After the Iowa loss, his campaign scrambled to send people to Maine and New Hampshire. These replacements often ran into the awkward problem of how to remove the personnel already in place.

Trippi was sent to Nashua and told to fire the five people at the Kennedy office there and install his own team of operatives who had worked in Iowa. Five minutes after he arrived and informed the campaign workers that their services were no longer needed, "the senator was on the phone yelling at me." The woman he had fired was Carol Geiger, the nanny for Teddy's kids. No one had told Trippi who she was. Wagner and the others likely didn't even know. It was a chaotic retreat.

Kennedy was now under the severest financial pressure. The $4 million he had started out with was down to $200,000, and most of that was already committed. Money from donors and from the Kennedy family was now slow in coming. The campaign had to make steep, slashing cuts. There was a staff of two hundred people. Most of them, if they wanted to keep working for the campaign, would have to do so for free. The $5,000-a-day private charter plane, with a "big blue executive chair" reserved for Kennedy, had to be canceled, just eight weeks into a twenty-week contract. The campaign saved another $125,000 by canceling the press charter plane.

In assessing the meaning of Iowa, no one was more blunt than the *New York Times*'s James Reston. "The Kennedy magic has now vanished," he wrote the day after the caucuses. Carter, having been "almost in despair" just a few months earlier, was now buoyed by advisers "talking cautiously about beating Kennedy in New Hampshire and knocking him out of the race before the industrial state elections later in the spring."

Reston added that while Kennedy had been "badly wounded," he would also "be around for a long time." "Stripped of the legend, he may now get ready for the future rather than relying on the past." At that moment, however, the future was already upon Kennedy. "The New Hampshire primary next month could be critical and even decisive," Reston wrote.

---

On the Republican side, Ronald Reagan was in a similar position after losing Iowa to George H. W. Bush. Like Kennedy, Reagan was under pressure to cut costs and make changes in his campaign.

He ended up firing his campaign manager, John Sears, to try to quiet the intense discord inside his operation.

Two days after the caucuses, on Wednesday, Carter delivered his third State of the Union address to Congress. It was shaped almost entirely by the Soviet Union's invasion of Afghanistan and marked an enormous change of course for Carter in his rhetoric and thinking about the communist nation. Clocking in at a relatively brief thirty-one minutes, the speech was also a shift away from Carter's first two addresses to Congress in which he focused on domestic affairs.

Carter devoted most of the speech to foreign affairs, putting inflation and the economy in the back half and making no news on those fronts. This happened to be the most politically advantageous subject matter for Carter. It kept the nation focused on issues that had benefited him dramatically in his primary fight with Kennedy, who sat listening in the House chamber with the other members of Congress.

Carter announced a handful of significant initiatives that clearly denoted his change of thinking on the Soviets. The first was a major shift in American foreign policy. America's stance toward the Middle East had been to charge regional nations with keeping order. But Carter extended a guarantee of U.S. military protection to the Persian Gulf region. He was the first American president to do so. He did it because he deemed the region "vital" to U.S. interests, due to America's reliance on imported oil. And Soviet forces in Afghanistan were only three hundred miles from the Strait of Hormuz, the chokepoint through which oil tankers passed.

"Let our position be absolutely clear," Carter said. "An attempt by any outside force to gain control of the Persian Gulf region will be regarded as an assault on the vital interests of the United States of America. And such an assault will be repelled by use of any means necessary, including military force."

Carter called on European nations to join what Hedrick Smith called "a collective effort to meet the 'radical and aggressive new Soviet threat.'" He also asked Congress to send military and economic aid to Pakistan, on Afghanistan's eastern border, and to reaffirm a 1959 defense commitment. Carter's saber-rattling included a call for the resumption of registration for the draft, a move Kennedy opposed. President Gerald Ford in 1975 had eliminated the registration requirement for eighteen-to-twenty-five-year-old males.

And finally, Carter—who had campaigned in 1976 on reducing military spending—reiterated the call he'd first made in December on Congress to approve a 5 percent increase in the defense budget, up from the 3 percent annual increases he had implemented earlier in his first term.

"Carter significantly raised defense spending to a level the Soviet economy could not match and launched a multifaceted campaign against the Soviets, especially focusing on human rights," Peter Bourne told me. "These policies had a significant effect in the collapse of the Soviet Union but their full impact was not apparent until Carter left office. Ironically, Reagan then claimed full credit for them."

Other significant foreign policy voices agree with that point of view. Robert Gates, who became CIA director under President George H. W. Bush and secretary of defense under President George W. Bush, added the Carter administration's covert actions that centered on anti-Soviet propaganda. Gates wrote in a 1996 memoir that Carter was "the first president since Truman to challenge directly the legitimacy of the Soviet government in the eyes of its own people." This, along with Carter's increased defense spending, produced "tiny fissures in the Soviet structure that ultimately helped bring about its collapse." Wrote Gates, "The Soviet leaders knew the implications for them of what Carter was doing, and hated him for it."

Carter's speech was the inception of the Carter Doctrine, a

policy that would be continued under subsequent presidents. It marked the end of the decade-long détente with the Soviets—a ratcheting down of Cold War tensions and an attempt to improve relations—that had originated with Richard Nixon in 1969 and continued under Gerald Ford.

Carter chose to end détente in part because of unrelenting pressure from his national security adviser, Zbigniew Brzezinski, the son of a Polish diplomat who had been posted in Germany during the rise of Hitler in the early 1930s and in the Soviet Union during the latter part of that decade, when the communist government murdered an estimated 600,000 to 1.2 million people during Joseph Stalin's "Great Purge."

Brzezinski had been pushing covert efforts to undermine Soviet legitimacy since the beginning of Carter's presidency. He met with resistance from the State Department, but did succeed in pushing large amounts of dissident literature behind the Iron Curtain, and the U.S. government helped boost the transmission of Voice of America and Radio Free Europe to overcome Soviet jamming. "The Carter administration waged ideological war on the Soviets with a determination and intensity that was very different from its predecessors," Gates wrote.

In the summer of 1979, Carter started arming Afghan rebels to aid their fight against the Soviet invasion. But to those who were not aware of the Carter administration's covert activities, his speech looked like a "gradual transformation from the optimism in his first two years of dealing with Moscow and the world, to the realism of power politics," as Hedrick Smith wrote.

There were short-term considerations for Carter's speech too. At a time when the hostage crisis in Iran was in its third month, taking such a hard line on the Soviets was a way for him to try to reassert his authority and the nation's power.

As Carter wound down his address to Congress, he quoted the

famous journalist Walter Lippmann, and called on the American people to make personal sacrifices in order to overcome the nation's challenges. "You took the good things for granted. Now you must earn them again," Lippmann had said. "For every right that you cherish, you have a duty which you must fulfill. For every good which you wish to preserve, you will have to sacrifice your comfort and your ease. There is nothing for nothing any longer."

Carter's challenge to the nation was an echo of his "malaise" speech just a few months earlier. But for Kennedy, there was nothing similar to the moment. If anything, he might have smiled at the bitter irony embedded in the Lipmann quote. He had been taking the presidency for granted, it seemed, just a few months earlier. But no longer. He might even have wondered if Carter was subtly taunting him after the Iowa results.

Carter wrote in his diary a few days later that there were "rumors... that Kennedy will get out of the campaign." It was in fact being considered. Guardians of the family name were alarmed at the damage already done to their brand. So a campaign trip to the next stage of the primary—New England—was canceled while Teddy and his advisers debated whether to continue.

There was a genuine split in the camp. Aging, more cautious Kennedy family allies like Steve Smith thought Teddy should get out before he diminished the family name and his own political reputation any more than he already had. The young idealist Shrum and others argued he should fight on. Smith at one point cornered Shrum and told the younger man he was going to "ruin" Kennedy if he kept egging the candidate on to keep up his campaign.

But by the time Carter was fantasizing in his journal about an end to the primary, Kennedy had already decided to keep going. He had made up his mind the day after Carter's speech, following a gathering of eight trusted aides: Paul Kirk, Steve Smith, Carey Parker, Larry Horowitz, Rick Burke, Carl Wagner, Eddie Martin, and Shrum.

Kennedy was upset about Carter's speech the previous evening, and what he saw as warmongering by a president trying to use foreign affairs for his own political purposes. But there were strong sentiments in the group that he should quit. Shrum argued that he should stay the course because if he didn't, he'd be "labeled a quitter forever." Shrum wanted Kennedy to rebuke the doubters who said he always ran away when things got tough. The memory of Chappaquiddick, even then, hovered over the meeting and over Shrum's comment.

The eight advisers were split on whether Kennedy should go on, and so Teddy, with the deciding vote, said they were moving ahead with his candidacy. They pegged the relaunch of his campaign to a speech scheduled for one week after the Iowa caucuses, at Georgetown University.

The day before the speech, a *Boston Globe* poll in New Hampshire showed that—just as had happened in Iowa—Kennedy's lead over Carter from the previous fall had evaporated and been turned upside down. In September, Kennedy had led Carter 68 percent to 20 percent in the Granite State. Now he trailed by 25 points, down 56 percent to 31 percent. Of the greatest concern for Kennedy was the jump in voters' negative perceptions of him. His unfavorability rating had gone from 16 percent to 43 percent. Adam Clymer, in a preview of the speech, called it "a last ditch effort to set the themes and issues for the campaign, and to prove there still is one."

However, it was a turning point for Kennedy. Faced with the very real prospect of defeat, he became a new kind of candidate, unfettered by concerns about appearing presidential or refining his message. In Iowa, he had said repeatedly that the American people should speak with "one voice" during a time of national crisis. But with little left to lose, he threw caution to the wind and embraced his role as a kamikaze candidate.

Kennedy had been afraid to criticize the president over the hostage crisis in Iran. But in a speech to about seven hundred supporters, faculty members, and students in Gaston Hall at Georgetown, he lambasted Carter's handling of the hostage-taking. He even blamed Carter directly for the hostages being taken in the first place. "In the clearest terms, the administration was warned that the admission of the shah would provoke retaliation in Tehran. President Carter considered those warnings and rejected them in secret," Kennedy said. "Had he made different decisions, the shah would doubtless still be in Mexico, and our diplomats would still be going about their business in Tehran."

It was a grave accusation at the time. But even Hamilton Jordan would come to agree with Kennedy's assessment. "The Shah had been allowed into the states because a doctor believed he was dying and needed emergency medical treatment 'available only in the United States.' We had not adequately questioned that judgment, and as a result, our people were captives in Tehran," he wrote in his book *Crisis*, published in 1982.

On the domestic front, Kennedy—who the *Times* said had been hesitant to embrace liberalism—let loose his inner progressive, calling for an anti-inflation six-month freeze on wages, the price of goods, dividends, interest rates, and rent, and then government control of those things for "as long as necessary." He also endorsed bailouts for collapsing farms, and his signature issue, nationalized public health care. He accused Carter of bringing the nation "Republican inflation . . . Republican interest rates . . . and Republican economics." He called for gas rationing and reduced oil imports, a position similar to Carter's. And he called for a United Nations commission to be created to study the reign of the shah and to hear Iranians' grievances against their former ruler, in exchange for the release of the hostages. Aides called it "the kitchen sink speech."

Kennedy also slammed the president for avoiding debates with him and hiding from voters. Carter had yet to spend any time campaigning, maintaining his Rose Garden strategy of staying in Washington to manage the hostage crisis. Two days later, he would again decline to debate Kennedy.

The Georgetown speech transformed Kennedy from a candidate to a cause, the leader liberal activists had been waiting for as they languished in frustration during the Carter presidency. He had "recovered his political voice," the *Globe* said. The speech reassured supporters, and frustrated the Carter campaign, by making clear that Kennedy was not going to quit. "I intend to stay the course," Kennedy said. "I have only just begun to fight." The Georgetown speech was broadcast in New England that evening, along with an appeal from Kennedy for donations, and a special message addressing Chappaquiddick.

There was dissatisfaction with Kennedy's refusal to tackle the issue of Chappaquiddick head-on in a major speech, despite advice in the fall of 1979 from New York political consultant David Garth to do so. Paul Kirk, too, wanted Kennedy to address it. And the issue continued to be a huge problem for him as the New Hampshire primary approached. The *New Hampshire Union Leader*, run by the fiercely conservative William Loeb, kept the story alive day after day. And so a special introductory message was added to the TV broadcast, preceding a truncated version of the Georgetown speech.

"Over ten years ago, I testified in court in detail under oath to God to the truth about the accident at Chappaquiddick that caused the death of Mary Jo Kopechne," Kennedy said. "That sworn testimony has been published and reprinted many times since then. I know that there are many who do not believe it. But my testimony is the only truth I can tell because that is the way it happened. I alone feel in my conscience the loss of Mary Jo Kopechne's life and the failure to report the accident immediately. I carry that burden with sorrow and regret." He asked the voters in Maine, New Hampshire, and Massachusetts to judge him "by the basic American standard of fairness, not on the basis of gossip and speculation."

Volunteers, and some money, returned to the campaign. Questions about Chappaquiddick had been addressed, the bugs had been worked out, and liberal Democrats finally had the candidate they had wanted all along.

"He has been freed from the shadow of his brothers. His campaign has acquired a moral imperative that has nothing to do with them. Someone has to speak out against the 'war hysteria' emanating from the White House, and the other liberals have fallen silent," Mary McGrory wrote after watching him campaign in Maine with a nineteen-year-old John F. Kennedy Jr. "The man who could not shake Chappaquiddick is being reborn as the conscience of his party."

But Kennedy couldn't escape the reality that he was a "once-confident candidate . . . now flinging charges in a desperate, post-Iowa attempt to catch up," as Clymer put it. Kennedy's criticisms of Carter "would have been more effective two weeks ago."

Kennedy had squandered much of 1979 organizationally, and was now paying the price. He needed an efficiently run campaign, now that he was trying to come from behind and was running low on money. But his effort was beleaguered by having too many cooks in the kitchen, a problem made worse by its glaring lack of a clear general.

Steve Smith was technically running the campaign. He was the Kennedy family consigliere whom Teddy trusted most, the fixer he'd called eleven years before in those desperate moments in the hours after his car had gone off the Dike Bridge and into the water with Mary Jo Kopechne in it. But Smith's formative political experiences were all from a completely different era. Since JFK's run in 1960, and Bobby's in 1968, presidential politics had changed dramatically. Campaign finance was different, the role of TV was bigger and more influential, and perhaps most important, the nominating system had been radically democratized.

Carl Wagner and Richard Stearns understood the changes to the nominating system, and adviser Morris Dees was an expert on how money had to be used differently. But these younger men were not empowered enough—either by Smith or by Kennedy himself or by both—in the fall and winter of 1979 as the Kennedy train was leaving the station, bound inevitably, they thought, for the White House. Top spots in the campaign had been filled with the many Kennedy characters from the political operations that had grown up around Teddy's two older brothers.

"You had layers upon layers upon layers of advisers, counselors, head geezers," said Harold Ickes. "John Kennedy men were there. . . . You had Bob Kennedy's men there. You had Ted Kennedy's Senate staff there."

Continued Ickes, "I remember being in a meeting with the top political people in the campaign with Steve, and we decided on a course of action—Rick Stearns, myself, and Carl Wagner went out and started to implement it—and Steve walked into the next room and had another meeting and the decisions were reversed! So it was a fucking nightmare."

Shrum agreed, telling Burton Hersh in 1993 that "there might be twenty-eight people in the room and everybody would have a vote" in the campaign's early days. "The problem," Hersh wrote, "was melding three generations of Kennedy advisers into something that worked. . . . Sixties veterans like Ted Sorensen and Dick Goodwin were in and out."

Paul Kirk, a longtime Senate aide, and his allies Larry Horowitz,

Tony Podesta, and Joe Crangle represented another power center in the campaign. Shrum and Carey Parker were constantly with Kennedy on the plane, along with the senator's body man, Rick Burke. "It was never quite clear who was really in charge of the campaign," Jim Flug, another Kennedy aide, said afterward.

Smith didn't want to spend a lot of money on polling or on creating TV ads, and didn't understand modern media. The first round of ads created for Teddy were "probably the worst television ever produced for a presidential candidate in American history," consultant Joe Napolitan told Hersh.

And "there was no centralized campaign authority capturing names of donors, workers—no framework to fall back on," said Bill Carrick, who oversaw Kennedy's campaign in South Carolina and then in Texas. The campaign's finances were so badly managed that a week before the New Hampshire primary, they were still looking for an election-night hotel after their original location, the Merrimack Hilton hotel—canceled their reservation for lack of payment. "Kennedy, known for the best staff in the Senate, had not created—or seen to Smith's creating—a campaign operation worthy of a president," Adam Clymer wrote.

Nevertheless, the February 10 Maine caucuses were something of a wash. Three weeks after Iowa was long enough to set expectations that Carter could re-create his overwhelming margin of victory, despite Kennedy's regional advantage. A poll one week out had given Carter a 19-point advantage. But instead, he won just 46 percent of the popular vote to Kennedy's 40 percent. Jerry Brown garnered just under 15 percent and was ineligible for delegates.

Yet Kennedy still trailed in the polls as New Hampshire approached. And the president came after him hard three days after the Maine voting, asserting that Kennedy's criticisms of him since the Georgetown speech were undermining the efforts to free the hostages. "The thrust of what Senator Kennedy has said throughout the last few weeks is very damaging to our country and to the establishment of our principles and the maintenance of them, and to the achievement of our goals to keep the peace and get our hostages released," Carter said at a press conference.

When a reporter asked if he thought the increasingly bitter back-and-forth between him and Kennedy was helping the Republicans, Carter shot back, with a smile that provoked laughter from the press, "Well, I might point out to you that I'm an incumbent Democratic president. I didn't ask for a challenger."

Kennedy said the next morning in New Hampshire on the campaign trail that he was "not going to be silenced in making what I consider constructive and positive recommendations." He went on, "We will all rally around the flag. But we need not, we must not, rally around the failures of a president that threaten the real interests of the nation. I will reject the course of false patriotism." But Carter, helped by Pat Caddell's polling data, knew what he was doing. The attacks on Kennedy's patriotism were effective, and Teddy had to back off. He focused instead on Carter's refusal to campaign or debate him.

The White House had one final trick up its sleeve in the days before the New Hampshire primary. On the Friday before the vote, the U.S. hockey team pulled off one of the great moments in American sports history, the "Miracle on Ice." They beat the heavily favored Soviet team in Lake Placid, New York, to advance to the gold medal game of the Winter Olympics. The game was a national sensation, and Carter moved quickly to capitalize on the patriotic fervor being created. He sent Vice President Walter Mondale to the gold medal game on Sunday, which the U.S. team won, and called in to the locker room afterward during a live TV broadcast of the celebration.

Then, on Monday, one day before New Hampshire voted, Carter

hosted the gold medal winners at the White House for a televised celebration in their honor. It would have been effective politics for any state's primary, but was especially so in a big hockey state like New Hampshire.

Carter whipped Kennedy the next day. The margin was much closer than in Iowa, but still a resounding victory for Carter at 47 percent to 37 percent. Brown took in a surprising 10 percent, largely on the back of his opposition to nuclear power and to Carter's proposal for resuming registration for the draft. Kennedy allies like Shrum blamed Brown for robbing Kennedy of the opportunity to have claimed they were gaining momentum in the event of a closer finish.

But Carter beat Kennedy among Catholic voters—who should have been Kennedy's natural constituency—on his way to winning blue-collar Manchester, and also won the more liberal Concord area. Kennedy won younger voters and the city of Portsmouth.

Speaking to supporters at a recently closed department store on Elm Street in Manchester, Kennedy tried to lighten the mood. "Well, the results are in. I have a very serious announcement to make," he said, and paused for several moments. "Tomorrow is my daughter's twentieth birthday. Let's sing for Kara!"

In his remarks, Kennedy had to reach so far for a silver lining that it bordered on the absurd. "Four years ago Jimmy Carter got 28 percent and he claimed victory," he said, not mentioning that Carter had finished first among several candidates then, not second among three like he had. Kennedy told the crowd he was "claiming victory."

But young Patrick's tears were a better indication of how the Kennedy camp felt about the result. Kennedy's finance committee had told him the day before that they had enough money to get him through the Illinois primary on March 18, three weeks away, and no further.

Kennedy won Massachusetts easily on March 4, despite some worries that he might lose even his home state. But he then faced a series of southern states, a primary calendar arranged craftily by Carter aide Tom Donilon. Kennedy was completely unprepared to deal with Carter's southern firewall.

The March 11 primaries, in Alabama, Florida, and Carter's home state of Georgia, were indeed a gauntlet. And it was no accident that Donilon, Carter's twenty-five-year-old phenom, had made sure that these three Deep South states were scheduled after New Hampshire. Even if Kennedy had had the resources to compete, geography was stacked against him. But money was so low that a number of staffers, in lieu of a paycheck, received Andy Warhol screenprints of Kennedy. (The prints are now worth thousands of dollars.)

Carter swept the three southern primaries easily on March 11. That got plenty of attention in the press. What went less noticed at the time was the commanding lead in delegates that Carter had racked up. Most primary states awarded delegates proportionally to the popular vote. So Carter's massive margins in the South—60 percent to 23 percent in Florida, 81 to 13 in Alabama, and 88 to 8 in Georgia—translated into huge delegate hauls for the president. Even more disturbing for Kennedy was that Carter got more support from African American and union households and that Jewish voters did not show up in large numbers to vote. All three groups were key Kennedy constituencies.

Meanwhile, Carter forces were dominating caucus states. On March 11, Carter took thirty-six delegates to Kennedy's three in the Oklahoma caucuses. Four days later, on March 15, Carter took home all of Mississippi's thirty-two delegates, and all of South Carolina's thirty-seven delegates, completely shutting Kennedy out. It was a foreshadowing of Barack Obama's campaign in 2008, where he picked off delegates from Hillary Clinton in caucus states where Clinton had not bothered to organize. And like Obama's reelection effort in 2012, Carter had the advantage of incumbency, which gave him four years to prepare operations in each state.

"Ham Jordan really understood the new nominating process and proportional representation much better than we on the Kennedy side did," Ickes said. "The Kennedy high command, meaning Steve Smith and others, didn't have the foggiest idea about how it worked."

But the Carter campaign didn't have time to relax. They needed to lock things up quickly. Ronald Reagan, the ex–Hollywood actor and suave politician, was solidifying his position and would soon be turning his attention to the general election. Reagan had rebounded in New Hampshire, crushing Bush 50 percent to 23 percent, and then reeled off a series of wins in the southern states.

Kennedy tried to ignore the obstacles. He looked to the primary on March 18 in Illinois, a northern industrial state that suited him. He had the endorsement of Chicago mayor Jane Byrne, a champion of progressive causes, who had been elected a year earlier. But on the day before the primary, Kennedy marched in the St. Patrick's Day Parade in Chicago and was booed several times. People followed him along the route, shouting, "Where's Mary Jo?"

Illinois, perhaps more than anywhere, showed the cracks that had developed in the old Democratic coalition with big labor since FDR and JFK. "There was a misplaced sense that because Chicago elected JFK, it would do the same for Teddy twenty years later. But times had changed," said David Axelrod, then an up-and-coming young political reporter at the *Chicago Tribune*. The white ethnic vote in the city had turned more conservative. And Byrne's support turned out to be a hindrance. She had launched battles with the black community, the firefighters, and the Daley clan, and all her liabilities became Teddy's. Locked in a battle for survival, the Daleys sided with Carter, and helped deliver for him.

Carter whipped Kennedy 65 percent to 30 percent in Illinois. The delegate total now looked hopeless for Teddy. The president took a massive haul: 163 delegates to Kennedy's 16. It was a new low point for Kennedy. Surely, he would now have to get out of the race. Once again, he faced a choice: Admit defeat, or plunge forward in a divisive, increasingly hopeless endeavor.

"Kennedy ought to get out," Robert Strauss, the former U.S. trade rep chairing Carter's campaign, told Hamilton Jordan. "I think so too, and this ought to do it," Jordan agreed. But then he caught himself. "I've quit predicting he'll get out because I'm not sure he ever will.... When you drop out you are saying that you are quitting and that you're beaten," Jordan told Strauss. "That's hard for a Kennedy to say."

The Carter campaign was pushing memos to the press showing their lead in delegates and the impossibility of Teddy catching them. But Kennedy was unmoved, even as Carter's numbers continued to grow through the spring. Four days after the Illinois primary, Carter picked up fifty-nine more delegates to Kennedy's five in Virginia. The fact was that math and delegates didn't mean much to Kennedy, or to most of his senior advisers. "He tended to see the campaign the way most aspiring presidential candidates that I've known see it," said Rick Stearns, who was in charge of Kennedy's delegate operation. "They judge their success by their popularity in a very broad way. I don't think they really think of a campaign in terms of assembling delegates."

In fact, after Illinois, Stearns told Kennedy that Carter had an insurmountable lead that Kennedy under no conceivable set of circumstances would overtake before the convention. But Kennedy vowed to take his campaign to the convention even if Carter had the majority of delegates, and hinted for the first time that he had a new plan. He suggested that he might try to change the rules at the convention binding delegates to vote in line with the primary or caucus result.

Normally there would have been people around Kennedy who could have made it clear to him as the race went on that he had no chance of winning enough delegates to secure the nomination. But after his loss in Iowa, he shrunk his inner circle and stopped talking to any advisers who had not been with him for many years. "After Iowa he shut down," Peter Edelman, the policy adviser, said. "I think he felt so humiliated [after losing the caucuses] that he didn't want to deal with anybody outside his inner circle."

As a result, Kennedy was talking mainly to advisers who were holdovers from his brothers' political operations. And here the idiosyncrasies of history played an enormous role: These older advisers did not understand that the Democratic Party's rules for the nominating process had dramatically changed in the previous two-plus decades, and were completely different from the way the party had nominated presidential candidates when JFK and RFK had run in 1960 and 1968.

Before 1968, the nominee had been decided by party bosses, usually at the convention. In the 1968 Democratic primary, Bobby Kennedy's candidacy had gained popular momentum because of his famous last name, but also because he had come out against the Vietnam War. After Bobby's death, Senator Eugene McCarthy of Minnesota, the only other antiwar candidate, won nearly three million votes in the primaries. But at the convention in Chicago at the end of August, the party bosses controlled their delegates and made Hubert Humphrey the nominee, while outside the hall Chicago police beat and gassed antiwar protesters. Young Democratic antiwar activists were outraged; Humphrey had not run in any of the fourteen primaries held earlier in the year.

The Democratic nominating process would never work the

same way again. After the 1968 election, the McGovern-Fraser Commission changed the rules to make the process more open and inclusive, more like the modern system. State caucuses would now be open and advertised; before, they had been essentially closed in most states to all but party insiders and officeholders. And in states that held primaries, the popular vote rather than the party bosses would have more impact on whom the delegates from that state supported.

Carter also understood that there were better ways to control and lock down the loyalty of delegates than relying on local political machines. Teachers' unions, especially the National Education Association (NEA), were a rising political force that sent hundreds of delegates to the convention, and Carter owned most of them because he had created the Department of Education. He had also won the loyalty of many others through federal largesse dispensed to their state or locality.

The Kennedy old guard "still thought it was five bucks and a pint of whiskey in West Virginia," Ickes said, referring to JFK's infamous victory in the 1960 West Virginia primary, which had been won with the aid of suitcases of cash dispersed throughout the Mountain State. Many of Kennedy's top advisers had only ever known the old system. But the younger set of advisers knew that there was a problem. "At some point it became clear that the emperor had no clothes in the context of the numbers," Ickes said.

Kennedy needed a miracle.

James Earl Carter Jr. was born in Plains, a small town in southwest Georgia, on October 1, 1924, to James Earl Carter and his wife, Lillian, a nurse. There was no running water in the Carter house until Jimmy, the firstborn, was nine years old. This photo shows Jimmy with his mother, Lillian, and his younger sister Gloria. *(Courtesy of Carter Library in Atlanta)*

Edward Moore Kennedy was born on February 22, 1932, the youngest of nine children of wealthy banker and Hollywood financier Joseph P. Kennedy Sr. When Teddy was six, his father—who harbored presidential ambitions—was named ambassador to the United Kingdom. This picture shows Joe Sr. with his wife, Rose, and five of their nine children not long after their arrival in London in March 1938. Left to right: Kathleen, Joe Sr., Edward, Rose, Patricia, Jean, and Robert. *(Photo by H. F. Davis/Topical Press Agency/Getty Images)*

When John F. Kennedy was elec[...] president in 1960, Teddy w[...] instructed by his father to run [...] Jack's U.S. Senate seat in Massach[...]setts. Teddy was a recent law sch[...] graduate and his candidacy was cal[...] "preposterous and insulting." But w[...] the help of his father's money and [...] brother's political machine, he w[...] elected a U.S. senator in 1962. He[...] Teddy speaks at a dinner in honor [...] President Kennedy at the Comm[...]wealth Armory in Boston in Octo[...] 1963. Standing at left: Speaker of [...] House of Representatives John [...] McCormack (Massachusetts) a[...] co-chairman of the dinner Thoma[...] White. *(Cecil Stoughton. White Ho[...] Photographs. John F. Kennedy Presid[...] tial Library and Museum, Boston)*

Jimmy Carter willed himself to the U.S. Naval Academy, and after six years in the service he was on track to become a submarine commander, having reached the rank of lieutenant. But his father's premature death in 1953 brought Carter to a crossroads. He chose to come home and take over the family farm, against the wishes of his wife, Rosalynn. He stepped into a rural southern community roiled by the 1954 Supreme Court ruling in *Brown v. Board of Education* to desegregate

public schools, and chaired the county school board during that time. In 1962, the same year [...] Kennedy won election to the U.S. Senate, Carter mounted an unlikely candidacy for the state Sen[...] and overcame a corrupt small-town political boss to win a recount. This photo shows him on his fa[...] which he built into a financially successful business, around 1965, a few years into his time as a st[...] senator. *(Photo courtesy of Carter Library in Atlanta)*

President John F. Kennedy was assassinated in 1963. Five years later, Bobby Kennedy was shot and killed in the kitchen of the Ambassador Hotel in Los Angeles on June 5, 1968. It was a heavy blow for all the Kennedys, and Teddy—shown here slumped in a pew at St. Patrick's Cathedral in New York while Bobby's body lay in state—was now the only living son of Joe Kennedy Sr. He mourned by spending much of the summer alone on a sailboat in Cape Cod, but in the fall Democrats tried to draft him to accept the party's nomination for president. He considered the idea, but concluded he was "not yet qualified to be president." *(Photo by Joe Dennehy/The* Boston Globe *via Getty Images)*

ear after Bobby's death, Teddy left a party on rtha's Vineyard with twenty-eight-year-old ry Jo Kopechne in a black four-door Oldsmo- Delmont 88. Her body was discovered in t same car the next morning next to the Dike dge on Chappaquiddick Island. Kennedy told ice he had become confused and driven off the dge, but did not report the incident until 10:00 .. Authorities never performed an autopsy on echne's body, and a week after the accident, nedy was let off with a slap on the wrist, ding guilty to leaving the scene of an acci- t after causing an injury, and receiving a two- nth prison sentence that the judge suspended. s photo shows Senator Edward Kennedy and wife, Joan, at the Hyannis airport on their way he funeral of Mary Jo Kopechne. *(Photo by Joe nehy/The* Boston Globe *via Getty Images)*

A year after Chappaquiddick, Jimmy Carter was elected governor of Georgia. Four years earlier, he had run a campaign that reached out to blacks in the state, and evoked comparisons to John F. Kennedy. But he fell short and white supremacist Lester Maddox won instead. Carter was devastated by the loss, but during this time he experienced a spiritual rebirth. In 1970, he ran again, and this time he won the white supremacist vote. "I never made a racist statement but...I never did anything to alienate them," Carter told the author. In his inaugural address, there were audible groans in the audience when Carter announced, "The time for racial discrimination is over." *(Photo courtesy of Carter Library in Atlanta)*

Carter began plotting a run for president in 1972, and expected—like Richard Nixon had—that Ted Kennedy would likely be his chief competition. But Kennedy decided against a run. Carter won the Iowa caucuses and outlasted a crowded field. He appealed to America's desire to heal after the Watergate scandal and the Vietnam War. Kennedy, here with Carter in the Oval Office in 1978, was at first

an ally in the Senate but quickly grew frustrated with Carter's lack of progress toward a national health care proposal. *(Courtesy of the National Archives)*

Carter's first two years had their ups and downs. In 1979, however, things fell apart. An energy shortage created gas lines and violent confrontations. Inflation skyrocketed, along with unemployment. The murder rate reached its highest point in the nation's history. Carter retreated to Camp David for ten days of meetings. His speech to the nation afterward was initially well received. But on the advice of his chief of staff, Hamilton Jordan—shown here with Carter four days after the speech—Carter also fired the majority of his cabinet. The firings backfired, and the speech became known as the "malaise" speech. *(Photo by Keystone/Hulton Archive/Getty Images)*

Teddy finalized his decision to challenge the sitting president of his own party over Labor Day weekend. Days before his campaign kickoff, in late October, Kennedy and Carter came face-to-face at the dedication of John F. Kennedy's presidential library in Boston. Carter gave one of the finest speeches of his career, using JFK's own words to send Teddy a

warning that he would not roll over simply at the sight of the Kennedy name, and that Teddy would be in for the political fight of his life. Ted Kennedy, Joan Kennedy, and Carter are pictured here seated on the stage. *(Photo by Chuck Fishman/Getty Images)*

Kennedy was a stunning two-to-one favorite over Carter in the fall of 1979, as the president's approval rating dropped to a staggering 19 percent. Kennedy here greets a large crowd outside Faneuil Hall in Boston after announcing his candidacy on November 7. *(Photo by Ted Dully/The* Boston Globe *via Getty Images)*

After Iranian radicals seized the American embassy in Tehran and took hostages, Americans rallied around Carter. That complicated Kennedy's challenge, and made for some tough days in Iowa, like this tour of a farm in Indianola. *(Bettman via Getty Images)*

Carter refused to campaign or debate Kennedy, citing the hostage crisis. But as Kennedy surged in the spring, Carter's handling of the issue appeared exploitative to many. He gave a press statement (pictured) on April 1, the day of the Wisconsin primary, that left the impression that the hostages might be released imminently. *(Bettman via Getty Images)*

Kennedy's convention speech is known as one of the greatest speeches in modern American politics. "For all those whose cares have been our concern the work goes on, the cause endures, the hope still lives, and the dream shall never die," Kennedy thundered as he closed. "Kennedy's words triggered open the floodgates of memories: Camelot, magic rhetoric, and the shock of the assassinations," Ham Jordan said. *(Photo by Frank Leonardo/*New York Post *Archives /(c) NYP Holdings, Inc. via Getty Images)*

On the final night of the convention, Kennedy humiliated Carter on live television by refusing to clasp raised hands together with him. It was, wrote Teddy White, "as if [Kennedy] had appeared at the wedding of his chauffeur." *(Photo by © Wally McNamee/CORBIS/Corbis via Getty Images)*

Kennedy gave some help to Carter against Ronald Reagan, but only after Carter helped Kennedy retire his debts. By January 1981, Carter was a private citizen again. Here, he speaks to the press for the first time after leaving the presidency. *(Photo by Chuck Fishman/Getty Images)*

The idea of Camelot—of returning a Kennedy to the presidency—had slipped away. But Teddy could now follow his own path. During the 1980s Kennedy became the standard-bearer for the Democratic Party in exile under Reagan's presidency. This photo shows Caroline Kennedy, Edward Kennedy, and Jackie Onassis at the JFK Library on December 5, 1983. *(Photo by Greg Derr/The* Boston Globe *via Getty Images)*

Carter returned to Georgia with Rosalynn and his daughter, Amy, and discovered that his family farm was $1 million in debt. He sold the farm, began work on his first post-presidency book, and then created the Carter Center in Atlanta. He threw himself into the work of conflict resolution and election monitoring, like in this photo, where he watches a polling booth in Panama City on May 8, 1994. *(RODRIGO ARANGUA/ AFP/Getty Images)*

Teddy remarried in 1991 and his life and career entered a new phase of stability. He led the Kennedy clan through continued tragedies in the 1990s, and in the Senate, he worked with President Bill Clinton and then George W. Bush as a respected Democratic leader. And in the 2008 presidential race, Kennedy threw his endorsement behind Barack Obama, shown here with Teddy and Caroline Kennedy (far left) on February 4, 2008, in East Rutherford, New Jersey. *(Photo by Charles Ommanney/ Getty Images)*

Jimmy Carter set a new standard for what a president could accomplish after leaving office. He fought disease in Africa, wrote thirty books, and mediated conflicts around the world. Here, Carter looks on as Aijalon Mahli Gomes, an American imprisoned in North Korea whose release he negotiated, is greeted by family members on August 27, 2010, at Logan International Airport in Boston, Massachusetts. *(JOHN MOTTERN/ AFP/Getty Images)*

The two men tried to put on a show of unity in 1988 for their party's sake, but Carter could not play the part. Years later however, in an interview with the author, Carter reflected on Kennedy—who had passed away a few years earlier—and offered heartfelt, deeply respectful words of praise. *(BOB PEARSON/AFP/Getty Images)*

# CHAPTER 13

---

# Civil War

Maybe, just maybe, this thing could be over by April, Carter hoped. Losses for Kennedy in both New York and Connecticut on March 25 would undoubtedly be the end of his candidacy. Then Carter would be able to devote his full energies to resolving the hostage crisis, which was now dragging toward its sixth month. The president still refused to campaign because of the crisis, and he spent the week leading up to the important New York and Connecticut primaries completely distracted by it.

The shah was in Panama but wanted to leave and get cancer treatment in Egypt. However, Carter knew that such a move would enrage the revolutionaries in Iran and might provoke them to harm the hostages. Ham Jordan, the president's top political adviser, should have been focused on how to deal with ending Kennedy's candidacy. But instead he spent four days leading up to March 25 in Panama, trying to persuade the shah not to leave Central America. It "could mean the death of the hostages," he told the shah's physician.

It wasn't as if the Carter high command could afford to ignore the looming primaries. The president's pollster, Pat Caddell, had told Carter that his standing was deteriorating in New York in particular because of three factors: inflation, the hostages, and a March 1 vote at the United Nations. The United States had joined in denouncing Israel and calling on it to dismantle settlements in Gaza and the West Bank. Carter had backtracked afterward, saying his ambassador to the United Nations had cast the vote by mistake, but New York's Jewish community was enraged.

The Carter campaign had locked down support from the New York political establishment, including Lieutenant Governor Mario Cuomo and New York City mayor Ed Koch. Governor Hugh Carey and Senator Daniel Patrick Moynihan, who had worked closely with Kennedy in the past, stayed on the sidelines. But as the primary drew nearer, "one could almost feel the increasing apprehension and tension at the White House," wrote Elizabeth Drew.

Public polling in the days before the New York primary showed Carter ahead by more than 20 points. But Pat Caddell's internal numbers had Kennedy ahead by 9 points, with the president's support "in a free fall." "Everyone says we're going to win big, but it doesn't feel good," said Joel McLeary, the Carter campaign's organizer in New York. Carter's people were furious at the way that they felt the press was helping Kennedy stay alive.

The Kennedy campaign didn't have their own polling numbers because they didn't have enough money to pay for them. They were expecting to lose, and many around Kennedy were hoping that a New York defeat would convince him to exit the race. Senator Wendell Ford, a Kentucky Democrat who chaired the Democrats' Senatorial Campaign Committee, was planning to tell Kennedy that he was endangering his colleagues' reelection chances if he continued to run against Carter after losses in New York and Connecticut.

Steve Smith, Kennedy's sisters, and Kennedy's top aides all met to talk over how to persuade Kennedy to drop out. Smith called the Parker House, a hotel in Boston often used to host political events, and reserved a room under an assumed name where Kennedy could finally admit defeat. He had fought bravely, his brain trust concluded, but to keep going past New York would be madness.

Smith had been there from the beginning with JFK. He had seen the glory years and experienced all the Kennedy highs. He had been with Bobby during his rise and at his bedside the night he succumbed to his wounds in Los Angeles. Teddy's embarrassing defeat would be sad, but tragedy had come to mean something much larger to Smith and others in the Kennedy orbit. At least Teddy was still alive.

Smith instructed speechwriter Bob Shrum to draft a statement: "I have withdrawn from the campaign, but I have not withdrawn from my commitment to speak for those who have no voice, to stand for those who are weak or exploited, to strive for those who are left out or left behind."

President Carter began primary day with a visit to the White House dentist. He lunched with Vice President Walter Mondale. He held a ninety-minute afternoon meeting with Christian Bourguet, a French attorney acting as a go-between with the Iranian government. "Our patience is beginning to look like a demonstration of cowardice!" he told Bourguet, expressing his frustration that the hostages had still not been released. He spent most of the afternoon on the phone with lawmakers and influence holders in New York and Connecticut, trying to get a sense of where things were headed.

As returns came in, Carter was in the State Dining Room, hosting a buffet dinner with members of Congress to go over his anti-inflation program. At 7:15 p.m., Caddell called and broke the news to the president. He was being crushed in New York. It was a 20-point loss. Jewish voters sided with Kennedy three-to-one. More alarming, concerns about Kennedy's character were fading. In Illinois, 64 percent of Catholics had voted against Kennedy, but in New York only 47 percent had. Questions about the president's competency had come to the fore. The ongoing hostage crisis, which had at first rallied Americans to the president, was now making Carter look impotent and weak. And Kennedy's criticism of Carter's refusal to campaign among the voters or to debate was working.

Kennedy was buoyant. But it was Joan who made it clear that the New York win had ended any talk of quitting. "I like New York in March, how about August?" she sang to reporters. It was a reference to the convention, to be held in Madison Square Garden that summer. Kennedy intended to be there as the nominee, not as an observer.

Carter's people were shaken. "We blew it," Bob Strauss, Carter's puckish campaign chairman, told Tom Brokaw on the night of the primary. But, again, there was a silver lining for the Carter forces: Kennedy's delegate haul was small. In New York, Kennedy won 58.9 percent to 41.1 percent, but only netted 46 delegates. Because of proportional representation, Carter won 118 delegates, to Kennedy's 164. Carter had run up the score in southern states, and the rules of the primary meant that those lopsided victories gave him a far bigger delegate edge than Kennedy's narrow wins in big states.

Four days after his New York win, Kennedy traveled to Pittsburgh, where he was greeted by a crowd of ten thousand at a noontime rally in Mellon Square. His speech showed that he was firing on all cylinders. It was a full-throated, all-out liberal assault on Carter's attempts to keep inflation down, and his continued refusal to campaign while the hostages remained in Iran.

"You can't remain in the White House for six months without underestimating the anguish and pain that millions are feeling as a result of runaway inflation," Kennedy said. "You just can't do it, Mr. Carter. You've got to come out and face the people."

Carter used some deception to slow the bleeding a week later in the Wisconsin primary. On the morning of April 1, he brought reporters into the Oval Office at 7:13 a.m. and announced a "positive development" in the negotiations, suggesting the hostages were about to be released. It was a false alarm, and Carter would be ripped in the press later for exploiting the hostage situation for political gain. But the positive news that day helped him in Wisconsin, where he easily won the primary, despite Jordan's predictions that he would lose. He also won Kansas that same day, and Louisiana four days later. Everything looked to be back under control.

But then Kennedy won the Arizona caucuses on April 12. And he edged out Carter in the Pennsylvania primary on April 22. Kennedy also won the Vermont caucuses that same day, and the Michigan caucuses a few days later.

At 10:43 p.m. on the night of the Pennsylvania primary, Kennedy stood at a podium in a Philadelphia hotel, his wife, Joan, to his right and his three children standing to his left, and addressed supporters. "Tonight, it appears like we have a narrow victory," he said with a smile, and then began to cackle as the crowd in the ballroom broke into raucous cheering. He leaned over, still smiling, said something to his kids, and then motioned for the crowd to quiet down, holding both arms up with his palms facing down.

Once the crowd had quieted, he launched into a version of the stump speech he had been delivering all over the Keystone State for the previous few weeks. The bumbling, unprepared candidate who could not give a straight answer to Roger Mudd the previous fall had found his voice and his message.

"If our campaign speaks for anyone, it speaks for the workers of this country that are caught—" here he was interrupted by applause, forcing him to repeat himself "—that are caught in the extraordinary position of seeing their wages constantly eaten up by inflation, or the real possibility of losing their jobs, as so many autoworkers, steelworkers, coal miners, and others across the length and breadth of this country have." He spoke with the loud, bullish voice of a man spoiling for a fight. "If our campaign speaks for anyone, it speaks for the elderly people of this great nation, who today—" there was more applause "—who today are making extremely difficult and cruel choices, whether they can make ends meet with their narrow incomes being eaten up by inflation."

He paused to take a breath, and then lunged back into his cadence. "If this campaign speaks for anyone, it speaks for the young people who really wonder whether they can afford the tuition to go to their schools and colleges," he said, his voice rising again. There was more cheering and applause, and again he motioned for quiet. "And if this campaign stands for anything, it stands for a rejection of the hand-wringing that has been done by this administration about the great problems that we are facing here at home and across the seas." The crowd went nuts.

However, Kennedy's win in Pennsylvania was costly. Carter's campaign had made a point of resurrecting voter concerns about Kennedy's character by going after him more directly in campaign ads that showed regular people on the street voicing doubts about him. "I don't believe him," one of the people said. If the electorate had shifted during the New York primary from a focus on Kennedy to a question of whether Carter was a competent president, the Pennsylvania primary moved the spotlight back onto Kennedy and the character issue: personal infidelities, Chappaquiddick, and his marriage. "Teddy's character, it had left the equation entirely [in New York]. So, in Pennsylvania it was a matter of bringing it back," Caddell said. "We thought we were going to leave Pennsylvania with a 20-point loss."

And for all the enthusiasm around Kennedy's win, he had a

razor-thin margin in Pennsylvania's popular vote. He netted exactly one delegate, winning 93 of them to Carter's 92. In fact, Carter won the Missouri caucuses that day and came away with 54 delegates there to Kennedy's 10. Carter's inability to put Kennedy away in key contests, and his ongoing unpopularity, continued to put him in danger of going into free fall. But as Sam Donaldson accurately reported from the White House, "The president will win more delegates today than Senator Kennedy will win." Carter was getting closer and closer to the magic number of 1,666 delegates.

But events in Iran once again intruded. Two days after the Pennsylvania primary, a convoy of six U.S. military cargo planes took off from Oman, crossed the Persian Gulf into Iran, and landed in a remote desert location. They were followed by eight Sea Stallion helicopters.

The planes carried U.S. Delta Force soldiers, members of an elite unit that had just been formed in 1977. They were the tip of the spear of an incredibly ambitious and complicated plan to rescue the hostages from Iran. The first leg of the trip was a four-hour, seven-hundred-mile journey to a makeshift airstrip in the middle of the Iranian desert, set up by advance personnel. The second step was to refuel the helicopters at the landing strip with gasoline carried in massive bladders on the cargo planes, then take the choppers to another rendezvous point closer to Tehran. They would hide during the day, and then travel by truck into the heart of Tehran the next night, mount an attack on the embassy, and seize the hostages. The helicopters would pick them up at nearby Shahid Shiroudi Stadium, fly to a little-used airstrip, and then everyone would flee the country aboard C-141 airplanes. Many Delta soldiers believed that even if they were lucky enough to get the hostages out, they'd be killed in the process or be left behind to try to fight their way out of Tehran.

As the planes and helicopters moved into Iranian airspace, Carter kept up the appearance of a president going through a normal day. Between updates from the military, he held a meeting on inflation with Hispanic leaders and also attended a bill-signing ceremony.

The helicopter pilots had been warned by some C-130 pilots to avoid flying through huge clouds of desert sand that were held suspended in the air, referred to as haboobs. But because of a communications blackout, the warning did not reach the chopper pilots. The fine dust enveloped the helicopters for three hours, putting a huge strain on their engines. One chopper had to turn back. Another Sea Stallion had to be grounded and abandoned, and a third arrived at the landing zone too damaged to fly farther.

The mission required six helicopters in order to proceed, and they were down to five. The officers on the ground in the desert relayed the bad news back to Washington. "Damn, damn," Carter said when he heard the news. Zbigniew Brzezinski was loath to abandon the mission. But as he and Carter discussed whether to ask Charlie Beckwith, the Delta Force commander, whether he could keep going anyway, they got word that Beckwith had made a final call to abort. Carter put his head in his arms, but took solace in the fact that there had been no loss of life.

Back in the Iranian desert, however, a chaotic scene unfolded as the U.S. troops tried to leave the landing zone. As one of the Sea Stallion helicopters maneuvered at low altitude, the pilot lost his bearings in all the sand that was kicked up into the air. The aircraft's rotor hit one of the C-130s and it crashed on top of the plane, igniting a fireball that lit up the desert sky. Eight servicemen were killed, and many others injured. A bad night had quickly turned into a horrific disaster.

The news landed like a bomb at the White House. "A tremendous wave of nausea gripped me," Ham Jordan said of the moment he found out. "I ducked into the president's private bathroom and vomited my guts out. But I didn't feel any better."

The president went on television the morning of April 25 to inform the nation of the debacle. He stressed that there had been no fighting, and no aggression toward Iran, in an attempt to minimize the chances that any of the hostages might be harmed. Carter deemed the operation "a humanitarian mission." He added, "It was not directed against Iran. It was not directed against the people of Iran. It was not undertaken with any feeling of hostility toward Iran or its people. It has caused no Iranian casualties."

Carter's strained positivity was at its worst in the aftermath of the failed hostage rescue. He called the operation "an incomplete success." But the wife of one of the hostages more bluntly summarized things. "I just find it hard to believe that they could have been so uncoordinated, so clumsy. It doesn't sound like our army," she told the *Washington Post*.

The debacle would haunt military and intelligence officials for decades. In 2011, when President Barack Obama debated whether to send special operations officers into Pakistan to kill al Qaeda leader Osama bin Laden, Secretary of Defense Robert Gates opposed the mission. Gates had been a high-ranking official at the CIA in 1980, and he feared a repeat.

The failed hostage rescue would be a permanent black mark on Carter's presidency. The political consequences were grave, but they were not immediate. The month of May, counterintuitively, turned out to be a good one for Carter. Kennedy's wins in Pennsylvania, Vermont, and Michigan had been accompanied by a relatively meaningless victory in Washington, D.C., on May 6. Other than that, Carter won all eleven of the following primaries. It was a brutal stretch for Kennedy.

There was one more day of primaries, on June 3, with eight states going to the polls. The president stood just 11 delegates short of the magic number, 1,666, and was guaranteed to go over the top on June 3. Kennedy had only 860 delegates. Surprisingly, the failed mission, as horrific as it was, had actually helped Carter in the polls. "People wanted the president to do something, and something happened," Caddell said.

There was talk again of Kennedy looking for a way out. Perhaps if Carter agreed to debate him, it would be a graceful path to an exit for Kennedy, after he stood as an equal to the president onstage in front of a televised audience. One of Kennedy's close advisers came to Jordan's apartment in D.C., according to Jordan, and discussed, "for the sake of the senator's ego and his own future, and for the sake of the party," how to "find an honorable way for him to get out of the race" after the June 3 Super Tuesday set of eight primaries.

Kennedy's team was urging him to quit, but he was not making any noises about retreat. "I'm committed to going to the convention and making the effort for the nomination," he told Elizabeth Drew. "It isn't just a campaign, it's a cause." A close friend of Kennedy's told Drew that "the divisions are too deep" for the senator to exit the race.

Carter ended his Rose Garden strategy and held his first official campaign event on May 29 in Columbus, Ohio, almost seven months after Kennedy announced his candidacy. Carter arrived in downtown Columbus for a noontime rally at Nationwide Plaza, in front of the Nationwide Insurance office building, a massive structure with windows that stretched up and down its face in vertical stripes. The heat was intense, forcing him to take off his suit jacket. The Carter campaign had prepared for the event and turned out a massive crowd. The building behind him was decorated with bunting, a huge American flag, and a large green-and-white "Support

President Carter" banner. He spoke of America "turning the tide," and predicted an economic resurgence in the country. He did a few other events in Columbus, a few more in Cleveland, and then flew home.

It would be Carter's only day of campaigning during the primary, and its enduring effect was negative. In the days afterward the nation received a raft of negative economic news, and Caddell would later conclude that Carter's talk of "turning the tide" in the economy would cost him 5 to 7 points in the June 3 primary states.

Kennedy, meanwhile, was plodding toward the finish line like an Irish fatalist poet. When he described his intent to Elizabeth Drew to go all the way to New York in August, he appeared driven by fate, destiny, the ghosts of his family and his last name, and the weight of history. But he had also found his voice over the course of the campaign, and some part of him did believe that he was fighting for the soul of the Democratic Party, standing up for the poor and the underprivileged in America against a president too feckless to do anything for them. At one stop in San Francisco he articulated perfectly what had so enraged him when watching Carter give his "malaise" speech a year earlier. "We have a president now that doesn't really believe that a president of the United States or an individual can make a difference. I reject that suggestion. That runs alien to everything that I believe," Kennedy thundered.

Yet the fundamental question remained: Why was he still in the race if he could not catch Carter in delegates? That question receded for a bit when the returns came in from California and New Jersey on June 3. Kennedy won both convincingly, and five of the eight contests in all. "Today Democrats from coast to coast were unwilling to concede the nomination to Jimmy Carter. And neither am I," Kennedy said defiantly at his election-night rally.

Carter held an overwhelming delegate lead, 1,988 to Kennedy's 1,220. Kennedy would have to win a procedural vote at the convention to release all the Carter delegates from voting for the president, but if the idea gathered enough momentum, it could happen. After the New York primary, Ham Jordan had comforted himself with the fact that "it was mathematically a near impossibility that [Kennedy] could overcome our lead in delegates." The next moment, he voiced a deep fear. "But if he started beating us regularly, a mood could develop in the Democratic party to take the nomination away from us."

As the two Democrats bloodied each other over the winter, through the spring, and into the summer, Ronald Reagan had locked up the Republican nomination and was gathering strength. He was a laughingstock to many Democrats, but Reagan had a knack for connecting with large audiences, especially on television. He was the first national Republican figure to have that talent. TV had been the dominant medium shaping politics since around 1960, but every Republican standard-bearer since then—Richard Nixon, Barry Goldwater, and Gerald Ford—had been unappealing on the small screen.

Reagan may have been advanced in years at the age of sixty-nine, but he was a folksy, optimistic charmer of a man. Four years earlier, he had been where Teddy Kennedy was now, the insurgent. Reagan had challenged the incumbent president within his own party, Gerald Ford, and the fight had gone all the way to the convention. Reagan narrowly lost, and his political career was declared over. It had been his second failed attempt to win the nomination. The hatred between Ford and Reagan was visceral, and lasted well beyond the 1976 election, which Ford had lost to Carter. Some in Reagan's camp had been pleased by Ford's demise.

Though after his failed 1976 bid many thought Reagan was finished, he was determined to stay in the national conversation. He had a daily radio commentary that was carried by more than five hundred stations, with an audience of roughly forty million people. He wrote a weekly column that appeared in hundreds of newspapers. He gave speeches across the nation. And Carter's troubled and often bungling presidency offered endless opportunities for Reagan to tell his listeners how he would do things differently. Carter was Reagan's ticket back into politics and toward a third attempt at the White House.

Carter was "pleased" when Reagan became the nominee. He and his staff had feared Senator Howard Baker of Tennessee as the most formidable Republican. "At the time, all my political team believed that [Reagan] was the weakest candidate the Republicans could have chosen," he wrote. Carter recognized Reagan's speaking ability but was contemptuous of it. "He has his memorized tapes. He pushes a button, and they come out," he wrote in his diary. He would later call Reagan "both dumb and incompetent." Reagan had a different way of dealing with Carter. He mocked him with easygoing humor, a contrast to Carter's self-serious zealotry. Reagan jokingly referred to Carter as "a man who tells you he enjoys a cold shower in the morning."

It was an apt metaphor for Carter's predicament. He held a significant mathematical advantage over Kennedy. If his opponent were anyone else, or had a different last name, the contest would almost certainly be over. But he could not finish the job, and Kennedy wouldn't quit. In fact, there was growing talk that Carter might lose the nomination to Kennedy at the convention. If this wasn't the political equivalent of a cold shower, nothing was. It was getting damn hard to keep smiling every day.

# CHAPTER 14

# Robot Rule

On June 5, two days after the California primary, Kennedy and Carter met at the White House. Publicly, Carter had told the press the day before the meeting that he expected Kennedy to keep running all the way until the convention.

But privately, the Carter White House hoped that Kennedy would arrive with the welcome news that he would no longer sustain his challenge to the president. Surely, he had exhausted whatever had driven him to prolong a hopeless cause. Carter held a commanding lead in delegates, with over 1,900, having easily surpassed the 1,666-delegate threshold. Kennedy had just over 1,200.

The meeting with Kennedy was scheduled for late in the afternoon, and Carter had a full day of business to deal with before that, including a trip to Baltimore for a White House conference on families. In addition, it was going to be a bad day for the president on Capitol Hill. Carter planned to veto a bill his own party had passed rejecting a fee on oil imports of $4.62 per barrel. He wanted to reduce consumption and increase revenue for the strained budget.

But Congress, in an election year, didn't want to anger American drivers by increasing the cost of gas. Congress was expected to quickly and easily override Carter's veto. It would be a historic rebuke, the first time since 1952 that a president's veto would be overridden by a Congress controlled by his own party.

At 4:35 in the afternoon, Kennedy strutted into the Oval Office. He wore a handsome dark suit that hugged his tall, sturdy frame. His graying hair was thick and in need of a trim, but swept back and disheveled enough that it looked vaguely glamorous. The only thing out of place was his left collar, which was missing a stay and jutting up. Carter, on the other hand, looked every bit the sober librarian. His hair was neatly combed to the side, his collar was perfectly turned down and tight against his neck, and his striped tie had a smaller knot than Kennedy's.

Whatever hopes Carter had for a positive outcome evaporated rather quickly. Kennedy wanted him to commit to a debate. It was obvious he wasn't getting out of the race. But eventually, Carter could not contain himself. "Ted, are you going to get out or not?" the president demanded. Kennedy rebuffed him, walked out of the West Wing with a big smile, and was enveloped by a huge media throng.

A reporter asked how much of a chance he had of becoming the party's nominee. "More than a prayer," he said. As he climbed into his car, the sun illuminated his wide grin, and a *New York Times* photographer captured the moment. Kennedy looked like he was the one with a delegate lead and the best shot at winning the nomination.

Carter, on the other hand, looked like he was facing a firing squad when he spoke with reporters. He signed the veto message on the oil import bill, and then told reporters that he continued to reject Kennedy's demands for a public debate. "The primary season is over," he said.

Carter said their differences on health care, wage and price controls, and spending priorities could be worked out "through the platform process" leading up to the convention in August. "If there are still differences after that," he said, "they can be taken to the floor of the convention itself." Down the street at the Capitol, the House overwhelmingly rebuked Carter by overriding his veto of the oil import fee, 335 to 34.

The president underestimated Kennedy's kamikaze-like state of mind that would drive him to keep fighting as long as possible. Many in the Kennedy camp were disgusted by Carter. They felt he was no better than Reagan, and almost preferred to see Reagan win.

Some thought Kennedy's buoyancy was unrelated to a primary comeback. "His return to his broth-of-a-boy, preannouncement self leads to speculation that the reason he is showing such spirit in the last act of the primary drama is that he will soon be a free man, free at last of the 20-year family burden of having to run for the presidency," Mary McGrory wrote. "There is, too, a counter theory: that he is turning in a class performance against hopeless odds so that he can try again in 1984—when it is said Chappaquiddick memories will be dimmed, and overcome by this year's display of character."

After the meeting, some of Carter's advisers urged the president to debate Kennedy, granting the challenger his top demand. At first, Carter agreed. Mondale was opposed, but the others in Carter's inner circle thought it was a good idea. But in the course of a day or two, Carter heard from Charles Kirbo, his old Georgia political adviser, who strongly advised against it. And that swung Carter against it once again.

Things were going better in the other political party. That same day, in Rancho Mirage, California, Ronald Reagan and former president Gerald Ford met for ninety minutes at Ford's home. They had been bitter foes four years earlier. Ford had said Reagan was "unelectable."

But the weakness being projected by the Democrats' infighting was the greatest invitation imaginable to unity among Republicans. Ford pledged his full support to Reagan and said he would "wholeheartedly campaign" for him. The front page of the next day's *New York Times* showed a side-by-side photo at the top of the page, contrasting a sharp-eyed, thick-haired Kennedy with a downcast, tired president wielding an impotent veto pen. At the bottom of the page a relaxed Reagan sat resting on Ford's couch, smiling and looking over at the former president.

There was another complication for Carter now that the primary season was over, as he surveyed the path to reelection. John B. Anderson, a Republican congressman from Illinois, had announced an independent run for president in late April, just over a month earlier, and he was standing up a serious political operation to get his name on the ballot in many states. His chief consultant was David Garth, the same New York politico who had counseled Kennedy the previous fall to tackle the Chappaquiddick issue head-on. Garth was one of the top media consultants in the country.

Anderson, fifty-eight, was raised in an ultra-conservative Christian home. He had grown up working in his Swedish immigrant father's grocery store in Rockford, Illinois. Anderson described Rockford as "a mecca for Swedish immigrants" in the early twentieth century. He'd seen combat as a staff sergeant in World War II, and gone on to be a lawyer and a congressman for two decades. He had been a member of the House Republican leadership for some time, rising to the third most powerful position. He mixed economic conservatism with social liberalism in a way that appealed to northeastern moderates and threatened to cost Carter key states like New York, Massachusetts, and Connecticut.

Anderson had put a scare into Ronald Reagan during the Republican primary, nearly winning Massachusetts and Vermont. He'd gained respect for his direct answers to questions, his willingness to speak his mind and buck conventional wisdom, and his substantive ideas. He had been the first Republican to call for President Nixon's resignation during the Watergate scandal. But Anderson was no loose cannon. "There's a meticulousness about him—the way he combs his snow-white hair, the way his suit is pressed, the way he chooses words. He emits candor in these meetings, but little that's off the cuff," wrote the *Globe*'s Al Larkin.

Anderson was critical of Carter's "gyrations" on economic policy, and thought the president had been unprepared in general for the job. But he also did not believe Americans needed the tax cuts that Reagan wanted. He was, however, proposing a 50-cent-a-gallon gas tax to reduce consumption, and wanted to simultaneously slash Social Security taxes in half, to increase take-home pay for average Americans, and to stimulate the economy. Anderson favored modest gun control efforts, supported the Equal Rights Amendment, and was vociferously in favor of abortion.

It was quite the change from his ultra-conservative days in the early 1960s, when he'd offered proposals to amend the Constitution so that the United States would "devoutly" recognize "the authority and law of Jesus Christ." He now denounced the pro-life movement as "extremists" and said he was "fed up with the zealots' attempt to impose compulsory pregnancy on America." It was the product of a decade-long conversion to a more liberal political worldview that had begun during the civil rights era in the late 1960s.

Anderson was growing more and more popular on college campuses, and he played up his appeal to younger voters in part because they were eager volunteers. Getting his name on the ballot in as many states as possible required a lot of manpower to go out and gather a sufficient number of signatures. He'd talk up his support for a moratorium on new nuclear energy plants, not mentioning that he opposed halting projects already under construction.

Anderson was in talks at the time with famous CBS newsman Walter Cronkite to consider serving as his running mate. It would have been an unconventional and bold choice, to say the least. Anderson also talked to former senator Edward Brooke, a Massachusetts Republican who had been the first African American popularly elected to the Senate in American history. "Fully 40 percent of the American people think there ought to be a third party," Anderson told Larkin, citing a Gallup poll. "We need a new centrist force in this country that will be more effective in dealing with the nation's problems than either of our two major parties have been to date."

The Carter White House was taking Anderson seriously enough that they tried to knock him off the ballot in Massachusetts. His appeal to liberal voters promised to subtract votes from Carter in the fall. The Democratic National Committee spent $225,000 to mount a legal challenge against Anderson's inclusion, but failed to keep him off the ballot.

The day after Kennedy's meeting with Carter at the White House, the Senate also overwhelmingly rejected Carter's veto on the oil import fee, 68 to 10, completing his humiliation. And the embarrassments kept coming. The following Monday, Carter flew to Miami and held meetings at the headquarters of the James E. Scott Community Association, the same group that had helped him beat Kennedy in a straw poll of the state's voters the previous fall, his first organizational win over the challenger.

Carter was there to discuss the race riots that had taken place the month before, which were the worst since the 1960s. The fatal beating of a black man by Miami police had outraged the city's black population, and eighteen people had been killed in the resulting unrest. Carter was jeered and booed as he left the meeting, and his presidential motorcade was pelted with bottles. One hit the back of the president's limousine, and other cars in the motorcade were struck by numerous bottles. One vehicle's window was shattered by the projectiles. Police had trouble keeping the mob away from Carter's vehicle.

A community leader said he was "appalled and embarrassed" by the actions of those who threw bottles at the president, but that Carter's stance that $1 billion in private capital would have to be raised for repair and rebuilding after the riots to trigger federally funded aid "may have actually inflamed the already desperate situation."

The following week, "talk of an 'open convention' swept Washington," Hamilton Jordan wrote. The Carter campaign redoubled their efforts to "stroke" their delegates, planning special mailings, regular telephone calls, and briefings for them in Washington. After all Carter and his campaign had done to secure the nomination, to lose it now would be catastrophic. He had spoken on the night of the final primaries of turning "what eight months ago was a prediction of absolute defeat into a wondrous victory." But the open convention speculation meant that Carter's nomination was not a sure thing.

Many observers thought Kennedy's gambit had no chance. "The 'open convention' was closed to manipulation a decade ago by the McGovern Commission. The process was opened to the people, and the people have spoken," wrote Marty Nolan of the *Boston Globe*. Nolan described a scene in San Francisco ahead of the June 5 primary where Kennedy was greeted by a midday throng of three thousand people but failed to rouse much enthusiasm from the crowd, which responded to much of his speech with silence or polite applause.

Nolan wrote that Kennedy's liberal ideas were an easy sell in a place like the West Coast, but that he was not winning over any more moderate voters. "His basic litany of Carter-caused economic miseries has failed to sway blue-collar voters, as primary results from blue-collar precincts in Ohio show," Nolan said. "The Kennedy candidacy has not been able to include more moderate elements of the party in endorsements and, equally important, in political help." Nolan compared Kennedy's campaign to McGovern's "ideologically pure but unpersuasive" effort in 1972.

Some thought that Kennedy's old-guard liberalism was on the rise, and that McGovern's defeat in 1972 had laid the groundwork for big congressional gains in 1974 and 1976, and taking back the White House in 1976 as well. However, another school of thought held that Democrats had won mostly because of Nixon and Watergate. The party's victories had blinded many Democrats from seeing the bigger, deeper splintering of their coalition that had kept them in power since the New Deal, argued Thomas and Mary Edsall in their 1991 book *Chain Reaction*.

Whereas white voters from the middle and working class had seen Democrats as protecting them from powerful business interests from the New Deal era through the 1950s, the Edsalls argued, they now saw Democrats as trying to raise their taxes in order to give government benefits to blacks and other minorities, even as plants were closing and jobs were disappearing in the Rust Belt.

"The Republican party, in developing a populist stance around the issues of race and taxes," the Edsalls wrote, "has partially resolved one of the central problems facing a political party seeking to build a conservative majority: how to persuade working and lower-middle-class voters to join in an alliance with business interests and the affluent."

Kennedy's support for an open convention was highly ironic. He had supported the reforms of 1968 that gave regular voters access to the primary process, taking control away from political machines that had been dominated by older white men and handing it to activists and ordinary citizens, many of them women and ethnic minorities. The "open convention" that Kennedy's forces argued for would be a return to the kind of system in which party bosses gathered behind closed doors to determine whom the party would nominate.

There was an argument for this approach. By 2016, Donald Trump would illustrate quite well the danger to a party of giving up control of its nomination to a primary system. Trump's win was a reminder that the old model, where parties chose nominees in a private process and then submitted them to the voters, was in line with the constitutional design of the government.

But voters had gone to the polls believing they were choosing a party's nominee, even though the rules did leave room for delegates at the convention to nominate whomever they wanted. Carter wanted the delegates bound by the votes of the primary. Kennedy wanted them to be free to use their own discretion, and if that meant defying the will of the primary voters, then so be it.

Nonetheless, supporters of the open convention had a point: If delegates were to merely reflect the popular vote in the primary, what was the point of even holding a convention? In truth, there wasn't much of one. Since the advent of television in the 1950s and the changes to primary rules prior to 1972, conventions had become increasingly little more than media spectacles, a giant and very expensive show, rather than an event with some actual determinative party purpose.

The *New York Times*'s Tom Wicker wrote that the binding requirement "eviscerates delegate responsibility, further diminishes the usefulness of the convention and the party itself." And the rule requiring delegates to vote according to the primary result was a new one, passed in 1978 by the Democratic National Committee and reaffirmed in a similar vote by the convention rules committee in early July.

The full convention would have to approve the rule in a vote during the official proceedings. Kennedy supporters began to refer to the new rule as the "robot rule." Wicker wrote that it would "[convert] the primacy of the primaries into a virtual tyranny." The debate went to the heart of what the American republic was designed to be at the nation's founding: How much direct democracy should there be?

Kennedy and Carter continued bickering in the days after their meeting. The White House made clear that Carter would not appear at a U.S. Conference of Mayors meeting in Seattle if Kennedy was onstage the same day. Kennedy ditched the mayors and rolled out a $12 billion jobs package in a different venue, during a speech in Anaheim, California, to the public employee union AFSCME (the American Federation of State, County and Municipal Employees). And Carter's forces tried to elect their own loyalist as a co-chairman of the Pennsylvania delegation, but fell short. Days later, another fight erupted in the Massachusetts delegation, with the White House successfully blocking two Kennedy aides from becoming delegates, but failing to stop Richard Stearns, Kennedy's delegate counter, from joining the delegation.

The day that Carter was in Miami being pelted with glass bottles, Kennedy's top aides met in D.C. to devise a plan to peel off delegates from the president. But they were behind the Carter operation, which already had a robust operation with fourteen regional leaders reporting to Donilon and monitoring state whips in each delegation. Those whips, in turn, had their own whips in each congressional district.

Kennedy, one week after his meeting with Carter, met with House Speaker Tip O'Neill and afterward told the press, "I have every intention of continuing in the race." He said the platform adopted by the pro-Carter forces was "Democratic in name only." He began comparing Carter to Reagan. Ham Jordan was worried about this line of attack, because a lot of Americans did not see much difference between Carter and Reagan. Bob Strauss, the DNC chairman, called Kennedy "spoiled." "It's pretty obvious Sen. Kennedy perceives his position on these issues as a holy writ. To be right on the issues you almost have to take a litmus test and agree with him on every one," he said.

For ten days following Carter's meeting with Kennedy, he was at the White House most of the time, except for the quick trip to Miami and a day trip to Seattle for the mayors' meeting. While in Washington State, he also met with disaster relief officials to review the response to the Mount St. Helens eruption on May 18, the worst volcanic eruption in recorded U.S. history, that had killed fifty-seven people and caused $1 billion in damage.

But then on June 19 he skipped town, and was gone for almost an entire month. With the primaries officially over, and the Democrats' own convention still nearly two months away, Carter would put some distance between himself and Kennedy, to get away from the relentless sniping still going on. While he did so, Hamilton Jordan retreated to his favorite haven—Maryland's Eastern Shore—to think, read books, and work on a memo for the president about the challenges ahead. It was the kind of radical step away from the daily grind that within a decade or so would become unthinkable to political strategists and presidential counselors in an election year. The first twenty-four-hour cable news network, CNN, had started that year. Its pace would create a more relentless news cycle and more demand for "news," regardless of whether it was news*worthy* or not. That would be just the first step toward the minute-by-minute news cycle of thirty and forty years later that would make the 1980s and '90s look almost medieval in terms of technological "progress." Jordan's memo informed the president that his yearlong battle with Kennedy, dating back to news coverage of Teddy's deliberations about a run for president in that awful summer of 1979, had "damaged severely" Carter's standing with the American people.

Carter would spend five days in Italy, then a few more in Yugoslavia, Spain, and Portugal. He'd come back for a three-day retreat at Camp David, spend three days in Washington, sign a bill deregulating the trucking industry with Kennedy, who'd sponsored the legislation, looming behind him, and then be off again, this time to California, then back to Miami for a speech to the NAACP, where the eight thousand members of the minority group would chant his name. (It was another sign of lackluster support for Kennedy among African Americans. Many resented his support for Senator Paul Tsongas, who had turned Edward Brooke out of office two years earlier.)

From Miami, Carter would go back to his roots, spending three days in Plains—his first trip back in ten months—before taking off on a three-day trip to Tokyo. And then it would be a weeklong vacation in Georgia, on Sapelo Island and at a fishing cabin in Hiawassee, a small town on the North Carolina border sandwiched between the massive Chattahoochee National Forest to the south and Nantahala National Forest to the north. If all went well, Carter would return to D.C. just after the Republican convention to find Anderson's candidacy gone and his own nomination in New York fully secured, free of the Kennedy nuisance.

Kennedy, however, didn't plan on going away quietly.

# CHAPTER 15

—∞∞∞—

# Losing Altitude

The only unpaved street in Plains, Georgia, while he was
governor, was the street in front of Billy Carter's house.
And it should have been paved.

—*Bert Lance*

Carter himself was hoping for some rest and relaxation on his
fourth day of vacation on Sapelo Island off the coast of Georgia,
on July 14. But that didn't mean sleeping in. He was up at 5:15
and went jogging twenty minutes later with friends Jim Bishop
and Carlton Hicks. He did not shower before meeting up with
Rosalynn and Charles Kirbo to board a vessel called the *Bagby* to
spend several hours deep-sea fishing. Even after eight hours on the
water, he and Rosalynn that evening spent another hour fishing
just by themselves at a nearby pond. The president ended his day
with a jeep ride on the beach.

In Detroit, the Republicans were kicking off their convention.
But in Washington, D.C., trouble was brewing. That same day the
Justice Department filed a civil complaint against the president's
younger brother, Billy Carter, for violating the Foreign Agents Registration Act. Billy, who was thirteen years younger than the president,

had failed to report to the government services he had rendered to the Libyan government by waging a "propaganda campaign" on behalf of the Arab country's foreign policy objectives. The Libyan government, which was deeply hostile to the United States and to Israel, had paid Billy $220,000 in cash, arranged two all-expenses paid trips to Libya in 1978 and 1979, and given him four gold bracelets, an expensive saddle, a serving platter, a suit, and a ceremonial sword.

For a year and a half, Billy had tried to help the Libyans gain access to key officials in the U.S. government who could help them obtain shipment of military aircraft. The United States had sold Libya the planes in 1973 but then refused to ship them because of Libya's support for anti-Israel terrorism. Billy had also been working for the Charter Oil Company of Jacksonville, Florida, seeking to help the company obtain crude oil from Libya. President Carter had asked his brother in April 1979, in a phone conversation, and in a formal letter, not to travel to Libya anymore, and yet Billy had continued to pursue financial dealings with the country, and did in fact make a second trip there in late August 1979.

On the day that the Justice Department filed their complaint, following a seven-month investigation, Billy Carter registered as an agent of Libya. So the president's brother was officially working for a country whose citizens had a few months earlier stormed the American embassy in Tripoli and set it ablaze. The White House tried to distance the president from his younger brother. White House spokesman Ray Jenkins announced that the issue was "a matter between the Justice Department and a private individual who happens to be the president's brother." Still, the president made a public statement condemning his brother's actions. "I do not believe it is appropriate for a close relative of the president to undertake any assignment on behalf of a foreign government," Carter said.

Billy Carter had always been different. He owned and operated a gas station in Plains. He started his own brand of beer called Billy

Beer. It had been funny for the first year or two of Jimmy Carter's presidency, but in 1979 Billy became a major embarrassment for his older brother, and a political problem. In January of that year, he had hosted a delegation of Libyans in Atlanta. As he waited for them at the airport, he urinated on the runway in full view of a reporter.

When the Jewish community in Atlanta complained about Billy's behavior, he responded, "All I can say is there is a hell of a lot more Arabs than there is Jews." He also accused the mayor of Atlanta, Maynard Jackson, of refusing to meet with the Libyan contingent because of pressure from "the Jews."

In late February 1979, Billy Carter was hospitalized for eleven days in Americus for alcoholism and acute bronchitis. He admitted himself in early March for alcoholism treatment at a naval hospital in Long Beach, California. He was facing enormous debts, and his income from public appearances and product endorsements had dried up thanks to his public behavior.

On Tuesday, July 15, 1980, news of the Justice Department complaint against Billy Carter hit the front page of the *New York Times*, sharing space with news of the Republican convention's first day and Reagan's promise to make America "great again." A week later, the story hit the headlines again, this time with reports possibly linking Billy to a plot by Libyan operatives in the United States to bribe American government officials. On Wednesday, July 23, the front page of the *Times* blared, BILLY CARTER SET UP BRZEZINSKI MEETING WITH LIBYAN ON IRAN. Carter's national security adviser, Zbigniew Brzezinski, had used Billy as a go-between to start talks with the Libyan government to see if they would be helpful in getting the Iranians to release the American hostages. That same day, Senate leaders agreed to launch a bipartisan investigation into the matter.

And so three weeks before the Democratic convention—and just months before the fall election—the Senate Judiciary Committee and the Justice Department opened investigations into whether Billy had broken the law and whether the White House had done anything improper as well. And the day after the Senate agreed to investigate, the *New York Times* headline put the president's wife, Rosalynn, at the center of the story. WIFE OF PRESIDENT ASKED BILLY CARTER FOR AID ON HOSTAGES, the front page screamed. PLAN REPORTEDLY WAS HERS.

Rosalynn had called Billy two weeks after the hostages were taken, without talking to Jimmy first, and asked him to see if his Libyan contacts could help get the hostages out of Iran. In his diary entry the next day, Jimmy Carter wrote that Rosalynn was "quite upset about headlines in the paper." The president suggested to her that she read John 14:1: "Let not your heart be troubled."

Carter allies downplayed the imbroglio. "Rare is the family that doesn't have a black sheep," said Tip O'Neill. As if to illustrate the point, federal officials seized Billy Carter's deed to a fifty-eight-acre property in Buena Vista, Georgia, twenty-five miles north of Plains, because of back taxes that Billy owed.

The debacle breathed new life into Kennedy's hopes of winning the nomination at the convention. It wasn't just Billy Carter. The patriotic fervor of the winter had waned and been replaced by anger over a still stagnant economy, high inflation, and rising unemployment. Carter was trailing Reagan in the polls by 25 or 30 points. "A few weeks ago, most of us didn't think there was a chance. Now there's some hope that we can pull it off," said one Kennedy aide. As Kennedy campaign staffers met in Hyannis Port, one of them wore a button that said, "Win with Ted or Lose with Carter."

⚬⚬⚬

The Republicans didn't expect much drama at their convention one month before the Democrats'. But Reagan was unable to choose a running mate before it started, and that was all the suspense the press needed to turn the convention into a soap opera. The media seized on the idea that Reagan might pick former president Gerald

Ford. Over the course of two days, the GOP proceedings in Detroit went from a sleepy affair to a frenzied mob scene.

Reagan asked Ford to consider the vice presidency on Tuesday evening, the second night of the convention. George H. W. Bush was a far more logical choice to moderate Reagan's image as a hard-line conservative, but Reagan couldn't stand him. Ford was initially skeptical of Reagan's request, but he didn't reject the idea. The conversation between the two men presented an opening for their staffs to begin a negotiating process that quickly became a vehicle for Ford advisers, especially former secretary of state Henry Kissinger, to attempt a power grab.

In a series of meetings that began late Tuesday and then escalated into Wednesday, the two sides discussed giving Ford what amounted to a co-presidency: "veto power over Reagan's cabinet choices... authority over the budget, the Domestic Council, the National Security Council, the Pentagon, and the State Department." A growing number of Reagan advisers were alarmed by the talks with Ford's men. But what became known as the "dream ticket" took on a life of its own as delegates swooned over the idea, as Reagan and Ford toyed with it, and as the media sprinted with the story.

The three TV networks vied to outdo each other with breathless speculation on live air, trying to hold the attention of viewers and hoping to be the first to break the big story. "We heard," ABC's Lynn Sherr reported live from the floor, "from Senator [Richard] Schweiker that Senator [Paul] Laxalt told someone else who then told Senator Schweiker that it would be Gerald Ford!"

On Wednesday evening, around 7:15 p.m., Ford and his wife, Betty, trekked to the CBS News booth inside Joe Louis Arena for a live interview with Walter Cronkite. The broadcasting legend, wearing a dark suit and red tie, asked Ford about his feelings toward a "co-presidency." The sixty-seven-year-old former president, who had clashed so bitterly with Reagan just four years earlier at the

1976 convention, made his most favorable public comments about the idea yet. He certainly seemed to be warming to it. "I would not go to Washington, Walter, and be a figurehead vice president," Ford said, with Betty sitting to his right on the other side of a large round table, out of the camera shot.

The former president's thinning blond hair was combed back over his bald pate. His pale, ruddy complexion and bullheaded appearance complemented his light blue suit and dark blue tie. "If I go to Washington—and I'm not saying that I'm accepting—I have to go there with the belief that I will play a meaningful role across the board in the basic and the crucial and the important decisions that have to be made in a four-year period," Ford said.

Reagan, moments earlier, had told a friend that he planned to pick Ford. But when Cronkite mentioned a co-presidency and Ford did not shoot down the term or the idea, Reagan blanched. "Did you hear what he just said?" he said to those around him. It was dawning on Reagan, who perhaps had not fully grasped or even been told the full details of the talks between his camp and Ford's, that this was not a good idea.

Reagan continued to resist the idea of selecting Bush. But he was running out of time. At 11:13 p.m., he was officially nominated for president by the party. The delegates in the hall now expected him and Ford to appear together onstage, as the media had been reporting all day would happen. But Ford's advance team told reporters the former president was not coming to the hall that night, and Reagan's communications trailer asked the band to keep playing music to stall and give Reagan time to make a decision.

Five minutes before clocks struck midnight, Cronkite tossed to Lesley Stahl on the floor, who he said had more information "on why this demonstration is being prolonged." As the camera cut to Stahl, she was looking over her right shoulder with a breathless expression. She hesitated, and the live feed showed Cronkite gazing at a monitor that showed Stahl looking around her on the floor, surrounded by dancing delegates waving signs to the band's music. "Uh, Lesley," Cronkite prompted her. Stahl let loose a bombshell, speaking as if she could not believe what she was saying.

"Uh, Walter, I am just being told by a high lieutenant the choice is Bush!" Her eyes went wide as she said it. "I am being told that the choice is Bush and he's telling me that I can go with it." She smiled breathlessly, as if she couldn't believe both the surprise and the fact that she was the one breaking the news.

"Uhhh, I'm being told for sure," she said again, looking to her right at whoever was talking to her as she reported the news live to millions of Americans. "Apparently the deal fell through. A couple of senators were just pulled off the floor. . . . I'm sorry I can't get to a second person to get it confirmed, but they just came running over to me, shouting at me, and said, 'Go with it, it's absolutely true.'"

Stahl flashed a huge smile and gulped a big breath of air as she finished. Cronkite had to pick himself up off the floor. "Lesley Stahl, that's the most amazing piece of news we've heard since we heard it was Ford," he said. "Now hold on just a second. Who told you that?" He still couldn't quite comprehend what he was hearing.

"Walter, a top lieutenant came and said, 'It's not Ford,'" Stahl said, still astounded. "They're all yelling Bush all around me. Everybody's yelling Bush." She looked up at someone passing in front of her and asked them simply, "Bush?" She got their response and nodded. "They're telling me Bush, Walter. Reagan lieutenants, men with colored hats all around, telling me Bush."

"Well they better bring the adrenaline up here to the anchor booth," Cronkite said. Stahl just laughed and looked around her, and said nothing more. The camera came back to Cronkite, who laughed, then put his head in his left hand for a moment, passing it over his face in a split second that revealed his mortification at the network's reporting over the previous few hours.

Bush, who had been stewing all evening about being passed over, was shocked by the phone call he received from Reagan at 11:37 p.m., a few minutes after Reagan and Ford met to agree that they would not run together. He wasn't even dressed in a proper shirt and tie when reporters arrived in his suite. The *Times*'s Clyde Haberman described him as "haggard-looking" and wearing a polo shirt. Nevertheless, Bush gladly accepted Reagan's offer.

Thirteen minutes after midnight, the band playing in the hall abruptly stopped and there was a moment of quiet, then cheering as the Reagans emerged from backstage and strode to the microphones. After Reagan had quieted the wild cheers from the audience, he gave a brief but unequivocal speech.

"I know that I am breaking precedent to come here tonight," he said. "But in watching at the hotel the television and seeing the rumors that were going around and the gossip that was taking place here, I felt that it was necessary to break with tradition, just as probably in this campaign we're going to break with tradition a lot."

There was a hint of sheepishness in Reagan's body language. "Let me, as simply as I can, straighten out and bring this to a conclusion," he said, bowing his head a little and extending his hands apologetically. "It is true that a number of Republican leaders, people in our party, officeholders, felt...that a proper ticket would have included the former president of the United States, Gerald Ford, as second place on the ticket." The crowd broke into cheers, but Reagan motioned for quiet, with a look of disappointment and slight alarm.

"And it is true also that we have gone over this and over this and over this, and he and I have come to the conclusion, and he believes deeply, that he can be of more value as the former president campaigning his heart out, which he has pledged to do, and not, and not as a member of the ticket," Reagan said. The hall rang with respectful but disappointed applause.

Then, rather informally, Reagan announced his choice. "I talked to a man we all know and a man who was a candidate, a man who has great experience in government"—there were the rumblings of cheers in the hall—"and a man who told me that he can enthusiastically support the platform across the board. I have asked, and I am recommending to this convention, that tomorrow, when the session reconvenes, that George Bush be nominated." Pandemonium erupted, and Reagan couldn't get the rest of his sentence out. There were screams, horns, cheering, and Reagan's closing words were swallowed by the din.

Reagan's convention speech the next night made up for much of the ground he had lost during the chaos of the convention's first few days. The energy of the crowd conveyed a sense that the GOP felt they had a man to lead them to victory in the fall. The imagery sent a message to the nation that this was a different kind of Republican. Beneath the podium, in big white letters on a blue background, a massive cloth banner said, "Together . . . A New Beginning." It was communal, progressive language, the kind uttered more often historically by liberal Democrats.

Reagan's speech was an effective tableau of appeals to groups usually neglected by the Republican Party—minorities and women in particular—and attacks on Carter's "mediocre leadership" at home and abroad. Reagan charged that with Carter at the helm, "the ship has no rudder."

He rejected the idea that America was destined for decline, and pledged to restore the nation's greatness. He promised to run a government with "the capacity to do the people's work without dominating their lives." He spoke out against discrimination against women. He told minorities that in the fight to move forward "we're not going to leave anyone behind." He castigated Carter for instituting a registration for the draft while cutting veterans' benefits.

Reagan ended with a bit of stagecraft that was catnip for the religious right. "I'll confess that I've been a little afraid to suggest what I'm going to suggest," he said, and then he choked up. "I'm more afraid not to." His voice had a slight tremor as he asked the rapt audience, "Can we begin our crusade joined together in a moment of silent prayer?" He closed his eyes, bowed his head, and breathed in deeply. He was quiet for a full eleven seconds.

Reagan broke the silence, and ended the speech, with three simple words: "God bless America." He paused, and as the audience took it in, he nodded emphatically and stepped back from the lectern. After the brief delay, there was an uproarious cheer. It was a triumphant night for Reagan, for conservatives, and for the Republican Party.

Hamilton Jordan and other Carter advisers had watched the Ford co-presidency chaos with satisfaction. But they had also noted Reagan's ability to quickly regain control, and his mastery of television.

---

BillyGate continued to spiral at the end of July, with new information dripping out daily to a political press still drunk from the rush of Watergate. Attorney General Benjamin Civiletti admitted that, contrary to prior statements, he actually had briefly discussed with the president the Justice Department's investigation into Billy Carter in mid-June. A little over a week earlier, Civiletti had been asked by the *New York Times* whether he had discussed the Billy Carter investigation with anyone at the White House. "No, it was never discussed with anybody over there," the attorney general had said.

Civiletti now admitted he had told the president that Billy was a "damn fool" for not registering as an agent of the Libyan government. Carter had then asked the attorney general what would happen if Billy registered, and Civiletti told him that as long as someone had registered, "the previous failure to register has not been prosecutable." This, however, was not necessarily true, as

Justice Department officials were in the process of considering a criminal complaint. Nonetheless, the president had called his brother June 28 and then again on July 1 and urged him to sign the foreign agents permit.

The same day as Civiletti's admission, Senator Sam Nunn, a Democrat from Carter's own state of Georgia, and Senator Henry "Scoop" Jackson, a Washington State Democrat, told Carter's organizers they would decline to speak at the convention. "Scoop is obviously trying to get himself promoted as the nominee," Carter wrote in his diary.

Also that day, a group of forty junior members of Congress met in Washington to discuss opening up the convention so delegates could vote for whoever they wanted, rather than according to their state primaries. However, this group didn't want Carter or Kennedy. They were unimpressed with both, and talk increasingly was of drafting Vice President Mondale or Secretary of State Edmund Muskie to unite the fractured wings of the party to take on Reagan in the fall. Nonetheless, any talk of an "open convention" was an opportunity for the Kennedy forces to exploit. Muskie, like Jackson, was making small gestures that indicated openness to such a scenario.

Senior Democratic leaders in Congress and across the country had held off on breaking with the president, but then on Monday, July 28, the dam began to burst. New York Democrats voiced support for the open convention movement. New York governor Hugh Carey traveled to Washington to bolster the Committee for an Open Convention started by members of Congress. Carey said he would begin traveling the country to promote the effort. New York mayor Ed Koch said Carter might lose the state and that he might withdraw his support for the president.

At Camp David, Carter and his advisers discussed an even more concerning development. Senate Majority Leader Robert Byrd, a West Virginia Democrat, was trying to organize an effort to get

Carter to drop out of the race. He'd held a lunch with other senators, but failed to persuade them to talk to the president.

The next day, Carter said he would respond "in person" to the Senate's inquiry into Billy Carter, and was "eager" to do so. But the public chorus for an open convention continued to grow. Connecticut governor Ella Grasso endorsed the idea. James Reston wrote in the *New York Times* that Carter's best hope to unite his party and have any hope of winning in the fall was to release his delegates and try to win the nomination at the convention. "He didn't really 'run' in the primaries at all," Reston wrote. "He stayed in the White House. He didn't run against Kennedy, but against Ayatollah Khomeini."

And on July 30, a Louis Harris/ABC News poll showed Carter with a 77 percent disapproval rating, "the worst rating of any American President in the history of polling," Jordan wrote. It was "worse even than Nixon at the height of Watergate." Another poll showed Carter losing California two-to-one to Reagan. Anderson, at 23 percent, had more support in the state than did the president. Democratic senators and congressmen up for reelection were terrified that they would be dragged down to defeat by Carter's unpopularity.

On July 31, Kennedy and John Anderson held a strange meeting in Washington. Anderson by this point had managed to get his name on the presidential ballot in all fifty states in a matter of weeks after he went independent, a highly impressive organizational feat. He and Kennedy emerged from their meeting and Anderson said he would consider dropping out if President Carter gave up the presidency after his one term.

Privately, Carter was still confident. "I have a lot of problems on my shoulders," he wrote in his diary. "But strangely enough, I feel better as they pile up." He was confident that the answers he was compiling for the Senate inquiry into his brother's relationship with Libya would vindicate him. But he noted that his aides and advisers were very worried. "My main concern is propping up the people around me who tend to panic," he wrote. However, he allowed for a moment of self-doubt. Those who were more concerned, he wrote, "might possibly have a better and clearer picture of the situation than I do."

Two days later Byrd publicly backed an open convention, saying Carter would have "a stronger mandate" if he won the nomination based on "the personal preference of delegates based on current circumstances." Byrd also rapped Carter, saying his decision to involve Billy Carter in the hostage crisis response showed "bad judgment" and was "rather amateurish." Six Democratic governors and 113 Democratic members of Congress also supported choosing the nominee at the convention.

Carter was on the verge of losing control of his party and the presidency. The Carter campaign did a "hard count" of how many delegates they could count on to vote with them against an open convention. Their margin was down to "a few delegates," Donilon told me years later. The Illinois and New York delegations were tottering, and if their support evaporated, it could trigger an avalanche away from Carter. "We absolutely felt we could lose the convention," Donilon said.

In a panic, Carter's advisers, as well as Vice President Mondale and his advisers, were summoned back from their August vacations to try and save him. "We've got a full-fledged revolt on our hands," Hamilton Jordan said.

Kennedy was cautiously hopeful. On a flight to Los Angeles to meet with wavering delegates in California, he told reporters he "hope[d] the right chemistry develops." He dangled the possibility that he would announce a running mate as the convention in New York was beginning, to build a positive energy.

"Conventions have a certain momentum of their own," he said.

# CHAPTER 16

———◆◆◆———

# Giant Killer

The six temporary trailers were set up in a circle deep within the bowels of Madison Square Garden, like a series of covered wagons on the western frontier. The arrangement said everything: The people inside this makeshift camp were hunkered down, and under duress.

Hamilton Jordan walked into one of the trailers on the afternoon of Monday, August 11. Inside were Jody Powell, Carter's press secretary and confidant; Jerry Rafshoon, his media consultant; and Bob Strauss, his campaign chairman. All of them had spent the day shuttling from one hotel ballroom to another, meeting with state delegations to ensure that Carter's support stayed firm. President Carter was at Camp David. He had gone fishing around 2:30 in the afternoon and would be gone for roughly two hours.

As the four men gathered in the trailer, the air was thick with anxiety. They believed they had more than enough rock-solid support among the delegates to win a vote that evening on whether to open the convention. After the panic in late July and early August over the Justice Department investigation of Billy Carter, the president himself had calmed the waters. His impressive hour-long press conference on August 5 was reassuring to many. He had laid out all the facts and argued persuasively that no impropriety had occurred.

Carter's lieutenants went over their detailed count again. They had a lead of several hundred delegates over Kennedy, based on the primary vote totals in each state. They had a database with each delegate's age, employment, key issues, hobbies, and a record of who their friends and enemies were. There was a Carter volunteer, called a "whip," for every ten delegates, who was in constant contact with his or her assigned targets. They had phones in every state delegation with red lights that blinked when the command post was calling, because nobody would hear the phone ringing over the din of the convention. The phone lines that ran from the Carter trailers to each state delegation were encased in copper, to prevent anyone from cutting the cords. They had thought of just about everything.

But there was one thing they couldn't prevent: what Jordan called "a stampede." So they spent each minute scanning the state delegations for small leaks, plugging them as quickly as possible to prevent a flood.

Rumors flew all day of defections away from Carter. As soon as the news reached the Carter compound, one of the "gerbils" in a separate trailer would call the whip assigned to those delegates. The whips, wearing green-and-white vests and hats, would check in with their delegates. If there was a legitimate concern, it would be relayed back to the trailers, and the delegates would be contacted by someone higher up in Carter world. When one of the leaders of the Illinois delegation began to waffle, Jordan conferred with Tom Donilon, the twenty-five-year-old Carter aide in charge of the delegate operation. Donilon told Jordan to relax. "He's been bought off," he said.

"What the hell did you promise?" Jordan asked, bemused. "A federal judgeship or an ambassadorship?"

"No," Donilon said. "This guy had a lot of family and friends in for the convention. I gave him a handful of VIP passes." Other delegates asked simply for more tickets. Some asked for friends to be released from prison.

The Carter forces were especially worried about the Pennsylvania and Illinois delegations. Kennedy had spoken to them on Sunday evening and promised them victory. Then, a little after 6 p.m., Jordan received notice of a serious problem in a different state: The entire Maine delegation was about to desert Carter. It wasn't even to support Kennedy. The Mainers were preparing to join a movement to draft Edmund Muskie, the former Maine governor, U.S. senator, and presidential candidate in 1972, to enter his name into nomination. Muskie was at this time Carter's secretary of state. Jordan quickly called Carter at Camp David. Three minutes later the president was on the phone with Muskie. Within fifteen minutes, Muskie had called the Maine delegation and instructed them not to join the movement trying to draft him into the race.

The fact that there was a Draft Muskie movement at all showed how odious the idea of renominating Carter for a second term had become to many Democrats. But it also showed that Kennedy was not the righteous white knight he believed himself to be. There had been talk for days leading up to the convention of attempts to draft a multitude of figures in addition to Muskie, including Scoop Jackson, the senator from Washington, and Senator Robert Byrd of West Virginia. In fact, some argued that Kennedy's candidacy may have actually stymied the move for an open convention, because many Democrats who did not want to nominate Carter were now disillusioned with Kennedy. But despite all that, Carter's lieutenants knew that a revolt in any state delegation, for any reason, would open the door to chaos and to a loss. "If this thing gets open, anything can happen," Jordan told Donilon.

The debate over the rule to forbid an open convention went on

for some time. The Carter forces held down their support dog-
gedly, hour by hour. Finally, around 8 p.m., it was time to vote.
Elizabeth Drew noted a "limpness" inside Madison Square Garden as the vote went forward. The Democratic Party had reached
the end of a brutal, unsatisfactory process, and didn't have the will
or appetite for a convention that went off the rails. If the Republican convention had demonstrated anything, it was that chaos
didn't help a party's brand. Carter won the final vote on the rule,
with 1,936 votes to Kennedy's 1,390.

At 9:46 p.m., Kennedy called Carter and told him he was
dropping out. After Carter got off the phone, Jordan asked the
president if Kennedy had assured him of his support in the general
election against Reagan. "I didn't press him, Ham," Carter said.
"It was an uncomfortable call for him. I'm not sure what he'll do
Thursday or in the fall."

Kennedy, looking emotional and grave, made a brief statement
to the TV cameras. "I'm deeply gratified by the support I received
on the rules fight tonight—but not quite as gratified as President
Carter," he said. "I'm a realist and I know what this result means. I
have called President Carter and congratulated him. The effort on
the nomination is over. My name will not be placed in nomination."

The repetition and redundancy in Kennedy's words signaled a
certain amount of disbelief. This was new ground for a Kennedy,
admitting defeat in a high-stakes contest, much less the biggest
stage in American politics. It was shocking. He had entered the
race less than a year before believing he was virtually assured of
victory. And now he was the first Kennedy to lose a major political contest. In addition, he had torn the Democratic Party in two,
leaving the sitting president badly wounded and vulnerable to his
Republican challenger.

But Kennedy was not in a regretful mood. If he could not have the nomination, he would have his revenge, and he would fight Carter on the platform tooth and nail. The president would pay for having defeated and humiliated him. "I continue to care deeply about the ideals of the Democratic Party. I continue to care deeply about where this party stands, and I hope the delegates will stand with me for a truly Democratic platform," Kennedy then said, sounding a note of defiance.

"Tomorrow, I will speak to the convention about the economic concerns that have been the heart of my campaign, and about the commitments in the future of the Democratic Party. I will speak again for the people I have seen in the cause I have carried across this country," he said. And that was that.

True to Kennedy's word, the fight was just getting started. A week earlier, the morning after Carter's press conference to deal with his brother's Libyan connections, Kennedy's top aides had secured a prime-time speaking slot for the senator. They had met with Ham Jordan at the Capital Hilton in Washington, and agreed to forgo most of the procedural maneuvers they had planned to disrupt the convention. They had threatened to tie up the proceedings with endless minority reports. Carter wanted to show a strong, united party to the national television audience. So he gave Kennedy his speaking slot, and the Kennedy campaign agreed to withdraw most of their minority reports.

That would have been enough for most politicians. But Kennedy and his operation seethed at their defeat, and continued to undermine Carter. The morning after Kennedy withdrew, his team was intent on embarrassing Carter on the convention's second night, when the delegates would vote for a party platform. Kennedy's camp was pushing to include planks that were a rebuke to the president: a call for a $12 billion stimulus spending program, a measure to fight unemployment, and an endorsement of wage and price controls.

The vote would come right after Kennedy was slotted to speak to the convention. The Carter forces knew that the senator's speech would create an atmosphere highly favorable for his platform proposals to pass, and that many of their delegates were already leaning toward doing so. The delegates had had to say no over and over to Kennedy whips on Monday, and were exhausted. They wanted to say yes to something.

Strauss could not understand why Kennedy insisted on continuing to fight. "If you have any wisdom and judgment at all, you know you don't get carried away by personalities and pettiness in a political fight," he said. "Politics is tough enough...that you don't cut each other's throats." But Jody Powell, Carter's press secretary, thought he knew. "We neglected to take into account one of the most obvious facets of Kennedy's character, an almost childlike self-centeredness," he recounted with great bitterness after the election.

Tensions were so high that high-ranking members of the dueling factions almost got into a fistfight on Tuesday. Harold Ickes, who was running the floor operation for Kennedy, used an obscure procedural rule to call a halt to the proceedings. It was a gesture done purely out of spite. "We just said, 'Fuck 'em.' This had turned into a real grudge match," Ickes said. "I mean, we weren't thinking about the country. We weren't even thinking about the general election. It was, 'Fuck 'em.' You know? To be blunt about it."

Tom Donilon was livid. The Carter aide was personally responsible for seeing that the 1980 Democratic convention went off without any major hitches, and he had just been blindsided. The convention had been stopped, for no apparent reason, on the second day of proceedings, by Kennedy forces. Donilon threw down his headset and stormed toward the stage, where he found a Carter lawyer named Tim Smith physically grappling with Ickes as they came down the stairs from the stage. "What the fuck are you doing? You can't do this!" Donilon yelled at Ickes. His outrage caused his already ruddy complexion to glow red.

Ickes, then forty, sneered at the younger political operative. "Go fuck yourself. I'm shutting this convention down, Tom," he said. For a few moments, the two men were on the verge of blows. Several minutes went by. The phone on the podium rang. It was Kennedy, calling for Ickes from his room at the Waldorf Astoria. Several Kennedy advisers were also on the phone. "Harold, I'm watching the convention, what's going on down there?" Kennedy asked Ickes.

"Well, Senator, you know they didn't comply with this rule," Ickes responded, explaining the technicality he had used to stop the proceedings.

"How long do you expect this convention to be shut down?" Kennedy said.

"For two hours," Ickes said.

There was a long pause. Then Kennedy spoke, gently, but pointedly.

"Harold, I think it's time we got on with the convention," he said.

When Kennedy reached the platform later that evening, the mood inside the Garden was electric. He began with a joke: "Well, things worked out a little different from the way I thought, but let me tell you, I still love New York." Those in the hall laughed, with a tinge of sadness. In his next breath, he said, "I have come here tonight not to argue as a candidate but to affirm a cause." It was a subtle but unmistakable distancing of himself from Carter. The cause, he said, was to fight for what Andrew Jackson referred to as "the humble members of society—the farmers, mechanics, and laborers." He went on to attack Reagan heartily as "no friend of labor...no friend of this city and our great urban centers across this nation...no friend of the senior citizens of this nation...no friend of the environment."

Kennedy acknowledged and rebuffed the critique that the left's ideas were stale. "The great adventures which our opponents offer is a voyage into the past. Progress is our heritage, not theirs," Kennedy said. "The commitment I seek is not to outworn views but to old values that will never wear out. Programs may sometimes become obsolete, but the ideal of fairness always endures."

But even the *New York Times* editorial page wrote in response to Kennedy's speech that "a big reason Senator Kennedy did not win is that many people feared his answers to social problems are too liberal, by which they mean, obsolete or too expensive or both." The editorial argued, "One can regret the turn to conservatism in America; one can rail against it; one can work to reverse it. But through much of his campaign, the Senator pressed on as though it didn't exist."

However, the final minutes of Kennedy's remarks made it one of the most memorable political speeches in modern political history. "There were hard hours on our journey, and often we sailed against the wind," he said. When he had first used that phrase, almost two years earlier in Memphis, it was a defiant signal that he intended to fight Carter for the nomination. He had been a sailor in a racing vessel, gaining speed, looking at the headwinds and feeling himself ready to take them on.

When he had used it a year after that, at the dedication of his older brother's presidential library, it had been an almost flippant dismissal of an incumbent president whom he, and most others, expected to be easily swept aside. But now the phrase meant something entirely different. Kennedy's quest was now similar to that of Santiago, from Hemingway's *The Old Man and the Sea*. He made it back to the shore, utterly exhausted, and defeated.

But, like Santiago, Kennedy took pride in what he had fought to accomplish, even in a losing effort.

"But always we kept our rudder true, and there were so many of you who stayed the course and shared our hope," Kennedy said, thanking his die-hard supporters. He had not been an enthusiastic campaigner in Iowa, but after he was forced by early defeats to work for votes, his travels across the country to seek support had made their mark, one handshake, one face, one conversation at a time. "You gave your help, but even more, you gave your hearts. And because of you this has been a happy campaign. You welcomed Joan, me, and our family into your homes and neighborhoods, your churches, your campuses, your union halls."

Kennedy mentioned people he had met in his time crisscrossing the states: a father of ten children in West Virginia who lost his job after thirty-five years, three years short of receiving his full pension; a family in Iowa struggling to keep their farm; a grandmother in Oakland who in order to pay the rent had given up her phone service and couldn't call her grandchildren.

"I have listened to workers out of work, to students without the tuition for college, and to families without the chance to own a home. I have seen the closed factories and the stalled assembly lines of Anderson, Indiana, and South Gate, California, and I have seen too many, *far* too many, idle men and women *desperate* to work," Kennedy said, and here he shifted into a different gear. His face bore the strain of a long fight coming to an end, and his voice echoed throughout the silent hall.

"I have seen too many, *far* too many, working families *desperate* to protect the value of their wages from the ravages of inflation. Yet I have also sensed a yearning for a new hope among the people in every state where I have been," he said. "Tonight, in their name, I have come here to speak for them, and for their sake I ask you to stand with them."

Even the Carter trailer compound was quiet, in uneasy awe. Hamilton Jordan could feel the power of the Kennedy magic working its will on him. "For a long year, Ted Kennedy had been the enemy...but it was difficult for me to see him in the convention setting without thinking of his family and its tragedies, of Bobby Kennedy's emotional appearance at the 1964 convention, when he stood looking sad while Democrats cheered and cried for half an hour," Jordan wrote.

Now, sixteen years later, another Kennedy stood before a Democratic convention, not the same as his brothers, not their equal, but having shown himself to be unique in a way that many found admirable. "Ted Kennedy's words triggered open the floodgates of memories: Camelot, magic rhetoric, and the shock of the assassinations," Jordan wrote.

For Kennedy, that night was the halfway point of an uneven career, one that careened between mediocrity and disaster until evening out into a place of respectability, and then great achievement. In the moment, all he knew was that he had not quit, not admitted defeat, and had, at last, perhaps come to want the presidency as badly as others had wanted it for him.

Kennedy gave a brief acknowledgment of President Carter. But there was a caveat in his promise of party unity. It was not an unqualified support for Carter. He said the unification would happen "on the basis of Democratic principles."

Finally, Kennedy's last words were a eulogy for his campaign. He sought to capture its essence as having upheld something bigger and greater even than politics. He cast himself in defeat as a prophetic figure, a Jeremiah whose intransigence and bullheadedness was an effort to call his brothers and sisters in the party back to their faith, an attempt to redeem and redirect his wayward party and a wayward president.

"And someday, long after this convention, long after the signs come down and the crowds stop cheering, and the bands stop playing, may it be said of our campaign that we kept the faith. May it be said of our party in 1980 that we found our faith again," he said.

Kennedy's final words transcended politics and connected with his family's past. "And may it be said of us, both in dark passages and in bright days, in the words of Tennyson that my brothers quoted and loved, and that have special meaning for me now," he said, his voice breaking just slightly. "'I am a part of all that I have met. Too much is taken, much abides. That which we are, we are: one equal temper of heroic hearts, strong in will to strive, to seek, to find, and not to yield.'"

As he quoted from pieces of Tennyson's poem "Ulysses," Kennedy evoked the memory and grief of all the losses and tragedies in the Kennedy family and his own life. "Too much is taken" spoke to the death of Joe Jr. in World War II, JFK's assassination, Bobby's assassination, his sister Kathleen's fatal plane crash, his sister Rosemary's lobotomy, the cancer that cost his son Teddy Jr. his right leg, and the tragic plane crash that nearly killed Kennedy himself. "Much abides" spoke to his sense of gratefulness for what he still had left. "That which we are, we are" was a poetic way of stating what was clearly true: He was a deeply blemished human being, and could not change that. And the closing words of the poem spoke to what had been the driving theme of his candidacy—a determination "not to yield."

Kennedy's voice rose to a crescendo as he paid tribute to his family name and to the dream of Camelot: something that was too good to be true, a fairytale period that lasted only a short time and had its truest essence more in the minds of JFK's admirers than in reality.

"For me, a few hours ago, this campaign came to an end. For all those whose cares have been our concern, the work goes on, the cause endures, the hope still lives, and the dream shall never die," Kennedy said.

With one more nod to the audience—a wooden, almost formal nod—and a barely audible 'Thank you very much,'" he turned from the podium. The hall exploded and the delegates' applause and cheering lasted almost thirty minutes. It was "one of the great emotional outpourings of convention history."

The vote on the party platform was to come immediately after Kennedy's speech, and now the Carter forces were entirely disheartened. All the emotion in the hall was now with Kennedy, and he had made clear in his speech that he believed the party needed to come his way on policy. Jordan and Strauss entreated the whips to fight for their version of the platform, but they knew it was a lost cause. And so they accepted two out of Kennedy's three proposals: the $12 billion stimulus program, and a call for a jobs bill.

Carter's people cut a deal with the Kennedy camp to avoid an extended roll call vote on each measure, which they likely would have lost. House Speaker Tip O'Neill, who was chairing the convention, gaveled the results through quickly, ignoring the loud cries of support for the third measure from the floor. The deal that the Carter camp had reached with Kennedy's people ensured that there would be no official protest or complaint. Still, a sitting president had accepted a platform at his own convention that included measures he opposed.

—✺—

Carter now had to unite the party in his speech on the convention's final night. He got off to a rough start. As he began, a loud series of firecrackers went off in the crowd less than a hundred feet to his left, set off by a woman named Signe Waller from the Communist Workers Party. The explosions caused the president to flinch and to pause his delivery, and rattled everyone in the hall.

Just after that, another woman from the communist group—thirty-one-year-old Dale Sampson—stood and began shouting at Carter. She and Waller were both demonstrating to bring attention to the deaths of their husbands in a violent confrontation with the Ku Klux Klan the previous fall. Dr. James Waller and Bill Sampson had been organizing mostly black textile workers in Greensboro, North Carolina, and had been shot and killed by members of the KKK and the American Nazi Party during a confrontation on November 3, 1979.

Secret Service agents removed both women, but outside the hall police clashed with another hundred or so CWP members who tried to storm the convention hall carrying sticks and Mace, sending six officers to the hospital with head injuries.

Carter also reinforced his image as a bumbler by making a hilarious verbal gaffe when thanking people at the beginning of his speech. "We're the party... of a great man who should have been president, who would have been one of the greatest presidents in history, Hubert Horatio Hornblower!" he shouted. The crowd reacted with confused applause, and Carter reached for the words to try to pull them back in with a shouted correction. "Humphrey!" he said. He had mistakenly referred to the former vice president, senator, and Democratic nominee for president, who had died of cancer in 1978, as the fictional protagonist of C. S. Forester's popular series of novels.

After these distractions, Carter made an overture to Kennedy. "Ted, your party needs, and I need, your idealism and dedication working for us," he said. After appealing to Kennedy for unity, Carter launched into a series of attacks on Reagan and the Republicans, portraying the GOP nominee as an unreliable warmonger.

The speech was immediately panned by some. "This was a speech that brought the crowd to its seats, not to its feet. This was a memo, not a speech," Jeff Greenfield said on CBS afterward. But in fact, the most talked-about few moments of the convention had yet to transpire.

When Carter finished his speech, Kennedy was still at the Waldorf Astoria in his room, about twenty blocks away from Madison Square Garden. That was by agreement. The Kennedy and Carter camps had haggled beforehand over where Kennedy would watch the speech. Kennedy had refused to be in the hall, and he had also decided he did not want to watch from a suite or holding room inside the Garden.

But Ham Jordan and others insisted that if he was going to watch the speech from his hotel, he couldn't leave the hotel until after Carter's speech was over. They were worried Kennedy would walk out while the president was still speaking and some of the TV networks would cut away to a live shot of Kennedy. So there was always going to be a delay in Kennedy arriving at the hall.

Carter finished his speech at 10:19 p.m., and the band struck up "Happy Days Are Here Again" as Rosalynn, and then Vice President Mondale and his wife, Joan, joined the president onstage. But comedic disaster struck almost immediately. The balloons hoisted above the floor from the ceiling became stuck when the mechanism to release them wouldn't work. Only a trickle of balloons fell to the floor.

"Whoever's in charge of balloons at this convention had better find themselves a new job," cracked ABC's Ted Koppel. Even Carter came in for abuse from some in the crowd. "Forget the hostages, he can't get the balloons down," said one person on the floor, according to Dan Rather.

At 10:22 p.m. the networks' live feed showed Kennedy emerging from the Waldorf Astoria and making his way past a crush of reporters down a few steps and into the backseat of his car. A Secret Service agent got in behind him, and he sat sandwiched between two agents. It took about ten minutes for Kennedy's motorcade to make the trip to the Garden. ABC News cameras showed the procession of a few dark sedans, escorted by police vehicles, cruising through Times Square, and then slowing as they neared the Garden and encountered a sea of yellow taxicabs outside the hall, waiting for the mass exodus of convention delegates and attendees.

But even before Kennedy's vehicle had made it to the Garden, the cheering inside the hall had died down. It was quite a contrast to the response for Kennedy's speech two nights earlier. The delegates had cheered and danced and sung for thirty minutes then. But for Carter, it took less than ten minutes for things to quiet down.

Carter's aides scrambled to keep the party going, to avoid the embarrassment of several minutes of quiet prior to Kennedy's arrival. Still, it was clear what was happening. "Even on this night, this president, after just delivering his acceptance speech, is going to be upstaged again," Frank Reynolds said on ABC.

The music had literally stopped. Carter campaign chairman Bob Strauss began calling political figures up onto the stage to keep the crowd cheering and the TV audience watching. It quickly got ridiculous. He was calling names no one had heard of or cared about. "This convention right now needs [Kennedy]," Koppel said. "This demonstration here has kind of fizzled out."

Onstage, Carter was shaking hands and giving a big hug to Tom Bradley, the mayor of Los Angeles, a large black man who looked slightly perplexed to be on the stage and confused as to why Carter was so enthusiastically squeezing him. Strauss called out many politicians who had opposed Carter, like California governor Jerry Brown, or who had undermined him by advocating for an open convention, like New York governor Hugh Carey. "They're calling them up in an effort to whip up the crowd. It's not doing it," Koppel noted.

"Bob Strauss will call up every politician he can find, including the county commissioner from Bernalillo, New Mexico, if necessary, to keep this thing going," cracked Sam Donaldson, who was positioned on the floor near the podium.

At 10:32, Kennedy's motorcade pulled into a garage entrance under the Garden. Kennedy hopped out, ran his hand through his hair, turned and waved to people applauding, and then was pushed forward into a back hallway by his entourage.

But Strauss had to keep the hit parade going on the stage, and Kennedy was still a few minutes from reaching the floor. Carter, almost an afterthought at this point, was now standing with both his hands resting on the wooden railing of the stage, next to Mondale. He was looking around, trying to keep a smile on his face.

Strauss was desperate now. He was calling up cabinet secretaries, hauled from their VIP seats and rushed to the stage. Secretary of Veterans Affairs Max Cleland, who had lost both of his legs and part of his right arm in Vietnam, had to be carried down a flight of stairs to get to the stage. Carter looked to his left and started clapping as the aging bureaucrats came forward. The president had been reduced to a guy desperately looking around a party for people he knows.

"This entire hall, and I guess the country too, it's almost as if they were waiting for the nominee of the party to arrive," Koppel said. "But of course they're waiting for the challenger, the loser!" Finally, at 10:36 p.m.—nearly twenty minutes after Carter's speech had ended—Kennedy reached the doorway to the hall and waited for Strauss to call him up. The buzz of his arrival emanated out into the hall. Loud chants of "We want Ted" rose up.

Donaldson began doing play-by-play on live TV: "Takes a moment for Strauss to get the word. [Kennedy] seems to be in fairly good spirits just judging from his facial expression. He clearly is going to be brought on with a roar when the moment arrives. An aide is patting down his hair in a last-minute gesture to make certain that not one is out of place." And then, as if aware of how banal he sounded talking about Kennedy's hair, Donaldson reached, too far, for some more grand and important-sounding thing to say. "Not since Caesar came into the Forum after one of the great battles has there been a scene like this, I suppose, although I must admit I was not there for the Forum scene."

Strauss announced Kennedy's name, and the hall drowned out all else with its roar. Kennedy walked into the hall "like an engine coming up the ramp," Donaldson said. He made his way through the crush of bodies around the stage, and up the three or four stairs onto the podium. Carter awaited him at the top. It was almost like he was a state official standing at the bottom of the stairs outside Air Force One, waiting for the president to come down and shake his hand. Kennedy's mouth was taut, his eyes were dead, and his brow was slightly furrowed.

Kennedy shook hands with Carter, and then with Rosalynn, and then finally his expression softened a little and he smiled as he greeted ten-year-old Amy. Then he moved to his right on the crowded stage and saw a familiar face: Mondale. The two men, formerly friends, now turned rivals, exchanged words and smiles and handshakes. "It does look all kind of backwards, though, doesn't it, Frank?" Koppel said to Reynolds. Tip O'Neill was now giving a side hug to Kennedy.

Then Carter made his move. He took a few steps toward center stage in front of the microphone. It was a clear attempt to bring Kennedy with him and to pose for the cameras, the two of them, hands together and aloft: a long-awaited, badly needed moment of victory for Carter. All the humiliation of the previous twenty minutes would be worth it, and all the acrimony and bitterness of the past nine months would be put behind the two men and their respective camps.

Kennedy could not, would not do it. He realized what Carter was doing, and stayed where he was, a few paces away from the podium. He waved to the crowd, nodding his head in a rhythmic way in acknowledgment of them. Carter reached the microphone, apparently thinking or hoping that Kennedy was right behind him. He realized that Kennedy had not come with him, and looked over his left shoulder. He turned back, took a step back and to his left, and extended a hand to Kennedy for a handshake, but he did so with his hand almost at shoulder level. It was a clear invitation to take his hand and raise it high.

The announcers expected Kennedy to give the president what he wanted. "There it is, there's the moment," Reynolds said. "Let's see if we—there it is." Kennedy stepped forward and shook Carter's hand, but he did not raise it, and his expression remained an almost somber one. His mouth remained closed, he let go of Carter's hand, and then he raised his hand again to the crowd. "What we are still lacking," Koppel said, "is that classical political photograph of the two men arm in arm, holding their hands up together."

Kennedy moved over to the right side of the stage, as Carter aides rushed to empty it of all the dignitaries whom they had moments ago been rushing forward. They wanted to clear the space for Carter and Kennedy, still in hopes of a unifying, triumphant image. Kennedy moved back toward the microphone and shook Carter's hand again, for the third time. And then he moved past him like he was at a rally and the president was just another nobody on the rope line waiting to shake his hand. He shook hands with Joan Mondale and a few other people behind Carter. The president continued applauding, and then turned back to the microphone, standing at the podium alone. He mouthed the words to the song being sung in the hall. He was completely by himself.

"If this was meant to be the display of Kennedy's support for Carter it is slightly underwhelming," Koppel said. "The senator is being very polite about it, but what is lacking here is any enthusiasm."

Kennedy was behind Carter and then began moving to his left, toward the stairs. Rosalynn joined Carter at the podium while Kennedy continued to talk and shake hands behind them. The first couple shared a quick word. He pulled her close and said something in her ear; she looked at him and nodded nervously. At this point, Kennedy was off by himself on the right side in the corner of the stage, with no one within five feet of him. The president, along with his wife and daughter, stood at the podium doing nothing. It was absurdist theater in the extreme. "It's a bizarre sight, it really is," ABC's Reynolds said.

Rosalynn looked over at Kennedy as he raised his hand again to the still-applauding crowd. Kennedy saw her, and they both reached to shake hands with each other, the second time for both of them. He leaned in, patted her hand with his left, and said a word. The president sidled over. He shook hands with those near Kennedy, and then with Kennedy for a fourth time. And then Kennedy quickly walked down the steps, flashing a raised fist to the crowd before he descended. The cameras caught him shaking hands with Arkansas governor Bill Clinton as he made his way away from the stage.

Moments later, Kennedy emerged back on the stage for a curtain call. He shook hands with Carter again, a fifth time, then slipped behind him on the stage while the president applauded almost spastically, with his hands held high. Carter faced forward but kept looking over his shoulder in both directions to see what Kennedy was doing. Kennedy smirked as he nodded rhythmically toward the crowd. Finally, he made his way off the stage for good. He walked behind Rosalynn and Amy, raised his left hand to the crowd, and then saw Carter walking over to stand next to him, still hoping for a moment of unity. The incumbent president of the United States was groveling on live TV, in front of the nation, for a photo with the man he had defeated for his own party's nomination. Roughly twenty million people were watching on live TV. "Well, this is slightly awkward," intoned NBC's David Brinkley.

But Kennedy just chuckled in amusement, patted the still-applauding president on the back, and turned to walk down the stairs. Carter was left pumping his right fist in the air to the crowd as Kennedy exited. It was, Teddy White wrote, "as if he had appeared at the wedding of his chauffeur."

As soon as Kennedy was off the stage and out of sight, the cheering died down. Carter was still on the stage, but the hall was filled only with the dull rumble of conversation. Rosalynn and Mondale looked flustered. Jimmy pulled his wife close and took a deep breath as Martin Luther King Sr. came to the podium for the benediction.

"It is still going to be a difficult job for President Carter to bring these Democrats together," Koppel said. As MLK Sr. prayed, NBC showed Kennedy going to his car, this time looking like a weight was off him: smiling, laughing, gesturing to people in the crowd who had gathered around his car in the bowels of the Garden. "I think," Koppel said, "it almost would have been better from the Carter point of view if he had not come."

Friends of Carter's like Bert Lance, his former budget chief and Georgia ally, sat watching on television, horrified. "I can't believe he's standing there, waiting around for Kennedy," Lance told his wife. Years later, he still couldn't believe it. "The Jimmy Carter that I know under normal circumstances . . . would have gone up to the microphone and said, 'Now folks, this guy can show up or not show up, I'm the president of the United States and I'm going to be reelected and hell, he can come when he wants to,'" Lance said.

"I think that it presented a sense of weakness on his part that was totally and completely out of character for him. . . . What he presented to the country that night was that little fellow standing up there on the platform milling around waiting for this big fellow to show up," Lance continued. "People saw supposedly the most powerful man on the face of the earth cooling his heels up there waiting for a fellow he's just whipped."

For Carter, hopes of capping off a long, agonizing primary fight with a triumphant ending to the convention had been dashed. Powell later accused the Kennedy camp of planning out ahead of time in Kennedy's hotel suite that night how they would embarrass Carter. "After the election, some of those aides took great glee in describing at length how they had choreographed [Kennedy's] final performance of the 1980 convention," Powell wrote. He added that the Kennedy camp's plan to humiliate Carter "worked like a charm."

Donilon lamented many years later that Carter had never been perceived as a winner because he never definitively knocked Kennedy down and out. "If he could have been the giant killer," Donilon said, things might have been different. It might have changed the perception of Carter. It might have helped him later on in the general election.

The irony was, Carter *was* the giant killer. He had defeated Kennedy. But after the convention, it didn't really feel like it.

# CHAPTER 17

———— ❧ ————

# Mr. Mean

The day after the convention, Kennedy met with a small group of reporters at his home in northern Virginia. Joan sat next to him. Relaxed and jovial, he was asked what he had learned from his run for president. He paused for several moments, and then said, "I suppose that you learn to live with your disappointments."

He told the reporters, "I'm not going to disappear." He said he planned to campaign for Carter now that the fall general election was approaching. But he made his support contingent on the degree to which the president endorsed some of his core ideas. "I have strong views about a lot of issues, and I get more enthusiastic as those issues are embraced and campaigned on," he said.

Aides to Kennedy and Carter were just starting negotiations over where and when Kennedy might campaign for the president's reelection. But as something of a down payment, he appeared a week later with Carter at Logan International Airport in Boston. Kennedy greeted Carter, who was in town for a speech to the American Legion, and followed him down a receiving line of state politicians, and then made brief remarks. "I'm determined that [Carter will be] reelected as the president of the United States," Kennedy said.

Kennedy immediately jetted to Detroit to speak to the American Federation of Teachers, which had backed his candidacy, to urge them to support Carter. He did so with caveats, noting that there were "forces of retreat" that must be resisted. It was language he had used to describe Carter before, and he said he would keep reminding Carter of "Democratic principles." With that in mind, he asked the group to "support and work for" Carter.

It took an hour of debate after Kennedy's thirty-minute speech, but the AFT did vote to back the president, though not with much passion. Their enthusiasm remained with Teddy. As Kennedy left the stage, the educators chanted, "We want Teddy" and "Eighty-four, eighty-four, eighty-four," already hopeful that Kennedy would run again for president in four years.

The following Monday, August 25, Kennedy traveled to the White House to meet with Carter. They discussed Carter's plans for reducing unemployment, and Kennedy said afterward that he thought the president was moving closer to the $12 billion program he had forced into the party platform at the convention. He left the White House saying he would "actively" campaign for Carter. However, it would be more than two weeks until an agreement was reached for him to do so.

Regardless, Carter was able to finally turn his attention to Ronald Reagan, whom he despised. Carter's lack of respect for Reagan would hamper his reelection efforts. But at first, Reagan played to type. The Republican nominee was embroiled in a series of controversies during the last two weeks of August. His propensity for sticking his foot in his mouth dominated the news. It highlighted Reagan's greatest vulnerability: the idea that he was a lightweight, made-for-TV candidate with no substance.

Reagan made a comment supporting the teaching of creationism alongside evolution in public schools, said that the Vietnam War was a "noble cause," declared the American economy to be in a "severe depression," and announced that he would recognize Taiwan again, reversing Carter's 1978 decision to cancel relations with the island country and angering the Chinese government.

The comments on Taiwan came as his running mate, George H. W. Bush, was in China. When Bush—a former U.S. ambassador to China—was asked about Reagan's comment, he disagreed. Reagan backed off, and lawyered his way out of the conundrum by arguing that the existing relationship with Taiwan met the standard of "official" recognition, contradicting his own prior statements.

Of course, not all of Reagan's comments were gaffes. He believed very firmly that the Vietnam War had been a noble effort. He had put that phrase into his speech to the Veterans of Foreign Wars himself. But regardless, in a day when the political press had far more enormous power to shape the public's perception of political figures than it would three decades later, each of these comments violated the establishment view. And they put Reagan on the defensive.

Reagan's advisers wanted him to shift gears, and his identity, from that of a conservative ideologue well suited for primary voters, to a more practical, moderate Republican who could win over independents and Democrats. As the *Globe*'s Thomas Oliphant put it, Reagan's advisers wanted him to be "a conservative in liberal's clothing." (Oliphant would describe Carter as "an enigma in conservative clothing.")

But the conversion was not going smoothly as of yet. There were "signs of frustration and disorganization" inside the Reagan campaign, Howell Raines wrote in the *Times*. Raines recounted the candidate's own irritation with his press coverage, as he stood in the press cabin of his campaign plane arguing that he was being unfairly covered, "in shirtsleeves, ignoring a junior aide who kept urging him to quit talking." The campaign began to limit his interactions with the press. Reagan "wasted August," wrote his biographer Craig Shirley.

As a result, Reagan's lead over Carter had evaporated, and the race was tied as summer drew to a close. Carter was eager to portray Reagan as dangerous, both to racial minorities and to the nation's national security. One Carter adviser said the president would take a "blowtorch" to Reagan once the campaign began in earnest after Labor Day.

———— ✠ ————

Carter kicked off the fall campaign on Labor Day in Tuscumbia, Alabama. Reagan spoke at the Michigan State Fair the same day. He told his crowd that Carter was "opening his campaign down in the city that gave birth to and is the parent body of the Ku Klux Klan." His clumsy attempt to associate Carter with the racist group was compounded by the fact that he was factually incorrect. Tuscumbia did headquarter one branch of the KKK, but Pulaski, Tennessee, was its birthplace. In addition, Carter had at his rally in Tuscumbia publicly criticized the Klan, which had sent members in full white hood and robe regalia.

Reagan's response to the inevitable backlash was to again claim he'd been misinterpreted, and to call on Carter to distance himself from allies of his who had associated Reagan with the KKK. But he also called Alabama governor Fob James to apologize for the remark, James claimed, and put out a statement that clarified that Tuscumbia was the "birthplace of Helen Keller."

"For two weeks it was delicious, watching Reagan on the news each night stumble from one controversy to another," Ham Jordan said. Carter's pollster Pat Caddell joked that if Reagan kept it up for another week, they could close down campaign headquarters. And then on September 12, Ayatollah Khomeini issued demands for the release of the hostages that Carter said a few days later "may very well lead to a resolution" of the crisis.

But Reagan retained a lead in key states, even as Carter closed in national and statewide polling. And Carter still didn't have a positive argument to make. The main thrust of the case he was making to the nation was that Reagan was a warmonger. Carter thought Reagan an empty-headed buffoon who would "lead our country toward war" through needless machismo. Reagan didn't have much respect for Carter either. He mocked the president's piety. "I wonder whether he's confusing some of his own statements with having come from God," he told Teddy White.

Reagan was on to something. Carter's self-certainty would get him in trouble, exposing one of his biggest personal flaws for the entire country to see. Carter utterly lacked a gift that Reagan, for all his own flaws, had in some abundance: a feel for nuance. "The President eschews the light touch. He prefers the disemboweling approach," the *Globe* wrote. Jimmy Carter's own mother, Lillian, once described him as "a beautiful cat with sharp claws." Gonzo journalist Hunter S. Thompson called Carter "one of the three meanest men I've ever met." The other two were boxer Muhammad Ali and Sonny Barger, leader of the Hells Angels. Carter, Thompson said, "would cut my head off to carry North Dakota. He'd cut both your legs off to carry a ward in the Bronx....He will eat your shoulder right off if he thinks it's right."

Carter's presidency had been derailed time and again by the impression that he was powerless and inept, especially as inflation raged on and the hostage crisis dragged out. But he wasn't some kind of political pacifist who was afraid of a fight. In fact, attacks on Reagan would be his downfall. On September 16, he spoke at Ebenezer Baptist Church in Atlanta, Martin Luther King Sr.'s church. "You've seen in this campaign the stirrings of hate and the rebirth of code words like 'states' rights' in a speech in Mississippi, in a campaign reference to the Ku Klux Klan," Carter said. "This is a message that creates a cloud on the political horizon."

He continued, "Hatred has no place in this country. Racism

has no place in this country." He didn't mention Reagan, but he was clearly calling his opponent a racist, even though Jody Powell tried to deny it. The backlash was immediate. "Mr. Carter has abandoned all dignity," wrote the *Washington Post* editorial board, maligning Carter's "miserable record of personally savaging political opponents." Former president Ford said Carter's comments "demean the office of the presidency." New York lieutenant governor Mario Cuomo criticized the president, calling the remarks "not nice." Carter was forced to call a press conference at the White House two days later to tamp down the brushfire. The last time he had met the press had been in early August, that time to deal with BillyGate.

Carter stated unequivocally that Reagan was not a racist, and was anxious for the media to move on from the topic altogether. "The press seems to be obsessed with this issue," he complained. But Lisa Myers of the *Washington Star* pointed out that Carter's own secretary of health and human services, Patricia Harris, was the one who had first injected the KKK into the campaign, remarking in early September, "When I hear Reagan's name, I see the specter of white sheets." Carter argued that Reagan's talk of states' rights was code for a return to the nation's segregationist past.

Carter aides admitted the president had "gone overboard" with his accusations of racism, and Jody Powell said Carter had "overstated" the degree to which Reagan might be a warmonger, but Carter's advisers rationalized that they believed the attacks on Reagan were working. Carter's "Georgia Mafia" knew what kind of things made the evening news broadcasts and what did not. "The networks' judgment has less to do with real news value than it has to do with personalities," the *Boston Globe*'s Curtis Wilkie observed. "There is also a recognition by the Carter media team that the networks need drama." Wilkie wrote that "no administration in the television age has studied the methods of the medium more religiously than this one. And none has designed its actions more accordingly.... It has all been orchestrated with TV in mind."

But Carter's aides did want him to use some restraint. Two weeks later, however, he overdid it again. The election, he said at a speech in Chicago, would "determine whether or not this America will be unified or, if I lose the election, whether Americans might be separated, black from white, Jew from Christian, North from South, rural from urban." Reagan, asked about the comment, shook his head sadly and said the president was reaching a "point of hysteria." Carter needed to walk himself back again, and this time chose to do an interview with Barbara Walters. Her first question pointed out to him that he had in recent days "been characterized as mean, vindictive, hysterical, and on the point of desperation."

She asked, "Is it in your nature to be so emotional that you become mean?"

"I don't think I'm mean, Barbara," Carter said. "Some of the issues are just burning with fervor in my mind and in my heart.... I have gotten carried away on a couple of cases."

"The meanness issue," Ham Jordan wrote, "had...sunk in." Eugene McCarthy, the insurgent antiwar Democratic candidate for president in 1968 and former Minnesota senator, endorsed Reagan. Leon Jaworski, the former Watergate prosecutor who had called Reagan an extremist in the spring, agreed to head up Democrats for Reagan, saying a competent extremist was better than an incompetent moderate.

Carter further hurt himself during this period, in two ways, when he refused to join a debate with Reagan and independent candidate John Anderson in Baltimore. Reagan benefited by coming across as far more charming and reasonable than the bogeyman that Carter had made him out to be. And Anderson, who was taking support away from Carter but had indicated he would drop out if the president would debate him, stayed in the race.

Carter needed help from Teddy Kennedy, but it was slow in coming. The Kennedy camp wanted a pound of flesh first. At the end of August, after Kennedy's initial good-faith appearances with Carter just after the convention, Ham Jordan traveled to meet Steve Smith at Kennedy's Senate offices, to talk about plans for Kennedy to campaign for Carter.

Jordan said he wanted to set up a "master schedule" that began with a joint appearance and then would dispatch Kennedy to some key states. Smith told Jordan that was "reasonable," but then informed him that Kennedy would require help retiring his campaign debt if he were going to help Carter. In fact, Smith said, before Kennedy scheduled any events, the White House would have to sign an agreement.

"We are going to need some help getting rid of this debt," Smith said. "If we have to raise it ourselves, it won't leave us any time to help the ticket." He smiled. Jordan seethed, but returned the smile, wishing they didn't need Kennedy's help. Carter hit the roof when he learned of the agreement. "He's blackmailing us!" he stormed at Jordan.

Kennedy did hit the hustings for Carter, and he taped TV and radio advertisements for the president. But his message on the stump was more about opposing Reagan than it was about supporting Carter, and he regularly toyed with supporters to pump them up about his own political advancement rather than the president's. In mid-September, he campaigned in Brookline, Massachusetts, for Representative Barney Frank and Representative James Shannon, greeting a boisterous crowd with the words, "I accept your nomination!"

Joked Kennedy, "I've been waiting for a chance to say that for so long." Carter was at that time refusing to debate Reagan and Anderson, so Kennedy added, "I support Jimmy Carter, but if he doesn't want to get out there and debate Ronald Reagan and John Anderson, I'm ready to go." At another event in McAllen, Texas, a crowd of Hispanic steelworkers screamed, "Viva Kennedy! Viva Kennedy!" Teddy leaned into the microphone and repeated the phrase "Viva Kennedy!" with a big grin.

And when Carter appeared at a fund-raiser in Los Angeles that was part of the joint fund-raising agreement, Kennedy couldn't resist zinging the president. He referred to a controversy over the leaked disclosure of the Pentagon's secret "Stealth" plane that was built to evade Soviet radar. "You've heard about the Stealth project, the invisible plane. That's what Jimmy Carter was to me for four months during the primary: invisible," Kennedy told a crowd at the Beverly Hilton. It was a shot at Carter for refusing to campaign against him, but it carried a fresh edge, coming one day after the debate between Anderson and Reagan that Carter had refused to join.

On October 15, Kennedy appeared with Carter at a pair of rallies in Boston and then two more in Secaucus, New Jersey. Once again, he unleashed his greatest energies on mocking Reagan and used the same boilerplate language to ask Democrats who had supported him to do the same for Carter. He made a number of other appearances on Carter's behalf over the final days of the campaign—including a campaign stop with Carter and heavyweight boxing champion Muhammad Ali in Brooklyn—but otherwise stayed out of the news. He was doing enough to avoid being labeled a sore loser and to be seen as a loyal Democrat, but not much more.

The day after Kennedy and Carter's joint appearances, the president and Reagan appeared together in person for the first time during the campaign. A debate between them was still being considered by both sides, but nothing had yet been settled. And so their appearance at the annual Al Smith Dinner in New York took on an even bigger significance than it otherwise would have. The dinner, a tradition since 1945 in honor of former New York governor Alfred E. Smith, was the kind of venue perfectly suited to Reagan's urbane wit, which had been shaped by his time in Hollywood, but profoundly less so to Carter's self-seriousness. It was a showcase for the contrast between the two men, especially their personalities and communication styles. It would demonstrate why, policies aside, many people just found Reagan more likable.

Reagan, who spoke first, was brief, funny, and self-deprecating, while working in a few moments of sincere tribute to the hostages still being held in Iran and to the dinner's namesake. "There's no truth to the rumor that I was at the original Al Smith Dinner," he joked, in a crack at his own age. He was to turn seventy the following February.

Carter skipped the dinner and arrived merely in time for the speeches, unlike Reagan. He was tone-deaf and censorious, and could spare no jokes at himself. He only took shots at Reagan. Carter said he had told New York mayor Ed Koch, who repeatedly undercut him during the primary fight with Kennedy, "not to get too close to Governor Reagan." He explained, "It has nothing to do with politics, but only that the governor's 'I Love New York' button—the paint is still wet." The white-tie crowd took offense and booed the president.

Carter plowed on, and delivered a speech within a speech, talking for ten minutes about the need for religious tolerance and the dangers posed by the religious right. "In our zeal to strengthen the moral character of this nation, we must not set ourselves up as judges of whom God might hear or whom he would turn away," he said. It was an apparent reference to Liberty University president Jerry Falwell, who had been reported to have said earlier in the fall that God heard the prayers only of Christians, not those from people of other faiths. Reagan had publicly disagreed with Falwell's comment.

The *Times*'s Anthony Lewis, in a column just one day before the dinner, had put his finger on what it was Carter showed that night. "There is no fun in Jimmy Carter," Lewis wrote. "[He] has acted as if his job were a pious duty. . . . He has uplifted practically no one." The columnist argued that Carter had successes to tout, but his lack of vision prevented him from doing so.

And yet the polls were tightening. And so after the dinner, Reagan's top aides huddled in the Waldorf Astoria and decided to drop their insistence that Anderson—who had polled in the low 20s at his zenith but was now below 15 percent—be included in any debate. The date was set for October 28, just one week to the day before voters would go to the polls. And while Kennedy was out campaigning for Carter, an associate of his family was causing trouble for Carter.

Paul Corbin, a longtime fixer and operative for the Kennedy family, and a former member of the Communist Party, was known for specializing in dirty tricks. He had never had a formal role in Teddy Kennedy's campaign, but Steve Smith appreciated his skills and kept him around. After Teddy conceded the race in New York, Corbin did something unthinkable: He agreed to work for the Reagan campaign and was put on retainer. He set to work obtaining the briefing books being used by Carter to prepare for his debate with Reagan, and delivered them to the Reagan campaign, according to Craig Shirley's account.

The theft was not discovered until 1983, when Washington went into an uproar and a congressional investigation was launched. Suspicion centered on Corbin at the time. But Shirley's 2009 book *Rendezvous with Destiny* assembled all the evidence against Corbin, including interviews with multiple sources who said Corbin claimed to have been the culprit. But the Carter camp had long suspected Kennedy people of being behind the theft. Carter spokesman Jody Powell speculated in 1984 that Steve Smith had directed Corbin to sabotage Carter, or at least green-lighted it. It's not clear that the briefing book made a significant difference, whatever the case. But the theft, and Corbin's apparent role, showed the bitterness that some in Kennedy world felt toward Carter.

———— ✎ ————

On October 22, comments from a top Iranian cleric and from Iranian prime minister Mohammad Ali Rajai raised the prospect that a resolution, and a release of the fifty-two Americans still in Tehran, could be imminent. It raised the prospect of a dramatic turnaround for Carter's fortunes that would be beyond belief. He had been saved from the Kennedy challenge by the seizure of the hostages. Would he now be saved by the Iranians a second time, and retain the presidency with their help? Some thought so.

Others, like the *Washington Post*'s Haynes Johnson, did not. "What's taking place now, as Election Day approaches, appears to be a confirmation of the most cynical exploitation of the most emotional issue in years—and by the most powerful person in the land, purely for political purposes," Johnson wrote. He said he thought the release of the hostages would "work against" Carter, and quoted unemployed steelworkers in Youngstown, Ohio, as telling him, "This valley will not be fooled by some rabbit out of a hat."

On October 28, Kennedy settled in with Shrum and some others to watch the debate at the Century Plaza Hotel in Los Angeles. He had just returned from Puerto Rico, where United Press International reported he had spent three days "campaigning and fund raising." It must have been a very generous use of those terms.

As Kennedy watched, he saw along with millions of others that Reagan was the more relaxed of the two debaters. Ham Jordan, watching the TV broadcast from a back room at the debate site in Cleveland, didn't like what he saw: "Reagan looking relaxed, smiling, robust; the President, erect, lips tight, looking like a coiled spring, ready to pounce, an overtrained boxer, too ready for the bout."

The two men grappled over their different approaches to the Soviet

Union. Carter had increased defense spending and wanted to negotiate from a place of strength, but he wanted to try to work out arms reduction agreements. Reagan's emphasis was heavier on outpacing the Soviets' arms production. Carter described Reagan's approach as "dangerous and belligerent in its tone, although it's said with a quiet voice."

Carter tried to end this portion of the debate on a poignant note, invoking his daughter to drive home the need for sobriety and expertise in handling national security. But it didn't quite come out right. "I think to close out this discussion it would be better to put it into perspective what we're talking about," he said. "I had a discussion with my daughter, Amy, the other day before I came here, to ask her what the most important issue was. She said she thought nuclear weaponry and the control of nuclear arms."

The way Carter delivered the line, it sounded like he was asking his thirteen-year-old daughter for advice. By the distortionary standards of television, it reinforced the image of him as a bumbling dope. Backstage, Carter adviser Rafshoon clapped his hand to his head and exclaimed, "Oh my God—not that!" He and others had told Carter not to use the anecdote, and the president had ignored them.

Moments later, Reagan hit Carter with a jab that again made a mockery of the president. Carter accused Reagan of campaigning "against Medicare" earlier in his career. Reagan, knowing his medium, was too smart to put substance ahead of style. He paused, smiled, looked askance at Carter, and said with a practiced chuckle, "There you go again."

It was the equivalent of a boxer knocking out his opponent with a feather. Kennedy, watching in L.A., knew it. He turned to Shrum in their car on the way to the airport and said of Carter, "He just got killed."

He was right. Polls showed Reagan pulling away from Carter in the days following the debate. "You could feel it drifting away," Mondale said.

# CHAPTER 18

◦◦◦◦◦◦

# Aftermath

Reagan's campaign grew giddy over the final days, as their candidate felt the wind at his back and relentlessly mocked Carter for consulting his middle school daughter on nuclear weaponry. And yet there were still the hostages.

The Iranian parliament released its demands two days before the American election. Carter took the dramatic step of coming off the campaign trail. He returned very early Sunday morning, November 2, to Washington from Chicago to review and discuss the four conditions set out by the Iranian assembly. He asked Mondale and Kennedy to fill in for him at rallies in Detroit and Philadelphia that day. Carter and his aides had hoped the news from Tehran would provide a way for the hostages to be freed. Reagan and his team feared a last-minute release in the days before the election, and reporters were besieged with calls from Reagan campaign officials accusing Carter of reaching an agreement and holding it in reserve until the last day or two of the campaign.

But after reviewing the Iran parliament's message with his team on Sunday, Carter's assessment of the situation was not optimistic. He didn't feel much had changed since September when the Ayatollah had set out the four conditions, which the parliament had simply approved. Carter was generally amenable to the conditions, which dealt mostly with undoing a freeze on financial assets that was retaliation for the hostage-taking, and agreeing not to interfere in Iran's internal affairs, but didn't think any negotiations over such a framework would ever happen before the election. "This should bring our people home, eventually," he told advisers Sunday morning. There wasn't much reason for optimism, but Carter nonetheless made a nationally televised statement that evening—cutting into NFL games—and said the Iranian actions were "a significant development." But he had to admit that he could not predict when the hostages would return.

Nonetheless, public polls showed the race razor tight, as did the Carter campaign's own internal voter surveys. Carter left nothing in reserve down the home stretch. On his final day of campaigning, he spoke at seven rallies, with stops in Akron, Ohio; St. Louis; Springfield, Missouri; Detroit; Portland; and Seattle.

He arrived in Seattle for the last rally of his campaign at 10:41 p.m. Pacific time. As the plane approached Boeing Field International Airport, Ham Jordan and Pat Caddell phoned Air Force One and reached Jody Powell. "Jody, brace yourself, because it looks like it's gone. And it could be bad," Jordan told Powell.

It was a shock. Caddell's final survey Monday night had shown a wild break toward Reagan, and he was now predicting an 8-to-10-point loss. It was a dramatic, heartbreaking shift. Jordan and the other Carterites thought the three major TV networks had played a big role in the turn. Each of their Monday night broadcasts had reviewed the previous year's hostage crisis, since election day would, unfortunately for Carter, be the one-year anniversary of when the hostages had been taken. Jordan, Caddell, Rafshoon, and DNC chair Bob Strauss had watched the evening news in horror. But the action by the Iranian parliament had also fixated the nation on the hostages as well, and reminded Americans of Carter's failure to bring them home.

Out in Seattle, the rally inside an airport hangar went well. Powell, standing on the rainy tarmac outside and nursing a stiff drink, ruefully observed that it might have been Carter's best of the year. Curtis Wilkie agreed, calling it "one of his finest speeches of the campaign." As the crowd cheered the president during the rally, Powell turned to another aide and said despondently, "It's gone." Afterward, Air Force One took off, headed for the East Coast, at 11:40 Pacific time. Powell waited to catch Carter alone to break the news. But the president was in a good mood. He was sipping a double martini—a rare indulgence for him—and bantering with staff. He then invited some reporters into his private quarters to talk. It was getting close to 5 a.m. on the East Coast by the time Caddell, Jordan, and Rafshoon finally reached the president on Air Force One.

"Mr. President, I am afraid that it's gone," Caddell said. Carter was taken aback. He was silent as Caddell explained what had happened to so suddenly dash their dreams of winning a second term. Then, with no emotion in his voice, Carter asked his advisers to draft some remarks for the morning when he'd be in Plains. After hanging up, he called Rosalynn, who was waiting for him back in Georgia, and told her they were going to lose.

And then the president went to be by himself, where he quietly wept.

Carter slept for about an hour, and after a four-hour flight, Air Force One landed at dawn just before 7 a.m. at Robins Air Force Base in Warner Robins, Georgia. The president and a few aides, including Powell, then hopped on Marine One for the forty-minute helicopter ride to Plains.

A heavy ground fog covered the brown southwest Georgia landscape as Carter choppered toward his boyhood home. Rosalynn met him upon landing, and they went to vote at Plains High School. Reporters asked the dejected-looking president if he thought he would win. "I hope so," was all he could muster.

After voting, he and Rosalynn went to the Plains Railroad Depot, and he mounted the platform to speak to supporters from the same place where he'd wept with joy four years earlier the morning after winning the presidency. It was a quieter occasion now, and he talked in the past tense of the difficult and unpopular things he'd done as president, as if building a defense for his defeat before it had even happened.

As he drew his remarks to a close, Carter focused on the people in front of him, and spoke with gratefulness of the pride his fellow Georgians had always shown in him. "People from Plains, from Americus, from Richland, from Preston, from Schley County, from around this area have gone all over the nation to speak for me and shake hands with people in other states, to tell them that you have confidence in me and that I would not disappoint them if I became president," Carter said.

As the word "disappoint" hung in the air, Carter's jaw trembled. "I've tried to honor your commitment to those other people," he said. He had to stop to collect himself. "In the process, I've tried to honor my commitment—" He couldn't finish the sentence. His eyes filled with tears as he tried to regain his composure and get out his last two words: "—to you."

In closing he said, "God bless you. Thank you. Don't forget to vote, everybody."

Carter returned to Washington to grimly await the results. He won only six states plus the District of Columbia: his home state of Georgia, Hawaii, Maryland, Mondale's home state of Minnesota, Rhode Island, and West Virginia. Reagan won forty-four states. It was an Electoral College landslide: 489 to 49. Anderson took votes from both candidates, but his share of the vote was greater than

Reagan's margin of victory in fourteen states. Nonetheless, even if Carter had won all those and picked up 168 electoral votes, he still would have been crushed, 321 to 217, in the Electoral College.

As he searched for causes of his defeat that night, Carter pointed the finger directly at Kennedy. "The Kennedy attacks for eight months hurt a lot. I spent a major portion of my time trying to recruit back the Democratic constituency that should have been naturally supportive: Jews, Hispanics, blacks, the poor, labor, and so forth," he wrote in his journal the day of the election.

Ham Jordan was equally angry. "I never really resented Kennedy's challenge to us, for, at the time he decided to run, it seemed that he had good prospects for winning," Jordan wrote. "Later, as it became mathematically impossible for him to be nominated, I developed an enormous resentment of what his continuing in the race would do to our chances of beating Reagan. Kennedy was demonstrating how little he cared for the Democratic party."

In other moments, however, Carter was more honest with himself. "I lost it myself," he admitted.

But of course, the hostages had also played a massive role. The crisis had rescued him from the Kennedy challenge, and then over time dragged him down. "Events had mocked us," Rosalynn said.

After speaking to weeping supporters at the Sheraton Washington that evening, Carter and Rosalynn returned to the White House. Before going to bed, the president spoke to two people on the phone. He placed a call to his brother, Billy, and they spoke for two minutes. Just before that, he received a call from Kennedy. The two men spoke for ten minutes. It's not known what was said.

Kennedy made another call that night, to congratulate President-elect Ronald Reagan. The Democrats might have been kicked out of the White House and lost their Senate majority, but they were in need of leadership, and Kennedy was not waiting for someone else to step up and claim the mantle. He felt he'd earned it.

—⊶⊷—

The impact of the collision between Jimmy Carter and Teddy Kennedy was intense but not disabling. It injured each of them significantly, but also freed them. Over time, both picked up the pieces, went their separate ways, and reached some of their greatest and highest achievements in the following years. For Kennedy, in particular, it was a process he had to go through.

The contrast between the direction of the two men in the years after 1980 was stark, just like the personal differences between them. Carter, after an initial period of depression and searching, spent decades in a frenetic and solitary pursuit of global peacemaking and healing, though Rosalynn was of course always at his side and as much a partner as ever. Kennedy's course was more linear. He spent the rest of his life working inside an institution, the Senate, on behalf of a cause bigger than himself, through the same entity, the Democratic Party. Unlike Carter, he colored within the lines in his professional life, even as he did the opposite for another decade in his personal life.

The 1980 election was marked by apathy. Reagan beat Carter amid the lowest turnout in a presidential election since 1948. Only 52.4 percent of eligible voters went to the polls. But it was a significant historical election because the coalition that Democrats had relied on for decades since FDR's presidency—combining union members and ethnics in the big cities, poor rural voters, racial minorities, Catholics, and the South—had splintered for good. It was a realigning event. Carter's total loss of support among white Baptist voters in the South demonstrated how badly his coalition from 1976 had been turned upside down. Baptists in the South had supported Carter 56 to 43 percent against Gerald Ford, but turned against him overwhelmingly. In 1980, Reagan got the 56 percent support from the Baptists that Carter had received just four years earlier, and Carter got even less than Ford, just 34 percent.

Carter, by beating Kennedy, avoided joining the lowly ranks of Franklin Pierce and Andrew Johnson, the only two presidents who failed to even be renominated for a second term by their own party. But with the loss to Reagan, he became only the eighth popularly elected president in U.S. history to lose a reelection campaign. Jimmy and Rosalynn took the loss extremely hard, as did those closest to them. "A part of my soul died that night," Ham Jordan told Douglas Brinkley many years later. Injury was added to insult when Carter broke his collarbone while cross-country skiing at Camp David a few days after Christmas.

But there was still the matter of the hostages for Carter to attend to, and he threw himself into that work with abandon in his final weeks. The shah had died in June 1980, removing one provocation. And with the beginning of a war between Iran and Iraq in September, there was now an incentive for Ayatollah Khomeini to negotiate, primarily because arms shipments and military "spare parts" were part of that negotiation, and they would come in handy against Iraq.

Carter finished out his term working obsessively to get a hostage deal done. He began making preparations to ask Congress for a declaration of war, which was never needed. Khomeini issued a demand for $24 billion a few days before Christmas. Although Carter rejected that, it was the beginning of a final negotiation. The number was whittled down to $8 billion, with $5 billion of that going to pay Iran's debts to U.S. and European banks. Carter signed a series of executive orders executing the deal, and spent his last weekend in office waiting for word on whether the deal would go through. He announced its completion at 4:44 a.m. on Monday, January 19, the day before Reagan's inauguration.

Carter aides hoped the deal would be done so quickly that he could go to meet the hostages in Germany on Monday evening and be back in Washington on inauguration day to transfer power to Reagan. But it was not to be. Still, Carter and his most loyal aides were "obsessed" with the idea of getting the hostages out of Iran before Reagan took office, and Ham Jordan fantasized about Carter interrupting the inauguration to announce the good news. On Tuesday, Carter stayed in the Oval Office until the last possible moment on the day of Reagan's inauguration, hoping to get word that the hostages were free. In one final indignity, the Iranians released the hostages only after Reagan had been sworn in as the nation's fortieth president.

Carter, years later, would imply that he believed Reagan had made a deal with Khomeini to wait until the inauguration to free the hostages, in exchange for military equipment that Tehran needed to fight Saddam Hussein's troops. Gary Sick, an Iran expert who served on Carter's National Security Council staff at the White House, wrote a book in 1991 called *October Surprise*, which made the case that Reagan had colluded with the Iranians. Carter told Brinkley in 1995 that "if you try to dig further into Gary's *October Surprise* revelations, and are successful, you may not like what you find."

Nonetheless, Carter was deeply relieved when the hostages were released as he flew home to Plains. He flew, at Reagan's request, to meet them in Frankfurt, Germany, at a U.S. Air Force hospital. The meeting was tense. Carter, perhaps uneasy and too eager to remind the group of his efforts for them, held up a front page he had brought with him from Georgia. The *Americus Times-Recorder*, his hometown newspaper, had blared, "Carter Efforts Bring Freedom to Hostages." The room reacted less than enthusiastically to this, and the first two former hostages to speak asked Carter why he had allowed the shah into the United States and why he had attempted the rescue mission. But by and large, the former hostages were grateful for Carter's appearance and his attempts to earn their release.

On the flight back to Georgia, Carter and his aides drank toasts to the end of the ordeal. Carter was in a reflective mood, and in a private moment with Jordan, he tried to persuade his closest adviser, and himself, that part of him was glad he had lost. "I wonder deep down if I would really want to go back to Washington," he told Jordan. "There are all these forces that compel an incumbent president to run again. You're surrounded by people who want to continue in their jobs, who want you to run. You get this sense of wanting to consummate what you started in your first term, and not to run would be considered by many as an indication that you don't think you could be reelected and an acknowledgment of failure."

He said, "I never seriously considered not running, but I've wondered what my true feelings were. I was disappointed, but I have to admit that I was also relieved."

Nevertheless, he was in agony. "I never admitted how deeply I was hurt and I still find it hard to do so," he later wrote. When he returned home to Georgia, he fell into a funk. Rosalynn was even worse off. To make matters worse, they had discovered that the trustees of the blind trust who had managed his family's peanut farm business had left it $1 million in debt. He sold the farm, moved back into their modest home in Plains—which had sat vacant for a decade—and faced an uncertain future. He was only fifty-six years old.

He and Rosalynn were not sure they would settle in Plains. Their daughter, Amy, certainly didn't want to. "You may be from the country but I'm not. I've been raised in the city!" she told Rosalynn.

While the Carters sorted all that out, Jimmy scored a multimillion-dollar deal to write a memoir, and got to work on *Keeping Faith: Memoirs of a President*. Rosalynn also won a book contract for her own memoir, *First Lady from Plains*. In typical fashion, Carter stipulated that he would only spend one year working on his book, and stayed pretty much on schedule. Rosalynn, meanwhile, took two and a half years to finish her book, which was well received.

After finishing his book, Carter turned his full energy to thinking about the rest of his life, and began planning and strategizing over what would eventually become the Carter Center, the hub of all his activity. He partnered with Emory University, headquartered in Atlanta, giving the center a research and academic institution with which to share resources. He and Rosalynn, together with John and Betty Pope, bought a cabin on ten acres in the mountains of northwest Georgia, where they could go fly fishing, and where he "read Gandhi and Thoreau; crafted furniture; painted scenes of rural Georgia life; and wrote highly personal poems."

Carter also connected that year with Ted Turner, who had started the Cable News Network during Carter's last year in office. It was a fortunate turn of events for the former president that CNN was headquartered in Atlanta and owned by a fellow Georgian. The upstart cable network would provide Carter with a huge platform in the subsequent years, increasing his influence and power in a way no other ex-president had experienced.

The stage was set for Carter to begin looking for problems to solve and ways to find purpose. His first major foreign trip with Rosalynn was to the Middle East, in early 1983. And in the months leading up to the trip, he dug into the Israeli-Palestinian conflict— something he already knew quite a bit about—with single-minded obsession. He studied the Torah and the Quran. And he became convinced that he had not fully appreciated the Palestinian plight. He grew angry with Israeli prime minister Menachem Begin for refusing to allow a Palestinian representative at the Camp David talks, and with himself for not insisting on it. "He saw more clearly how the establishment of present-day Israel in 1948, while resolving the problem of vulnerability and statelessness for Jews, had created a set of new problems for the Palestinian Arabs, whose land

and houses had been taken by Israelis," Brinkley wrote. This issue, and his point of view on it, would become one of the most lasting and dominant legacies of his ex-presidency.

In September 1983, his sister Ruth Stapleton Carter died of pancreatic cancer. She was just fifty-four years old. Nearly five weeks after Ruth's death, Carter's mother, Lillian, died, also of pancreatic cancer. At least she had lived to age eighty-five. Carter's father, Earl, had also died of pancreatic cancer thirty years earlier at age fifty-eight. And in 1990, the same disease would also claim Carter's other sister, Gloria Carter Spann, at age sixty-three, and his only brother, Billy, who died in 1988 at age fifty-one. Jimmy would outlive them all, and go on to survive liver and brain cancer himself at age ninety-one.

Carter traveled to Latin America in 1984, marking the beginning of his relationship with another region where he would play a significant role in the coming years. It was also that year that he and Rosalynn first were introduced to Habitat for Humanity and its founders, Millard and Linda Fuller, who had started the nonprofit in 1976 only a few miles from Plains. The Fullers were a southern couple motivated by an intensely evangelistic Christian faith. And while they bonded with the Carters over that, Carter would grow concerned over the years that his association with Habitat—which provided affordable housing to needy families through labor from volunteers and the families buying the homes—was overshadowing the work of his center. But after his first trip with Habitat, a well-publicized build in the drug-infested Alphabet City neighborhood in New York's East Village, he was "addicted" to Habitat work.

As president, Ronald Reagan had disregarded Carter. But as Carter's former vice president, Walter Mondale, ran against Reagan that year, the former president was snubbed by his own party as well. Democratic officials reluctantly invited him to speak at the 1984 convention, but gave him an early slot on opening night, and his remarks were ignored both on TV and on the floor of the convention. It was a humiliation, largely motivated by a desire to forget the party's loss of the White House in 1980.

But Carter had never been a part of the Democratic Party establishment either. He was referred to as a "partyless president." On the night of his defeat at Reagan's hands, he had ignored his advisers' requests to wait until polls had closed on the West Coast before conceding, to help party candidates who would be hurt if Democratic voters saw Carter throwing in the towel and decided not to go to the polls. "He wants to get it over with," Carter spokesman Jody Powell told Ham Jordan that night. House Speaker Tip O'Neill, the Massachusetts Democrat who had supported Carter during the challenge from his own state's favorite son, wanted to keep the Democratic advantage in the House. He exploded in anger during a phone call with Frank Moore, a Carter aide. "You guys came in like a bunch of jerks, and I see you're going out the same way," O'Neill yelled at Moore.

On one of his last Sundays as president, Carter—a defeated politician—had taught Sunday school at First Baptist Church in Washington, D.C., one final time. His text had been Luke 9:46–48, where Jesus rebukes his disciples as they bicker over who among them would be the greatest. Jesus, bringing a child to stand by him, tells the disciples, "Whoever welcomes this little child in my name welcomes me; and whoever welcomes me welcomes the one who sent me. For it is the one who is least among you all who is the greatest." That day in January 1981, Carter had said, "Is greatness being a president? An emperor?" No, he said. "The foundation of greatness is service to others."

By that definition, the always ambitious Carter achieved greatness in his post-presidency. His work around the world more than sustained him, especially since he increasingly saw a role for himself easing suffering through mediating conflicts and bringing medical aid to places badly in need of it. In 1985, he held an arms control summit in Atlanta at the Carter Center that was well attended by top officials in the new Soviet government headed by Mikhail Gorbachev. Also that same year, he launched a public health initiative in Africa called Global 2000. The year after that, the center set a goal of eradicating the painful guinea worm disease from the earth. Dracunculiasis afflicted roughly 3.5 million people at that time, most of them in sub-Saharan Africa, and the United Nations estimated that 100 million people were at risk of the disease. It was transmitted through unsanitary drinking water, through which worm larvae were ingested and emerged from the host's body as two- to three-foot-long worms, usually around the ankles and feet. The worms produced burning blisters and sores on the skin as they were secreted, and often led to infection. Victims were often crippled for months, sometimes for life.

The Carter Center spearheaded an education effort to help villages use filtered water—distributing a simple cloth filter throughout Africa—and to keep disease sufferers from walking into water sources to ease their pain, and in the process releasing larvae into the water that led to infections in others. In 2015, there were only twenty-two cases in Africa, and Carter thought they would eradicate the disease within a year. But then a surprise development set them back. Dogs with guinea worm disease were discovered in the nation of Chad, setting back the hopes for its imminent elimination. Nevertheless, Carter's work on the disease has been heroic.

Over the years, Carter used his work to make an opening for human rights and democracy promotion. He would meet with a foreign leader to discuss aid efforts, and bring with him the names of specific political prisoners held under that regime. It was a model similar to Habitat for Humanity's form of evangelism, which was intended in part to create receptivity to the Christian gospel:

Provide material and substantial relief and assistance to people in need, and then carry a larger message with you through the doors that open. Brinkley estimated that his efforts had resulted in the release of fifty thousand political prisoners around the world between 1981 and 1997, an astounding number. The Carter Center said they did not know where that number had come from, and in fact a Carter spokeswoman told me that Carter had advocated for the release of "hundreds" of political prisoners during his post-presidency. "But we do not have a definitive accounting here of the number of 'released prisoners' resulting from these efforts, and that would be a very large undertaking to produce," spokeswoman Deanna Congileo said.

Carter was not a central player in the biggest story of the late 1980s and early 1990s: the fall of communist governments in the Soviet Union and Eastern Europe. But he did enter the public eye as a key figure in some internationally known conflicts during that time. He stood up to Panamanian strongman Manuel Noriega in 1989. After observing elections there, Carter compiled evidence that Noriega had fraudulently stolen the election, and vigorously denounced him during a forty-five-minute press conference in Panama City.

In 1994, Carter was a force. He helped prevent a U.S. invasion of Haiti through last-minute negotiations, headed off a conflict with North Korea, and helped secure a four-month cease-fire in the bloody Balkan conflict between the Serbs, Croats, and Bosnians. But in the latter two cases, he alienated himself from the first Democratic president to take office since he had left it, Bill Clinton. Carter's freelancing on CNN—announcing details of a deal without consulting with Clinton—limited the president's choices and was viewed as deeply disloyal. It was similar to the way that Carter had ruined a healthy relationship with President George H. W. Bush's administration by publicly and privately seeking to undermine their coalition-building as they prepared to send troops to Kuwait in 1991 to throw the Iraqi invaders out of the small Gulf state.

Carter's strident criticism of Israel over the years has angered and dismayed many. His willingness to talk to and even befriend ruthless dictators like Hafez al-Assad of Syria and Daniel Ortega of Nicaragua, or questionable characters like Palestinian leader Yasser Arafat, left him open to charges that he was hypocritical or naive. He wrote an open letter in 2009 apologizing to the Jewish people for any offense he had given them, but he continued in his final years to push President Obama to recognize a Palestinian state. And as for the naiveté charge, Carter strongly believed that dialogue and mutual understanding were highly preferable and more effective in resolving disagreements than violence. And his Christian faith gave him a view of the human heart that was more complex than some Manichean worldview. He believed himself a sinner, and he believed the worst ruler to be redeemable.

Carter's lone attempt at urban renewal, in Atlanta, did not succeed. But he has led a robust and energetic life even into his nineties. He has published thirty books in his ex-presidency, including a novel (the first by a U.S. president), a book of poetry, a children's book, a book on fishing and other outdoor sporting activities, two on making the most of older years (one of which he cowrote with Rosalynn), a few on the Middle East, a few personal history books focused on different periods of his life, and a handful of religious devotional books. He won the Nobel Peace Prize in 2002.

In August 2015, he underwent cancer surgery. Miraculously, he was declared cancer-free three months later. He continued to teach Sunday school in Plains on a regular basis.

⁕⁕⁕

Kennedy, during all this time, followed a quite different path. In the immediate aftermath of 1980, he seemed to see the race as a cathartic personal experience, and a bridge toward future political opportunity. The damage done to the Democratic Party was the cost of doing business. The impact on his own family name came in exchange for a certain amount of freedom from his own demons.

He had proven something, to himself certainly, and to others. He had proven he was not a quitter, whatever the cost. He had proven himself to his dead father and his dead brothers. And he had proven that he, too, could summon the "invisible but solid" political electricity, that mixture of inspiration, passion, and liberalism, that had made his brothers famous and beloved. For a few brief moments on that stage, on a Tuesday night in August at the convention, he had embodied and resurrected the unique essence that had always made the Kennedy name something special. "The magic was finally on him" for those few brief moments.

But Kennedy would never fully outrun his family's past, even if sometimes he physically seemed to be trying to do so. One former Capitol Hill aide, Jon Haber, said that in the Capitol hallways Kennedy walked so fast that he and other staffers sometimes had to trot to keep up. "It was almost like the ghosts of his brothers were whispering in his ear, 'You're not worthy enough.' I've never seen anyone so driven," Haber said. Haber also did advance work for Kennedy at one point, and learned that one ironclad rule was never to take Kennedy through a kitchen at a hotel or restaurant to get him into an event. Bobby had been shot while exiting a kitchen.

And Kennedy's use of that magic also meant its diminishment. He had dinged and battered his legacy a great deal on his way to finding his meaning. After the loss, he kept his options open to run again in 1984. He set up a political operation and even hired Pat Caddell to do focus groups in Iowa and to test TV ads for New Hampshire. But Caddell thought Kennedy was just going through the motions, and Teddy formally decided against it at the end of 1982. He cut off any thoughts of a 1988 run at the end of 1985. And so with his exit from the world of presidential politics, the Kennedy name lost a good deal of raw power. The family name, still respected and revered by many, nonetheless transitioned into the realm of a historical object. By 1982, "Teddy had moved from the mythic to the human," according to his nephew, Christopher Kennedy Lawford. Most fundamentally, the fact that he would never be president made him a force much less to be feared.

It wasn't just a process of shedding unwanted psychological baggage. Teddy embraced an identity that was not in synch with the way American politics was going. The Democratic Party was tilting rightward, and he went left. That wasn't a given for him, since his own upbringing and family background was fairly conservative. But it was where his state was headed.

On the other side of 1980, Kennedy became a highly respected senator, and finally an elder statesman in U.S. politics. But not right away. Even as he became increasingly productive in the Senate during Reagan's two terms in office, his personal life became more and more chaotic. In 1990, Michael Kelly wrote that Kennedy had shown over the years "a childish belief that the rules of human behavior do not apply to himself, a casual willingness to place himself in a compromising positions [*sic*] with an attractive young woman and, most probably, a reckless use of alcohol."

Teddy divorced Joan in 1982, and so the 1980s became Kennedy's "second bachelorhood," the *Boston Globe* wrote. "Spiced by published reports of heavy drinking and sexual escapades, his personal life became punch-line fodder for late-night TV shows." Kelly's profile of Kennedy for *GQ* magazine in February 1990 detailed the senator's debauched and drunken escapades with fellow senator Chris Dodd of Connecticut at a French restaurant on Capitol Hill and elsewhere. Kennedy and Dodd were described by staff at the restaurant as having manhandled a waitress in 1985 to such a degree that it was sexual assault. In 1987, Kennedy was found having sex with a woman on the floor of a semiprivate dining room. Former *Star Wars* actress Carrie Fisher related in a recent book that in 1985 she went to a dinner with Dodd, whom she had never met. During the dinner, Kennedy asked her if she would be having sex with Dodd later.

"It was all part of my desire to escape, to keep moving, to avoid painful memories," Kennedy wrote in his autobiography. "And so I lived this string of years in the present tense, not despondently, because that is not my nature, but certainly with a sense of the void."

In 1991, Kennedy hit a new low point when his nephew, William Kennedy Smith, was accused of rape and accounts of the night included a description of Teddy himself wandering around a Palm Beach mansion with no pants on in the wee hours of the morning. The trial was televised nationally and Kennedy's part in the escapade rendered him conspicuously silent during the confirmation hearings of Supreme Court nominee Clarence Thomas after a former colleague, Anita Hill, stepped forward with sexual harassment charges.

"It seemed that Ted Kennedy had finally bottomed out," wrote the *New Yorker*'s Peter Boyer. Said *People* magazine, "In the long downward slope of Sen. Edward Kennedy's private life and public career, what happened at the family's Palm Beach, Fla., retreat last month may, in retrospect, mark the point at which sorry decline turned into free-fall." Kennedy sensed he had hit bottom—and saw that he had a 22 percent approval rating—and in late 1991 he gave a speech expressing contrition, in stark contrast to the defiance of his 1980 speech at the convention. "I recognize my own shortcomings—the faults in the conduct of my private life. I realize that I alone am responsible for them, and I am the one who must confront them." He had given such speeches before, after Chappaquiddick. There was plenty of reason to believe this was just another one. "He seemed a man whose life had long ago become overfull of incident, too eventful, yet the incidents and events never ceased," Boyer wrote.

During that time, Kennedy experienced a form of salvation: He met Victoria Anne Reggie. Kennedy began dating Reggie in the summer of 1991 and married her the next year. She was just thirty-seven years old when they met, and he was fifty-nine. She was a successful banking attorney and the mother of two children. Her first marriage, to telecom executive Grier Raclin, had ended in 1990. Their families had known each other for years, and they were acquaintances. Vicki had even worked as an intern in Kennedy's office in the 1970s, though he had no memory of it.

B. Drummond Ayres Jr., a *New York Times* reporter who covered Kennedy's 1980 run for president, observed seventeen years afterward that Kennedy was a uniquely solitary individual, because of who he was. "You were struck by the loneliness of this man," Ayres said. Kennedy agreed with that assessment. "I don't think I knew how lonely I was until I met Vicki," he said. She made him happy, and provided stability and guidance. She was a loving spouse who made Kennedy laugh but who also functioned as a sharp-eyed political consigliere. He described her as "the woman who changed my life."

In the 1980s and early 1990s, Kennedy had made steady progress on some issues that were important to him. But the best-known episode of his Senate career from that decade was his opposition to the Supreme Court nomination of Robert Bork in 1987. Kennedy hyperbolically charged that if Bork were nominated, America would resegregate blacks and whites, women would be forced into back alleys for abortions, and police would "break down citizens' doors in midnight raids." Kennedy helped tank Bork's nomination, but tarnished himself in the process. And the Bork nomination fight degraded and weaponized national politics. It enraged the right and provoked them, under Newt Gingrich in the 1990s, to view Congress as a battlefield rather than a place where elected representatives work together to solve problems. That dynamic has persisted and worsened since then.

After marrying Vicki, Kennedy would go on to the most productive years of his life. But first he faced one of the toughest electoral challenges of his career, when Boston businessman Mitt Romney challenged him for the seat in 1994. Kennedy overcame a slow start and finished strong to stave off the ambitious young private equity CEO, who would go on to become governor of Massachusetts eight years later, and the Republican nominee for president in 2012.

In his autobiography, Kennedy told a story about Vicki from this period that illustrated the way in which she supported him, as well as challenged him. The night after Thanksgiving, a few weeks after he dispatched Romney and won reelection to a sixth Senate term, Kennedy and Vicki were having dinner with her parents and two other couples. There were a number of toasts congratulating him on his election win, and he grew uncomfortable, he said, with the attention. So he stood and tried to deflect it, or play it down. "This victory really isn't about me," he said. "It's about my family, and it's about the people of Massachusetts and their residual goodwill that goes all the way back to Grampa's day—"

He was suddenly cut off by Vicki, who got to her feet and exclaimed, "Please excuse my language, but BULLSHIT! This is just ridiculous!" Kennedy could only stare at her, stunned. She paused, and then continued. "You know, Teddy, if you had lost, it would've been *you* that lost. It wouldn't have been your family that lost. *You* would've lost. You *won*. *You* won! Not your family. *You*."

Vicki sat back down. Kennedy's decision to include the anecdote in his book was significant. He was a private person, not given to sharing a multitude of colorful personal stories. But Vicki's words to him—endorsing him as his own person, as an individual—in a way that was both empowering and somewhat unsettling, meant a lot to him. "Her message to me was one I needed to hear—perhaps one I'd yearned to hear," he wrote.

The final fifteen years of Kennedy's life and Senate career saw him transformed into a liberal icon, into the unquestioned patriarch of the Kennedy clan, and then finally into a bipartisan elder of the Senate. In the 1990s, he worked with President Bill Clinton to expand government health care for children and to raise the minimum wage. He also led the Kennedy clan through its grief as they continued to deal with loss. Jackie—Jacqueline Bouvier Kennedy Onassis—died of cancer in May 1994, just sixty-four. Kennedy's mother, Rose, died several months later at the beginning of 1995. She was 104 years old, but her death hit Kennedy hard. The late 1990s brought another wave of tragedy. Michael Kennedy, the sixth of Bobby Kennedy's eleven children and the father of three, was killed in a skiing accident in 1997 at age thirty-nine. And then in 1999, JFK's only son, John F. Kennedy Jr., was killed in a plane crash at age thirty-eight, along with his wife, Carolyn Bessette Kennedy, and her sister, Lauren Bessette.

In the early years of George W. Bush's presidency, Kennedy collaborated with the Republican administration on a major overhaul of the federal education system. He was optimistic about the No Child Left Behind legislation, but grew disillusioned with Bush's implementation of it and with funding levels he saw as insufficient. He ultimately called the law "a spectacular broken promise" of Bush's.

Kennedy was a vocal opponent of Bush's decision to invade Iraq in 2003. But in Bush's second term, he tried to help the president pass comprehensive immigration reform. The far right of the Republican Party—and some last-minute Democratic defections—defeated that attempt.

Kennedy turned out to be a far better lawmaker than either John or Bobby, although he did have a much longer time to figure it out. "Far more than either of his brothers, who were lackluster senators, Kennedy, over the past three decades, has been responsible for changes in the complexion of this country and in the lives of its citizens," Michael Kelly wrote.

Kennedy said in the late 1980s of himself, "I define liberalism in this country." To some degree, though, he achieved his statesmanlike status by moderating his liberalism. He "abandoned the costly Utopian reforms he pushed in the Seventies—such as government-financed universal health insurance and welfare payments that guaranteed an income above the poverty level for all—and now focuses on less-budget-busting programs," wrote Kelly. He had been forced to do so by his experience in 1980, when his calls for bigger and more active government ran headlong into public sentiment that the government was too big and spent too much.

Ironically it was Carter who veered hard to the left in his post-presidency, becoming an outspoken critic of Israel in particular. Carter never sought office again, and being unconstrained by political concerns, he went in the opposite direction from the Democratic Party, which tacked to the center in the wake of his loss to Reagan. The president who had been nearly tossed from his own party for being too conservative was seen by many as one of the most liberal ex-presidents of the modern age.

But Kennedy was a model of what an effective senator could be. He was crafty at the legislative process and hardworking, he was renowned for the excellent staff he hired and utilized, but most of all he was patient. He pursued his legislative goals over years and decades, taking what he could get, very much an incrementalist. He was not a shooting star like his brothers, who flashed for a brief moment and then were extinguished. He was not impatient with the rhythms of the Senate. It was the approach best suited to him.

He wasn't a genius or an unparalleled political talent, but he took pride in working harder than others, in continuing to move forward no matter how hard life got or how brutal a tragedy he had to confront, and in persevering. "Perseverance" was the word he used when asked in 1994 what he thought his personal strengths were.

His son Teddy Jr. told a story at Teddy's funeral in 2009 of a time the two of them went sledding when Teddy Jr. was twelve and had recently had his leg amputated due to cancer. Teddy Jr. fell on an ice patch and began telling his father through tears that he couldn't function with his prosthetic limb. His voice wavering, he described how his father had picked him up "in his strong, gentle arms" and told him, "I know you can do it. There is nothing you can't do. We're going to climb that hill together, even if it takes us all day."

Said Teddy Jr., "My father taught me that even our most profound losses are survivable. And it is what we do with that loss, our ability to transform it into a positive event, that is one of my father's greatest lessons."

To the end, Teddy Kennedy knew there was much in his life to atone for, and hoped he had done enough to do so. "I know that I have been an imperfect human being, but with the help of my faith I have tried to right my path," he wrote in a 2009 letter to Pope Benedict XVI, just weeks before his death.

Kennedy had that letter hand-delivered to the pope by the newly elected president, Barack Obama. It had been his endorsement of Obama during the young senator's difficult primary battle with Hillary Clinton in 2008 that marked his final significant political moment. Endorsing Obama had been both a political risk for Kennedy and a huge boost for Obama, coming at a time when the race was still quite uncertain. But Obama moved quickly once in office to accomplish what Kennedy had been hoping to see happen during his lifetime: national health insurance.

Teddy did not live quite long enough to see that goal fulfilled. He died in August 2009, as Congress debated the legislation, of a malignant brain tumor. He had served in the Senate for almost forty-seven years, the fourth-longest-serving senator in American history.

In 1985, Kennedy's longtime friend and adviser Paul Kirk made an attempt to patch up the relationship between Teddy and Jimmy Carter. It took three more years and many phone calls to get the two men together. On the first day of the 1988 convention in Atlanta, Kennedy visited the Carter Center and the former rivals had a brief meeting to try to make a show of party unity.

"All of us know that we've had our difficulties in the past," Kennedy said to reporters, standing next to Carter. "But one thing has to stand out and that is Mr. Carter's record on the issue of human rights. All Americans are in his debt for that and history will demonstrate that Camp David was one of the great historical achievements."

Carter scraped for a compliment in return, and offered this: "I went to the dedication of his brother's library, and it was one of the nicest days of my life."

It was classic Kennedy, and classic Carter. Humbled by personal failure and tragedy, yet on his way to eventual redemption and transformation, Kennedy offered frank commentary and sincere praise. Carter, for all his achievements and personal success, for all his moral uprightness—perhaps precisely because of this—could not bring himself to do so.

Many years later, seated in his office in Atlanta, Carter had had more time to mellow, to observe his own life and career, and that of Kennedy, from a distant remove. I asked him if he thought Kennedy had redeemed himself by the end of his life. And to my surprise, Carter offered the compliment to Kennedy that he had been unable to twenty-five years earlier.

"I don't think he needed any redemption," Jimmy Carter said of Teddy Kennedy. "I think he is one of the best senators who ever served."

# Acknowledgments

None of this happens without Alison. I'd be lost without her. She is first in my heart and my life. I love you, Ali.

I have wondered what my children will think about all those times I told them I had to go work on "the book." Hopefully they will realize I did it in part to leave them some enduring part of myself. Of course we do that in many ways for those after us. But books have always appealed to me, in part because of the way they transform one's working hours into a form of legacy making that does have staying power.

I draw strength, purpose, and inspiration from each of my children. Jethro, Gwen, Etta, Juniper, and Susie: I do all this for you, and you are my world.

Sue Woodrow cared for our children after the birth of our fifth child and so many other times, often allowing me to steal away to do some reading or writing. And Bill Woodrow is the best grandfather in the world. His delight in our children is a gift to them and us. My father, Chip, gifted me many of my writer sensibilities, and he is one of my best friends. My mother, Diane, is probably the greatest hero in my life. I love you all.

In the early days of the book's gestation, Jeff Berman played a key role just by hearing me out, supporting the idea, and helping to arrange one of my first interviews, with Bill Carrick. Anita Dunn was also a key validator for me. It meant a lot to have people like Jeff and Anita encourage the project and be part of it.

Jerry Rafshoon was also a presence from start to finish of this journey, and a believer in the idea. He was instrumental in getting me time with President Jimmy Carter. And Jerry also helped me, if memory serves, attend the performance of the play *Camp David* at Arena Stage in 2014 with President Carter in attendance. President Carter himself was gracious and forthcoming during our time together, and I'm grateful for his cooperation. Others at the Carter Center in Atlanta who were helpful either during my visits there or over email and phone include Phil Wise, Steve Hochman, Deanna Congileo, and Karin Ryan. Tim Kraft helped me find Bill Romjue as I researched the 1980 Iowa caucuses.

Thanks to Pat Caddell for two memorable interviews in Chicago and Charleston. Peter Bourne was a true gentleman in our correspondence and during our interview, and his excellent biography of Carter was an absolutely vital resource. It was no easy task getting Tom Donilon to sit down for an interview, but once I finally did, Tom was full of helpful information, good stories, and kindness.

Barbara Ann Perry, the director of presidential studies at the University of Virginia's Miller Center, helped guide me through the resources available in the center's presidential oral history project. It was highly serendipitous that the Miller Center oral histories began with Jimmy Carter's presidency, and included only one oral history project for a political figure who was not a president: Teddy Kennedy. I took that as a sign of good fortune for this book.

When the Edward M. Kennedy Institute opened in Boston, Dan Reilly was an affable, skilled ambassador, and because of that I won't hold his collegiate loyalties against him. And although most of Teddy Kennedy's files at the John F. Kennedy Library in Boston were still sealed, Adam Clymer's papers were an indispensable resource largely because of all the interview transcripts. Clymer's Kennedy biography is a great contribution.

In Kennedy world, there were many who were eager to help. Bob Shrum was a regular source of encouragement throughout the process, and provided good insights. There were many who gave helpful interviews: Rick Stearns, Bill Carrick, Peter Edelman, Joe Trippi, Carl Wagner, Jon Haber, Susan Estrich, Matt Bennett, Steve McMahon, Harold Ickes, Jim Manley, and Ricki Seidman.

I'm grateful to have stumbled upon Sergio Bendixen, who connected me with Mike Abrams. Our conversations about the Florida straw poll in the fall of 1979, and the years leading up to that, were illuminating.

Vice President Joe Biden ran way over his allotted time with me in January 2015, maybe to the bemusement of Shailagh Murray, or maybe to her irritation. Either way, I enjoyed my time in the vice president's West Wing office very much, and thank you to Shailagh for arranging it.

Many people helped me understand the nuance and complexity of both Carter and Kennedy. Senator Orrin Hatch of Utah gave me a tour of Kennedy's old hideaway office in the U.S. Capitol, which he inherited, and showed me a painting Kennedy did for him. Former senator Alan Simpson and former Texas lieutenant governor Ben Barnes also shared their thoughts about the two men.

Al From and Sean Trende talked with me about what came after 1980 and helped me explore the broader historical and political context. David Axelrod and Chris Wallace shared their memories as journalists who covered the 1980 primary. And Roger Mudd graciously invited me to his McLean home and spent time talking about that famous and historic hour-long special he broadcast in the fall of 1979, the Teddy Kennedy interviews. Mudd became a journalistic hero of mine as I studied his career, and it's a shame he did not inherit Walter Cronkite's anchor chair at CBS News. But Roger's equanimity and kindness to this day—despite that career disappointment—only increased my estimation of him.

Elaine Kamarck was another invaluable guide to the history of the nominating process and to the intricacies of primary rules, and I've relied on her expertise and knowledge often.

Craig Shirley's book on Ronald Reagan's 1980 campaign, *Rendezvous with Destiny*, was another great resource, and I benefited from our conversations early in the process.

Two people among the most responsible for making this possible are Megan Liberman and Dan Klaidman. They hired me at Yahoo News in the fall of 2014, and that ushered in the happiest period of my journalism career to date. They hired the most talented group of journalists I'd ever worked with, and developed a positive, creative, affirming culture that helped all of us do our best work. Megan and Dan always had my back, and that included supporting my book. When I told Megan that our family would be adding a fifth child during the middle of the 2016 presidential election, she offered nothing but support. And thanks to Yahoo's generous paternity leave, having another kid meant that I got the kind of time I needed to take off from work and finish the book. After the election ended, I spent all of December writing the last few chapters. Megan and Dan are models of strong and inspiring leadership, and I call them my good friends as well.

Thanks also to Arianna Huffington, Tucker Carlson, Neil Patel, Mike Nizza, and Ken McIntyre for giving me every chance along the way to grow and advance in my career.

Thank you to all my journalist and political friends who encouraged me, asked about the book, and gave advice along the way, especially John Dickerson, Paul Kane, James Rosen, Miranda Kennedy, Jonathan Rauch, and Sasha Issenberg. A special thanks to Amy Sullivan for reading much of the manuscript and providing helpful feedback.

David Eldridge was my first mentor in journalism. He had just met me, and he handed me a press release and said, "Go cover this."

Day by day he molded me into something resembling a newspaper man for the next few years, and we remain good friends.

Michael Olmert was the college professor who baptized my imagination and my intellect with a fiery passion for learning and exploration. I will never forget my mornings in Olmert's lecture hall at the University of Maryland.

Mike Allen has been a friend, a mentor, and a champion. I simply wouldn't have had many of the opportunities I've had if it weren't for his generosity and friendship. Thank you, Mike.

I had always looked up to Matt Bai even before I met him. I thought he was one of the best journalists and political magazine writers around. Then one day in 2014, I reached out for advice on a story, and he told me I should come work at Yahoo News. Now that we have become friends, I'm an even bigger fan. No one has helped me more to think about the finer points of writing and reporting as a craft than Matt. And Matt always encouraged me to make time to take a walk, slow down, and really think about what I was doing. That was invaluable advice. I can't believe I get to have drinks and talk shop with him.

I'm also very lucky to be friends with Yuval Levin, whom I consider a kindred spirit. I suspect many people feel that way about Yuval. He may have one of the more incisive minds in American political thought, but he's also one of the most kind and decent people I've ever met. He's one of the few people I'll continue to meet on a regular basis without insisting we switch to a decent coffee shop, because the conversation is always stimulating.

My sister Catherine is one of my personal heroes, a strong and courageous woman with an irrepressible zest for life, and her passion for writing—and her skill—is an inspiration to me.

Mark Fedeli's steady friendship has been a constant source of support and encouragement for which I'm deeply grateful. He has one of the biggest hearts in the world. Phil Gallo and Joe

Walker just make me laugh. But they do it really well, and I love them for it.

Bridget Wagner Matzie is more than an agent. She's an editor, a trusted adviser and guide, an advocate, and a friend. I quite simply wouldn't have written this book if not for her belief in the project and her expert and skillful assistance every step of the way. Thank you, Bridget.

Sean Desmond, as well, has been for this book and for me from the beginning. It meant a lot to work with a publisher who, quite simply, treated me as more than just a writer and took an interest in who I was and what I cared about. Thanks to the whole team at Twelve Books: Rachel Kambury, Brian McLendon, Paul Samuelson, Rachel Molland, Jarrod Taylor, Carolyn Kurek, and Roland Ottewell.

And to Jonathan Allen, thank you for introducing me to Bridget, and for the occasional politics chat along the way. Every journey begins with a first step, and meeting Bridget was one of the key ones on mine.

# Sources

## Books

Anderson, John B. *A Congressman's Choice: Between Two Worlds.* Grand Rapids, MI: Zondervan, 1970.

Anderson, Patrick. *Electing Jimmy Carter: The Campaign of 1976.* Baton Rouge: Louisiana State University Press, 1994.

Balmer, Randall. *Redeemer: The Life of Jimmy Carter.* New York: Basic Books, 2014.

Bingham, Clara. *Witness to the Revolution: Radicals, Resisters, Vets, Hippies, and the Year America Lost Its Mind and Found Its Soul.* New York: Random House, 2017.

Bourne, Peter G. *Jimmy Carter: A Comprehensive Biography from Plains to Post-Presidency.* New York: A Lisa Drew Book/Scribner, 1997.

Bowden, Mark. *Guests of the Ayatollah: The Iran Hostage Crisis; The First Battle in America's War with Militant Islam.* New York: Grove Press, 2006.

Brinkley, Douglas. *The Unfinished Presidency: Jimmy Carter's Journey Beyond the White House.* New York: Penguin, 1998.

Broder, David. *The Party's Over: The Failure of Politics in America.* New York: Harper & Row, 1972.

Brzezinski, Zbigniew. *Power and Principle: Memoirs of the National Security Adviser, 1977–1981.* Revised edition. New York: Farrar, Straus & Giroux, 1985.

Burke, Richard E., with William and Marilyn Hoffer. *The Senator: My Ten Years with Ted Kennedy*. New York: St. Martin's, 1992.

Canellos, Peter S., ed. *Last Lion: The Fall and Rise of Ted Kennedy*. New York: Simon & Schuster, 2009.

Carson, Donald W., and James W. Johnson. *Mo: The Life and Times of Morris K. Udall*. Tucson: University of Arizona Press, 2001.

Carter, Dan. T. *The Politics of Rage: George Wallace, the Origins of the New Conservatism, and the Transformation of American Politics*. New York: Simon & Schuster, 1995.

Carter, Jimmy. *A Full Life: Reflections at Ninety*. New York: Simon & Schuster, 2015.

———. *Always a Reckoning, and Other Poems*. New York: Times Books, 1995.

———. *An Hour Before Daylight: Memories of a Rural Boyhood*. New York: Simon & Schuster, 2001.

———. *Keeping Faith: Memoirs of a President*. New York: Bantam, 1982.

———. *The Hornet's Nest: A Novel of the Revolutionary War*. New York: Simon & Schuster, 2003.

———. *The Virtues of Aging*. New York: The Library of Contemporary Thought/Random House, 1998.

———. *Turning Point: A Candidate, a State, and a Nation Come of Age*. New York: Three Rivers Press; Reissue edition, 2011.

———. *White House Diary*. New York: Farrar, Straus & Giroux, 2010.

———. *Why Not the Best?* Nashville: Broadman Press, 1977.

Carter, Jimmy, and Rosalynn Carter. *Everything to Gain: Making the Most of the Rest of Your Life*. Revised edition. Fayetteville: University of Arkansas Press, 1995.

Carter, Rosalynn. *First Lady from Plains*. New York: Ballantine, 1985.

Chellis, Marcia. *Living with the Kennedys: The Joan Kennedy Story.* New York: Simon & Schuster, 1985.

Clymer, Adam. *Edward M. Kennedy: A Biography.* New York: Harper Perennial, 2009 (originally published in 1999).

Cohen, Marty, David Karol, Hans Noel, and John Zaller. *The Party Decides: Presidential Nominations Before and After Reform.* Chicago: University of Chicago Press, 2008.

Cooper, Andrew Scott. *The Fall of Heaven: The Pahlavis and the Final Days of Imperial Iran.* New York: Henry Holt, 2016.

Cramer, Richard Ben. *What It Takes: The Way to the White House.* New York: Vintage, 1993.

DeFrank, Thomas M. *Write It When I'm Gone: Remarkable Off-the-Record Conversations with Gerald R. Ford.* New York: Berkeley, 2008.

Dickerson, John. *Whistlestop: My Favorite Stories from Presidential Campaign History.* New York: Twelve, 2016.

Drew, Elizabeth. *Portrait of an Election: The 1980 Presidential Campaign.* New York: Simon & Schuster, 1981.

Edsall, Thomas Byrne, and Mary Byrne Edsall. *Chain Reaction: The Impact of Race, Rights, and Taxes on American Politics.* New York: Norton, 1991.

Eizenstat, Stuart E. *President Carter: The White House Years.* New York: St. Martin's Press, 2018.

Frum, David. *How We Got Here: The 70's; The Decade That Brought You Modern Life.* New York: Basic Books, 2000.

Gates, Robert. *Duty: Memoirs of a Secretary at War.* New York: Vintage, 2015.

———. *From the Shadows: The Ultimate Insider's Story of Five Presidents and How They Won the Cold War.* New York: Simon & Schuster, 2011 (originally published in 1996).

Germond, Jack W., and Jules Witcover. *Blue Smoke and Mirrors:*

*How Reagan Won and Why Carter Lost the Election of 1980.* New York: Viking, 1981.

Godbold, E. Stanly Jr. *Jimmy and Rosalynn Carter: The Georgia Years, 1924–1974.* New York: Oxford University Press, 2010.

Halberstam, David. *The Powers That Be.* New York: Open Road Media (December 18, 2012).

———. *The Unfinished Odyssey of Robert Kennedy: A Biography.* New York: Open Road Media (March 5, 2013).

Hart, Gary. *Right from the Start: A Chronicle of the McGovern Campaign.* New York: Quadrangle/New York Times Book Co., 1973.

Harwood, Richard, ed., and the staff of the *Washington Post. The Pursuit of the Presidency, 1980.* New York: Berkeley, 1980.

Hersh, Burton. *Edward Kennedy: An Intimate Biography.* Berkeley, CA: Counterpoint, 2010.

Jordan, Hamilton. *A Boy from Georgia: Coming of Age in the Segregated South.* Athens, GA: The University of Georgia Press, 2015.

———. *Crisis: The Last Year of the Carter Presidency.* New York: G. P. Putnam's Sons, 1982.

Kamarck, Elaine C. *Primary Politics: How Presidential Candidates Have Shaped the Modern Nominating System.* Washington, DC: Brookings Institution, 2009.

Kennedy, Edward M. *True Compass: A Memoir.* New York: Twelve, 2009.

Kennedy, Patrick J., and Stephen Fried. *A Common Struggle: A Personal Journey Through the Past and Future of Mental Illness and Addiction.* New York: Blue Rider Press, 2015.

Lawford, Christopher Kennedy. *Symptoms of Withdrawal: A Memoir of Snapshots and Redemption.* New York: HarperCollins e-books; Reprint edition, 2009.

L'Engle, Madeleine. *The Irrational Season: (The Crosswicks Journal, Book 3).* New York: HarperOne, 1984.

Littlefield, Nick, and David Nexon. *Lion of the Senate: When Ted Kennedy Rallied the Democrats in a GOP Congress.* New York: Simon & Schuster, 2015.

Manchester, William. *The Death of a President: November 20– November 25, 1963.* New York: Little, Brown; Kindle edition, 2013.

Mattson, Kevin. *"What the Heck Are You Up to, Mr. President?": Jimmy Carter, America's "Malaise," and the Speech That Should Have Changed the Country.* New York: Bloomsbury USA, 2009.

McGinniss, Joe. *The Last Brother.* New York: Simon & Schuster, 1993.

Mudd, Roger. *The Place to Be: Washington, CBS, and the Glory Days of Television News.* New York: PublicAffairs, 2008.

Nasaw, David. *The Patriarch: The Remarkable Life and Turbulent Times of Joseph P. Kennedy.* New York: Penguin, 2012.

Oliphant, Thomas, and Curtis Wilkie. *The Road to Camelot: Inside JFK's Five-Year Campaign.* New York: Simon & Schuster, 2017.

O'Mara, Margaret. *Pivotal Tuesdays: Four Elections That Shaped the Twentieth Century.* Philadelphia: University of Pennsylvania Press, 2015.

O'Neill, Tip, with William Novak. *Man of the House: The Life and Political Memoirs of Speaker Tip O'Neill.* New York: Random House, 1987.

Perry, Barbara A. *Rose Kennedy: The Life and Times of a Political Matriarch.* New York: Norton, 2013.

Polsby, Nelson W. *Consequences of Party Reform.* New York: Oxford University Press, 1983.

Powell, Jody. *The Other Side of the Story.* New York: William Morrow, 1984.

Shapiro, Ira. *The Last Great Senate: Courage and Statesmanship in Times of Crisis.* New York: PublicAffairs, 2012.

Sherrill, Robert. *The Last Kennedy: Edward M. Kennedy of Massachusetts Before and After Chappaquiddick.* New York: Dial, 1976.

Shirley, Craig. *Rendezvous with Destiny: Ronald Reagan and the Campaign That Changed America*. Wilmington, DE: ISI Books, 2009.

Shogan, Robert. *Promises to Keep: Carter's First 100 Days*. New York: Thomas Y. Crowell, 1977.

Shrum, Robert. *No Excuses: Concessions of a Serial Campaigner*. New York: Simon & Schuster, 2007.

Sick, Gary. *October Surprise: America's Hostages in Iran and the Election of Ronald Reagan*. New York: Times Books, 1991.

Sorensen, Ted. *Kennedy: The Classic Biography*. New York: Harper Perennial Political Classics, 2009 (originally published in 1965).

Stanley, Timothy. *Kennedy vs. Carter: The 1980 Battle for the Democratic Party's Soul*. Lawrence: University Press of Kansas, 2010.

Tedrow, Richard L., and Thomas L. Tedrow. *Death at Chappaquiddick*. Gretna, LA: Pelican Publishing Company, 1980.

Thomas, Evan. *Robert Kennedy: His Life*. New York: Simon & Schuster Paperbacks, 2007.

Thompson, Hunter S. *The Great Shark Hunt: Strange Tales from a Strange Time*. New York: Simon & Schuster Paperbacks, 2003 (originally published in 1979).

Tsongas, Paul. *The Road from Here: Liberalism and Realities in the 1980s*. New York: Vintage, 1982.

Updike, John. *Rabbit Is Rich*. New York: Random House; Reissue edition, 2010.

White, Theodore H. *America in Search of Itself: The Making of the President, 1956–1980*. New York: Harper & Row, 1982.

———. *The Making of the President: 1960*. New York: Harper Perennial Political Classics, 2009 (originally published in 1961).

Witcover, Jules. *Marathon: The Pursuit of the Presidency, 1972–1976*. New York: Viking, 1977.

Wooten, James. *Dasher: The Roots and the Rising of Jimmy Carter*. New York: Summit Books, 1978.

Wright, Lawrence. *In the New World: Growing Up with America from the Sixties to the Eighties.* New York: Vintage, 2013 (originally published in 1987).

———. *Thirteen Days in September: The Dramatic Story of the Struggle for Peace.* New York: Alfred A. Knopf, 2014.


## Magazine Articles

Boyer, Peter J. "We're Not in Camelot Anymore." *New Yorker*, May 23, 1994.

Clift, Eleanor. "Kennedy Enters 1980 Presidential Race." *Newsweek*, September 23, 1979.

Drew, Elizabeth. "In Search of a Definition." *New Yorker*, August 27, 1979.

Fallows, James. "The Passionless Presidency." *Atlantic*, May 1979.

Kelly, Michael. "Ted Kennedy on the Rocks." *GQ*, February 1990.

Lessard, Suzannah. "Kennedy's Woman Problem. Women's Kennedy Problem." *Washington Monthly*, December 1979.

Sherrill, Robert. "Chappaquiddick +5: A Tragedy, an Enigma, a Political Achilles Heel." *New York Times Magazine*, July 14, 1974.

Tolchin, Martin. "New Pro in the White House." *New York Times Magazine*, December 17, 1978.

# Notes

## INTRODUCTION

**I entered Jimmy Carter's personal office**—President Carter's comments are from our interview on January 15, 2015, at the Carter Center in Atlanta.

**the Edward M. Kennedy Institute**—The institute's dedication ceremony took place on March 30, 2015.

**Bobby Kennedy's children were angry**—Adam Clymer and Don Van Natta Jr., "Family of Robert F. Kennedy Rethinks His Place at Library," *New York Times*, July 11, 2011.

**taxpayers pitched in $38 million**—Joshua Miller, "A Monument to Kennedy and the Power of the Senate," *Boston Globe*, March 28, 2015.

**Vicki said that Teddy had once told her**—Vicki Kennedy speech at Kennedy Institute opening ceremony, March 30, 2015.

**the Democratic Party's annual winter meeting**—The DNC winter meeting in 2013 took place at the Marriott Wardman Park hotel in Washington, D.C., on January 22.

**"It was ideological"**—Tom Donilon interview, March 3, 2017, Washington, D.C.

**"was searing for the party"**—Harold Ickes phone interview, July 22, 2013.

**"He's really been"**—Ben Barnes phone interview, March 14, 2017.

**"The period of '78 to '82"**—Peter Hart interview with Adam Clymer, January 9, 1988, John F. Kennedy Library, Adam Clymer Personal Papers, Box 3.

**"I cannot remember a time"**—Anita Dunn interview, August 6, 2013, Washington, D.C.

**an "anguished" decade**—Madeleine L'Engle, *The Irrational Season* (*The Crosswicks Journal, Book 3*) (San Francisco: Harper San Francisco, 1984), 33.

**"What we have"**—David Broder, *The Party's Over: The Failure of Politics in America* (New York: Harper & Row, 1972), xxv.

**Suicide rates were on the rise**—Sabrina Tavernise, "U.S. Suicide Rate Surges to a 30-Year High," *New York Times*, April 22, 2016.

# CHAPTER 1: Sailing Against the Wind

**"Ted Kennedy had inherited"**—Theodore H. White, *America in Search of Itself: The Making of the President, 1956–1980* (New York: Harper & Row, 1982), 272.

**he might someday inhabit the White House**—Adam Clymer, *Edward M. Kennedy: A Biography* (New York: William Morrow, 1999), 51.

**The temperature would sink well below freezing**—*The Old Farmer's Almanac*, "Weather History for Memphis, TN," https://www.alma nac.com/weather/history/TN/Memphis/1978-12-09.

**"eager to play a minimal role"**—Adam Clymer, "Democrats Girding for Midterm Parley," *New York Times*, December 7, 1978.

**"an extraordinary gesture"**—Associated Press, "Mondale Warns Inflation Is 'Vietnam of the 70's,'" December 11, 1978.

**"Let the people of the world know"**—Donald Pfarrer and John W. Kole, "Carter Tries to Calm Furor in Guns vs. Butter Debate," *Milwaukee Journal*, December 10, 1978.

**"As a young boy" to "mostly working people"**—Edward M. Kennedy, *True Compass: A Memoir* (New York: Twelve, 2009), 300–10.

**"More than most Americans" and all other speech quotes**—Kennedy speech to Memphis midterm convention, December 9, 1978.

**"No, no, no"**—Adam Clymer, "Kennedy Assails Carter on Budget at Midterm Meeting of Democrats," *New York Times*, December 10, 1978.

**hired Carl Wagner**—Carl Wagner interview, December 10, 2014.

**"The son of a bitch"**—Pat Caddell interview, April 27, 2017, Charleston, SC.

**"I am tired of telling you guys"**—Pat Caddell interview with Adam Clymer, January 1, 1998, John F. Kennedy Library, Adam Clymer Personal Papers, Box 3.

*What in the world are we going to do?*—Peter G. Bourne, *Jimmy Carter: A Comprehensive Biography from Plains to Post-Presidency* (New York: A Lisa Drew Book/Scribner, 1997), 438.

**Menachem Begin had arrived**—Bernard Gwertzman, "Begin Lands in U.S., Saying Peace Talks Are in 'Deep Crisis,'" *New York Times*, March 2, 1979.

**"I don't like Mondays"**—Associated Press, "School Sniper Suspect Bragged of 'Something Big to Get on TV,'" January 30, 1979.

**"It is just disgusting"**—Gwertzman, "Begin Lands in U.S."

**"The failure of the Camp David accords"**—*New York Times* (editorial), "Mr. Carter Flies to the Brink," March 7, 1979.

**He faced sharp questioning**—Terence Smith, "Mondale, Hailing Carter, Is Optimistic on 80 Race," *New York Times*, March 3, 1979.

**A full-page newspaper ad**—Wallace Turner, "Protest on Coast Exposes Carter Political Wounds," *New York Times*, March 1, 1979.

**"When Teddy wanted advice"**—Burton Hersh, *Edward Kennedy: An Intimate Biography* (Berkeley, CA: Counterpoint, 2010), 473.


## CHAPTER 2: Origins of Dirt and Riches

**admitted to reporters**—"Walker Says He Was State Executive Who Addressed National Klan Council," *Atlanta Constitution*, October 14, 1924.

**two and a half miles west of Plains**—Jimmy Carter, *An Hour Before Daylight: Memories of a Rural Boyhood* (New York: Simon & Schuster, 2001), 47.

**"We wiped with old newspapers"**—Ibid., 29.

**a can with holes**—Ibid., 31.

**a multidecade process**—Ibid., 5.

**"He developed the reputation"**—Bourne, *Jimmy Carter*, 21.

**He also ran a small store**—Ibid., 24.

**The family did not speak**—Ibid., 29.

**"I Wanted to Share My Father's World"**—from *Always a Reckoning, and Other Poems* (New York: Times Books, 1995), 99.

**"I don't remember"**—Carter, *Hour Before Daylight*, 44.

**When his parents went on trips**—Ibid., 39.

**saved around $125**—Ibid., 31.

**thirty other families**—Bourne, *Jimmy Carter*, 22.

**260 farmhands**—Ibid., 24.

**"above all, a Talmadge man"**—Jimmy Carter, *Turning Point: A Candidate, a State, and a Nation Come of Age* (New York: Three Rivers Press; Reissue edition, 2011), 237.

**one-ton truck**—Carter, *Turning Point*, 255.

**"For some reason"**—Ibid., 274.

**"There was an unvoiced suspicion"**—Hersh, *Edward Kennedy*, 24.

**When guests would spend the night**—Ibid., 23.

**a household staff of eight**—Barbara A. Perry, *Rose Kennedy: The Life and Times of a Political Matriarch* (New York: Norton, 2013), 62.

**called him "fat stuff"**—Hersh, *Edward Kennedy*, 34.

**bought the house in 1928**—Kennedy, *True Compass*, 31.

**"not only is there no evidence"**—David Nasaw, *The Patriarch: The Remarkable Life and Turbulent Times of Joseph P. Kennedy* (New York: Penguin, 2012), 79.

**just off Hyde Park**—Ibid., 285.

**Teddy's bedroom**—Kennedy, *True Compass*, 51.

**an American freezer**—Nasaw, *The Patriarch*, 286.

**"Anglo-Scottish Protestants"**—Ibid., 284.

**"remain an American"**—Ibid.

**they saw the sandbags**—Kennedy, *True Compass*, 57.

**"He believes that Germany"**—Nasaw, *The Patriarch*, 429.

**who warned Roosevelt**—Ibid., 316.

on three separate ships—Ibid., 410.

"The ambassador was too rich"—Ibid., 333.

running away from the bombs—Ibid., 480.

he returned to America—Ibid., 485.

"Democracy is finished"—Ibid., 498.

"These did not prove"—Kennedy, *True Compass*, 60.

"It was a recipe for disaster"—Ibid., 61.

his pet turtle—Ibid., 62.

a rather "nomadic" experience—Ibid., 66.

Teddy's dorm master was "an abuser"—Ibid., 63.

too tired to do with him—Hersh, *Edward Kennedy*, 23.

"As sick as I was"—Kennedy, *True Compass*, 66.

"always kissed us"—Ibid., 67.

"the first of the tragedies"—Nasaw, *The Patriarch*, 537.

for two decades—Ibid., 536.

told Teddy and his friend—Kennedy, *True Compass*, 86.

"tended to travel light emotionally"—Hersh, *Edward Kennedy*, 39.

claimed to have no anger—Kennedy, *True Compass*, 66.

"Even though it was spring"—Ibid., 90.

"The sudden death"—Nasaw, *The Patriarch*, 622.

## CHAPTER 3: The Pull of Home and Politics

to get drunk—Bourne, *Jimmy Carter*, 47.

age of seven—Ibid., 44.

Earl became a member—Carter, *Turning Point*, 237.

Julia Coleman—Bourne, *Jimmy Carter*, 37–41.

"I don't think"—Ibid., 40.

"settled into a strategy of anonymity"—Ibid., 49.

weighing only around 120 pounds—Ibid., 48.

"He did not make"—Ibid., 50.

applied for a Rhodes Scholarship—Ibid., 64.

**"She's the girl"**—Jimmy Carter, *A Full Life: Reflections at Ninety* (New York: Simon & Schuster, 2015), 38.

**their first son, Jack**—Bourne, *Jimmy Carter*, 63.

**his closest brush with death**—Ibid., 66.

**"not one of the guys"**—Ibid., 67.

**a different kind of leadership**—Ibid., 71.

**"not so much a manager"**—Ibid., 77.

**"Did you always do your best?"**—Ibid., 73.

**"We feared and respected him"**—Ibid., 76.

**more than five thousand acres**—Ibid., 78.

**"It was almost like a medieval idea"**—Ibid., 79.

**"He had to come back"**—Ibid., 81.

**"almost quit me"**—Ibid.

**"We don't want any losers"**—Clymer, *Edward M. Kennedy*, 13.

**"You can have a serious life"**—Kennedy, *True Compass*, 40.

**fight in the Korean war**—Ibid., 99.

**He suspected**—Ibid., 100.

**"stopped worrying about 'catching up'"**—Ibid., 112.

**ninety miles per hour**—Hersh, *Edward Kennedy*, 91.

**"a charge of energy"**—Kennedy, *True Compass*, 116.

**There were plenty of warning signs**—Clymer, *Edward M. Kennedy*, 23.

**Jack had forgotten he was wearing a microphone**—Joan Kennedy interview with Adam Clymer, October 12, 1998, from Clymer Papers at JFK Library.

**a group of ski jumpers**—Hersh, *Edward Kennedy*, 113.

**"he played a vital role"**—Kennedy, *True Compass*, 148–50.

**his mind set on the West**—Hersh, *Edward Kennedy*, 93.

**"seriously discussed living in California"**—Kennedy, *True Compass*, 128.

**"I paid for it"**—Hersh, *Edward Kennedy*, 127.

**"It's your turn"**—Joan Kennedy interview with Adam Clymer, December 12, 1996, from Clymer Papers at JFK Library.

**"Nobody forced me"**—Clymer, *Edward M. Kennedy*, 126.

**"never used the word 'ass'"**—Ted Kennedy interview with Adam Clymer, February 3, 1997, from Clymer Papers at JFK Library.

**wasn't sure if Joe Sr. would even approve**—Kennedy, *True Compass*, 170.

**"Dad didn't think too much of the idea"**—Ibid., 128.

**"Eventually, of course"**—Hersh, *Edward Kennedy*, 126.

**they took a political approach**—Bourne, *Jimmy Carter*, 88.

**White Citizens' Council**—Ibid., 96.

**"We wanted to have"**—Ibid., 88.

**he tried to consolidate**—Ibid., 106–8.

**"would have been unthinkable"**—Ibid., 115.

**with the same horror**—Ibid.

**"relatively unobtrusive"**—Carter, *A Full Life*, 78.

COONS AND CARTERS—Bourne, *Jimmy Carter*, 108.

**underground fuel tank**—Carter, *A Full Life*, 79.

**considered leaving Plains**—Ibid., 79; E. Stanly Godbold Jr., *Jimmy and Rosalynn Carter: The Georgia Years, 1924–1974* (New York: Oxford University Press, 2010), 92.

**new Fourteenth District**—Ibid., 95.

**Hurst used his political influence**—Bourne, *Jimmy Carter*, 117.

**on Election day**—Ibid., 118–19.

**"Everybody knows it's not right"**—Ibid., 120.

**connected Carter with an investigative reporter**—Ibid., 122.

**Kirbo took their case**—Ibid., 124.

**He won by a count**—Ibid., 129.

**made a veiled threat**—Ibid., 132.

**said succinctly: "None"**—Hersh, *Edward Kennedy*, 133.

**"His academic career is mediocre"**—Clymer, *Edward M. Kennedy*, 37.

**"widely regarded here"**—James Reston, "Pragmatism to Nepotism in One Easy Lesson," *New York Times*, September 21, 1962.

**"demeaning to the dignity of the Senate"**—*New York Times*, editorial, September 19, 1962.

**"hardly made a ripple"**—Clymer, *Edward M. Kennedy*, 34.

**O'Donnell was dead set against it**—Hersh, *Edward Kennedy*, 138.

**Bobby, too, reportedly**—Hersh, *Edward Kennedy*, 136.

**JFK himself had reservations**—Clymer, *Edward M. Kennedy*, 32.

**"If I'd been somebody else"**—Ibid., 139.

**"If there's a piece of cake"**—Clymer, *Edward M. Kennedy*, 31.

**"understood his own appeal"**—Hersh, *Edward Kennedy*, 132.

**"You're already running"**—Ibid., 131.

**he took a trip to Africa**—Clymer, *Edward M. Kennedy*, 31.

**another trip to Latin America**—Ibid., 34.

**a heavy blow**—Kennedy, *True Compass*, 178.

**meeting three different times**—Mark Feeney, "Robert L. Healy, at 84; Globe Editor, Columnist, Political Insider," *Boston Globe*, June 7, 2010.

**The president wanted Healy to bury the details**—Clymer, *Edward M. Kennedy*, 36.

**"We're having more fucking trouble"**—Hersh, *Edward Kennedy*, 137.

**softened its language**—Clymer, *Edward M. Kennedy*, 36.

**McCormack did indeed savage Teddy**—Hersh, *Edward Kennedy*, 154–55.

**Teddy's voice shook**—Kennedy, *True Compass*, 185.

**559,303 votes**—Hersh, *Edward Kennedy*, 159.

**"That was the question"**—Ibid., 146.

# CHAPTER 4: A Sense of the Void

**"A Sense of the Void"**—The chapter title comes from a phrase Kennedy used in his autobiography to describe his state of mind for many years after suffering the losses of his brothers. Kennedy, *True Compass*, 422.

**"the temperature was climbing"**—Weather Underground, "Weather History for KDCA—November, 1963," Friday, November 22, 1963, https://www.wunderground.com/history/airport/KDCA/1963/11/22/Daily History.html.

**He was signing letters; a female staffer to Oregon senator Wayne Morse; Richard Riedel; "AP photographer James W. Altgens"**—William

Manchester, *The Death of a President: November 20–November 25, 1963* (New York: Little, Brown, 2013), Kindle ed., location 4187.

a "strange expression"—Kennedy, *True Compass*, 208.

Other accounts of JFK's assassination—Clymer, *Edward M. Kennedy*, 52; Hersh, *Edward Kennedy*, 161.

He could barely hear—Kennedy, *True Compass*, 208.

"The world lurched apart"—Ibid., 209.

broke down and wept—Manchester, *Death of a President*, location 7823.

had not cried over the death of anyone—Jimmy Carter interview, January 15, 2015.

picked up his school desk—Bourne, *Jimmy Carter*, 140.

twenty young black girls—Ibid., 135.

worried about the political consequences—Ibid., 144.

Carter stood and spoke; "There was a testing time"—Ibid., 147.

resented those who were born into wealth—Ibid., 144.

still yearned to escape—Ibid., 153.

"Many think [Carter] resembles"—Ibid., 152.

"entirely devoid of any discussion of issues"—Ibid., 157.

"almost cult-like"—Ibid., 156.

"The bottom line"—Ibid., 157.

250,000 people—Ibid.

almost 800,000 people voted—Ibid., 164.

"A new Democratic star"—Ibid.

wept in a hallway—Ibid.

left his election-night rally—Hamilton Jordan, *Crisis: The Last Year of the Carter Presidency* (New York: G. P. Putnam's Sons, 1982), 371.

"whether I ever amount to much"—Ibid., 165.

"I had very little genuine interest"—Ibid., 167.

an inner peace—Jules Witcover, *Marathon: The Pursuit of the Presidency, 1972–1976* (New York: Viking, 1977), 270–71.

a quasi-pastoral calling—Bourne, *Jimmy Carter*, 113.

"political Bible"—Ibid., 171.

"a miracle"—Ibid., 176.

**"Increasingly, he conceptualized"**—Ibid., 178.

**a small two-engine plane**—Clymer, *Edward M. Kennedy*, 58.

**a dairy farmer's teenage daughter**—Hersh, *Edward Kennedy*, 177.

**found the Aero Commander**—Ibid., 173.

**two cracked ribs**—Clymer, *Edward M. Kennedy*, 59.

**"I guess the only reason"**—Hersh, *Edward Kennedy*, 180.

**"perhaps the only time"; "never really had"**—Ibid., 185.

**"I had a lot of time"**—Ibid., 187.

**"From 1965 to 1968"**—Clymer, *Edward M. Kennedy*, 63–99.

**"He avoided reporters"**—Hersh, *Edward Kennedy*, 195.

**"At a loss"**—Ibid., 195.

**had separate bedrooms**—Ibid., 226.

**"veered close to being"**—Kennedy, *True Compass*, 210.

**"Bobby's therapy"**—Hersh, *Edward Kennedy*, 262.

**he should wait until 1972**—Clymer, *Edward M. Kennedy*, 102.

**Scientologist Helga Wagner**—Maxine Cheshire, "The Mysterious Helga Wagner," *Washington Post*, March 13, 1980, https://www.washing tonpost.com/archive/lifestyle/1980/03/13/the-mysterious-helga -wagner/3f34b14f-ed77-4631-9253-03f112bf848d/.

**rallied campaign workers**—Clymer, *Edward M. Kennedy*, 109.

**"I am not yet qualified"**—Ibid., 121.

**"a stepping stone to the Presidency"**—Ibid., 129.

**"the first battle of '72"**—Ibid., 131.

**But then came a night**—Accounts of Chappaquiddick accident: Clymer, *Edward M. Kennedy*, 139–49; Hersh, *Edward Kennedy*, 344–80; Peter S. Canellos, ed., *Last Lion: The Fall and Rise of Ted Kennedy* (New York: Simon & Schuster, 2009), 156–73; Robert Sherrill, *The Last Kennedy: Edward M. Kennedy of Massachusetts Before and After Chappaquiddick* (New York: Dial, 1976); and Richard L. Tedrow and Thomas L. Tedrow, *Death at Chappaquiddick* (Gretna, LA: Pelican Publishing Company, 1980).

**"It marks the end of Kennedy"**—Clymer, *Edward M. Kennedy*, 145.

**a highly rehearsed speech**—Edward M. Kennedy, "Address to the People of Massachusetts on Chappaquiddick," July 25, 1969, American

Rhetoric, http://www.americanrhetoric.com/speeches/tedkenne dychappaquiddick.htm.

**her third miscarriage**—Marcia Chellis, *Living with the Kennedys: The Joan Kennedy Story* (New York: Simon & Schuster, 1985), 39, 43–44.

**had the promise taken out**—Clymer, *Edward M. Kennedy*, 147.


## CHAPTER 5: A Rivalry Begins

**At the front gate**—Hunter S. Thompson, *The Great Shark Hunt: Strange Tales from a Strange Time* (New York: Simon & Schuster Paperbacks, 2003 [originally published 1979]), 464.

**a weeklong trip to the Soviet Union**—Clymer, *Edward M. Kennedy*, 208–10.

**moving too fast**—Bourne, *Jimmy Carter*, 188.

**run for a lower office**—Ibid., 185.

**first white politician**—Ibid., 182.

**"Can you imagine?"**—Ibid., 189.

**"appears kind of meek"**—Patrick Anderson, *Electing Jimmy Carter: The Campaign of 1976* (Baton Rouge: Louisiana State University Press, 1994), 13.

**"proof of his allegations"**—Bourne, *Jimmy Carter*, 191.

**an overt reference to Wallace**—Ibid., 190.

**had been openly racist**—Margaret Shannon, "The Next President's Georgia Campaign," *Atlanta Journal-Constitution*, November 3, 1968.

**had distributed leaflets**—Dan T. Carter, *The Politics of Rage: George Wallace, the Origins of the New Conservatism, and the Transformation of American Politics* (New York: Simon & Schuster, 1995), photo section.

**Ham Jordan and press secretary Bill Pope**—Bourne, *Jimmy Carter*, 192–93.

**a "nigger campaign"**—George Lardner Jr., "Jimmy Carter—Promises… Promises," *Washington Post*, March 7, 1976.

**"Here's Carl Sanders"**—Bill Torpy, "The Political Grudge Carl Sanders Takes to His Grave," *Atlanta Journal-Constitution*, November 19, 2014.

**a Putnam county prison**—Bourne, *Jimmy Carter*, 193.

**he blocked Wallace**—Ibid., 192.

**a subtle signal**—Ibid., 191.

**"everything" he could for private schools**—James Wooten, *Dasher: The Roots and the Rising of Jimmy Carter* (New York: Summit Books, 1978), 292.

**"everything they could to defeat me"; "I never made a racist statement"**—Jimmy Carter interview, January 15, 2015.

**Roy Harris**—Bourne, *Jimmy Carter*, 197.

**Others followed Harris's lead**—Wooten, *Dasher*, 293.

**did refute Sanders's claim**—Bill Shipp, "Maddox Says He's Neutral," *Atlanta Journal-Constitution*, September 21, 1970.

**"running a Maddox-type campaign"**—Bill Shipp, "Carter Wins by Large Margin," *Atlanta Journal-Constitution*, September 24, 1970.

**"smiling hypocrite"**—Randall Balmer, *Redeemer: The Life of Jimmy Carter* (New York: Basic Books, 2014), 31.

**only 7 percent of the black vote**—Bourne, *Jimmy Carter*, 197.

**"Carter lacked enthusiasm"**—Wooten, *Dasher*, 295.

**"close friends" of Carter's**—Ibid.

**"Carter's only prospect for redemption"**—Ballmer, *Redeemer*, 32.

**"I realize that the test of a man"**—"Governor Jimmy Carter's Inaugural Address," January 12, 1971, Carter Center, https://www.jimmycar terlibrary.gov/assets/documents/inaugural_address_gov.pdf.

**plenty of groans**—Godbold, *Jimmy and Rosalynn Carter*, 170–71.

**the Kopechnes were "satisfied"**—Clymer, *Edward M. Kennedy*, 153.

**"The voters need reassurance"**—R. W. Apple, "Kennedy Is Running Hard Against His '64 Vote Total," *New York Times*, August 27, 1970.

**paraded Joan around; she felt "used"**—Clymer, *Edward M. Kennedy*, 164.

**walk around the Senate floor**—Ibid., 151.

**mocked by British newspapers**—Ibid., 173.

***Newsweek* and *Time***—Ibid., 150.

**why they were not more affectionate**—Ibid., 163.

**"a total animal"**—Ibid., 173.

**"royal family in exile"**—Witcover, *Marathon*, 124.

**running in 1976**—Clymer, *Edward M. Kennedy*, 192.

**pay tribute to George Wallace**—Ibid., 193.

**he praised Wallace**—"Synd 6 7 73 Kennedy Speech at Rally with Governor Wallace," AP Archive via YouTube, https://www.youtube.com/watch?v=XH6O6PjXhCI.

**"the height of political opportunism"**—*Jet* magazine, September 6, 1973, 30.

**"People had not forgotten"**—Witcover, *Marathon*, 121.

**Kennedy noticed a nasty red lump**—Kennedy, *True Compass*, 305.

**an early form of chemotherapy**—Ibid., 310.

**Bourne was with Carter in Washington**—Witcover, *Marathon*, 107.

**"President of what?"**—Bourne, *Jimmy Carter*, 251.

**"We all knew"**—Witcover, *Marathon*, 109.

**the need for "moral leadership"**—Ibid.

**a fifty-eight-page memo**—November 4, 1972, memo, Carter Library, 1976 Presidential Campaign, Campaign Director's Office, Container 199.

**"Carter had a thing"**—Peter Bourne interview, July 28, 2015, Washington, D.C.

**Wild Turkey bourbon**—Thompson, *The Great Shark Hunt*, 472.

**he laid bare what he thought**—Carter's Law Day speech is archived online: Jimmy Carter, "Georgia Law Day Address," May 4, 1974, http://www.americanrhetoric.com/speeches/jimmycarterlawday1974.htm.

**"king hell bastard of a speech"**—Thompson, *The Great Shark Hunt*, 474.

**"he was angry"**—Peter Bourne interview, July 28, 2015, Washington, D.C.

**"I had never seen"**—"Hunter S. Thompson Says Jimmy Carter Is Ruthless, 1977" (interview with Canadian Broadcasting Company), YouTube, https://www.youtube.com/watch?v=yvpPosKe-I0.

**"Kennedy had been impressed"**—Clymer, *Edward M. Kennedy*, 211.

**"It was a little bit"**—Peter Bourne interview, July 28, 2015, Washington, D.C.

**"I probably would have chuckled"**—Thompson, *The Great Shark Hunt*, 474.

## CHAPTER 6: The Outsider

**In the summer of 1975**—Sergio Bendixen phone interviews, August 13, 2013, and April 4, 2016.

**announced his candidacy**—Witcover, *Marathon*, 142.

**Their argument to each**—Bendixen interviews.

**"We just saw him"**—Donald W. Carson and James W. Johnson, *Mo: The Life and Times of Morris K. Udall* (Tucson: University of Arizona Press, 2001), 154.

**"I didn't think that the party"**—Witcover, *Marathon*, 258.

**Udall was beset by chaos**—Carson and Johnson, *Life and Times of Morris K. Udall*, 157.

**"the crisis of our lives"**—Witcover, *Marathon*, 252.

**"suddenly transformed"**—R. W. Apple Jr., "Ford Victor in Jersey and Ohio; Carter Is Set Back in Jersey," *New York Times*, June 9, 1976.

**a prolonged primary**—R. W. Apple Jr., "Carter Appears Near Goal in Last 3 Primaries Today," *New York Times*, June 8, 1976.

**"He's got courage"**—Witcover, *Marathon*, 349–50.

**He threw his delegates to Carter**—R. W. Apple Jr., "Shift to Georgian," *New York Times*, June 10, 1976.

**"the nearest thing"**—Tom Wicker, "Humphrey and Kennedy?," *New York Times*, June 1, 1976.

**"If I don't get but two votes"**—Witcover, *Marathon*, 196.

**on local newspapers**—Ibid.

**he visited it seven times**—Ibid., 197.

**The media had overlooked**—Ibid., 200.

**A strange calm**—Ibid., 178.

**"His speeches are mostly"**—Charles Mohr, "Carter and Audiences," *New York Times*, June 2, 1976.

**"I want a government"**—Witcover, *Marathon*, 198.

**"would listen long"**—Ibid., 198–99.

**Sally Quinn**—Ibid., 211.

**"Don't pay any attention"**—Bourne, *Jimmy Carter*, 218.

**"a simple, straightforward common man"**—Witcover, *Marathon*, 515.

**"I don't want a picture"**—Anderson, *Electing Jimmy Carter*, 40.

**"Have I answered your question?"**—Witcover, *Marathon*, 210.

**"curiosity about process"**—Bourne, *Jimmy Carter*, 206.

**Rosalynn Carter was also a huge asset**—Ibid., 262–64.

**"She wants to be first lady"**—Anderson, *Electing Jimmy Carter*, 12.

**"faith in Jimmy Carter"**—Bourne, *Jimmy Carter*, 344.

**"He asked of voters"**—Witcover, *Marathon*, 209.

**Voters wanted "nonideological change"**—Bourne, *Jimmy Carter*, 265.

**"the real issues in the campaign"**—Ibid., 328.

**"I want a government"**—Witcover, *Marathon*, 232.

**"He has tenaciously stuck"**—Mohr, "Carter and Audiences."

**rolled their eyes**—Anderson, *Electing Jimmy Carter*, 31.

**"He was a conservative"**—Bert Lance Oral History, Presidential Oral Histories, Miller Center, University of Virginia, May 12, 1982, https://millercenter.org/the-presidency/presidential-oral -histories/bert-lance-oral-history-campaign-advisor-office.

**"We lost Martin Luther King"**—Anderson, *Electing Jimmy Carter*, 32.

**"It could be slowed"**—Bourne, *Jimmy Carter*, 325.

**"An almost physical wave"**—Charles Mohr, "Spanning the Spectrum," *New York Times*, June 5, 1976.

**"I expect the nominee will be Mr. Carter"**—Apple, "Shift to Georgian."

**an eight-page piece**—Robert Sherrill, "Chappaquiddick +5: A Tragedy, an Enigma, a Political Achilles Heel," *New York Times Magazine*, July 14, 1974.

**"The piece attracted"**—Kennedy, *True Compass*, 344.

**Kennedy denied it**—"Stop-Carter Query Hedged by Kennedy," *New York Times*, May 26, 1976.

**In a prepared speech in Cincinnati**—Charles Mohr, "Carter Assails Opponents Who Seek to Block Drive," *New York Times*, May 28, 1976.

**"I'm glad I don't"**—Witcover, *Marathon*, 341.

**Kennedy offered to enter**—Bourne, *Jimmy Carter*, 334.

**"To those who for years"**—Witcover, *Marathon*, 358.

**called many of the pack's questions "frivolous"**—Ibid., 207.

**his flip-flopping answers**—Ibid.

**"It would be"**—Ibid., 226.

**"designed to conceal"**—Robert Shrum, *No Excuses: Concessions of a Serial Campaigner* (New York: Simon & Schuster, 2008), 69.

**"impugning their motives"**—Bourne, *Jimmy Carter*, 318.

**"sticking his love-coated needle"**—Witcover, *Marathon*, 294.

a **"moveable madhouse"**—Anderson, *Electing Jimmy Carter*, 30–31.

**increased the campaign's mistrust**—Bourne, *Jimmy Carter*, 319.

**"the dark side of the South"**—Ibid., 337.

**"Our candidate may have been"**—Anderson, *Electing Jimmy Carter*, 2.

**made racist jokes**—Bourne, *Jimmy Carter*, 315.

**"as hard-drinking"**—Anderson, *Electing Jimmy Carter*, 2.

**"a deeply embedded southern attitude"**—Bourne, *Jimmy Carter*, 315.

**"a bit more challenging"**—Witcover, *Marathon*, 564.

**"always makes me nervous"**—Ibid., 563.

**"I didn't run around"**—Ibid., 564.

**"I'm not trying"**—Ibid., 565–66.

**Religious conservatives were offended**—Ibid., 567–68.

**"increased the weirdo factor"**—Ibid., 570.

**"The spirit of this country"**—Ibid., 589.

**"even worse" than Nixon**—Ibid., 619.

**"callous indifference"**—Ibid., 625.

**led Ford by around 15 points**—R. W. Apple Jr., "Contrasting Campaign Symbols," *New York Times*, September 7, 1976.

**the lowest voter turnout**—Witcover, *Marathon*, 644.

**"the turning point"**—Anderson, *Electing Jimmy Carter*, 113.

**"It destroyed his lead"**—Ibid., 113.

**"arrived in Washington"**—White, *America in Search of Itself*, 196.

## CHAPTER 7: Lanced

**Jimmy Carter's inaugural address**—"Jimmy Carter, Inaugural Address," January 20, 1977, American Presidency Project, http:// www.presidency.ucsb.edu/ws/?pid=6575.

**"would become the most"**—Bourne, *Jimmy Carter*, 383.

**Carter's honeymoon period**—Ibid., 380–411.

**His approval rating was 75 percent**—Presidential Job Approval Center, Gallup, http://www.gallup.com/poll/124922/presidential-job-approval-center.aspx.

**"In his first two months"**—Quoted in James Fallows, "The Passionless Presidency," *Atlantic*, May 1979.

**the Group of Seven summit**—Bourne, *Jimmy Carter*, 397.

**a 10 percent pay cut**—Ibid., 368.

**turn off the lights**—Bert Lance Oral History, Presidential Oral Histories, Miller Center, University of Virginia, May 12, 1982.

**by car rather than helicopter**—Jimmy Carter, *White House Diary* (New York: Farrar, Straus & Giroux, 2010), 19.

**Rosalynn Carter did not want to see her staff cut**—Bert Lance Oral History, Presidential Oral Histories, Miller Center, University of Virginia, May 12, 1982; Charles Mohr, "Carter Advisers Ask Revision and 30% Cut in White House Staff," *New York Times*, July 7, 1977.

**to pitch his energy plan**—Edward Cowan, "Carter Energy Plan Said to Stress Efficiency Rise and Fuel Scarcity," *New York Times*, April 1, 1977.

**James Reston summed up**—James Reston, "Carter's Best Week," *New York Times*, April 24, 1977.

**Carter failed to build**—White, *America in Search of Itself*, 208.

**Anthony Lewis noted**—Anthony Lewis, "Carter and the Liberals," *New York Times*, August 18, 1977.

**"He has his eye"**—James T. Wooten, "Carter Gains in Confidence—and Gets a Few Lessons in the Limits of Presidential Power," *New York Times*, July 25, 1977.

**polling showed declining public support**—Anthony J. Parisi, "Poll Finds Doubt on Energy Crisis," *New York Times*, September 1, 1977.

**Byrd was in no rush**—James Reston, "Panama: What's the Rush?," *New York Times*, August 17, 1977.

**"I was the only person"**—Bert Lance Oral History, Presidential Oral Histories, Miller Center, University of Virginia, May 12, 1982.

**"He had very few personal relationships"**—Godbold, *Jimmy and Rosalynn Carter*, 127.

**"Apart from Rosalynn"**—Ibid., 174.

**"Simply did not like politicians"**—White, *America in Search of Itself*, 201.

**"South Georgia turtle"**—Bourne, *Jimmy Carter*, 218.

**"primarily to shame legislators"**—Ibid.

**"more of an outsider"**—Ibid., 260.

**the press picked up on a letter**—William Safire, "Carter's Broken Lance," *New York Times*, July 21, 1977.

**sell 190,000 shares**—"Senators Are Expected to Request 'Further Assurance' from Lance," *New York Times*, July 15, 1977.

**"The hands of the Carter entourage"**—Hedrick Smith, "Lance Inquiry: A Carter Test," *New York Times*, August 16, 1977.

**a pattern of massive overdrafts**—"Judging Mr. Lance," *New York Times*, September 5, 1977.

**he resigned his budget director job**—Charles Mohr, "President Is Somber," *New York Times*, September 22, 1977.

**"probably one of the worst days"**—Carter, *White House Diary*, 102.

**"Lance's departure was"**—Bourne, *Jimmy Carter*, 415.

**damaged Carter's moral authority**—Hedrick Smith, "In Lance Case, the 'New Morality' Echoes Some of the Old," *New York Times*, September 18, 1977.

**dropped from 66 percent to 54 percent**—Presidential Job Approval Center, Gallup, http://www.gallup.com/poll/124922/presidential-job-approval-center.aspx.

**118 of the 289**—White, *America in Search of Itself*, 210.

**"These people didn't come up"**—Ibid., 212.

**"The same emotions"**—Ibid., 213.

**"Hamilton Jerkin"**—Ibid., 212.

**"We simply had more"**—Bert Lance Oral History, Presidential Oral Histories, Miller Center, University of Virginia, May 12, 1982.

**"spokes of the wheel"**—Bourne, *Jimmy Carter*, 360.

**"It won't work"**—Ibid., 358.

**giving Carter "maximum control"**—Ibid., 360.

**"He made everything come through him"**—Ibid., 361.

**"writing thoughtful memos"**—Ibid., 362.

**"Whatever Hamilton pretty well laid out"**—Bert Lance Oral History, Presidential Oral Histories, Miller Center, University of Virginia, May 12, 1982.

**"a cohesive plan"**—Bourne, *Jimmy Carter*, 372.

**Ted Kennedy visited the White House**—Jimmy Carter Presidential Daily Diary, September 22, 1977, Carter Presidential Library online archives.

**"It is time"**—Clymer, *Edward M. Kennedy*, 249.

**Kennedy had floated rumors**—Ibid., 241.

**the one campaign rally**—Ibid., 243.

**Kennedy sent him a handwritten note**—Ibid., 248.

**He consulted with Zbigniew Brzezinski**—Ibid., 253.

**"a party whose coalition"**—Bourne, *Jimmy Carter*, 416.

**"the world had changed"**—Ibid., 417.

**approval rating had dropped**—Presidential Job Approval Center, Gallup, http://www.gallup.com/poll/124922/presidential-job-approval-center.aspx.

**53 percent to 40 percent; the U.S. Conference of Mayors**—Clymer, *Edward M. Kennedy*, 260.

**was running away from home**—Ibid., 245.

**Joan moved out**—Ibid., 252.

**When he visited a prison**—Ibid., 254.

**"deep down"**—Ibid., 205.

## CHAPTER 8: Malaise

**"The people out there"**—John Updike, *Rabbit Is Rich* (New York: Random House; Reissue ed., 2010), 2.

**began preparing for a primary challenge**—Jordan, *Crisis*, 20.

**"Suddenly, they're not laughing"**—Martin Tolchin, "New Pro in the White House," *New York Times Magazine*, December 17, 1978.

**Violent crime had been rising**—"State-by-state and national crime estimates by years," Uniform Crime Reporting Statistics, U.S. Department of Justice, https://www.ucrdatatool.gov/Search/Crime /State/RunCrimeStatebyState.cfm.

**the highest point in American history**—Ryan McMaken, "FBI: US Homicide Rate at 51-Year Low," Mises Institute, June 15, 2016, https://mises.org/blog/fbi-us-homicide-rate-51-year-low.

**"For the part of his job" and all Fallows quotes**—James Fallows, "The Passionless Presidency," *Atlantic,* May 1979.

**"seemed to believe"**—White, *America in Search of Itself,* 200.

**"who would step on some toes"**—Adam Clymer, "Carter's Standing Drops to New Low in Times-CBS Poll," *New York Times,* June 10, 1979.

**"He is a glamorous figure"**—Tom Wicker, "Ike and Teddy," *New York Times,* June 26, 1979.

**asked by Representative Toby Moffett**—Associated Press, "Carter 'Whip' Quote Must Be Wrong: Kennedy," *Montreal Gazette,* June 14, 1979.

**"which was kind of an insult"; "didn't intend"**—Jimmy Carter interview, January 15, 2015.

**there were multiple reports**—Jack W. Germond and Jules Witcover, *Blue Smoke and Mirrors: How Reagan Won and Why Carter Lost the Election of 1980* (New York: Viking, 1981), 52; Associated Press, "Carter 'Whip' Quote Must Be Wrong."

**Kennedy sniped back**—Associated Press, "Carter 'Whip' Quote Must Be Wrong."

**"upset at the glee"**—Walter F. Mondale Vice Presidential Papers, Minnesota Historical Society, Location: 153.J.8.4F, http://www2.mnhs .org/library/findaids/00697/pdfa/00697-00085-1.pdf.

**"The significance of this result"**—Collection: Office of the Chief of Staff Files; Series: Hamilton Jordan's Confidential Files; Folder: Caddell, Patrick (3); Container 33, https://www.jimmycarterlibrary .gov/digital_library/cos/142099/33/cos_142099_33_14-Caddell _Patrick_(3).pdf.

**"psychological crisis"**—White, *America in Search of Itself,* 258.

**one survey by Democratic pollster**—Ira Shapiro, *The Last Great Senate: Courage and Statesmanship in Times of Crisis* (New York: PublicAffairs, 2012), 302.

**Senator Daniel Patrick Moynihan said**—Steven R. Weisman, "Moynihan Feels Kennedy Moves Make Carter Act," *New York Times*, May 23, 1979.

**"dump Carter"**—Steven V. Roberts, "5 Congressmen Join to 'Dump' President," *New York Times*, May 22, 1979.

**A write-in effort; "It seems hardly debatable"**—Tom Wicker, "Dumping and Drafting," *New York Times*, May 25, 1979.

**assaulting a pregnant woman**—Robert Lindsey, "Panicky California Drivers Form Lines at Gas Stations," *New York Times*, May 5, 1979.

**an "I told you so" speech**—Richard Halloran, "Carter Says Public Refuses to Face Up to Crisis in Energy," *New York Times*, May 16, 1979.

**he tried to do damage control**—Martin Tolchin, "Carter Is Optimistic on June Gas Supply," *New York Times*, May 17, 1979.

**"This country is going to hell"**—White, *America in Search of Itself,* 259; Pat Caddell interview, April 20, 2017.

**A group of public intellectuals**—White, *America in Search of Itself,* 259.

**"The seeds of division"**—Tolchin, "Carter Is Optimistic on June Gas Supply."

**the day after Memorial Day weekend**—Pranay B. Gupte, "Most Gas Stations in City Are Closed," *New York Times*, May 28, 1979.

**Andrew Medosa**—Judith Cummings, "Suspect Accused of Slaying Man in Gasoline Line," *New York Times*, June 2, 1979.

**Fritz Boutain**—"Motorist, 29, Is Killed in Brooklyn Stabbing at a Gasoline Station," *New York Times*, June 10, 1979.

**gas station attendant**—Pranay B. Gupte, "Gas-Station Attendant Held in Gun Threat on Customer," *New York Times*, June 11, 1979.

**as long as five hours**—Pranay B. Gupte, "Gas Prices and Lines Are the Worst Ever on 'Driest Weekend,'" *New York Times*, June 24, 1979.

**was shot in the head**—Lee A. Daniels, "Much of U.S. Feeling Impact of Gas Crisis," *New York Times*, June 26, 1979.

**independent truckers went on strike**—Associated Press, "14 States Affected by Trucker Protest," *New York Times*, June 8, 1979.

**Carter adviser Stuart Eizenstat**—Ernest Holsendolph, "Independent Truckers Calling National Work Stoppage," *New York Times*, June 19, 1979.

**the strike cut off 40 percent**—"Long Angry Lines and Meetings of Ministers," editorial, *New York Times*, June 24, 1979.

**a sniper in Tennessee**—Holsendolph, "Independent Truckers Calling National Work Stoppage."

**shot and killed in Alabama**—Ernest Holsendolph, "Truckers' Protests Spread as Deadline for Stoppage Passes," *New York Times*, June 21, 1979.

**nine on a single block**—David M. Anderson, "Levittown Is Burning! The 1979 Levittown, Pennsylvania, Gas Line Riot and the Decline of the Blue-Collar American Dream," *Labor* 2, no. 3 (Fall 2005): 47–66.

**forty-four officers were injured**—Donald Janson, "Rioting Follows Protests by Truckers in Levittown, Pa.," *New York Times*, June 26, 1979.

**"There are two questions"**—Walter F. Mondale Vice Presidential Papers, Minnesota Historical Society, Location: 149.J.14.1B, http://www2 .mnhs.org/library/findaids/00697/pdfa/00697-00057.pdf.

**"I do not need"**—Terence Smith, "President Summons Aides to Camp David for a Broad Review," *New York Times*, July 7, 1979.

**a quick trip to Vienna**—Jimmy Carter Presidential Daily Diary, July 14, 1979.

**"Almost no one's body"**—White, *America in Search of Itself*, 261.

**"I didn't see"**—Carter, *White House Diary*, 337.

**"very easy for me"**—Ibid., 338.

**whittled down to less than two hours**—Jimmy Carter Presidential Daily Diary, July 1, 1979.

**"Why...the man"**—White, *America In Search of Itself*, 265.

**"Most White House officials"**—Smith, "President Summons Aides to Camp David."

**"My observation"**—Adam Clymer, "Governors at Camp David Parley Say Carter Still Bars Wage-Price Curbs," *New York Times*, July 8, 1979.

**Brock Adams; "He just obviously"; "When I came back"**—Bert Lance Oral History, Presidential Oral Histories, Miller Center, University of Virginia, May 12, 1982.

**two warring factions**—Pat Caddell interview, April 20, 2017.

**"Pat continues to argue"; "The speech is badly needed"**—Office of the Chief of Staff Files, Hamilton Jordan's Confidential Files, Speech, President's 7/15/79, Container 37.

**"America was afflicted"; Carter thought Caddell's memo; But Mondale called**—White, *America in Search of Itself*, 276.

**"Sinners in the Hands"**—Ibid., 277.

**"hype up" the situation**—Office of the Chief of Staff Files, Hamilton Jordan's Confidential Files, Speech, President's 7/15/79, Container 37.

**"a ten-day production"**—White, *America in Search of Itself*, 267.

**steeping himself**—Hedrick Smith, "Carter's View Beyond Crisis," *New York Times*, July 11, 1979.

**"a political and economic elite"**—David Broder, "The Denouement: Carter Faces Tough Audience at the End of Summit," *Washington Post*, July 15, 1979.

**"to revive ourselves"**—"Carter's View Beyond Crisis."

**"on the moon"**—David Broder, "Carter Seeking Oratory to Move an Entire Nation," *Washington Post*, July 14, 1979.

**mayors, state legislators**—Warren Weaver Jr., "Carter Ends Camp David Talks; Believed Drafting New Address," *New York Times*, July 12, 1979.

**Bill Clinton told him; "Somebody needs to pray"**—Terence Smith, "Theme at Camp David: Need to Lift Nation's Spirit," *New York Times*, July 12, 1979.

**"Good evening"**—The text of Carter's "malaise" speech can be found online at the American Presidency Project: "Address to the Nation on Energy and National Goals: 'The Malaise Speech,'" July 15, 1979, http://www.presidency.ucsb.edu/ws/?pid=32596.

**The speech's greatest weakness**—Kevin Mattson, *"What the Heck Are You Up To, Mr. President?": Jimmy Carter, America's "Malaise," and the Speech That Should Have Changed the Country* (New York: Bloomsbury USA, 2009), 165.

**It came from Clark Clifford**—Martin Schram and Edward Walsh, "Camp David Talks Cover Wide Range: Carter Wants to Improve His Leadership, Counter 'Malaise,'" *Washington Post*, July 10, 1979.

**Caddell had also used the word**—Stuart E. Eizenstat, *President Carter: The White House Years* (New York: St. Martin's Press, 2018), 672.

**"really an extraordinary speech"**—Vanderbilt Television News Archive, Clip #659804: CBS Special for Sunday, July 15, 1979, http://tvnews.vanderbilt.edu/program.pl?ID=659804.

**Jody Powell told reporters; "We've taken down"**—Vanderbilt Television News Archive, Clip #850327: ABC Special for Monday, July 16, 1979, http://tvnews.vanderbilt.edu/program.pl?ID=850327.

**"become an islander himself"**—Steven Roberts, "Washington Ponders 'Island' Description," *New York Times*, July 17, 1979.

**"There was a feeling"**—Germond and Witcover, *Blue Smoke and Mirrors*, 41.

**Jordan wrote Carter another long memo**—July 16, 1979, memo, Carter Library, Office of the Chief of Staff Files, Hamilton Jordan's Confidential Files, Image Analysis and Changes, 7/16/79, Container 34b.

**"Every single change"**—Elizabeth Drew, "In Search of a Definition," *New Yorker*, August 27, 1979, 68.

**"The firings were meant"**—Ibid., 70.

**"Suddenly, bang"**—Germond and Witcover, *Blue Smoke and Mirrors*, 41.

**"It was in the aftershocks"**—Kennedy, *True Compass*, 367.

**Kennedy had held two big meetings**—Germond and Witcover, *Blue Smoke and Mirrors*, 50–51.

**Kennedy remained "torn"; "I think we are"**—Lunch with the President talking points, July–December 1979, part 1, Walter F. Mondale Vice Presidential Papers, Minnesota Historical Society, Location: 153.J.8.4F, http://www2.mnhs.org/library/findaids/00697/pdfa/00697-00085-1.pdf.

**"We were losing"**—Clymer, *Edward M. Kennedy*, 275.

**"If the thing doesn't work out"**—Germond and Witcover, *Blue Smoke and Mirrors*, 54.

## CHAPTER 9: The Inevitable Return of Camelot

**"Heir to all the magic"**—Eleanor Clift, "Kennedy Enters 1980 Presidential Race," *Newsweek*, September 23, 1979.

**"loved government"; "the contempt of a master machinist"**—White, *America in Search of Itself*, 274.

**"This was remarkable enough"**—Ibid., 256.

**he had no intention of backing off**—Germond and Witcover, *Blue Smoke and Mirrors*, 53.

**a stunning 19 percent**—Elizabeth Drew, *Portrait of an Election: The 1980 Presidential Campaign* (New York: Simon & Schuster, 1981), 18.

**"It's amazing"**—Jordan, *Crisis*, 23.

**"The question Carter must ask himself"**—Patrick J. Buchanan, "What Argument Is Left for Carter?," *Ludington (MI) Daily News*, November 12, 1979.

**"We are not simply"**—Collection: Office of the Chief of Staff Files; Series: Hamilton Jordan's Confidential Files; Folder: Caddell, Patrick (3); Container 33, https://www.jimmycarterlibrary.gov/digital_library /cos/142099/33/cos_142099_33_14-Caddell_Patrick_(3).pdf.

**"We had evolved"**—Mike Abrams phone interview, April 5, 2016.

**a mysterious phone call; "He kept looking over his shoulder"**—Sergio Bendixen phone interviews, August 13 and August 20, 2013.

**monumental significance**—Rowland Evans and Robert Novak, "Working Florida Over," *Washington Post*, October 5, 1979.

**"You better win"**—Sergio Bendixen phone interview, August 13, 2013.

**decided by a few hundred votes**—Sergio Bendixen phone interview, August 20, 2013.

**a "hollow victory"**—David Broder, "Lessons in Florida for Carter, Kennedy," *Washington Post*, October 17, 1979.

**at her grandmother's house**—Anita Dunn interview, August 6, 2013, Washington, D.C.

**"a lively topic"**—Broder, "Lessons in Florida."

**Peter Hart and Morris Dees**—Clymer, *Edward M. Kennedy*, 279.

**"People here still think"**—Drew, *Portrait of an Election*, 18.

**"the realization that"**—Ibid., 22.

**"torn apart by Carter"**—Cubillos personal papers, Hoover Institute Archives, via Zach Dorfman, "How Henry Kissinger Conspired Against a Sitting President," *Politico*, January 6, 2017.

**Teddy was standing on the sidewalk**—Public-domain footage of the ceremony: "Jimmy Carter & Ted Kennedy at JFK Library," YouTube, https://www.youtube.com/watch?v=iWp-zOr2C_k.

**Some said they saw her wince**—Clymer, *Edward M. Kennedy*, 280.

**"I started to kiss"**—Jimmy Carter interview, January 15, 2015.

**"the Family"**—Vanderbilt Television News Archive, Clip #659098: CBS Special for Sunday, November 4, 1979, http://tvnews.vanderbilt.edu/program.pl?ID=659098.

**Teddy had informed Carter**—Clymer, *Edward M. Kennedy*, 276.

**"Response to Kennedy"**—September 10, 1979, memo, Carter Library, Office of the Chief of Staff Files, Landon Butler's Memoranda files, Container 148.

**"I never met him"**—From text of Carter speech at Kennedy Library dedication, October 20, 1979, https://www.jfklibrary.org/About-Us/About-the-JFK-Library/History/1979-Dedication-Remarks-by-President-Carter.aspx.

**Carter looked over again at Kennedy**—Public-domain footage of the ceremony: "President Jimmy Carter Presides over John F. Kennedy Library Dedication Oct 26 1979," YouTube, https://www.youtube.com/watch?v=YT1QBCWEOZg.

**"one of the best speeches of his career"**—Clymer, *Edward M. Kennedy*, 280.

**"removed the presidential seal"**—Clymer, *Edward M. Kennedy*, 281.

**Kennedy's turn to speak**—From text of Kennedy's speech at Kennedy Library dedication, October 20, 1979, https://www.jfklibrary

.org/About-Us/About-the-JFK-Library/History/1979-Dedication
-Remarks-by-Senator-Kennedy.aspx.

**crude sketches of the U.S. embassy**—Mark Bowden, *Guests of the Ayatollah: The Iran Hostage Crisis; The First Battle in America's War with Militant Islam* (New York: Grove Press, 2006), 4.

**on February 14**—Anna M. Tinsley, "Last American Seized at U.S. Embassy in Iran Recalls the Day," *Fort Worth Star-Telegram*, November 2, 2009.

**Around 4:30 a.m.**—Jordan, *Crisis*, 18.

**"island of stability"**—Jimmy Carter toast at a state dinner in Tehran, December 31, 1977, "Tehran, Iran Toasts of the President and the Shah at a State Dinner," December 31, 1977, American Presidency Project, http://www.presidency.ucsb.edu/ws/?pid=7080.

**"To hell with Henry Kissinger"**—Jordan, *Crisis*, 31.

**"What are you guys going to advise"**—Ibid., 32.

**"It'll be over in a few hours"**—Ibid., 19.

**Around eighty million of them**—Les Brown, " 'Jaws' Played to 80 Million on ABC," *New York Times*, November 7, 1979.

# CHAPTER 10: Mudd

**"Why do you want to be president?"**—All quotations and details from the Kennedy special are from Vanderbilt Television News Archive, Clip #659098: CBS Special for Sunday, November 4, 1979, http://tvnews.vanderbilt.edu/program.pl?ID=659098.

**refer to this interview as "uh-strewn"**—"The Kennedy Effort," editorial, *Washington Post*, August 13, 1980.

**sixteen million people**—Pew Research Center, "Network Evening News Ratings," March 13, 2006, http://www.journalism.org/numbers/network-evening-news-ratings/.

**"My discomfort and unhappiness"**—Kennedy, *True Compass*, 370.

**the car's left front fender**—Germond and Witcover, *Blue Smoke and Mirrors*, 63.

"address it as 'a political question' "; a "defiant" dare—Ibid., 64.

"a very sweaty moment"—Ibid., 65.

"He had never sat down"—Roger Mudd, *The Place to Be: Washington, CBS, and the Glory Days of Television News* (New York: Public-Affairs, 2008), 350.

"Oh my God"—Ibid., 356.

"It was like"—Germond and Witcover, *Blue Smoke and Mirrors*, 70.

"not the way you'd like to launch"—Fred Barnes, "Kennedy Bid Off to a Slow Start," *Baltimore Sun*, November 30, 1979.

tried to kill the special—Mudd, *The Place to Be*, 353.

"Everybody's going to be"—Jordan, *Crisis*, 21.

"It gave everybody pause"—Harold Ickes phone interview, July 22, 2013.

"was such a shock"—Anita Dunn interview, August 6, 2013, Washington, D.C.

"seventy-five percent of the country"—Mudd, *The Place to Be*, 354.

"felt anything he had to say"—Germond and Witcover, *Blue Smoke and Mirrors*, 51.

moments after Bobby was shot—Mudd, *The Place to Be*, 235.

"I'm sure he knew better"—Ibid., 351–52.

when he announced his candidacy—Clymer, *Edward M. Kennedy*, 283–84; Chellis, *Joan Kennedy Story*, 88–94.


# CHAPTER 11: Upended

"The Iranian revolution"—James Reston, "Beyond the Gas Lines," *New York Times*, May 27, 1979.

"He seems tired"—Drew, *Portrait of an Election*, 32.

"One day it's sunny"—Joe Trippi interview, July 10, 2014, Washington, D.C.

"The Carter campaign"—Canellos, *Last Lion*, 211.

Kennedy referred to "fam farmilies"—Shrum, *No Excuses*, 83.

"Roll up your sleeves"—Hersh, *Edward Kennedy*, 477.

**"one of the most violent regimes"**—Terence Smith, "Kennedy Chided by the Leaders of Both Parties," *New York Times*, December 4, 1979.

**"and at the same time say"**—Hersh, *Edward Kennedy*, 477.

**"Carter's approval rating"**—Shrum, *No Excuses*, 85.

**"thought out carefully"**—Rowland Evans and Robert Novak, "Ted Kennedy's Amateur Hour," *Washington Post*, December 7, 1979.

**"a phenomenon"**—Drew, *Portrait of an Election*, 39.

**The editorial boards**—Steven V. Roberts, "Kennedy Shifts Criticisms on Iran, Urging a Public Debate on Asylum," *New York Times*, December 6, 1979.

**"The president is entitled"**—Smith, "Kennedy Chided."

**"The roof caved in"**—Shrum, *No Excuses*, 85.

**"We all support"**—B. Drummond Ayres Jr., "Kennedy, After Criticizing Shah, Supports Carter's Efforts on Iran," *New York Times*, December 4, 1979.

**"the single most damaging"**—Adam Clymer, "Kennedy Discovers the Pain of Running as an Underdog," *New York Times*, January 27, 1980.

**But his heart wasn't in it**—Drew, *Portrait of an Election*, 52.

**"Nice, nice"**—Ibid., 52.

**columnist Ellen Goodman**—Ellen Goodman, "It's Very Plain to See: Ted Doesn't Want It," *Boston Globe*, January 24, 1980.

**"They don't trust his judgment"**—Drew, *Portrait of an Election*, 50.

**"fragile and vulnerable woman"**—Ibid., 57.

**did more harm than good**—Hersh, *Edward Kennedy*, 481.

**Doris Kearns Goodwin**—Ellen Goodman, "Joan: Nobody's Victim Anymore," *Boston Globe*, February 21, 1980.

**"regain my strength"**—Benjamin Taylor, "A Pledge from Joan Kennedy," *Boston Globe*, February 16, 1980.

**"Some people who did not like"**—Hersh, *Edward Kennedy*, 482.

**Suzannah Lessard**—Suzannah Lessard, "Kennedy's Woman Problem. Women's Kennedy Problem," *Washington Monthly*, December 1979.

**"I don't think"**—Drew, *Portrait of an Election*, 54.

**"Ted Kennedy leads"**—Clymer, *Edward M. Kennedy*, 290.

**did not believe Kennedy's tale**—Ibid., 288.

**"Our mistake was thinking"**—Bob Shrum phone interview, January 2, 2018.

**"He seemed to have lost"**—Clymer, *Edward M. Kennedy*, 280.

**"When he censored himself"**—Hersh, *Edward Kennedy*, 477.

**"Virtually each day"**—Drew, *Portrait of an Election*, 40.

**"I want these burned"**—Pat Caddell interview with Adam Clymer, January 1, 1998, John F. Kennedy Library, Adam Clymer Personal Papers, Box 3.

**"revert to a battle"**—Adam Clymer, "Carter Pulls Out of Forum in Iowa, Saying the Iran Crisis Gets Priority," *New York Times*, December 29, 1979.

**"there's no question"**—Adam Clymer, "Brown and Kennedy Aide Assail Carter for Pulling Out of Forum," *New York Times*, December 30, 1979.

**"slowly, in a sort of singsong"**—Drew, *Portrait of an Election*, 58.

**"being advised not to"**—Ibid., 62.

**"Geez, when can we"**—Ibid.

**sixty calls each**—Ibid., 38.

**"We're being smothered"**—Clymer, "Brown and Kennedy Aide Assail Carter."

**"very astute at having"; "We are being tested"**—Francis X. Clines, "Carter and 'the Patriot's Game' in Iowa," *New York Times*, January 11, 1980.

**ran an ad in the closing days**—David Broder, "Carter Victorious, Bush and Reagan Neck-and-Neck," *Washington Post*, January 22, 1980.

**Mondale was "strongly opposed"**—Carter, *White House Diary*, 388.

**"the patriotic route to take"**—Steven R. Weisman, "Mondale's Tough Stand on Grain Curb," *New York Times*, January 12, 1980.

**landing in the uncommitted lane**—Francis X. Clines, "Kennedy Camp Working on Farmer Anger," *New York Times*, January 14, 1980.

**"Here we are"**—David Nyhan, "In the Field, Kennedy's Fine—Nationally, It's Another Story," *Boston Globe*, February 21, 1980.

**its final poll**—Drew, *Portrait of an Election*, 70.

**Once again Elizabeth Drew**—Ibid., 72–75.

**"we'll show them"**—Ibid., 87.

**a fifteen-minute speech**—Bernard Weinraub, "Kennedy Makes a Blunt Attack on Carter Policy," *New York Times*, January 15, 1980.

**Reader's Digest published**—Linda Charlton, "New Chappaquiddick Challenges," *New York Times*, January 15, 1980.

**the Star's report**—B. Drummond Ayres Jr., "New Question Arises on Chappaquiddick," *New York Times*, January 16, 1980.

**Joan herself had to weigh in**—B. Drummond Ayres Jr., "Wife Backs Kennedy on Chappaquiddick," *New York Times*, January 19, 1980.

**"She didn't want the monkey on her back"**—Germond and Witcover, *Blue Smoke and Mirrors*, 53.

**The New York Post published**—Associated Press, "Kennedy Tale Rebutted," *Boston Globe*, January 22, 1980.

**"a chance to finish first"**—Adam Clymer, "Candidates Battle Snow and Rivals on Eve of Iowa Presidential Caucuses," *New York Times*, January 20, 1980.

**30,000 "hard ID's"**—Shrum, *No Excuses*, 90.

**"one of the most impressive"; had expected it to surge**—Broder, "Carter Victorious."

**"The polls weren't looking good"**—Shrum, *No Excuses*, 90.

**Kennedy spent caucus night**—Germond and Witcover, *Blue Smoke and Mirrors*, 145.

**speech to the National Association of Religious Broadcasters**—Jimmy Carter Presidential Daily Diary, January 21, 1980.

**had expected it to surge**—Broder, "Carter Victorious."

**In 1976, 38,000 people**—Adam Clymer, "Carter Wins Strong Victory in Iowa as Bush Takes Lead over Reagan," *New York Times*, January 22, 1980.

**expected to get 60,000 votes**—Bill Romjue phone interview, July 18, 2017.

**"You still have me"**—Timothy Stanley, *Kennedy vs. Carter: The 1980 Battle for the Democratic Party's Soul* (Lawrence: University Press of Kansas, 2010), 129.

# CHAPTER 12: "I Didn't Ask for a Challenger"

**"What wonderful words do we have?"**—Germond and Witcover, *Blue Smoke and Mirrors*, 145.

**"This baby's going down"**—Shrum, *No Excuses*, 90.

**a wry smile**—David Broder, "Carter Victorious, Bush and Reagan Neck-and-Neck," *Washington Post*, January 22, 1980.

**"Here and there"**—Hedrick Smith, "Senator Assesses Campaign," *New York Times*, January 23, 1980.

**"The whole idea"; "the Cornstalkers"; "the senator was on the phone"**—Joe Trippi interview, July 10, 2014.

**The $4 million; staff of two hundred; private charter plane**— B. Drummond Ayres Jr., "Kennedy Camp Starts to Lay Off Some of Its Staff," *New York Times*, January 24, 1980.

**"The Kennedy magic"**—James Reston, "The Myths of Iowa," *New York Times*, January 23, 1980.

**"thirty-one minutes"**—Terence Smith, "Carter Warns U.S. Would Use Armed Force to Repel a Soviet Thrust at Persian Gulf," *New York Times*, January 24, 1980.

**"Let our position"**—Text of Carter's State of the Union address, January 23, 1980, available at American Presidency Project, http://www.presidency.ucsb.edu/ws/?pid=33079.

**"Carter significantly raised defense spending"**—Peter Bourne email to the author, October 25, 2016.

**"the first president"**—Robert M. Gates, *From the Shadows: The Ultimate Insider's Story of Five Presidents and How They Won the Cold War* (New York: Simon & Schuster, 2011 [originally published in 1996]), 95.

**large amounts of dissident literature; "The Carter administration"**—Ibid., 94.

**"gradual transformation"**—Hedrick Smith, "The Carter Doctrine," *New York Times*, January 24, 1980.

**quoted the famous journalist Walter Lippmann**—Text of Carter's State of the Union address.

**"rumors...that Kennedy"**—Carter, *White House Diary*, 395.

**he was going to "ruin" Kennedy**—Shrum, *No Excuses*, 90.

**eight trusted aides**—Author's emails with Robert Shrum, Carl Wagner.

**"labeled a quitter forever"**—Shrum, *No Excuses*, 91.

**a *Boston Globe* poll**—"Carter Surges Ahead of Kennedy in New Hampshire Poll," *Boston Globe*, January 27, 1980.

**"a last ditch effort"**—Adam Clymer, "Kennedy Discovers the Pain of Running as an Underdog," *New York Times*, January 27, 1980.

**speak with "one voice"**—B. Drummond Ayres Jr., "Kennedy Cancels a Trip and Sets 'Major' Speech," *New York Times*, January 25, 1980.

**about seven hundred supporters**—Thomas Oliphant, "Kennedy States His Case," *Boston Globe*, January 29, 1980.

**"In the clearest terms"**—Text of Kennedy Georgetown speech published in *Washington Post*, "Sometimes a Party Must Sail Against the Wind," January 29, 1980.

**Jordan would come to agree**—Jordan, *Crisis*, 200.

**let loose his inner progressive**—Clymer, *Edward M. Kennedy*, 292.

**he would again decline**—"Carter Declines," *Boston Globe*, January 31, 1980.

**"recovered his political voice"**—"Kennedy Finds His Form," editorial, *Boston Globe*, January 29, 1980.

**political consultant David Garth**—*Boston Globe*, January 22, 1980.

**"Over ten years ago"**—"Statement on Chappaquiddick," *Boston Globe*, January 29, 1980.

**"He has been freed"**—Mary McGrory, *Boston Globe*, February 4, 1980.

**"once-confident candidate"**—Clymer, "Kennedy Discovers the Pain of Running as an Underdog."

**"You had layers upon layers"**—Harold Ickes phone interview, July 22, 2013.

**"there might be twenty-eight people"**—Hersh, *Edward Kennedy*, 480.

**"was melding three generations"**—Ibid.

**"It was never quite clear"**—Ibid.

**"probably the worst television"**—Ibid.

**"there was no centralized"**—Canellos, *Last Lion*, 216.

**finances were so badly managed**—"A Party with No Place to Go," *Boston Globe*, February 20, 1980.

**"Kennedy, known for"**—Clymer, *Edward M. Kennedy*, 286.

**he won just 46 percent**—David Nyhan, "Slim Maine Win for Carter," *Boston Globe*, February 11, 1980.

**"The thrust of what Senator Kennedy"**—Germond and Witcover, *Blue Smoke and Mirrors*, 148.

**"Well, I might point out"**—Transcript of President Carter press conference, February 13, 1980, available at American Presidency Project, http://www.presidency.ucsb.edu/ws/?pid=32928.

**"not going to be silenced"**—Thomas Oliphant, "Kennedy Defends Right to Speak Out on Policy," *Boston Globe*, February 14, 1980.

**"We will all rally"**—Germond and Witcover, *Blue Smoke and Mirrors*, 149.

**sent Vice President Walter Mondale**—Ibid., 150.

**Shrum blamed Brown**—Shrum, *No Excuses*, 97.

**Carter beat Kennedy among Catholic voters**—Charles Kenney, "Kennedy Vows to Fight On," *Boston Globe*, February 27, 1980.

**should have been Kennedy's natural constituency**—Robert Healy, "A Campaign of Surprises," *Boston Globe*, March 14, 1980.

**Kennedy tried to lighten the mood**—Thomas Oliphant, "Kennedy: 'We Continue,'" *Boston Globe*, February 27, 1980.

**Andy Warhol screenprints**—Peter Edelman interview, January 25, 2014, Washington, D.C.

**"Ham Jordan really understood"**—Harold Ickes phone interview, July 22, 2013.

**"Where's Mary Jo?"**—Canellos, *Last Lion*, 222.

**"There was a misplaced sense"**—David Axelrod email to the author.

**"Kennedy ought to get out"**—Jordan, *Crisis*, 199.

**"He tended to see the campaign"**—Richard Stearns interview, July 23, 2014, Boston.

**Stearns told Kennedy**—Clymer, *Edward M. Kennedy*, 295.

**"After Iowa he shut down"**—Peter Edelman interview, January 25, 2014.

**"still thought it was five bucks"**—Harold Ickes phone interview, July 22, 2013.

## CHAPTER 13: Civil War

**"It could mean the death"**—Jordan, *Crisis*, 198.

**cast the vote by mistake**—Edward Walsh and John M. Goshko, "Carter Says Error Led U.S. to Vote Against Israelis," *Washington Post*, March 4, 1980.

**"one could almost feel"**—Drew, *Portrait of an Election*, 143.

**"in a free fall"**—Clymer, *Edward M. Kennedy*, 297.

**"Everyone says we're"**—Jordan, *Crisis*, 200.

**Carter's people were furious**—Drew, *Portrait of an Election*, 145.

**Senator Wendell Ford**—Ibid., 143.

**Smith called the Parker House; instructed speechwriter Bob Shrum**—Clymer, *Edward M. Kennedy*, 297.

**a visit to the White House dentist**—Jimmy Carter Presidential Daily Diary, March 25, 1980.

**"Our patience is beginning"**—Jordan, *Crisis*, 232.

**only 47 percent had**—Clymer, *Edward M. Kennedy*, 298.

**"I like New York in March"**—Ibid., 297.

**Carter's people were shaken**—Ibid., 299.

**"We blew it"**—Vanderbilt Television News Archive, Clip #852767: Decision 80: The New York Primary, https://tvnews.vanderbilt.edu/broadcasts/852767.

**"You can't remain"**—Sherley Uhl, "Kennedy Raps Carter, Inflation at City Rally," *Pittsburgh Press*, March 28, 1980.

**despite Jordan's predictions**—Carter, *White House Diary*, 414.

**"Tonight, it appears"**—Vanderbilt Television News Archive, Clip #656859: *Nightline* ABC Special for Tuesday, April 22, 1980, https://tvnews.vanderbilt.edu/broadcasts/656859.

**resurrecting voter concerns**—Clymer, *Edward M. Kennedy*, 299.

**"Teddy's character"**—Pat Caddell interview with Adam Clymer, January 1, 1998, John F. Kennedy Library, Adam Clymer Personal Papers, Box 3.

**came away with 54 delegates**—Tom Donilon delegate count, April 27, 1980, Presidential Papers of Jimmy Carter, Staff Offices: Press/Powell, Box 9.

**"The president will win"**—Vanderbilt Television News Archive, Clip #656859: *Nightline*, April 22, 1980.

**seven-hundred-mile journey**—Bowden, *Guests of the Ayatollah*, 434.

**referred to as haboobs**—Ibid., 440.

**"Damn, damn"**—Ibid., 456.

**"A tremendous wave of nausea"**—Jordan, *Crisis*, 273.

**The president went on television**—Transcript of Carter statement, April 25, 1980, available at the American Presidency Project, http://www.presidency.ucsb.edu/ws/?pid=33322.

**"an incomplete success"**—Germond and Witcover, *Blue Smoke and Mirrors*, 161.

**"It doesn't sound like our army"**—William Greider, "8 U.S. Dead as Rescue Try Fails in Iran," *Washington Post*, April 25, 1980.

**he feared a repeat**—Robert M. Gates, *Duty: Memoirs of a Secretary at War* (New York: Vintage, 2015), 540.

**just 11 delegates short**—Tom Donilon delegate counts, May 13 and June 4, 1980, Presidential Papers of Jimmy Carter, Staff Offices: Press/Powell, Box 9.

**"People wanted the president"**—Drew, *Portrait of an Election*, 180.

**came to Jordan's apartment**—Jordan, *Crisis*, 293.

**"I'm committed to going"**—Drew, *Portrait of an Election*, 168.

**a noontime rally**—Steven R. Weisman, "Carter and Reagan 'Debate' in Ohio, Six Blocks Apart," *New York Times*, May 30, 1980.

**The building behind him**—Drew, *Portrait of an Election*, 181.

**Cadell would later conclude**—Clymer, *Edward M. Kennedy*, 300.

**"We have a president"**—Drew, *Portrait of an Election*, 171.

**"Today Democrats"**—David Broder, "Kennedy Vows He'll Press On," *Washington Post*, June 4, 1980.

**Carter held an overwhelming**—Tom Donilon delegate count, June 4, 1980, Presidential Papers of Jimmy Carter, Staff Offices: Press/ Powell, Box 9.

**"But if he started beating"**—Jordan, *Crisis*, 235.

**pleased by Ford's demise**—Craig Shirley, *Rendezvous with Destiny: Ronald Reagan and the Campaign That Changed America* (Wilmington, DE: ISI Books, 2009), 16.

**a daily radio commentary; a weekly column**—Ibid., 15.

**the most formidable Republican**—Ibid., 59.

**"At the time"**—Jimmy Carter, *Keeping Faith: Memoirs of a President* (New York: Bantam, 1982), 542.

**"He has his memorized tapes"**—Carter, *White House Diary*, 476.

**"both dumb and incompetent"**—Ibid., 492.

**"a man who tells you"**—Shirley, *Rendezvous with Destiny*, 67.

## CHAPTER 14: Robot Rule

**he expected Kennedy to keep running**—Hedrick Smith, "Carter and Kennedy to Meet Today to Cope with Democratic Breach," *New York Times*, June 5, 1980.

**Carter planned to veto**—Martin Tolchin, "House and Senate Vote Down Oil Fee by Large Margins," *New York Times*, June 5, 1980.

**The only thing out of place**—Vanderbilt Television News Archive, Clip #511285: *NBC Evening News* for Thursday, June 5, 1980, http://tvnews.vanderbilt.edu/program.pl?ID=511285.

**"Ted, are you going to get out"**—Jordan, *Crisis*, 299.

**"More than a prayer"; captured the moment; "The primary season is over"**—Terence Smith, "Kennedy Meets with the President and Declares He Is Still Candidate," *New York Times*, June 6, 1980.

**335 to 34**—Steven R. Weisman, "House, by 335 to 34, Overrides Carter on Oil-Import Fee," *New York Times*, June 6, 1980.

**almost preferred to see Reagan win**—Jordan, *Crisis*, 293.

**"His return to his"**—Mary McGrory, *Boston Globe*, June 2, 1980.

**Carter heard from Charles Kirbo**—Clymer, *Edward M. Kennedy*, 304.

**met for ninety minutes**—Leslie Bennetts, "Ford Vows to Back Reagan Fully," *New York Times*, June 6, 1980.

**There was another complication**—Adam Clymer, "Kennedy, Anderson and Recession Are Among Post-Primary Perils," *New York Times*, June 8, 1980.

**"a mecca for Swedish immigrants"**—John B. Anderson, *Between Two Worlds: A Congressman's Choice* (Grand Rapids, MI: Zondervan, 1970), 32.

**"There's a meticulousness"**—Al Larkin, "John Anderson: The Making of a Maverick," *Boston Globe*, June 15, 1980.

**critical of Carter's "gyrations"; 50-cent-a-gallon gas tax**—"Talking Politics: John B. Anderson," *New York Times*, January 21, 1980.

**"the authority and law"**—Larkin, "John Anderson: The Making of a Maverick."

**"extremists"; "fed up with the zealots"**—David Farrell, "Anderson: The Too Angry Man," *Boston Globe*, March 2, 1980.

**a decade-long conversion**—Larkin, "John Anderson: The Making of a Maverick."

**he played up his appeal; a moratorium**—Al Larkin, "John Anderson Knows Who He Is, but Do We?," *Boston Globe*, May 11, 1980.

**Anderson was in talks**—Robert Healy, "Brooke to Run with Anderson?," *Boston Globe*, June 18, 1980.

**"Fully 40 percent"**—Larkin, "John Anderson: The Making of a Maverick."

**"We need a new centrist force"**—Ibid.

**tried to knock him off**—Robert L. Turner, "A Key Battle for Anderson," *Boston Globe*, June 10, 1980.

**rejected Carter's veto**—Martin Tolchin, "Oil-Import Fee Dies as Senate Overrides Carter by 68 to 10," *New York Times*, June 7, 1980.

**One vehicle's window was shattered**—Steven R. Weisman, "Crowd Boos Carter in Riot-Torn Area," *New York Times*, June 10, 1980.

**"appalled and embarrassed"**—"Carter's Visit Found Lacking by Miami Black Leaders," *New York Times*, June 11, 1980.

**"talk of an 'open convention' swept Washington"**—Jordan, *Crisis*, 305.

**"stroke" their delegates**—Ibid., 305.

**"what eight months ago"**—Drew, *Portrait of an Election*, 187.

**"The 'open convention'"**—Marty Nolan, "The Future of a Party; Downs, Ups, Realities of a Challenger's Campaign," *Boston Globe*, June 5, 1980.

**had blinded many Democrats; they now saw Democrats; "The Republican party"**—Thomas Byrne Edsall and Mary D. Edsall, *Chain Reaction: The Impact of Race, Rights, and Taxes on American Politics* (New York: Norton, 1991), 17, 10, 13.

**"eviscerates delegate responsibility"**—Thomas Wicker, "Carter's 'Guarantee' Rule," *New York Times*, July 27, 1980.

**The White House made clear**—Associated Press, *Boston Globe*, June 10, 1980.

**rolled out a $12 billion jobs package**—Charles Claffey, "Kennedy Proposes $12 Billion Jobs Plan," *Boston Globe*, June 11, 1980.

**failing to stop Richard Stearns**—Chris Black, "Delegates Block Lang, Galbraith," *Boston Globe*, June 15, 1980.

**Kennedy's top aides met**—*Boston Globe*, June 11, 1980.

**"I have every intention"**—*Boston Globe*, June 13, 1980.

**"Democratic in name only"**—*Boston Globe*, June 27, 1980.

**began comparing Carter to Reagan**—"Reagan Urges Rapid U.S. Arms Buildup," *Boston Globe*, June 19, 1980.

**Ham Jordan was worried**—Jordan, *Crisis*, 307.

**called Kennedy "spoiled"**—*Boston Globe*, June 27, 1980.

**Hamilton Jordan retreated**—Jordan, *Crisis*, 305.

**had "damaged severely"**—Ibid., 307.

**looming behind him**—Associated Press, "Truck Bill Signing Brings Kennedy to the Rose Garden," via *Boston Globe*, July 1, 1980.

**would chant his name**—Steven R. Weisman, "Warm Greeting for President," *New York Times*, July 4, 1980.

**first trip back in ten months**—David Nyhan, "Next Attraction: A Game of Hardball," *Boston Globe*, July 10, 1980.

# CHAPTER 15: Losing Altitude

**"The only unpaved street"**—Bert Lance Oral History, Presidential Oral Histories, University of Virginia, May 12, 1982.

**went jogging twenty minutes later**—Jimmy Carter Presidential Daily Diary, July 14, 1980.

**filed a civil complaint**—Robert Pear, "Billy Carter Settles Charges by U.S. and Registers as an Agent of Libya," *New York Times*, July 15, 1980.

**working for the Charter Oil Company**—Robert Pear, "Civiletti Discloses He Spoke to Carter on Brother's Case," *New York Times*, July 26, 1980.

**asked his brother**—"Inquiry into the Matter of Billy Carter and Libya," Senate Judiciary Committee report, https://www.intelligence.senate .gov/sites/default/files/961015.pdf.

**"a matter between"**—Pear, "Billy Carter Settles Charges by U.S. and Registers as an Agent of Libya."

**"All I can say is"**—Associated Press, "Billy Carter Curbs Tongue," via *Spokane Daily Chronicle*, January 15, 1979.

**pressure from "the Jews"**—"Inquiry into the Matter of Billy Carter and Libya."

**hospitalized for eleven days**—"Inquiry into the Matter of Billy Carter and Libya."

**A week later**—Steven R. Weisman, "Billy Carter Set Up Brzezinski Meeting with Libyan on Iran," *New York Times*, July 23, 1980.

WIFE OF PRESIDENT—Philip Taubman, "Wife of President Asked Billy Carter for Aid on Hostages," *New York Times*, July 25, 1980.

**Rosalynn was "quite upset"**—Carter, *White House Diary*, 451.

**"Rare is the family"**—Hedrick Smith, "New Carter Embarrassment," *New York Times*, July 24, 1980.

**seized Billy Carter's deed**—Taubman, "Wife of President Asked Billy Carter for Help on Hostages."

**"A few weeks ago"**—Steven V. Roberts, "Carter's Problems Renew Hopes of Kennedy's Backers," *New York Times*, July 27, 1980.

**Reagan asked Ford**—Shirley, *Rendezvous with Destiny*, 351.

**In a series of meetings**—Ibid., 354–55.

**Lynn Sherr reported**—Clyde Haberman, "Convention Replay: When TV Runs Hot, Politics Boils Over," *New York Times*, July 20, 1980.

**Ford and his wife, Betty**—Vanderbilt Television News Archive, Clip #842699: CBS Special for Wednesday, July 16, 1980, https://tvnews.vanderbilt.edu/broadcasts/842699.

**"Did you hear what he just said?"**—Shirley, *Rendezvous with Destiny*, 358.

**Reagan continued to resist**—Ibid., 359.

**At 11:13 p.m.**—Ibid., 363.

**Ford's advance team told reporters**—Vanderbilt Television News Archive, Clip #842922: CBS Special for Wednesday, July 16, 1980, https://tvnews.vanderbilt.edu/broadcasts/842922.

**Cronkite tossed to Lesley Stahl**—Ibid.

**from Reagan at 11:37 p.m.**—Shirley, *Rendezvous with Destiny*, 365.

**described him as "haggard-looking"**—Haberman, "Convention Replay: When TV Runs Hot, Politics Boils Over."

**Thirteen minutes after midnight; a brief but unequivocal speech**—Vanderbilt Television News Archive, Clip #843021: CBS Special for Wednesday, July 16, 1980, https://tvnews.vanderbilt.edu/broadcasts/843021.

**"I know that I am breaking"**—Transcript of Ronald Reagan speech, July 17, 1980, available at the American Presidency Project, http://www.presidency.ucsb.edu/ws/index.php?pid=25970.

**Hamilton Jordan and other Carter advisers**—Jordan, *Crisis*, 311.

**Civiletti admitted; "No, it was never discussed"; a "damn fool"**—Robert Pear, "Civiletti Discloses He Spoke to Carter on Brother's Case," *New York Times*, July 26, 1980.

**considering a criminal complaint**—"Inquiry into the Matter of Billy Carter and Libya."

**urged him to sign**—Carter, *White House Diary*, 443.

**would decline to speak**—Ibid., 451.

**a group of forty**—Hedrick Smith, "Disgruntled Democrats in Congress Weigh Bid for New Party Nominee," *New York Times*, July 26, 1980.

**New York Democrats**—Joyce Purnick, "Carey Supports 'Open Convention;' Koch Trims His Backing for Carter," *New York Times*, July 29, 1980.

**Senator Majority Leader Robert Byrd**—*White House Diary*, 451.

**would respond "in person"**—Terence Smith, "President Is 'Eager' to Testify to Panel in Billy Carter Case," *New York Times*, July 30, 1980.

**Ella Grasso endorsed the idea**—Joyce Purnick, "Amid Others' Doubts, Gov. Grasso Joins Move for 'Open Convention,'" *New York Times*, July 30, 1980.

**"He didn't really 'run'"**—James Reston, "Carter's Garden Strategy," *New York Times*, July 30, 1980.

**77 percent disapproval rating; Another poll showed**—Hedrick Smith, "Senators Uneasy About President, Byrd Is Informed," *New York Times*, July 31, 1980.

**"worse even than Nixon"**—Jordan, *Crisis*, 313.

**held a strange meeting**—Warren Weaver Jr., "Anderson Says He Will Reconsider Candidacy If Carter Is Not Nominee," *New York Times*, August 1, 1980.

**"I have a lot of problems"**—Carter, *White House Diary*, 452.

**Byrd publicly backed**—Judith Miller, "Byrd Says He Backs 'Open' Convention; Assails Libyan Case," *New York Times*, August 3, 1980.

**"a few delegates"**—Tom Donilon interview, March 3, 2017.

**Illinois and New York delegations**—Martin Schram, "Hard-Nosed Hustling Choked Off Once-Feared Defections," *Washington Post*, August 12, 1980.

**"We absolutely felt"**—Tom Donilon interview, March 3, 2017.

**as well as Vice President Mondale**—Steven R. Weisman, "White House Mood: Anger and Frustration," *New York Times*, August 1, 1980.

**were summoned back**—Schram, "Hard-Nosed Hustling."

**"We've got a full-fledged"**—Jordan, *Crisis*, 316.

**"hope[d] the right chemistry develops"**—B. Drummond Ayres Jr., "Kennedy Pins Hopes on 'Right Chemistry,'" *New York Times*, August 3, 1980.

# CHAPTER 16: Giant Killer

**The six temporary trailers**—Martin Schram, "Hard-Nosed Hustling Choked Off Once-Feared Defections," *Washington Post*, August 12, 1980.

**gone fishing around 2:30**—Jimmy Carter Presidential Daily Diary, September 22, 1977.

**calmed the waters**—Adam Clymer, "Poll Finds Carter Gaining in Party After News Conference on Brother," *New York Times*, August 10, 1980.

**hour-long press conference**—Transcript of President Carter's News Conference, August 4, 1980, http://www.presidency.ucsb.edu/ws/index.php?pid=44875.

**a lead of several hundred delegates**—Elaine C. Kamarck, *Primary Politics: How Presidential Candidates Have Shaped the Modern Nominating System* (Washington, DC: Brookings Institution, 2009), 139.

**red lights that blinked; were encased in copper**—Tom Donilon interview, March 3, 2017.

**"a stampede"**—Jordan, *Crisis*, 319.

**Jordan conferred with Tom Donilon**—Ibid., 323.

**released from prison**—Drew, *Portrait of an Election*, 237.

**the Pennsylvania and Illinois delegations**—Ibid., 233, 236.

**The entire Maine delegation**—Jordan, *Crisis*, 323.

**Jordan quickly called Carter**—Jimmy Carter Presidential Daily Diary, August 11, 1980.

**attempts to draft a multitude**—Hedrick Smith, "Disgruntled Democrats in Congress Weigh Bid for New Party Nominee," *New York Times*, July 26, 1980.

**may have actually stymied**—Drew, *Portrait of an Election*, 241.

**"If this thing gets open"**—Tom Donilon interview, March 3, 2017.

**a "limpness"; won the final vote**—Drew, *Portrait of an Election*, 242–43.

**At 9:46 p.m., Kennedy called Carter**—Jimmy Carter Presidential Daily Diary, August 11, 1980.

**I didn't press him, Ham**—Jordan, *Crisis*, 324.

**"I'm deeply gratified"**—Drew, *Portrait of an Election*, 244.

**secured a prime-time speaking slot**—Jordan, *Crisis*, 319.

**pushing to include planks; an atmosphere highly favorable**—Drew, *Portrait of an Election*, 244–52; Jordan, *Crisis*, 327–28.

**"If you have any wisdom"**—Drew, *Portrait of an Election*, 232.

**"We neglected to take"**—Jody Powell, *The Other Side of the Story* (New York: William Morrow, 1984), 245.

**"We just said, 'Fuck 'em'"**—Harold Ickes phone interview, July 22, 2013.

**Donilon threw down his headset**—Tom Donilon interview, March 3, 2017.

**"Go fuck yourself"**—Harold Ickes phone interview, July 22, 2013.

**the verge of blows**—Tom Donilon interview, March 3, 2017.

**"Harold, I'm watching"**—Harold Ickes phone interview, July 22, 2013.

**When Kennedy reached the platform**—Text of Kennedy speech to the Democratic convention in Madison Square Garden, August 12, 1980, available at American Rhetoric, http://www.americanrhetoric.com/speeches/tedkennedy1980dnc.htm.

**"a big reason Senator Kennedy"**—"As Humphrey, as Stevenson, as Kennedy," editorial, *New York Times*, August 14, 1980.

**"For a long year"; "Ted Kennedy's words"**—Jordan, *Crisis*, 326.

**"one of the great emotional outpourings"**—"As Humphrey, as Stevenson, as Kennedy."

**they knew it was a lost cause**—Jordan, *Crisis*, 327–28.

**a woman named Signe Waller**—Tom Raum, Associated Press, "A Hot Night for Protests Inside and Out of Hall," *Boston Globe*, August 15, 1980.

**a confrontation on November 3, 1979**—Joe Killian, "Nov. 3, 1979: A Day That Still Divides City," *Greensboro News and Record*, January 25, 2015.

**"This was a speech"**—Vanderbilt Television News Archive, Clip #845294: CBS Special for Thursday, August 14, 1980, https://tvnews.vanderbilt.edu/broadcasts/845294.

**had haggled beforehand**—Shrum, *No Excuses*, 127; Powell, *The Other Side of the Story*, 249.

**"Whoever's in charge"**—Vanderbilt Television News Archive, Clip #860761: ABC Special for Thursday, August 14, 1980, https://tvnews.vanderbilt.edu/broadcasts/860761.

**"Forget the hostages"**—Vanderbilt Television News Archive, Clip #845294: CBS Special for Thursday, August 14, 1980, https://tvnews.vanderbilt.edu/broadcasts/845294.

**the networks' live feed**—Vanderbilt Television News Archive, Clip #860761: ABC Special for Thursday, August 14, 1980, https://tvnews.vanderbilt.edu/broadcasts/860761.

**"Even on this night"**—Ibid.

**"This convention right now"; "They're calling them up"; "Bob Strauss will call up every politician"; quotes by Koppel, Donaldson, and Reynolds; descriptions of Kennedy and Carter onstage**—Ibid.

**Roughly twenty million people**—Nielsen, "Democratic and Republican Conventions," http://www.nielsen.com/content/dam/corporate/us/en/newswire/uploads/2012/08/Conventions-Historic-TV-Ratings-Track.pdf.

**"Well, this is slightly awkward"**—Vanderbilt Television News Archive, Clip #857719: NBC Special for Thursday, August 14, 1980, http://tvnews.vanderbilt.edu/program.pl?ID=857719.

**"as if he had appeared"**—White, *America in Search of Itself*, 342.

**"I can't believe he's standing there"**—Bert Lance Oral History, Presidential Oral Histories, Miller Center, University of Virginia, May 12, 1982.

**"After the election"**—Powell, *The Other Side of the Story*, 250.

**"If he could have been"**—Tom Donilon interview, March 3, 2017.

## CHAPTER 17: Mr. Mean

**"I suppose that you learn"**—B. Drummond Ayres Jr., "Kennedy Indicates His Zeal for Ticket Depends on Carter," *New York Times*, August 17, 1980.

**he appeared a week later with Carter**—Adam Clymer, "President Tells Legion U.S. Could Win an Arms Race," *New York Times*, August 22, 1980.

**the American Federation of Teachers**—Douglas E. Kneeland, "Kennedy Bids Union Support President," *New York Times*, August 22, 1980.

**Kennedy traveled to the White House**—Steven R. Weisman, "Kennedy Warms to Plan by President to Add Jobs," *New York Times*, August 26, 1980.

**embroiled in a series of controversies**—Howell Raines, "Reagan Campaign Problems," *New York Times*, August 27, 1980.

**Reagan backed off**—Howell Raines, "Reagan, Conceding Misstatements, Abandons Plan on Taiwan Office," *New York Times*, August 26, 1980.

**put that phrase into his speech**—Howell Raines, "Reagan Campaign Runs into Unexpected Obstacles," *New York Times*, August 24, 1980.

**"a conservative in liberal's clothing"**—Thomas Oliphant, "The Reagan Conservatism," *Boston Globe*, September 10, 1980.

**"signs of frustration"**—Raines, "Reagan Campaign Runs into Unexpected Obstacles."

**Reagan "wasted August"**—Shirley, *Rendezvous with Destiny*, 454.

**take a "blowtorch"**—Timothy D. Schellhardt, "President to Stress His Wide Differences with Reagan," *Wall Street Journal*, August 29, 1980.

**"opening his campaign"; Reagan's response**—Terence Smith, "Carter Assails Reagan Remark About the Klan as an Insult to the South," *New York Times*, September 3, 1980.

**"For two weeks it was delicious"**—Jordan, *Crisis*, 338.

**Pat Caddell joked**—Ibid., 339.

**Ayatollah Khomeini issued demands**—Martin Schram, "President Voices Optimism, Muskie Wary on Hostages," *Washington Post*, September 16, 1980.

**"lead our country toward war"**—Drew, *Portrait of an Election*, 307.

**"I wonder whether he's"**—White, *America in Search of Itself*, 310.

**"The President eschews the light touch"**—*Boston Globe*, October 13, 1980.

**"a beautiful cat with sharp claws"**—Drew, *Portrait of an Election*, 307.

**"one of the three meanest men"**—"Hunter S. Thompson Says Jimmy Carter Is Ruthless, 1977" (interview with Canadian Broadcasting Company), YouTube, https://www.youtube.com/watch?v=yvpPosKe-I0&list=TLZWbkHkjpkhw.

**he spoke at Ebenezer Baptist Church; "Racism has no place in this country"**—Curtis Wilkie, "Carter Warns Blacks on Reagan," *Boston Globe*, September 17, 1980.

**Jody Powell tried to deny it**—Shirley, *Rendezvous with Destiny*, 475.

**"Mr. Carter has abandoned all dignity"**—"Running Mean," editorial, *Washington Post*, September 18, 1980.

**"demean the office of the presidency"**—Shirley, *Rendezvous with Destiny*, 475.

**calling the remarks "not nice"**—Ibid.

**"The press seems to be obsessed"; But Lisa Myers**—Ibid., 476.

**had "gone overboard"**—Steven R. Weisman, "Carter Campaign Says Attack Strategy Is Working," *New York Times*, September 26, 1980.

**"The networks' judgment"**—Curtis Wilkie, "Carter's Televised Presidency: And Now, This Season's Final Episode," *Boston Globe*, November 2, 1980.

**at a speech in Chicago**—Drew, *Portrait of an Election*, 306.

**"been characterized as mean"**—Jordan, *Crisis*, 349.

**"I don't think I'm mean"**—Germond and Witcover, *Blue Smoke and Mirrors*, 263.

**"The meanness issue"**—Jordan, *Crisis*, 351.

**Eugene McCarthy**—Shirley, *Rendezvous with Destiny*, 520.

**Leon Jaworski**—T. R. Reid, "Jaworski Announces He Will Lead 'Democrats for Reagan' Effort," *Washington Post*, September 30, 1980.

**he would drop out if the president would debate him**—James Reston, "Carter's Curious Campaign," *New York Times*, October 6, 1980.

**Ham Jordan traveled**—Jordan, *Crisis*, 335–36.

**"I accept your nomination!"**—Chris Black, "Kennedy Lauds Frank, Shannon," *Boston Globe*, September 13, 1980.

**"Viva Kennedy!"**—Anthony Marro, "Faint-Praise Politics by Ford and Kennedy," *Newsday/Boston Globe*, October 24, 1980.

**couldn't resist zinging the president**—Terence Smith, "Carter, in California Visit, Sharpens Reagan Attack," *New York Times*, September 23, 1980.

**On October 15**—Joseph F. Sullivan, "Kennedy Urges Followers in Jersey to Back Carter's Re-election Drive," *New York Times*, October 16, 1980.

**Muhammad Ali in Brooklyn**—Steven R. Weisman, "Carter Promises Aid on Welfare Costs," *New York Times*, October 21, 1980.

**their appearance at the annual Al Smith Dinner; Reagan, who spoke first**—David Nyhan, "A N.Y. Weigh-In: Reagan's Jabs vs Carter's Punches," *Boston Globe*, October 17, 1980.

**"It has nothing to do with politics"**—Terence Smith, "Carter and Reagan Trade Quips on Same Dais at Al Smith Dinner," *New York Times*, October 17, 1980.

**God heard the prayers only of Christians**—Howell Raines, "Reagan Is Balancing Two Different Stances," *New York Times*, October 4, 1980.

**"There is no fun in Jimmy Carter"**—Anthony Lewis, "Carter Against Himself," *New York Times*, October 16, 1980.

**Reagan's top aides huddled**—Shirley, *Rendezvous with Destiny*, 509.

**was put on retainer**—Ibid., 436.

**assembled all the evidence against Corbin**—Craig Shirley, "New Book Pins 'Debategate' on Dem," *Politico*, October 15, 2009.

**Jody Powell speculated in 1984**—Powell, *The Other Side of the Story*, 287.

**Mohammad Ali Rajai raised the prospect**—Loren Jenkins, "Cleric Sees Release as Early as Monday," *Washington Post*, October 23, 1980.

**Some thought so**—David Broder, "Carter Riding the Hostage Issue, Either to Triumph or Humiliation," *Washington Post*, October 26, 1980.

**"What's taking place"**—Haynes Johnson, "Americans Feel Held in Thrall by President and Iran," *Washington Post*, October 26, 1980.

**the Century Plaza Hotel**—Shirley, *Rendezvous with Destiny*, 548.

**He had just returned from Puerto Rico**—United Press International, "Puerto Ricans Cheer Kennedy," via *New York Times*, October 27, 1980.

**"Reagan looking relaxed"**—Jordan, *Crisis*, 355.

**"dangerous and belligerent"**—Carter-Reagan Presidential Debate, October 28, 1980, Debate Transcript, Commission on Presidential Debates, http://www.debates.org/index.php?page=october-28-1980 -debate-transcript.

**"Oh my God—not that!"**—Jordan, *Crisis*, 356.

**"He just got killed"**—Shirley, *Rendezvous with Destiny*, 548.

**"You could feel it drifting away"**—Ibid., 555.

## CHAPTER 18: Aftermath

**He asked Mondale**—Les Lescaze, "Mondale Takes Over Campaigning So Carter Can 'Manage Our Side,'" *Washington Post*, November 3, 1980.

**and Kennedy to fill in**—Jordan, *Crisis*, 362.

**were besieged with calls**—Bernard Gwertzman, "Muskie Asserts Khomeini's Terms Could Lead to Accord on Hostages," *New York Times*, November 2, 1980.

**was not optimistic**—Jordan, *Crisis*, 362.

**was generally amenable**—Gwertzman, "Muskie Asserts Khomeini's Terms Could Lead to Accord on Hostages."

**"This should bring our people home"**—Jordan, *Crisis*, 362.

**cutting into NFL games**—Robert Kaiser, "Carter's Last Roll at Big Media Audience Ricocheted into the Ether," *Washington Post*, November 4, 1980.

**"a significant development"**—"Text of the President's Statement on the Hostages," *Washington Post*, November 3, 1980.

**showed the race razor tight**—Jordan, *Crisis*, 364.

**he spoke at seven rallies**—Jimmy Carter Presidential Daily Diary, November 3, 1980.

**"Jody, brace yourself"**—Jordan, *Crisis*, 367.

**TV networks had played a big role**—Ibid., 364.

**nursing a stiff drink**—Ibid., 367.

**"one of his finest speeches"; "It's gone"**—Curtis Wilkie, "Plains Knew When Carter Wept," *Boston Globe*, November 5, 1980.

**close to 5 a.m.**—Jimmy Carter Presidential Daily Diary, November 4, 1980.

**"Mr. President, I'm afraid that it's gone"**—Jordan, *Crisis*, 368.

**Carter slept for about an hour**—Curtis Wilkie, "Exhausted President in Plains After 5000-Mile Trip," *Boston Globe*, November 4, 1980.

**A heavy ground fog; "I hope so"**—Wilkie, "Plains Knew When Carter Wept."

**"The Kennedy attacks"**—Carter, *White House Diary*, 480.

**"I never really resented"**—Jordan, *Crisis*, 315.

**"I lost it myself"**—Shirley, *Rendezvous with Destiny*, 570.

**"Events had mocked us"**—Jimmy and Rosalynn Carter, *Everything to Gain: Making the Most of the Rest of Your Life*, Revised ed. (Fayetteville: University of Arkansas Press, 1995), 6.

**spoke to two people**—Jimmy Carter Presidential Daily Diary, November 4, 1980.

**Kennedy made another call that night**—Shirley, *Rendezvous with Destiny*, 579.

**was marked by apathy**—Douglas Brinkley, *The Unfinished Presidency: Jimmy Carter's Journey Beyond the White House* (New York: Penguin, 1998), 3.

**white Baptist voters**—"Polls Indicate Election Was Not Shift to the Right," *Boston Globe*, November 13, 1980.

**"A part of my soul died"**—Brinkley, *The Unfinished Presidency*, 2.

**there was now an incentive**—Ibid., 11.

**arms shipments and military "spare parts"**—Rowland Evans and Robert Novak, "Carter's Hostage Ploy," *Washington Post*, November 5, 1980.

**a declaration of war**—Carter, *White House Diary*, 503.

**a demand for $24 billion; was whittled down**—Brinkley, *The Unfinished Presidency*, 34.

**hoped the deal would be done so quickly**—Jordan, *Crisis*, 393.

**Carter and his most loyal aides were "obsessed"**—Ibid., 16.

**Reagan had made a deal; "if you try to dig further"**—Brinkley, *The Unfinished Presidency*, 44.

**The meeting was tense**—Ibid., 41.

**the first two former hostages**—Jordan, *Crisis*, 412.

**"I wonder deep down"**—Ibid., 416.

**"I never admitted"**—Carter, *Everything to Gain*, 6.

**left it $1 million in debt**—Wayne King, "Carter Redux," *New York Times*, December 10, 1989.

**had sat vacant for a decade**—Carter, *Everything to Gain*, 3.

**"You may be from the country"**—Ibid., 7.

**a multimillion-dollar deal**—Edwin McDowell, "Carter Sells Memoirs to Bantam Books," *New York Times*, March 14, 1981.

**two and a half years**—Brinkley, *The Unfinished Presidency*, 48.

**planning and strategizing**—Ibid., 73–74.

**"read Gandhi and Thoreau"**—Ibid., 94.

**a huge platform**—Ibid., 97.

**dug into the Israeli-Palestinian conflict; "He saw more clearly"**— Ibid., 102.

**traveled to Latin America**—Ibid., 131–36.

**introduced to Habitat for Humanity; had started the nonprofit in 1976**—Ibid., 146–49.

**drug-infested Alphabet City**—Sam Roberts, "Renovated Tenement Awaits the Return of One of Its Carpenters, Jimmy Carter," *New York Times*, October 8, 2013.

**he was "addicted"**—Brinkley, *The Unfinished Presidency*, 157.

**reluctantly invited him**—Ibid., 130.

**a "partyless president"**—Ibid., 2.

**"He wants to get it over with"**—Jordan, *Crisis*, 373.

**exploded in anger**—Brinkley, *The Unfinished Presidency*, 2.

**had taught Sunday school**—Ibid., 30.

**"Whoever welcomes this little child"**—Luke 9:46–48, New International Version.

**an arms control summit**—Brinkley, *The Unfinished Presidency*, 138.

**roughly 3.5 million people**—Carter Center, "Guinea Worm Eradication Program," https://www.cartercenter.org/health/guinea_worm/.

**estimated that 100 million people were at risk**—Brinkley, *The Unfinished Presidency*, 222.

**a surprise development**—Michaeleen Doucleff, "Dogs Block President Carter's Dream of Wiping Out Guinea Worm," National Public Radio, August 9, 2016.

**fifty thousand political prisoners**—Brinkley, *The Unfinished Presidency*, 212.

**"But we do not have a definitive accounting"**—Email from Deanna Congileo, Carter Center Director of Communications, January 3, 2017.

**a forty-five-minute press conference**—Brinkley, *The Unfinished Presidency*, 284–85.

**was viewed as deeply disloyal**—Ibid., 407.

**seeking to undermine their coalition-building**—Ibid., 339–41.

**He wrote an open letter**—Associated Press, "Ex-President Carter Offers Apology to Jews," NBC News, December 23, 2009.

**a view of the human heart**—Brinkley, *The Unfinished Presidency*, 112.

**urban renewal, in Atlanta**—Ibid., 362–63.

**was declared cancer-free**—Gillian Mohney, "The Remarkable Cancer Treatment That Helped Jimmy Carter Combat Brain Tumor," ABC News, March 7, 2016.

**"invisible but solid"; "The magic was finally on him"**—White, *America in Search of Itself*, 337.

**"It was almost like"**—Jon Haber interview, March 31, 2017, Washington, D.C.

**hired Pat Caddell**—Pat Caddell interview with Adam Clymer, January 1, 1998, John F. Kennedy Library, Adam Clymer Personal Papers, Box 3.

**"Teddy had moved"**—Christopher Kennedy Lawford, *Symptoms of Withdrawal: A Memoir of Snapshots and Redemption* (New York: HarperCollins e-books, Reprint ed., 2009), 272.

**"a childish belief"**—Michael Kelly, "Ted Kennedy on the Rocks," *GQ*, February 1990.

**Kennedy's "second bachelorhood"**—Joseph P. Kahn, "An Untidy Private Life, Then a Turn to Stability," *Boston Globe*, February 12, 2009.

**During the dinner, Kennedy asked**—Sheila Marikar, "Carrie Fisher's Top 3 Crazy Tales: Senators, Prostitutes and Michael Jackson," ABC News, November 10, 2011.

**"It was all part"**—Kennedy, *True Compass*, 422.

**Kennedy hit a new low point; "It seemed that Ted Kennedy"**—Peter J. Boyer, "We're Not in Camelot Anymore," *New Yorker*, May 23, 1994.

**"In the long downward slope"**—Michelle Green, "Boys Night Out in Palm Beach," *People*, April 22, 1991.

**he gave a speech expressing contrition**—Alessandra Stanley, "Facing Questions of Private Life, Kennedy Apologizes to the Voters," *New York Times*, October 26, 1991.

**He met Victoria Anne Reggie; had even worked as an intern**—Kennedy, *True Compass*, 422–23.

**"You were struck by the loneliness"**—Interview with B. Drummond Ayres Jr., August 28, 1997, John F. Kennedy Library, Adam Clymer Personal Papers, Box 3.

**"I don't think I knew how lonely I was"**—Kennedy interview with Natalie Jacobson, October 29, 1994, John F. Kennedy Library, Adam Clymer Personal Papers, Box 5.

**"the woman who changed my life"**—Kennedy, *True Compass*, 421.

**"break down citizens' doors"**—James Reston, "Washington: Kennedy and Bork," *New York Times*, July 5, 1987.

**tarnished himself in the process**—Clymer, *Edward M. Kennedy*, 408.

**he stood and tried to deflect it**—Kennedy, *True Compass*, 449.

**"a spectacular broken promise"**—Ibid., 494.

**"Far more than either of his brothers"; "I define liberalism"; "abandoned the costly Utopian reforms"**—Michael Kelly, "Ted Kennedy on the Rocks," *GQ*, February 1990.

**ran headlong into public sentiment**—White, *America in Search of Itself*, 7.

**"Perseverance" was the word he used**—Clymer, *Edward M. Kennedy*, 543.

**Teddy Jr. told a story**—Canellos, *Last Lion*, 424.

**a 2009 letter to Pope Benedict**—Ibid., 426.

**Paul Kirk made an attempt to patch up the relationship**—Brinkley, *The Unfinished Presidency*, 249.

**"All of us know"; "I went to the dedication"**—Maureen Dowd, "Convention Chronicle: Stars Twinkle Amid Glitches in a Show of Unified Strength," *New York Times*, July 19, 1988.

**"I don't think he needed any redemption"**—Jimmy Carter interview, January 15, 2015.

# Index

# About the Author

**Jon Ward** has written about American politics and culture for nearly two decades, as a city desk reporter in Washington, D.C., as a White House correspondent who traveled aboard Air Force One to Africa, Europe, and the Middle East, and as a national affairs correspondent who has traveled the country to cover two presidential campaigns and the ideas and people animating our times. He is a national correspondent for Yahoo News, he has been published in the *Washington Post*, the *New Republic*, the *Huffington Post*, and the *Washington Times*, and has appeared on TV programs from *Good Morning America* to *Morning Joe*. He and his family live in Washington, D.C.